hindi

Rupert Snell

with

Simon Weightman

TEACH YOURSELF BOOKS

For UK order queries: please contact Bookpoint Ltd, 130 Milton Park, Abingdon, Oxon OX14 4SB. Telephone: (44) 01235 400414, Fax: (44) 01235 400454. Lines are open from 9.00–6.00 Monday to Saturday, with a 24 hour message answering service. Email address: orders@bookpoint.co.uk

For U.S.A. & Canada order queries: please contact NTC/Contemporary Publishing, 4255 West Touhy Avenue, Lincolnwood, Illinois 60646–1975, U.S.A. Telephone: (847) 679 5500, Fax: (847) 679 2494.

Long renowned as the authoritative source for self-guided learning – with more than 30 million copies sold worldwide – the *Teach Yourself* series includes over 200 titles in the fields of languages, crafts, hobbies, and other leisure activities.

British Library Cataloguing in Publication Data
A catalogue entry for this title is available from The British Library.

Library of Congress Catalog Card Number: On file

First published in UK 1989 by Hodder Headline Plc, 338 Euston Road, London, NW1 3BH.
Second edition 2000

First published in US 1989 by NTC/Contemporary Publishing, 4255 West Touhy Avenue, Lincolnwood (Chicago), Illinois 60646–1975, U.S.A.

Printed in Great Britain for Hodder & Stoughton Educational, a division of Hodder Headline Plc, 338 Euston Road, London NW1 3BH, by Cox & Wyman Ltd, Reading, Berkshire.

Impression number	10 9 8 7 6 5 4 3
Year	2005 2004 2003 2002 2001

CONTENTS

INTRODUCTION

This course is designed to enable those with no previous knowledge of Hindi to learn to read, write and converse in the language with confidence and enjoyment. The course has also proved effective as teaching material for both class tuition and individual study.

The Hindi presented in this course is primarily colloquial and practical. To start by learning a very formal linguistic register, such as the purists might prefer, would be to invite looks of incredulity (and incomprehension) during everyday encounters with Hindi-speakers

An advantage of the colloquial approach is that it gives greater access to Urdu, Hindi's sister-language. Hindi and Urdu share a virtually identical grammar and much of their vocabulary. In the higher registers they do part company, because Hindi looks to the classical Indian language of Sanskrit for its higher vocabulary, script and general cultural orientation, while Urdu looks to Persian and Arabic for these things. But at the everyday spoken level, Hindi and Urdu are virtually identical, and you should not be surprised if you are complimented on your spoken 'Urdu' when you complete this course in 'Hindi'!

How to use the course

The course is divided into 18 units, each of which is based on (usually two) dialogues which exemplify and bring to life the new grammar introduced in that particular unit. Transliteration in the roman script is provided for the first five units and for all words in the Hindi-English glossary. The dialogues form a kind of soap opera based on the life of a Delhi family; the English translations are deliberately close and literal, so as to function as a key to the Hindi. The book ends with some additional material in the appendixes, together with a Key to the exercises and complete Hindi-English and English-Hindi glossaries.

Once you have worked carefully through the introductory section on script and pronunciation, taking help from the cassette and/or a native speaker if possible, you should turn to Unit 1. Familiarise yourself with the vocabulary of the first dialogue (given beneath it) before reading the dialogue and working towards an understanding of it by means of the translation; then work through the grammatical explanations and the examples; alternatively, you may prefer to start with the grammar sections, and then turn back to the dialogue. Either way, learning the dialogues by heart will give you a sound basis for conversations of your own. When you have completed the whole unit in this way, learn the vocabulary (no short cuts here – this is essential!), and then do the exercises, checking your work against the key. Don't forget to revise earlier sections as you progress through the book.

The grammatical explanations are meant to be as accessible and non-technical as possible. A book of this kind cannot aim to be exhaustive, but the main grammatical structures of Hindi are all presented here. Learn as much as possible by heart and augment your vocabulary from other sources whenever you can. Hindi is not a particularly difficult language to learn and you will find your efforts amply rewarded by the warm reactions of the Hindi-speaking world. A note on further learning material is included in Exercise 18b.3, which you can read in translation in the Key to the exercises.

Acknowledgements

The authors wish to thank Dr A.S. Kalsi, Mr M.D. Mundhra and Dr R.D. Gupta for their invaluable comments and suggestions on the Hindi text.

RS and SCRW

Acknowledgements to the new edition

The number of students, teachers and other readers whose suggestions over the last decade have influenced the content of this second edition is too great for them all to be named individually. I am however particularly indebted to my friend Dr A.S. Kalsi for his close reading of the new text and for teaching me Hindi as we teach it together at the School of Oriental and African Studies; such colleagues are among the greatest boons of academic life. Professor Frances Pritchett of the University of Columbia also deserves special thanks.

The Macintosh fonts 'Jaisalmer' (Devanagari) and 'Taj' (roman with diacriticals) have been kindly provided by their designer, Professor K.E. Bryant of the University of British Columbia; and the illustrations to the dialogues are by Kavita Dutta. Sue Hart, of Hodder & Stoughton, has been the most supportive of commissioning editors. Many thanks to these people.

RS

The dialogues: meet the Kumar family

The 37 dialogues tell the story of the Kumar family, who live in Delhi, and their paying guest Pratap, who is from London; many of the exercises also form part of the same narrative.

Pratap (21) has come to India to study Hindi at a private college run by Sharma ji. Pratap's divorced mother Anita, living in London, has arranged for him to stay as a paying guest with the Kumars. The Kumar family consists of the strong-willed Kamala and her obedient husband Prakash, their daughter Sangeeta (19), sons Rishi (14) and Raj (12) and Prakash's elderly but spry mother, whom everybody addresses as Dadi ji ('Grandma'). Tensions between Kamala and Prakash are not helped by their shared concern about the future of Sangeeta: they would like to see her married, but she strongly cherishes her independence. Sweet-natured Dadi ji, meanwhile, has a calming effect on the whole family.

Prakash's younger brother, the aspiring author Arun, often stays with them; he speaks a rather Sanskritised or formal Hindi (whereas his co-author Prem speaks a Hindi liberally sprinkled with English). Suresh, a neighbour of the Kumars, is another frequent visitor; he is closer to Kamala than to Prakash.

Prakash works in a company recently taken over by Mr Khanna, who has a rather pathetic office peon called Chotu. Khanna's younger sister Pinkie is a close friend of Sangeeta Kumar. Khanna's son Harish, like Pratap, admires Sangeeta from afar; but Sangeeta's heart is engaged elsewhere.

THE HINDI SCRIPT AND SOUND SYSTEM

Hindi is written in the Devanagari script, which is also used by Marathi and Nepali and is the main script for Sanskrit (India's classical language). Devanagari is pronounced as it's written, so 'what you see is what you get'. This makes it quite easy to learn. The script is written from left to right and has no capital letters.

Vowels have two forms: an independent *character* used when a vowel stands at the beginning of a syllable, and a dependent *sign* used for a vowel immediately following a consonant. Here's an example:

आ is the independent character form of the long vowel *ā*, pronounced as in the English word 'calm'. Placed before the consonant म *m* it forms the word आम *ām*, 'mango'. But in the name 'Ram', the same vowel sound is written with its dependent form (the sign ा), because the vowel now follows 'r' (र) as part of the syllable *rā*: hence राम *Rām*.

Consonants that are *not* followed by a dependent vowel sign are automatically followed by the short vowel *a*, pronounced as in 'alive'. It's called the 'inherent vowel' because it is *inherent* in the consonant character. This is why the Hindi consonants in the following table are transliterated *ka, kha, ga* etc. and not *k, kh, g* etc. The inherent vowel can be cancelled by writing the sign ् (called *virām* or *halant*) below the consonant: क *ka*, क् *k*.

You may have noticed that no inherent vowel was shown just now after the *m* character in the name राम; this is because the inherent vowel is dropped at the end of a word (and sometimes elsewhere, as we shall see later on). But this dropping doesn't occur in Sanskrit, where the name राम has two full syllables – *Rāma*, not *Rām*.

Two important contrasts lie at the heart of correct Hindi pronunciation. First, you must distinguish between 'dental' and 'retroflex' consonants. Dental consonants are pronounced with the tip of the tongue touching the upper teeth, giving a 'soft' sound: Hindi तीन *tīn* 'three' has much softer consonants than English 'teen'. Retroflex consonants are pronounced with the tongue curled back to touch the roof of the mouth, which it touches further back than in English, giving a 'hard' sound: Hindi लूट *lūṭ* has a harder 't' than English 'loot' (which, incidentally, derives from the Hindi word). To Hindi-speakers, English consonants sound more retroflex than dental; so they'll pronounce 'David' as डेविड *ḍeviḍ*.

The second important contrast is in the amount of breath that's released when a consonant is pronounced: 'aspirated' consonants contrast with 'unaspirated' ones. The same effect sometimes occurs in English: put your hand in front of your mouth and say 'pit, spit' loudly (when alone!), and you'll probably feel that the 's' reduces the aspiration accompanying the adjacent 'p'. Hindi has several pairs of aspirated/unaspirated consonants; English-speakers must try hard to curb their aspiration in pronouncing the unaspirated ones (practise saying 'Panjab' and 'Pakistan' with minimum aspiration in the 'p').

When pronouncing Hindi vowels, English-speakers must take care to avoid English-style diphthongs: words like से *se* ('from') and को *ko* ('to') are pure vowels that can be held unchanged as long as you have breath to hold them (try it!); they must not be pronounced like 'say' and 'Co', in which the quality of the vowel changes as you utter it.

You should now practise the shapes of the Devanagari characters. Using lined paper, begin on the left of each character and follow through to the right, completing the character with the headstroke, which should fall on the printed line; your words should hang from the printed line like washing put out to dry, not standing on the lower line as the Roman script does. Maintain the overall proportions of the characters carefully, not letting them get too straggly; each one should fill two-thirds of the space between your printed lines.

The Devanagari syllabary

Independent vowel characters

अ *a*	आ *ā*	इ *i*	ई *ī*
उ *u*	ऊ *ū*	ऋ *ṛ*	
ए *e*	ऐ *ai*	ओ *o*	औ *au*

Consonants

क *ka*	ख *kha*	ग *ga*	घ *gha*	(ङ् *ṅ*)*
च *ca*	छ *cha*	ज *ja*	झ *jha*	(ञ् *ñ*)*
ट *ṭa*	ठ *ṭha*	ड *ḍa*	ढ *ḍha*	ण *ṇa*
त *ta*	थ *tha*	द *da*	ध *dha*	न *na*
प *pa*	फ *pha*	ब *ba*	भ *bha*	म *ma*
य *ya*	र *ra*	ल *la*	व *va*	
श *śa*	ष *ṣa*	स *sa*	ह *ha*	

*These bracketed forms rarely occur and can be ignored for now.

Dependent vowel signs, based on क् as an example

क *ka*	का *kā*	कि *ki*	की *kī*
कु *ku*	कू *kū*	कृ *kṛ*	
के *ke*	कै *kai*	को *ko*	कौ *kau*

The Devanagari script and phonetics

The phonetic organisation of the Devanagari script was laid down by the grammarians of ancient India, who codified the Sanskrit language in order to preserve the effectiveness of its sacred mantras or prayer formulae. As a result, the main block of consonants from क *ka* to म *ma* has a very precise layout: the vertical columns show the *manner* of articulation (voiceless unaspirated and aspirated; voiced unaspirated and aspirated; nasal) while the horizontal rows show the *place* of articulation in the mouth (velar, palatal, retroflex, dental, labial).

Some Devanagari characters have 'dotted' versions which show sounds not occurring in Sanskrit. Thus the guide to pronunciation that follows includes seven characters that don't appear in the syllabary: क़ *qa*, ख़ *kha*, ग़ *ga*, ज़ *za*, ड़ *ṛa*, ढ़ *ṛha*, and फ़ *fa*. These characters are not distinguished in dictionary order from their undotted equivalents; and the dots are often omitted in both handwriting and print.

Vowels

Shown first in their independent forms, then in their dependent forms, again using the consonant क् by way of example.

अ	*a*	क	*ka*	as in 'alive'; inherent in any consonant not bearing a dependent vowel sign
आ	*ā*	का	*kā*	as in 'palm'
इ	*i*	कि	*ki*	as in 'hit'
ई	*ī*	की	*kī*	as in 'heat'
उ	*u*	कु	*ku*	as in 'foot'
ऊ	*ū*	कू	*kū*	as in 'fool'
ऋ	*ṛ*	कृ	*kṛ*	as 'ri' in 'critic'; in Sanskrit loanwords only
ए	*e*	के	*ke*	as in French *é*; a pure vowel sound, *not* a diphthong as in English
ऐ	*ai*	कै	*kai*	as in 'hen'
ओ	*o*	को	*ko*	as in the first part of 'o' in 'hotel'; a pure vowel sound, *not* a diphthong as in English

Ka, kha, Ga, Gha, Anga.

औ	*au*	कौ	*kau*	as in 'off'

A consonant can support only one dependent vowel. When two vowels appear in sequence, the second is written in its independent form: हुआ *huā,* जाओ *jāo,* लिए *lie,* कई *kaī,* दाऊद *daud,* etc.

The character र *ra* is something of a maverick; *ru* and *rū* have special forms – रु *ru,* and रू *rū.*

Velar consonants (produced in the throat)

क	*ka*	as in 'skit', with minimal release of breath
क़	*qa*	a 'k' sound produced further back than क *ka*
ख	*kha*	aspirated form of क *ka*: as in 'kit', but more aspirated
ख़	*kha*	as 'ch' in Scottish 'loch', or German 'Bach'
ग	*ga*	as in 'gift'
ग़	*ga*	a 'g' sound produced further back than ग *ga*
घ	*gha*	aspirated form of ग *ga*: as in 'dog-house'
ङ	*ṅ*	used only with a velar consonant; as in 'ink'; it is rarely seen in Hindi but is included here for completeness

Palatal consonants (produced at the palate)

च	*ca*	as in 'cheese', but with less release of breath
छ	*cha*	aspirated form of च *ca*: as in 'pitch-hook'
ज	*ja*	as in 'jeer'
ज़	*za*	as in 'zip'
झ	*jha*	aspirated form of ज *ja*: as in 'large house'.
ञ्	*ñ*	used only with a palatal consonant; as in 'inch' – rarely seen, but included here for completeness

Retroflex consonants (tongue curls back to touch the palate: 'hard' sounds)

ट	*ṭa*	as in 'train', but harder
ठ	*ṭha*	aspirated form of ट *ṭa*; as in 'at home'
ड	*ḍa*	as in 'drum', but harder

ड़ *ṛa* a flapped hard 'r'– the tongue makes a ड *ḍa* sound as it moves past the palate

ढ *ḍha* aspirated form of ड *ḍa*

ढ़ *ṛha* flapped equivalent of ढ *ḍha*

ण *ṇa* the retroflex nasal; a hard 'n' sound

Dental consonants (tongue touches the upper teeth: 'soft' sounds)

त *ta* as in 'at' within the phrase 'at the'

थ *tha* aspirated form of त *ta*

द *da* as in 'breadth'

ध *dha* aspirated form of द *da*

न *na* the dental nasal: as in 'anthem'

Labial consonants (produced with the lips)

प *pa* as in 'spin', with minimal release of breath

फ *pha* like 'p' in 'pin', but more aspirated, as in 'top-hat'

ब *ba* as in 'bin'

भ *bha* aspirated form of ब *ba*: as in 'club-house'

म *ma* as in 'mother'

Semi-vowels etc.

य *ya* as in 'yet', but less tense

र *ra* as in 'roll'

ल *la* a dental 'l'; softer than the first 'l' in 'label', and *much* softer than the second

व *va* between English 'v' and 'w'; the teeth don't touch the lip as in 'vest', but neither are the lips rounded as in 'west'

Sibilants

श *śa* as 'sh' in 'ship'

ष *ṣa* a retroflex 'sh'; usually not distinguished from श *śa* in pronunciation (found in Sanskrit loanwords only)

स *sa* as in 'sip'

Aspirate

ह *ha* This 'h' sound is always fully voiced, as in 'ahead'. It often 'lightens' an adjacent *a* vowel: both vowels in महल *mahal* ('palace') are similar to the 'e' in 'melt'.

Visarga

Visarga looks like a colon with widely spaced dots; it occurs without a headstroke within or at the end of a word, and is pronounced as ह *ha*. It's transliterated as *ḥ*, as in दुःख *duḥkh*, छः *chaḥ*. Mostly limited to Sanskrit loanwords.

Conjunct characters

Just when you thought you had mastered the script, along come the conjunct characters! When two consonants come in succession with no vowel between them, they are physically joined together as a 'conjunct'. In the word *sthān* ('place') for example, no vowel separates the 's' from the 'th', so स *sa* is reduced to a special half-form, स्‍ *s*, which is attached to the following थ *th* to form स्थ *stha* (स्थान *sthān*). Without the conjunct, the word would be read as '*sathān*'.

Most conjuncts are formed on this principle; but some are a little more complicated, and some don't resemble either of their component parts.

As already noted, र *ra* is a bit of a wild card. As the first member of a conjunct it appears in the 'flying' form र् above the headstroke, as in धर्म *dharm* (let's be very clear: the 'r' *precedes* the 'm' here). It's written at the very end of the syllable that it precedes in pronunciation: शर्मा *śarmā*, बर्फ़ी *barfī*. As the second member of a conjunct its characteristic sign is ्र as in प्र *pra*; but its location changes according to its partner:

ग्र *gra* ट्र *ṭra* ड्र *ḍra* त्र *tra* श्र *śra* स्र *sra* ह्र *hra*

The common conjuncts are shown in the following tables. In the first column the consonants are written initially with the *halant* sign ् introduced earlier; it cancels the inherent vowel. This list is meant for reference: have a look through it to familiarise yourself with the basic principle, but don't feel you have to learn all the forms immediately. You will pick them up gradually, as you encounter them.

To begin with, here are all the conjuncts that appear in Unit 1

क्	+	य	=	क्य
क्	+	र	=	क्र, क्र
ग्	+	र	=	ग्र
च्	+	च	=	च्च
च्	+	छ	=	च्छ
त्	+	थ	=	त्थ
न्	+	द	=	न्द
प्	+	र	=	प्र
र्	+	त	=	र्त
र्	+	फ़	=	र्फ़
र्	+	म	=	र्म
स्	+	त	=	स्त

And here is a list of the 100 most common conjuncts, numbered for convenience. (Two forms are regarded as independent characters in their own right: क्ष (क् + ष), pronounced 'ksha'; and ज्ञ (ज + ञ), pronounced 'gya'.)

1	क्	+	क	=	क्क	5	क्	+	र	=	क्र
2	क्	+	ख	=	क्ख	6	क्	+	ल	=	क्ल
3	क्	+	त	=	क्त, क्त	7	क्	+	व	=	क्व
4	क्	+	य	=	क्य	8	क्	+	श	=	क्श

9	क्	+	ष	=	क्ष	32	त्	+ त् +	व	=	त्त्व
10	क्	+ ष् +	म	=	क्ष्म	33	त्	+	थ	=	त्थ
11	क्	+	स	=	क्स	34	त्	+	न	=	त्न
12	ख्	+	य	=	ख्य	35	त्	+	म	=	त्म
13	ग्	+	द	=	ग्द	36	त्	+	य	=	त्य
14	ग्	+	न	=	ग्न	37	त्	+	र	=	त्र
15	ग्	+	र	=	ग्र	38	त्	+	व	=	त्व
16	ग्	+	ल	=	ग्ल	39	त्	+	स	=	त्स
17	ग्	+	व	=	ग्व	40	द्	+	ग	=	द्ग
18	घ्	+	र	=	घ्र	41	द्	+	द	=	द्द
19	च्	+	च	=	च्च	42	द्	+	ध	=	द्ध
20	च्	+	छ	=	च्छ	43	द्	+	भ	=	द्भ
21	ज्	+	ञ	=	ज्ञ	44	द्	+	म	=	द्म
22	ज्	+	र	=	ज्र	45	द्	+	य	=	द्य
23	ट्	+	ट	=	ट्ट	46	द्	+	र	=	द्र
24	ट्	+	ठ	=	ट्ठ	47	द्	+	व	=	द्व
25	ट्	+	र	=	ट्र	48	ध्	+	य	=	ध्य
26	ड्	+	ड	=	ड्ड	49	ध्	+	व	=	ध्व
27	ड्	+	र	=	ड्र	50	न्	+	त	=	न्त
28	ण्	+	ट	=	ण्ट	51	न्	+	द	=	न्द
29	ण्	+	ठ	=	ण्ठ	52	न्	+ द् +	र	=	न्द्र
30	त्	+	क	=	त्क	53	न्	+	न	=	न्न, न्न
31	त्	+	त	=	त्त	54	न्	+	य	=	न्य

55	न्	+	ह	=	न्ह	78	श्	+	क	=	श्क
56	प्	+	त	=	प्त	79	श्	+	च	=	श्च, श्च
57	प्	+	न	=	प्न	80	श्	+	य	=	श्य
58	प्	+	प	=	प्प	81	श्	+	र	=	श्र
59	प्	+	य	=	प्य	82	श्	+	व	=	श्व, श्व
60	प्	+	र	=	प्र	83	ष्	+	ट	=	ष्ट, ष्ट
61	प्	+	ल	=	प्ल	84	ष्	+ ट्	+ र	=	ष्ट्र
62	ब्	+	ज	=	ब्ज	85	ष्	+	ण	=	ष्ण
63	ब्	+	द	=	ब्द	86	स्	+	क	=	स्क
64	ब्	+	ध	=	ब्ध	87	स्	+	ट	=	स्ट
65	ब्	+	र	=	ब्र	88	स्	+	त	=	स्त
66	भ्	+	य	=	भ्य	89	स्	+ त्	+ र	=	स्त्र
67	भ्	+	र	=	भ्र	90	स्	+	थ	=	स्थ
68	म्	+	न	=	म्न	91	स्	+	न	=	स्न
69	म्	+	र	=	म्र	92	स्	+	प	=	स्प
70	र्	+	त	=	र्त	93	स्	+	य	=	स्य
71	र्	+	थ	=	र्थ	94	स्	+	र	=	स्र
72	र्	+	म	=	र्म	95	ह्	+	न	=	ह्न
73	र्	+	फ	=	र्फ	96	ह्	+	म	=	ह्म
74	र्	+	व	=	र्व	97	ह्	+	य	=	ह्य
75	र्	+	स	=	र्स	98	ह्	+	र	=	ह्र
76	ल्	+	म	=	ल्म	99	ह्	+	ल	=	ह्ल
77	व्	+	र	=	व्र	100	ह्	+	व	=	ह्व

Nasalised vowels, and conjuncts beginning with *n* or *m*

Any Hindi vowel (except ऋ *ṛ*) can be nasalised – some of the breath flows through the nose. Nasalised vowels bear the sign ँ, a moon and a dot, called *candrabindu* (*candra* 'moon', *bindu* 'dot', logically enough!). This is transliterated with a tilde (~) as in मुँह *mũh* 'mouth, face', and हाँ *hā̃* 'yes'.

Any vowel sign that protrudes above the headline eclipses the *candra* moon, so the *bindu* dot has to appear alone – नहीं *nahī̃* 'no', हैं *haĩ* 'are'. Some people replace *candrabindu* with *bindu* for all nasalised vowels, writing हां for हाँ *hā̃*. Should you do this? नहीं *nahī̃* 'No'! Should you write *candrabindu* in full where there's no superscript vowel? हाँ *hā̃* 'Yes'!

The *bindu* dot has a second function: it can replace any of the nasal consonants (ङ, ञ, ण, न, म) when they appear as the *first* member of a conjunct. Note its position in the following:

रंग	=	रङ्ग	*raṅg*	colour
पंजाब	=	पञ्जाब	*pañjāb*	Panjab
अंडा	=	अण्डा	*aṇḍa*	egg
हिंदी	=	हिन्दी	*hindī*	Hindi
लंबा	=	लम्बा	*lambā*	long, tall

Both spellings are correct and either may be used freely – although in the first two pairs, the simple *anusvār* forms (रंग, पंजाब) are *much* more common than their complicated alternatives. In this book, no special symbol is used for *anusvār*: both हिन्दी and हिंदी are transliterated as '*hindī*'.

Pronunciation

Do try to use the cassette, or better still get help from a native speaker, when practising pronunciation. Some watchpoints:

1 Short and long vowels in the pairs *a/ā, i/ī, u/ū* must be clearly distinguished, especially the *a/ā* pair as in कम *kam* 'less'/ काम *kām* 'work'; दल *dal* 'political party' / दाल *dāl* 'lentils'.

2 A doubled consonant is 'held' momentarily – as in English 'night train', whose 't...t' is held to distinguish it from 'night

rain'. So बच्चा *baccā* 'child' sounds different from बचा *bacā* 'survived'. The same effect occurs with repeated sounds in adjacent words: उस से *us se* 'from that' sounds different from उसे *use* 'to that'.

3 As we've seen, the inherent vowel is not pronounced at the end of a word. But there's an exception: it may be lightly pronounced when the word ends in a conjunct. Thus मित्र *mitr(a)* 'friend', अवश्य *avaśy(a)* 'of course'.

4 There are occasions when an inherent vowel is not pronounced in the *middle* of a word, even though the spelling involves no conjunct. As a general rule, the inherent vowel remains silent in the second syllable of a word whose third character either includes a vowel sign (thus समझ *samajh* 'understanding', but समझा *samjhā* 'understood') or is followed by a fourth syllable (thus मानव *mānav* 'human being', but जानवर *jānvar* 'animal'). This rule does not apply when the second or third syllable of the word has a conjunct.

5 Inherent vowel + य *ya*, as in समय *samay* 'time' and जय *jay* 'victory', is pronounced *ai* (indeed, the spellings समै *samai* and जै *jai* were once current).

6 The pattern of stress across a sentence is more even in Hindi than in English – emphasis is usually carried by the addition of 'particles' (short indeclinable words) rather than through the voice.

Punctuation and other signs

The 'full stop' is a vertical line (।) called *daṇḍ* 'stick' or *khaṛī pāī* 'perpendicular line'. Other punctuation follows English usage.

In writing abbreviations, a small circle (०) follows the first entire *akṣar* or syllable of the abbreviated word:

उ० प्र०	=	उत्तर प्रदेश Uttar Pradesh
पं० गो० ना० शर्मा	=	पंडित गोपाल नारायण शर्मा Pandit Gopal Narayan Sharma

The ० is dropped when the initials cohere as an acronym:

भाजपा	=	भारतीय जनता पार्टी Bharatiya Janata Party
नभाटा	=	नवभारत टाइम्स NavBharat Times (newspaper)

Sometimes abbreviations are merely transliterations of the English:

यू० पी०	=	*(yū. pī.)*	UP
जी० एन० शर्मा	=	*(jī. en. śarmā*	G.N. Sharma
बी० जे० पी०	=	*(bī. je. pī*	BJP

English 'o' sounds as in 'chocolate' or 'sorry' are pronounced by some Hindi speakers as similar to *ā*; and Devanagari spellings of such sounds may use a special *candra* character (without dot) over the vowel: चॉकलेट, सॉरी.

Alternative spellings

ए *e* following a vowel in verb endings can have different forms (the standard form is shown in the left-hand column):

जाए *jae*	=	जायें *jāye*, जाय *jāy* may go
जाइए *jāie*	=	जाइये *jāiy* please go
चाहिए *cāhie*	=	चाहिये *cāhiye* needed

The use of conjuncts in loans from Persian is not fully standardised:

उमर *umar*	=	उम्र *umr* age
गरम *garam*	=	गर्म *garm* warm, hot
परदा *pardā*	=	पर्दा *pardā* curtain, purdah

Numerals

०	१	२	३	४	५	६	७	८	९
0	1	2	3	4	5	6	7	8	9

The so-called 'Arabic' numerals (which originated in India!) are used at least as commonly as the Devanagari numerals.

Dictionary order

The dictionary order of the script follows the pattern shown in the Devanagari syllabary section, reading horizontally. Three principles apply:

1 Syllables with *candrabindu* or *anusvār* precede those without: गाँव *gā̃v* 'village' precedes गाड़ी *gāṛī* 'train, car', and तंग *tang* 'narrow' precedes तक *tak* 'up to'.

2 Non-conjunct forms precede conjunct forms: छाता *chātā* 'umbrella' precedes छात्र *chātr* 'pupil', and बचा *bacā* 'survived' precedes बच्चा *baccā* 'child'.

3 'Dotted' forms (e.g. क़ *qa*, ड़ *ṛa*, ज़ *za*) are not distinguished in sequence from 'undotted' equivalents (क *ka*, ड *ḍa*, ज *ja*).

Note: Transcriptions of the Hindi sounds on the cassette are given at the beginning of the Key to the exercises on page 260.

1 I AM PRATAP
मैं प्रताप हूँ

In this unit you will learn how to

- greet and identify people
- ask and answer 'yes/no' questions
- ask people how they are
- use adjectives

1a Pratap, from London, meets his Delhi host

प्रताप नमस्ते । मैं प्रताप हूँ । क्या आप कमला जी हैं ?

कमला जी हाँ, मैं कमला हूँ । नमस्ते । यह लड़का राज है ।

प्रताप नमस्ते राज । तुम ठीक हो ?

राज जी हाँ, शुक्रिया, मैं ठीक हूँ । क्या आप अँग्रेज़ हैं ?

प्रताप जी नहीं, मैं अँग्रेज़ नहीं हूँ, हिन्दुस्तानी हूँ ।

राज अच्छा, आप हिन्दुस्तानी हैं !
प्रताप जी हाँ । क्या वह गाड़ी जापानी है ?
राज नहीं, वह जापानी नहीं है, वह मारुति है ।

Pratāp *namaste. maĩ Pratāp hũ. kyā āp Kamalā jī haĩ?*
Kamalā *jī hā̃, maĩ Kamalā hũ. namaste. yah laṛkā Rāj hai.*
Pratāp *namaste Rāj. tum ṭhīk ho?*
Rāj *jī hā̃, śukriyā, maĩ ṭhīk hũ. kyā āp ā̃grez haĩ?*
Pratāp *jī nahī̃, maĩ ā̃grez nahī̃ hũ, hindustānī hũ.*
Rāj *acchā, āp hindustānī haĩ!*
Pratāp *jī hā̃. kyā vah gāṛī jāpānī hai?*
Rāj *nahī̃, vah jāpānī nahī̃ hai, vah Māruti hai.*

नमस्ते *namaste* hello
मैं *maĩ* I
हूँ *hũ* am
क्या *kyā* question-marker
आप *āp* you (formal)
जी *jī* respect-marker
हैं *haĩ* are
जी हाँ *jī hā̃* yes
यह *yah* this
लड़का [m] *laṛkā* boy
है *hai* is
तुम *tum* you (familiar)
ठीक *ṭhīk* all right
हो *ho* are
शुक्रिया *śukriyā* thank you
अँग्रेज़ *ā̃grez* English
जी नहीं *jī nahī̃* no
नहीं *nahī̃* not
हिन्दुस्तानी *hindustānī* Indian
अच्छा *acchā* good, really?, I see!
हाँ *hā̃* yes
वह *vah* it, that
गाड़ी [f] *gāṛī* car
जापानी *jāpānī* Japanese
मारुति [f] *māruti* Maruti (make of car)

Pratap Hello, I am Pratap. Are you Kamala ji?
Kamala Yes, I'm Kamala. Hello. This boy is Raj.
Pratap Hello Raj. Are you OK?
Raj Yes, thank you, I'm OK. Are you English?
Pratap No, I'm not English, I'm Indian.
Raj Oh, you're Indian!
Pratap Yes. Is that car Japanese?
Raj No, it's not Japanese, it's a Maruti.

Grammar

1.1 Personal pronouns and the verb 'to be'

SINGULAR			PLURAL		
मैं हूँ	*maĩ hū̃*	I am	हम हैं	*ham haĩ*	we are
तू है	*tū hai*	you are (intimate)	तुम हो	*tum ho*	you are (familiar)
			आप हैं	*āp haĩ*	you are (formal)
यह है	*yah hai*	he, she, it, this is	ये हैं	*ye haĩ*	these, they are; he, she is (formal)
वह है	*vah hai*	he, she, it, that is	वे हैं	*ve haĩ*	those, they are; he, she is (formal)

Hindi has a subtle system of 'honorific' levels – like French tu/vous, or German du/Sie. There are three second-person pronouns, each with its own verb form as shown in the table.

> **तू** ***tū*** indicates great intimacy and is used in addressing a close loved one or a small child.
>
> **तुम** ***tum*** is informal and casual and is used with a person expecting no formality or deference – a friend, child or servant.
>
> **आप** ***āp*** is relatively formal; it indicates the respect one shows towards equals (and above!) and is the natural choice in conversations with all people not falling into the previous categories.

Both तुम *tum* and आप *āp* are grammatically plural; but either may indicate several people (numerical plural) or a single individual (honorific plural).

The honorific system extends into the third person: when referring to a person whom you would address face-to-face as आप *āp*, use the plural forms ये *ye* / वे *ve*.

यह *yah* and its plural ये *ye* refer to a subject that's nearby, while वह *vah* (which is often pronounced '*vo*') and वे *ve* refer to a subject that's more remote – rather like English 'this' and 'that'. Unless a specific sense of 'nearness' is involved, use वह/ वे *vah*/*ve*.

The honorific system can indicate disdain as well as respect: to use a lower-grade honorific than expected by the person you're talking to can imply severe disrespect. So you must observe the usages of others and learn from them. When in doubt, stick to आप *āp*!

मैं गुजराती हूँ ।	*maĩ gujarātī hū̃.*	I am Gujarati.
वह जर्मन है ।	*vah jarman hai.*	He/she is German.
हम पंजाबी हैं ।	*ham panjābī haĩ.*	We are Panjabi.
तुम अँग्रेज़ हो ?	*tum ãgrez ho?*	You're English?
आप हिन्दुस्तानी हैं ।	*āp hindustānī haĩ.*	You are Indian.
वे भारतीय हैं ।	*ve bhāratīy haĩ.*	They are Indian. (or He/she is Indian.)

1.2 Questions and answers

Questions expecting a 'yes/no' answer are formed by simply prefixing a statement with क्या *kyā*:

तुम ठीक हो ।	*tum ṭhīk ho.*	You're OK. (statement)
क्या तुम ठीक हो ?	*kyā tum ṭhīk ho?*	Are you OK? (question)

In speech, a question can be conveyed by a rising tone, as in English:

तुम ठीक हो ?	*tum ṭhīk ho?*	You're OK?

1b Kamala shows Pratap his room

प्रताप	यह कमरा बहुत बड़ा है ! क्या दूसरे कमरे छोटे हैं ?
कमला	जी नहीं । सिर्फ़ एक कमरा छोटा है, दूसरे बड़े हैं ।
प्रताप	क्या यह बड़ी अलमारी ख़ाली है ?
कमला	जी हाँ, ज़रूर, दोनों अलमारियाँ ख़ाली हैं ।
प्रताप	और यहाँ एक मेज़ और दो कुरसियाँ हैं । क्या पंखा नहीं है ?
कमला	पंखा नहीं है; लेकिन खिड़की काफ़ी बड़ी है ।
प्रताप	बहुत अच्छा । कमरा साफ़ और बहुत हवादार है ।

Pratāp	*yah kamrā bahut baṛā hai! kyā dūsre kamre choṭe haĩ?*
Kamalā	*jī nahĩ. sirf ek kamrā choṭā hai, dūsre baṛe haĩ.*

Pratāp	*kyā yah baṛī almārī khālī hai?*
Kamalā	*jī hā̃, zarūr, donõ almāriyā̃ khālī haĩ.*
Pratāp	*aur yahā̃ ek mez aur do kursiyā̃ haĩ. kyā pankhā nahī̃ hai?*
Kamalā	*pankhā nahī̃ hai; lekin khiṛkī kāfī baṛī hai.*
Pratāp	*bahut acchā. kamrā sāf aur bahut havādār hai.*

कमरा^{m}	*kamrā*	room	और	*aur*	and
बहुत	*bahut*	very	यहाँ	*yahā̃*	here
बड़ा	*baṛā*	big	मेज़^{f}	*mez*	table
दूसरा	*dūsrā*	other	दो	*do*	two
छोटा	*choṭā*	small	कुरसी^{f}	*kursī*	chair
सिर्फ़	*sirf*	only	पंखा^{m}	*pankhā*	fan
एक	*ek*	one, a	लेकिन	*lekin*	but
अलमारी^{f}	*almārī*	cupboard	खिड़की^{f}	*khiṛkī*	window
ख़ाली	*khālī*	empty, vacant	काफ़ी	*kāfī*	quite
ज़रूर	*zarūr*	of course	साफ़	*sāf*	clean
दोनों	*donõ*	both	हवादार	*havadar*	airy

Pratap	This room is very big! Are the other rooms small?
Kamala	No. Only one room is small, the others are big.
Pratap	Is this big cupboard empty?
Kamala	Yes, of course, both cupboards are empty.
Pratap	And here there's a table and two chairs. Isn't there a fan?
Kamala	There's no fan; but the window is quite big.
Pratap	Very good. The room is clean and very airy.

Grammar

1.3 Nouns

Hindi nouns are either masculine or feminine; the gender of every new noun must be learnt. There is no definite article 'the'; एक *ek*, the number 'one', sometimes functions as the indefinite article 'a'.

Masculine nouns are of two types: those ending *-ā* in the singular, changing to *-e* in the plural; and all others, which are the same in both singular and plural.

Masculine type 1

लड़का	*laṛkā*	boy	लड़के	*laṛke*	boys
कमरा	*kamrā*	room	कमरे	*kamre*	rooms

Masculine type 2

मकान	*makān*	house	मकान	*makān*	houses
आदमी	*ādmī*	man	आदमी	*ādmī*	men

Not all nouns ending in *-ā* are masculine: many Sanskrit loanwords such as आशा *āśā* 'hope' and भाषा *bhāṣā* 'language' (and names like कमला *Kamalā*) are feminine. A few masculines ending in *-ā* belong to type 2 and therefore don't change in the plural; these are mostly relationship terms like पिता *pitā* 'father', चाचा *cācā* 'uncle' – but also राजा *rājā* 'king'.

Feminine nouns are also of two types: those ending *-ī*, *-i* or *-iyā* in the singular, all changing to *-iyā̃* in the plural; and all others, which add *-ẽ* in the plural.

Feminine type 1

लड़की	*laṛkī*	girl	लड़कियाँ	*laṛkiyā̃*	girls
प्रति	*prati*	copy (of book)	प्रतियाँ	*pratiyā̃*	copies
चिड़िया	*ciṛiyā*	bird	चिड़ियाँ	*ciṛiyā̃*	birds

Feminine type 2

मेज़	*mez*	table	मेज़ें	*mezẽ*	tables
माता	*mātā*	mother	माताएँ	*mātāẽ*	mothers

Feminine nouns ending *-ū* are of type 2, but shorten the *-ū* to *-u-* in the plural: बहू *bahū* 'daughter-in-law', बहुएँ *bahuẽ* 'daughters-in-law'.

> **!** आदमी *ādmī* 'man' derives from Arabic and means 'descendant of Adam'; compare मानव *mānav* 'man, human being', derived from Sanskrit and meaning 'descendant of Manu' (the progenitor of the world in Hindu belief).

1.4 Adjectives

Adjectives agree with the nouns they qualify. They are of two types: those that inflect (change their endings), and those that are invariable.

Inflecting adjectives follow the pattern of बड़ा *baṛā* 'big': *-ā* masculine singular, *-e* masculine plural, *-ī* feminine singular and plural.

बड़ा लड़का	*baṛā laṛkā*	big boy
बड़े लड़के	*baṛe laṛke*	big boys
बड़ी लड़की	*baṛī laṛkī*	big girl
बड़ी लड़कियाँ	*baṛī laṛkiyā̃*	big girls
छोटा मकान	*choṭā makān*	small house
छोटे मकान	*choṭe makān*	small houses
छोटी मेज़	*choṭī mez*	small table
छोटी मेज़ें	*choṭī mezẽ*	small tables

Invariable adjectives, of course, remain unchanged:

ख़ाली कमरा	*khālī kamrā*	vacant room
ख़ाली कमरे	*khālī kamre*	vacant rooms
लाल कुरसी	*lāl kursī*	red chair
लाल कुरसियाँ	*lāl kursiyā̃*	red chairs
सुन्दर मकान	*sundar makan*	beautiful house
सुन्दर मकान	*sundar makān*	beautiful houses
साफ़ मेज़	*saf mez*	clean table
साफ़ मेज़ें	*sāf mezẽ*	clean tables

One or two adjectives ending *-ā*, such as बढ़िया *baṛhiyā* 'excellent', are invariable; these are marked 'inv.' in the Glossary.

1.5 The simple sentence

A typical sentence begins with the subject and ends with the verb. The question-word क्या *kyā* usually precedes the subject; the negative नहीं *nahī̃* precedes the verb.

क्या यह मूर्ति है ?	*kyā yah mūrti hai?* Is this a statue?
यह मूर्ति नहीं है । पत्थर है ।	*yah mūrti nahī̃ hai. patthar hai.* It's not a statue. It's a stone.

The last example shows how a pronoun can be dropped if its reference is entirely clear: [यह] पत्थर है *[yah] patthar hai*. Similarly a verb can be dropped when negated: मैं अमरीकन नहीं [हूँ], रूसी हूँ *maĩ amrīkan nahī̃ [hū̃], rūsī hū̃* 'I'm not American, I'm Russian'.

Word order: note the very important difference in meaning between the following:

यह कमरा बड़ा है।	*yah kamrā baṛā hai.*	This room is big.
यह बड़ा कमरा है।	*yah baṛā kamrā hai.*	This is a big room.

The first sentence answers the question 'What is this room like?', and gives the information 'big'; the second answers the question 'What is this?', and gives the information 'a big room'.

EXERCISE 1a Fill the gap with हूँ *hū̃*, हो *ho*, है *hai*, or हैं *haĩ*. Then translate.

१ वह आदमी पंजाबी... ।

२ क्या ये आदमी पाकिस्तानी... ?

३ राज, तू अच्छा लड़का नहीं... ।

४ मैं जर्मन नहीं... , रूसी... ।

५ हम लोग हिन्दू नहीं... , लेकिन यह आदमी हिन्दू... ।

६ पीटर, क्या तुम अँग्रेज़... ? नहीं, मैं जर्मन... ।

७ क्या तुम दोनों अँग्रेज़... ? नहीं, हम अमरीकन... ।

८ सुशीला गुजराती... , लेकिन सुशील और रवि दोनों पंजाबी... ।

९ क्या आप प्रताप... ? जी हाँ, मैं प्रताप... ।

१० क्या वे दो आदमी जर्मन... ? नहीं, वे अँग्रेज़... ।

1 *vah ādmī panjābī... .*
2 *kyā ye ādmī pākistānī... ?*
3 *Rāj, tū acchā laṛkā nahī̃... .*
4 *maĩ jarman nahī̃... , rūsī... .*
5 *ham log hindū nahī̃... , lekin yah ādmī hindu... .*
6 *Pīṭar, kyā tum ãgrez... ? nahī̃, maĩ jarman... .*
7 *kyā tum donõ ãgrez... ? nahī̃, ham amrīkan... .*
8 *Suśīlā gujarātī... , lekin Suśīl aur Ravi donõ panjābī... .*
9 *kyā āp Pratāp... ? jī hā̃, maĩ Pratāp... .*
10 *kyā ve do ādmī jarman... ? nahī̃, ve ãgrez... .*

EXERCISE 1b Translate this entry from Pratap's diary.

रविवार, १५ जनवरी

कमला और प्रकाश कुमार बहुत अच्छे लोग हैं । तीन बच्चे हैं – एक लड़की, संगीता, और दो लड़के, ऋषि और राज । संगीता बहुत सुन्दर है । ऋषि बड़ा है, राज छोटा है । दादी जी बूढ़ी हैं लेकिन बहुत अच्छी हैं । मकान साफ़ है और बग़ीचा बहुत सुन्दर है । मेरा कमरा काफ़ी बड़ा है । एक पलंग, दो अलमारियाँ (दोनों ख़ाली), एक छोटी मेज़, दो कुरसियाँ हैं । पंखा नहीं है, लेकिन कमरा हवादार है । एक सफ़ेद मारुति गाड़ी और दो-तीन पुरानी साइकिलें हैं ।

ravivār, 15 janvarī

Kamalā aur Prakāś Kumār bahut acche log haĩ. tīn bacce haĩ – ek laṛkī, Sangītā, aur do laṛke, Ṛṣi aur Rāj. Sangītā bahut sundar hai. Ṛṣi baṛā hai, Rāj choṭā hai. dādī jī būṛhī haĩ lekin bahut acchī haĩ. makān sāf hai aur bagīcā bahut sundar hai. merā kamrā kāfī baṛā hai. ek palang, do almāriyā̃ (donõ khālī), ek choṭī mez, do kursiyā̃ haĩ. pankhā nahī̃ hai, lekin kamrā havādār hai. ek safed Māruti gāṛī aur do-tīn purānī sāikilẽ haĩ.

Vocabulary

अँग्रेज़ m, f *ãgrez* English person
अच्छा *acchā* good, nice; really?, o I see!
अमरीकन *amrīkan* American
अलमारी f *almārī* cupboard
आदमी m *ādmī* man, person
आप *āp* you (formal)
आशा f *āśā* hope
और *aur* and
एक *ek* one, a
कमरा m *kamrā* room
काफ़ी *kāfī* quite
कुरसी f *kursī* chair
क्या *kyā* (question-marker)
ख़ाली *khālī* empty, vacant
खिड़की f *khiṛkī* window
गाड़ी f *gāṛī* car
गुजराती *gujarātī* Gujarati
चाचा m *cācā* paternal uncle
चिड़िया f *ciṛiyā* bird
छोटा *choṭā* small
जनवरी f *janvarī* January
ज़रूर *zarūr* of course, certainly
जर्मन *jarman* German
जापानी *jāpānī* Japanese
जी *jī* (respect-marker)

जी नहीं *jī nahī̃* no
जी हाँ *jī hā̃* yes
ठीक *ṭhīk* all right, OK
तीन *tīn* three
तुम *tum* you (familiar)
तू *tū* you (intimate)
दादी [f] *dādī* grandmother
दूसरा *dūsrā* other, second
दो *do* two
दोनों *donõ* both
नमस्ते *namaste* hello; goodbye
नहीं *nahī̃* not
पंखा [m] *pankhā* fan
पंजाबी *panjābī* Panjabi
पत्थर [m] *patthar* stone
पलंग [m] *palang* bed
पाकिस्तानी *pākistānī* Pakistani
पिता [m] *pitā* father
पुराना *purānā* old (of things)
प्रति [f] *prati* copy
बग़ीचा [m] *bagīcā* garden
बच्चा [m] *baccā* child
बड़ा *baṛā* big
बहुत *bahut* very
बहू [f] *bahū* daughter-in-law
बूढ़ा *būṛhā* elderly
भारतीय *bhāratīy* Indian
भाषा [f] *bhāṣā* language
मकान [m] *makān* house
माता [f] *mātā* mother
मानव [m] *mānav* human being
मारुति [f] *māruti* Maruti (car make)
मूर्ति [f] *mūrti* statue, image
मेज़ [f] *mez* table
मैं *maĩ* I
यह *yah* this, he, she, it
यहाँ *yahā̃* here
ये *ye* these, they; he, she (formal)
रविवार [m] *ravivār* Sunday
राजा [m] *rājā* king
रूसी *rūsī* Russian
लड़का [m] *laṛkā* boy
लड़की [f] *laṛkī* girl
लाल *lāl* red
लोग [m. pl] *log* people
वह *vah* that, he, she, it
वे *ve* those, they; he, she (formal)
शुक्रिया *śukriyā* thank you
सफ़ेद *safed* white
साइकिल [f] *sāikil* bicycle
साफ़ *sāf* clean
सिर्फ़ *sirf* only
सुन्दर *sundar* beautiful
हम *ham* we
हवादार *havādār* airy
हाँ *hā̃* yes
हिन्दुस्तानी *hindustānī* Indian
हिन्दू *hindū* Hindu
हूँ *hū̃* am; है *hai* is; हैं *haĩ* are;
हो *ho* are

2 QUESTIONS AND ANSWERS

सवाल और जवाब

In this unit you will learn how to

- ask and answer questions about quality and number
- describe things
- use adjectives
- use conversational conventions

2a Pratap in his Hindi teacher's office

प्रताप अध्यापक जी, यहाँ कितने विद्यार्थी हैं ?

शर्मा जी अभी चौदह हैं – नौ लड़कियाँ और पाँच लड़के ।

प्रताप यह "टीच योरसेल्फ़ हिन्दी" कैसी किताब है ? क्या यह अच्छी है ?

शर्मा जी हाँ, बुरी नहीं है । लेकिन सस्ती नहीं है, काफ़ी महँगी है ।

प्रताप क्या ये शब्दकोश भी महँगे हैं ?

शर्मा जी नहीं, बिलकुल नहीं । बहुत सस्ते हैं ।

प्रताप	और वह मोटी किताब क्या है ? क्या वह भी शब्दकोश है ?
शर्मा जी	नहीं नहीं, वह शब्दकोश नहीं है, रामायण है !

Pratāp	*adhyāpak jī, yahā̃ kitne vidyārthī haĩ ?*
Śarmā jī	*abhī caudah haĩ – nau laṛkiyā̃ aur pā̃c laṛke.*
Pratāp	*yah 'ṭīc yorself hindī' kaisī kitāb hai? kyā yah acchī hai?*
Śarmā jī	*hā̃, burī nahī̃ hai. lekin sastī nahī̃ hai, kāfī mahãgī hai.*
Pratāp	*kyā ye śabdkoś bhī mahãge haĩ?*
Śarmā jī	*nahī̃, bilkul nahī̃. bahut saste haĩ.*
Pratāp	*aur vah moṭī kitāb kyā hai? kyā vah bhī śabdkoś hai?*
Śarmā jī	*nahī̃ nahī̃, vah śabdkoś nahī̃ hai, rāmāyaṇ hai!*

अध्यापक m	*adhyāpak*	teacher	**सस्ता**	*sastā*	cheap
कितना	*kitnā*	how much/many	**महँगा**	*mahãgā*	expensive
विद्यार्थी m, f	*vidyārthī*	student	**शब्दकोश** m	*śabdkoś*	dictionary
अभी	*abhī*	at the moment, just now	**भी**	*bhī*	also, too
चौदह	*caudah*	fourteen	**बिलकुल**	*bilkul*	quite
नौ	*nau*	nine	**बिलकुल नहीं**	*bilkul nahī̃*	not at all
पाँच	*pā̃c*	five	**मोटा**	*moṭā*	fat, thick
कैसा	*kaisā*	of what kind, what like	**क्या**	*kyā*	what
किताब f	*kitāb*	book	**रामायण** m	*rāmāyaṇ*	Ramayan (epic poem)
बुरा	*burā*	bad			

Pratap	Teacher ji, how many students are there here?
Sharma ji	At the moment there are 14 – nine girls and five boys.
Pratap	What kind of book is this *Teach Yourself Hindi*? Is it good?
Sharma ji	Yes, it's not bad. But it's not cheap, it's quite expensive.
Pratap	Are these dictionaries also expensive?
Sharma ji	No, not at all. They're very cheap.
Pratap	And what is that thick book? Is it a dictionary too?
Sharma ji	No no, it's not a dictionary, it's the Ramayan!

Grammar

2.1 Interrogative words

Interrogative words – often beginning 'wh' in English – begin with क् *k* in Hindi:

क्या	*kyā*	what?
कौन	*kaun*	who?
कैसा/ कैसी/ कैसे	*kaisā/kaisī/kaise*	of what kind?
कितना/ कितनी/ कितने	*kitnā/ kitnī/ kitne*	how much, how many?

> **!** क्या *kyā* 'what?' has a different role here from the 'yes-no' question-maker role that we met in 1.2.

यह क्या है ?	*yah kyā hai?*	What is this?
तुम कौन हो ?	*tum kaun ho?*	Who are you?
मौसम कैसा है ?	*mausam kaisā hai?*	What's the weather like?
कितने विद्यार्थी हैं ?	*kitne vidyārthī haĩ?*	How many students are there?

> **!** मौसम *mausam*, an Arabic loanword, is the ultimate source of the English word 'monsoon'.

2.2 Agreement of adjectives with mixed genders

A plural adjective qualifying a group of people of mixed gender is masculine:

ऋषि और संगीता लंबे हैं ।	*Ṛṣi aur Sangītā lambe haĩ.* Rishi and Sangeeta are tall.
राज और कमला दुबले नहीं हैं ।	*Rāj aur Kamalā duble nahī̃ haĩ.* Raj and Kamala are not thin.

With inanimate nouns of mixed gender, a plural adjective agrees with the nearest noun:

ये चप्पलें और जूते गंदे हैं ।	*ye cappalẽ aur jūte gande haĩ.* These sandals and shoes are dirty.
वे काग़ज़ और चिट्ठियाँ पुरानी हैं ।	*ve kāgaz aur ciṭṭhiyā̃ purānī haĩ.* Those papers and letters are old.

In the first sentence, गंदे *gande* agrees with masculine plural जूते *jūte;* and in the second sentence, पुरानी *purānī* agrees with feminine plural चिट्ठियाँ *ciṭṭhiyā̃.*

> **!** Learning a new noun *with* an adjective helps you learn the noun's gender: अच्छी किताब *acchī kitāb,* बड़ा मकान *baṛā makān,* and so on.

2b Pratap's little problem

प्रताप	हलो राज, क्या हाल है ? सब ठीक है ?
राज	हाँ, सब ठीक है । और आप कैसे हैं ?
प्रताप	मैं भी अच्छा हूँ, शुक्रिया । ऋषि और संगीता कैसे हैं ?
राज	ऋषि अच्छा है, लेकिन संगीता अच्छी नहीं है ।
प्रताप	क्यों ? क्या बात है ? क्या वह बीमार है ?
राज	नहीं, वह नाराज़ है क्योंकि... क्योंकि आप यहाँ हैं !
प्रताप	अच्छा ? यह बहुत बुरी बात है ! पर संगीता क्यों परेशान है ?
राज	मालूम नहीं । लड़की है, न ?

Pratāp	*halo Rāj, kyā hāl hai? sab ṭhīk hai?*
Rāj	*hā̃, sab ṭhīk hai. aur āp kaise haĩ?*
Pratāp	*maĩ bhī acchā hū̃, śukriyā. Ṛṣi aur Sangītā kaise haĩ?*
Rāj	*Ṛṣi acchā hai, lekin Sangītā acchī nahī̃ hai.*
Pratāp	*kyõ? kyā bāt hai? kyā vah bīmār hai?*
Rāj	*nahī̃, vah nārāz hai kyõki... kyõki āp yahā̃ haĩ!*
Pratāp	*acchā? yah bahut burī bāt hai ! par Sangītā kyõ pareśān hai?*
Rāj	*mālūm nahī̃. laṛkī hai, na?*

हलो *halo* hello
हाल m *hāl* condition, state
सब *sab* everything, all
क्यों *kyõ* why
बात f *bāt* matter, thing
बीमार *bīmār* ill
नाराज़ *nārāz* angry, displeased
क्योंकि *kyõki* because
पर *par* but
परेशान *pareśān* troubled, upset
मालूम नहीं *mālūm nahī̃* [I] don't know
न *na* not; isn't that so?

Pratap	Hello Raj, how're things? Everything OK?
Raj	Yes, everything's OK. And how are you?
Pratap	I'm well too, thank you. How are Rishi and Sangeeta?
Raj	Rishi is well, but Sangeeta isn't all right.
Pratap	Why? What's the matter? Is she ill?
Raj	No, she's in a huff because... because you're here!
Pratap	Really? This is a very bad thing! But why is Sangeeta upset?
Raj	[I] don't know. She's a girl, isn't she?

Grammar

2.3 Some conversational features

The greetings नमस्ते *namaste* or नमस्कार *namaskār*, often said formally with the hands folded in front of the chest, mean 'Hello', 'Good morning', 'Goodbye' etc.

The word जी *jī* following a surname means roughly 'Mr' (e.g. शर्मा जी *śarmā jī* 'Mr Sharma'), although its tone is rather more cordial. जी *jī* can also be used with first names, both male and female, equivalent in formality to use of the pronoun आप *āp*; it is often attached to terms of relationship – पिताजी *pitājī* 'Father', माताजी *mātājī* 'Mother' etc. जी *jī* also occurs alone, roughly in the sense 'sir' (but with either gender), and the loanwords सर *sar* 'sir' and मैडम *maiḍam* 'madam' are also common. साहब *sāhab* is an alternative to जी *jī*, especially common with Muslim names.

भाई *bhāī* 'brother' is used in addressing males of similar age to oneself; the more formal भाई साहब *bhāī sāhab* is useful in addressing strangers. Similarly बहिन जी *bahin jī* for females.

श्री *śrī* and श्रीमती *śrīmatī* mean 'Mr' and 'Mrs' respectively. श्री *śrī* also means 'lord'(with a deity): श्री कृष्ण *śrī kṛṣṇa* 'Lord Krishna'.

क्या हाल है? *kyā hāl hai?* means literally 'What's [your] condition?' – a colloquial alternative to the more literal आप कैसे (कैसी) हैं? *āp kaise (kaisī) haĩ ?* 'How are you?'.

Honorific usages such as आप *āp* are innately polite, often making equivalents for 'please' and 'thank you' redundant. In formal contexts you will hear कृपया *kṛpayā* 'please' and धन्यवाद *dhanyavād* 'thank you', while प्लीज़ *plīz* 'please' and शुक्रिया *śukriyā* 'thanks' have a more colloquial ring. मेहरबानी है *meharbānī hai* (literally 'it is [through your] kindness') also means 'thank you'.

अच्छा *acchā* 'good' bears various meanings, depending on tone: 'Good!', 'Really?' 'Ah, I see!' etc.

मालूम नहीं *mālūm nahī̃* '[I] don't know' (lit. 'not known') is introduced more fully in 4.4.

The negative न *na* after a verb invites confirmation, as in 'is it not so?' – तुम ठीक हो, न? *tum ṭhīk ho, na?* 'You're all right, aren't you?'. It's like the French 'n'est ce pas?'.

As well as meaning 'and', और *aur* means 'more, else, other': और कौन? *aur kaun?* 'who else?'; और क्या *aur kyā* 'what else/of course'; और लोग *aur log* 'more/other people'. In this meaning, और *aur* is stressed in speech.

The position of भी *bhī* 'also' is essential – *it qualifies the word(s) immediately preceding it:*

ऋषि भी होशियार है ।	*Ṛṣi bhī hośiyār hai.* Rishi too is clever.
ऋषि होशियार भी है ।	*Ṛṣi hośiyār bhī hai.* Rishi is clever too. [as well as e.g. tall]

2.4 More on adjectives and nouns

Remember that the pronouns आप *āp* and तुम *tum* are grammatically plural, even when referring to just one person. So adjectives agreeing with them must also be in the plural. The question आप कैसे (कैसी) हैं? *āp kaise (kaisī) haĩ?* 'How are you?' can, as in English, address one person or a group of people.

Adding the pluralising word लोग *log* 'people' will specify a *numerical* plural:

हम लोग बहुत ख़ुश हैं ।	*ham log bahut k͟huś haĩ.* We are very happy.
तुम लोग कैसे हो ?	*tum log kaise ho?* How are you lot?
वे लोग पागल हैं ।	*ve log pāgal haĩ.* They (those people) are crazy.

A masculine noun of type 1 (see 1.3) will show its *-e* plural in honorific plurals as well as numerical ones: thus तुम लड़के *tum laṛke* means both 'you boy' and 'you boys'. By contrast, feminine nouns show plural forms in numerical plurals only.

तुम अच्छे बेटे हो ।	*tum acche beṭe ho.* You are a good son/good sons.
तुम अच्छी बेटी हो ।	*tum acchī beṭī ho.* You are a good daughter.
तुम अच्छी बेटियाँ हो ।	*tum acchī beṭiyā̃ ho.* You are good daughters.

EXERCISE 2a.1 Answer these questions on Dialogue 2a.

१ शर्मा जी कौन हैं ?
२ कितने छात्र और छात्राएँ हैं ?
३ क्या "टीच योरसेल्फ़ हिन्दी" सस्ती किताब है ?
४ क्या शब्दकोश महँगे हैं ?
५ रामायण कैसी किताब है – क्या वह पतली है ?

1 *Śarmā jī kaun haĩ?*
2 *kitne chātr aur chātrāẽ haĩ?*
3 *kyā 'ṭīc yorself hindī' sastī kitāb hai?*
4 *kyā śabdkoś mahãge haĩ?*
5 *rāmāyaṇ kaisī kitāb hai – kyā vah patlī hai?*

EXERCISE 2a.2 Translate Pratap's postcard home.

सोमवार १६ जनवरी; नई दिल्ली
यहाँ सब ठीक है । शर्मा जी अच्छे आदमी हैं, पर काफ़ी सख़्त भी हैं । हम १४ छात्र हैं । दूसरे छात्र ज़्यादातर अँग्रेज़, जर्मन या अमरीकन हैं । दो जापानी लड़कियाँ भी हैं । दोनों बहुत दुबली-पतली हैं ! दिल्ली सुन्दर है लेकिन हवा साफ़ नहीं है – बहुत गंदी है । प्रदूषण बहुत ख़राब है । पर आज मौसम ठीक है । वहाँ मौसम कैसा है ?

प्रताप

somvār 16 janvarī; naī dillī

yahā̃ sab ṭhīk hai. Śarmājī acche ādmī haĩ, par kāfī sakht bhī haĩ. ham 14 chātr haĩ. dūsre chātr zyādātar ãgrez, jarman yā amrīkan haĩ. do jāpānī laṛkiyā̃ bhī haĩ. donõ bahut dublī-patlī haĩ! dillī sundar hai lekin havā sāf nahī̃ hai – bahut gandī hai. pradūṣaṇ bahut kharāb hai. par āj mausam ṭhīk hai. vahā̃ mausam kaisā hai?

Pratāp

EXERCISE 2b.1 Translate.

1 Sangeeta is tall; Rishi is tall too.
2 The teacher is strict; he's crazy too.
3 The new fan is cheap; and it's good too.
4 These shoes are dirty; the sandals are dirty too.
5 That girl is fat; she's beautiful too.
6 These newspapers are good; they're cheap too.

EXERCISE 2b.2 Convert singular to numerical plural, as shown.

वह बूढ़ा आदमी दुबला-पतला है । > वे बूढ़े आदमी दुबले-पतले हैं ।

vah būṛhā ādmī dublā-patlā hai. > ve būṛhe ādmī duble-patle haĩ.

१ यह बच्चा अच्छा नहीं है, बीमार है ।

२ मैं लंबा नहीं हूँ, छोटा हूँ । (हम...)

३ वह किताब कैसी है ? क्या वह अच्छी है ?

४ वह मेज़ साफ़ नहीं है, बहुत गंदी है ।

५ यह नया अख़बार बहुत अच्छा नहीं है ।

६ यह शब्दकोश सस्ता है । हाँ, और काफ़ी अच्छा भी है ।

1 *yah baccā acchā nahī̃ hai, bīmār hai.*
2 *maĩ lambā nahī̃ hū̃, choṭā hū̃. (ham...)*
3 *vah kitāb kaisī hai? kyā vah acchī hai?*
4 *vah mez sāf nahī̃ hai, bahut gandī hai.*
5 *yah nayā akhbār bahut acchā nahī̃ hai.*
6 *yah śabdkoś sastā hai. hā̃, aur kāfī acchā bhī hai.*

Vocabulary

अख़बार m *akhbār* newspaper
अध्यापक m *adhyāpak* teacher
अभी *abhī* at the moment, right now
आज *āj* today
और *aur* more, else, other
काग़ज़ m *kāgaz* paper; a piece of paper
कितना *kitnā* how much/many
किताब f *kitāb* book
कृपया *kṛpayā* please
कैसा *kaisā* of what kind, what like, how
कौन *kaun* who
क्या *kyā* what
क्यों *kyõ* why
क्योंकि *kyõki* because
ख़राब *kharāb* bad
ख़ुश *khuś* happy
गंदा *gandā* dirty
चप्पल f *cappal* sandal
चिट्ठी f *ciṭṭhī* letter, note, chit
छात्र m *chātr* student
छात्रा f *chātrā* female student
जवाब m *javāb* answer
जूता m *jūtā* shoe; pair of shoes
ज़्यादातर *zyādātar* mostly, most
दिल्ली f *dillī* Delhi
दुबला *dublā* thin; दुबला-पतला *dublā-patlā* thin, slight of build
धन्यवाद *dhanyavād* thank you
न *na* not; is it not so?
नमस्कार *namaskār* hello; goodbye
नया (नए, नई) *nayā (nae, naī)* new
नाराज़ *nārāz* angry, displeased
नौ *nau* nine
पतला *patlā* thin
पर *par* but
परेशान *pareśān* troubled, upset
पाँच *pā̃c* five
पागल *pāgal* mad, crazy
प्रदूषण m *pradūṣaṇ* pollution
बहिन f *bahin* sister
बात f *bāt* matter, thing
बिलकुल *bilkul* completely
बिलकुल नहीं *bilkul nahī̃* not at all
बीमार *bīmār* ill
बुरा *burā* bad
बेटा m *beṭā* son
बेटी f *beṭī* daughter
भाई m *bhāī* brother
भी *bhī* also, too
महँगा *mahā̃gā* expensive
मालूम नहीं *mālūm nahī̃* [I] don't know
मेहरबानी f *meharbānī* kindness
मैडम f *maiḍam* madam
मोटा *moṭā* fat, thick
मौसम m *mausam* weather
या *yā* or

रामायण^{m} *rāmāyaṇ* Ramayan (epic poem)
लंबा *lambā* tall, high
विद्यार्थी$^{m, f}$ *vidyārthī* student
शब्दकोश^{m} *śabdkoś* dictionary
श्री *śrī* Mr; Lord (with deity)
श्रीमती *śrīmatī* Mrs
सख़्त *sakht* strict, severe
सब *sab* everything, all
सर *sar* sir
सवाल^{m} *savāl* question
सस्ता *sastā* cheap
साहब^{m} *sāhab* Mr; sir
सोमवार^{m} *somvār* Monday
सोलह *solah* sixteen
हलो, हेलो *halo , helo* hello
हवा^{f} *havā* air
हाल^{m} *hāl* condition, state
हिन्दी^{f} *hindī* Hindi

3 ROOMS IN THE HOUSE
घर में कमरे

In this unit you will learn how to

- describe locations –'in', 'on' etc.
- use a fuller range of pronouns
- develop conversational skills

3a Pratap's mother phones from London

अनीता कैसे हो प्रताप ? तुम्हारी तबियत ठीक है न ? और वह मकान कैसा है ?

प्रताप बिलकुल ठीक हूँ माँ । और यह घर भी बुरा नहीं है ।

अनीता कुमार परिवार कितना बड़ा है ? सिर्फ़ पति-पत्नी हैं, या बच्चे भी हैं ?

प्रताप परिवार में कई लोग हैं – प्रकाश और कमला, दादी जी, एक लड़की और दो लड़के ।

अनीता अच्छा, काफ़ी बड़ा परिवार है ! मकान में कितने कमरे हैं ?

प्रताप नौ बड़े कमरे हैं, और एक छोटा । सब कमरों में सामान नया है ।

अनीता और तुम्हारा कमरा ? कमरे में पंखा वग़ैरह है न ?

प्रताप हाँ, अब मेज़ पर नया पंखा है । और फ़र्श पर नई दरी भी है ।

Anītā *kaise ho Pratāp? tumhārī tabiyat ṭhīk hai na? aur vah makān kaisā hai?*

Pratāp *bilkul ṭhīk hū̃ mā̃. aur yah ghar bhī burā nahī̃ hai.*

Anītā *Kumār parivār kitnā baṛā hai? sirf pati-patnī haĩ, yā bacce bhī haĩ?*

Pratāp *parivār mẽ kaī log haĩ – Prakāś aur Kamalā, Dādījī, ek laṛkī aur do laṛke.*

Anītā *acchā, kāfī baṛā parivār hai! makān mẽ kitne kamre haĩ?*

Pratāp *nau baṛe kamre haĩ, aur ek choṭā. sāb kamrõ mẽ sāmān nayā hai.*

Anītā *aur tumhārā kamrā? kamre mẽ pankhā vagairah hai na?*

Pratāp *hā̃, ab mez par nayā pankhā hai. aur farś par naī darī bhī hai.*

तुम्हारा *tumhārā* your, yours	छह *chah* six
तबियत f *tabiyat* health	सारा *sārā* all, whole
घर m *ghar* house, home	सामान m *sāmān* furniture, things
परिवार m *parivār* family	वग़ैरह *vagairah* and so on, etc.
पति m *pati* husband	अब *ab* now
पत्नी f *patnī* wife	फ़र्श m/f *farś* floor
कई *kaī* several	दरी f *darī* floor rug, mat

Anita How are you, Pratap? Your health is OK isn't it? And what's that house like?

Pratap I'm absolutely fine, Mum. And this house too isn't bad.

Anita How big is the Kumar family? Is it just husband and wife, or are there children too?

Pratap There are six in the family – Prakash and Kamala, Grandma, a girl and two boys.

Anita Oh, it's quite a big family. How many rooms are there in the house?

Pratap There are nine big rooms and one small. And the furniture in all the rooms is new.

Anita And your room? There's a fan etc. in the room isn't there?

Pratap Yes, there's a new fan on the table now. And there's a new rug on the floor too.

Grammar

3.1 Simple postpositions

In English, words like 'in' and 'from' are called *pre*positions because they precede a noun or pronoun ('in the house'); in Hindi they *follow* a noun or pronoun, so they're called *post*positions (मकान में *makān mẽ*). There are five 'simple' or single-word postpositions:

में *mẽ* 'in' पर *par* 'on' तक *tak* 'up to, as far as'
को *ko* 'to' etc. से *se* 'by, with, from' etc.

घर में *ghar mẽ* in the house	राम को *Rām ko* to Ram
मेज़ पर *mez par* on the table	रात को *rāt ko* at night
समय पर *samay par* on time	बस से *bas se* by bus

आज तक	*āj tak*	until today	आराम से	*ārām se*	with ease, easily
यहाँ तक	*yahā̃ tak*	up to here	भारत से	*bhārat se*	from India

3.2 Nouns with postpositions

Hindi has two main cases. In Units 1 and 2, all nouns were in the *direct* case, which is obligatory for verb subjects. But when a noun is followed by a postposition, it must transform into a different case, known as the *oblique* case. Thus all the nouns in 3.1 above, shown with postpositions, are by definition in the oblique; but no change is apparent, because the nouns cunningly chosen there are all singular 'type 2' nouns (see 1.3), whose oblique form is identical to the direct singular.

For example, the word घर *ghar* 'house' remains the same in the following two sentences, although its case changes: in the first sentence it's the subject of the verb and is therefore in the direct case, while in the second it is followed by a postposition and is therefore in the oblique case.

घर ख़ाली है ।	*ghar khālī hai.*	The house is vacant.
घर में सामान है ।	*ghar mẽ sāmān hai.*	There is furniture in the house.

Not all nouns are so user friendly. Masculine 'type 1' nouns like कमरा *kamrā* 'room' change their final *-ā* to *-e* in the oblique singular (कमरे *kamre*):

कमरा ख़ाली है ।	*kamrā khālī hai.*	The room is vacant.
कमरे में सामान है ।	*kamre mẽ sāmān hai.*	There is furniture in the room.

Nouns of *all* classes change in the oblique plural, which ends in *-õ* (घरों में *gharõ mẽ*, कमरों में *kamrõ mẽ*):

घरों में सामान है ।	*gharõ mẽ sāmān hai.*	There is furniture in the houses.
कमरों में सामान है ।	*kamrõ mẽ sāmān hai.*	There is furniture in the rooms.

The following table gives all the noun types in the direct and oblique cases, singular and plural:

DIRECT CASE	OBLIQUE CASE + POSTPOSITION
Masculine type 1	
लड़का *laṛkā* boy	लड़के से *laṛke se* from the boy
कमरा *kamrā* room	कमरे में *kamre mẽ* in the room
लड़के *laṛke* boys	लड़कों से *laṛkõ se* from the boys
कमरे *kamre* rooms	कमरों में *kamrõ mẽ* in the rooms
Masculine type 2	
मकान *makān* house	मकान में *makān mẽ* in the house
आदमी *ādmī* man	आदमी को *ādmī ko* to the man
हिन्दू *hindū* Hindu	हिन्दू को *hindū ko* to the Hindu
मकान *makān* houses	मकानों में *makānõ mẽ* in the houses
आदमी *ādmī* men	आदमियों को *ādmiyõ ko* to the men
हिन्दू *hindū* Hindus	हिन्दुओं को *hinduõ ko* to the Hindus
Feminine type 1	
लड़की *laṛkī* girl	लड़की से *laṛkī se* from the girl
मूर्ति *mūrti* image	मूर्ति में *mūrti mẽ* in the image
चिड़िया *ciṛiyā* bird	चिड़िया से *ciṛiyā ko* to the bird
लड़कियाँ *laṛkiyā̃* girls	लड़कियों से *laṛkiyõ se* from the girls
प्रतियाँ *pratiyā̃* copies	प्रतियों में *pratiyõ mẽ* in the copies
चिड़ियाँ *ciṛiyā̃* birds	चिड़ियों को *ciṛiyõ ko* to the birds
Feminine type 2	
मेज़ *mez* table	मेज़ पर *mez par* on the table
माता *mātā* mother	माता से *mātā se* from Mother
मेज़ें *mezẽ* tables	मेज़ों पर *mezõ par* on the tables
माताएँ *mātāẽ* mothers	माताओं से *mātāõ se* from the mothers

> **!** Before the oblique plural *-õ* ending, *-ū* nouns shorten to *-u-* (हिन्दू *hindū* > हिन्दुओं *hinduõ*); and *-ī* nouns change to *-iy-* (आदमी *ādmī* > आदमियों *ādmiyõ*).

मकान में कई कमरे हैं ।	*makān mẽ kaī kamre haĩ.* In the house there are several rooms.
दीवारों पर तस्वीरें हैं ।	*dīvārõ par tasvīrẽ haĩ.* There are pictures on the walls.
फ़र्श पर दरी है ।	*farś par darī hai.* There is a rug on the floor.
अलमारियों में क्या है ?	*almāriyõ mẽ kyā hai?* What's in the cupboards?

Word order: look back to the vital word-order point made in 1.5; then note how the sense 'there is...' is conveyed through a similar inversion of word order. Compare the following two sentences:

मेज़ पर क़लम है । *mez par qalam hai.* There is <u>a pen</u> on the table.

This statement answers the question मेज़ पर क्या है ? *mez par kyā hai?* 'What is there on the table?'

क़लम मेज़ पर है । *qalam mez par hai.* The pen is <u>on the table</u>.

This statement answers the question क़लम कहाँ है *qalam kahā̃ hai?* 'Where is the pen?'

In both Hindi sentences, the answer words (क़लम *qalam*, मेज़ पर *mez par*) replace the respective question words (क्या *kyā*, कहाँ *kahā̃*).

3b Prakash has lost his glasses

प्रकाश	ऋषि, ओ ऋषि, तुम कहाँ हो ?
ऋषि	मैं अभी छोटे बाथरूम में हूँ, पिता जी । क्यों? क्या बात है ?
प्रकाश	तुम सुबह से वहाँ हो ? ख़ैर... मेरा चश्मा कहाँ है रे ?
ऋषि	बड़ी मेज़ पर नहीं है ? या उस छोटी अलमारी में, बड़े कमरे में ?

प्रकाश	नहीं है। शायद तुम्हारे कमरे में है।
ऋषि	नहीं पिताजी, मेरे कमरे में सिर्फ़ मेरा चश्मा है, आपका नहीं।
प्रकाश	और तुम्हारी दराज़ में भी नहीं है?
ऋषि	जी नहीं, मेरी दराज़ में बहुत-सारी चीज़ें हैं, पर आपका चश्मा नहीं है।

Prakāś	*Ṛṣi, o Ṛṣi, tum kahā̃ ho?*
Ṛṣi	*maĩ abhī choṭe bāthrūm mẽ hū̃, pitā jī. kyõ? kyā bāt hai?*
Prakāś	*tum subah se vahā̃ ho? khair... merā caśmā kahā̃ hai re?*
Ṛṣi	*baṛī mez par nahī̃ hai? yā us choṭī almārī mẽ, baṛe kamre mẽ?*
Prakāś	*nahī̃ hai. śāyad tumhāre kamre mẽ hai.*
Ṛṣi	*nahī̃ pitājī, mere kamre mẽ sirf merā caśmā hai, āpkā nahī̃.*
Prakāś	*aur tumhārī darāz mẽ bhī nahī̃ hai?*
Ṛṣi	*jī nahī̃, merī darāz mẽ bahut-sārī cīzẽ haĩ, par āpkā caśmā nahī̃ hai.*

ओ	*o*	o!
कहाँ	*kahā̃*	where?
बाथरूम m	*bāthrūm*	bathroom
में	*mẽ*	in
सुबह f	*subah*	morning
से	*se*	since, from
वहाँ	*vahā̃*	there
ख़ैर	*khair*	well, anyway
मेरा	*merā*	my, mine
आपका	*merā*	your, yours
चश्मा m	*caśmā*	glasses
रे	*re*	eh, hey
पर	*par*	on
उस	*us*	that
शायद	*śāyad*	perhaps
दराज़ f	*darāz*	drawer
बहुत-सारा	*bahut-sārā*	lots of
चीज़ f	*cīz*	thing

Prakash Rishi, o Rishi, where are you?
Rishi I'm in the small bathroom at the moment, Father. Why? What's the matter?
Prakash Have you been there since morning? Anyway... where are my glasses, eh?
Rishi Aren't they on the big table? Or in that small cupboard in the big room?
Prakash They're not. Perhaps they're in your room.
Rishi No, Father, in my room there's only my glasses, not yours.
Prakash And aren't they in your drawer either?
Rishi No, there are lots of things in my drawer, but your glasses aren't there.

Grammar

3.3 Adjectives in the oblique case

A noun before a postposition must be in the oblique case (3.2), and so must any adjective qualifying it. Inflecting adjectives like बड़ा *baṛā* 'big', ending in *-ā*, change to *-e* in the oblique (singular and plural); masculine adjectives not ending in *-ā* do not change. Similarly the feminine ending *-ī* (बड़ी *baṛī*) doesn't change in the oblique.

Note incidentally that the pronouns मेरा *merā* 'my, mine', तुम्हारा *tumhārā* 'your, yours' (relating to तुम *tum*) and आपका *āpkā* 'your, yours' (relating to आप *āp*) work just like adjectives, agreeing with the thing possessed (मेरा भाई, मेरी बहिन *merā bhāī, merī bahin* 'my brother, my sister'); they're introduced more fully in 6.2.

बड़े कमरे में	*baṛe kamre mẽ*	in the big room
बड़े कमरों में	*baṛe kamrõ mẽ*	in the big rooms
मेरे मकान में	*mere makān mẽ*	in my house
मेरे मकानों में	*mere makānõ mẽ*	in my houses
तुम्हारी अलमारी में	*tumhārī almārī mẽ*	in your cupboard
तुम्हारी अलमारियों में	*tumhārī almāriyõ mẽ*	in your cupboards
आपकी मेज़ पर	*āpkī mez par*	on your table
आपकी मेज़ों पर	*āpkī mezõ par*	on your tables
लाल दरवाज़े पर	*lāl darvāze par*	on the red door
लाल दरवाज़ों पर	*lāl darvāzõ par*	on the red doors

3.4 Pronouns in the oblique case

When a pronoun is followed by a postposition (3.1), it must of course take the oblique case (compare English: 'tell her' is correct, 'tell she' is not). Here are the pronouns with their oblique forms:

SINGULAR			PLURAL		
मैं *mai*	>	मुझ *mujh*	हम *ham*	>	हम *ham*
तू *tū*	>	तुझ *tujh*	तुम *tum*	>	तुम *tum*
—			आप *āp*	>	आप *āp*
यह *yah*	>	इस *is*	ये *ye*	>	इन *in*
वह *vah*	>	उस *us*	वे *ve*	>	उन *un*
कौन *kaun*	>	किस *kis*	कौन *kaun*	>	किन *kin*
क्या *kyā*	>	किस *kis*	क्या *kyā*	>	किन *kin*

Postpositions following pronouns may be written separately, or as one word: मुझ से *mujh se* / मुझसे *mujhse* ; आप को *āp ko* / आपको *āpko*.

> **!** A verb subject *must* be in the direct case (compare English: 'he is' is correct, 'him is' is not). Test this rule by identifing the subject in each sentence of Dialogues 3a and 3b.

EXERCISE 3a.1 Answer these questions on Dialogue 3a.

१ प्रताप कैसा है ?

२ कुमार परिवार में कितने लोग हैं, और वे कौन हैं ?

३ मकान में कितने कमरे हैं ? क्या वे सब बड़े हैं ?

४ कमरों में कैसा सामान है ?

५ पंखा कहाँ है ? वह कैसा है ?

६ क्या दरी पुरानी है ? वह कहाँ है ?

1 *Pratāp kaisā hai?*

2 *Kumār parivār mẽ kitne log haĩ, aur ve kaun haĩ?*

3 *makān mẽ kitne kamre haĩ? kyā ve sab baṛe haĩ?*

4 *kamrõ mẽ kaisā sāmān hai?*

5 *pankhā kahā̃ hai? vah kaisā hai?*

6 *kyā darī purānī hai? vah kahā̃ hai?*

EXERCISE 3a.2 Describe a room, using at least eight sentences based on the format of the descriptions in Dialogue 3a.

EXERCISE 3b.1 Translate.

1	this big room	in this big room	The boys are in this big room.
2	those black chairs	on those black chairs	The clothes are on those black chairs.
3	this dirty floor	on this dirty floor	There's a rug on this dirty floor.
4	these old tables	on these old tables	The books are on these old tables.
5	that big garden	in that big garden	There's a car in that big garden.
6	these new rooms	in these new rooms	Are there fans in these new rooms?
7	the old city	from the old city	Those girls are from the old city.
8	this little village	from this little village	Is that boy from this little village?
9	this clean kitchen	in this clean kitchen	There's a table in this clean kitchen.
10	those tall boys	from those tall boys	This letter is from those tall boys.

EXERCISE 3b.2 Using Dialogue 3b as your model, write a short dialogue in which Rishi asks his mother where his new book is.

Vocabulary

अब *ab* now

आपका *āpkā* your, yours

आराम m *ārām* rest, comfort;

आराम से *ārām se* comfortably, easily

इस *is* oblique of यह *yah*

इन *in* oblique of ये *ye*

उस *us* oblique of वह *vah*

उन *un* oblique of वे *ve*

ऐनक f *ainak* glasses

ओ *o* o!
कपड़ा m *kapṛā* cloth; garment
क़लम m/f *qalam* pen
काला *kālā* black
किस *kis* oblique singular of कौन *kaun* and of क्या *kyā*
किन *kin* oblique plural of कौन *kaun* and of क्या *kyā*
को *ko* to, on, at
ख़ैर *khair* well, anyway
गाँव m *gā̃v* village
गुसलख़ाना m *gusalkhānā* bathroom
घर m *ghar* house, home
चश्मा m *caśmā* glasses
चार *cār* four
चीज़ f *cīz* thing
छह *chah* six
तक *tak* up to, as far as
तबियत f *tabiyat* health
तस्वीर f *tasvīr* picture
तुझ *tujh* oblique of तू *tū*
तुम्हारा *tumhārā* your, yours
दरवाज़ा m *darvāzā* door
दराज़ f *darāz* drawer
दरी f *darī* floor rug, mat
दस *das* ten
दीवार f *dīvār* wall
पति m *pati* husband
पत्नी f *patnī* wife
पर *par* on
परदा m *pardā* curtain
परिवार m *parivār* family
फ़र्श m/f *farś* floor
बस f *bas* bus
बहुत-सारा *bahut-sārā* lots of
बाथरूम m *bāthrūm* *bathroom*
भारत m *bhārat* India
मुझ *mujh* oblique of मैं *maĩ*
में *mẽ* in; में से *mẽ se* from among, out of
मेरा *merā* my, mine
रसोईघर m *rasoīghar* kitchen
रात f *rāt* night
रे *re* eh, hey
लंदन m *landan* London
वग़ैरह *vagairah* etc., and so on
वहाँ *vahā̃* there
शहर m *śahar* town, city
शायद *śāyad* perhaps
समय m *samay* time
सामान m *sāmān* furniture, things
सारा *sārā* all, whole
सुबह f *subah* morning
से *se* by, since, from, with

4 WHO WAS THAT HANDSOME MAN?

वह ख़ूबसूरत आदमी कौन था ?

In this unit you will learn how to

- use the past tense
- make comparisons
- say you have a cold or fever
- use the vocative case – 'O children!'

4a Sangeeta's friend Suhas – just a friend?

पिंकी संगीता, आज तुम क्लास में क्यों नहीं थीं ? तुम कहाँ थीं ?

संगीता मैं घर पर थी; सुहास भी था । दूसरे लोग बाहर थे । हाँ, प्रताप भी था वहाँ ।

पिंकी सुहास – वह ख़ूबसूरत आदमी ? वह कौन है – दोस्त या रिश्तेदार ?

संगीता रिश्तेदार तो नहीं, वह मेरा बहुत पुराना दोस्त है ।

पिंकी यह तुम्हारा दोस्त उम्र में तुमसे काफ़ी बड़ा है !

संगीता हाँ मुझसे बड़ा तो है, पर बहुत प्यारा आदमी है ।

पिंकी क्या वह दिल्ली से है ? या विदेश से ?

संगीता वे लोग पहले लंदन में थे – मेरा मतलब है, बाल-बच्चे भी थे... पर अब तो सुहास अकेला है ।

पिंकी और सुहास सिर्फ़ तुम्हारा "दोस्त" है क्या ?

संगीता हाँ पिंकी, वह सिर्फ़ मेरा दोस्त है – मेरा मित्र है, फ़्रेंड है !

Pinkī *Sangītā, āj tum klās mẽ kyõ nahī̃ thī̃? tum kahā̃ thī̃?*

Sangītā *maĩ ghar par thī; Suhās bhī thā. dūsre log bāhar the. hā̃, Pratāp bhī thā vahā̃.*

Pinkī *Suhās – vah k͟hūbsūrat ādmī? vah kaun hai – dost yā riśtedār?*

Sangītā *riśtedār to nahī̃, vah merā bahut purānā dost hai.*

Pinkī *yah tumhārā dost umr mẽ tumse kāfī baṛā hai!*

Sangītā *hā̃ mujhse baṛā to hai, par bahut pyārā ādmī hai.*

Pinkī *kyā vah dillī se hai? yā videś se?*

Sangītā *ve log pahle landan mẽ the – merā matlab hai, bāl-bacce bhī the... par ab to Suhās akelā hai.*

Pinkī *aur Suhās sirf tumhārā 'dost' hai kyā?*

Sangītā *hā̃ Pinkī, vah sirf merā dost hai – merā mitr hai, freṇḍ hai!*

क्लास m/f *klās* class

था, थी, थे, थीं *thā, thī, the, thī̃* was, were

घर पर *ghar par* at home

बाहर *bāhar* out; outside

ख़ूबसूरत *k͟hūbsūrat* beautiful, handsome

दोस्त m, f *dost* friend

रिश्तेदार m, f *riśtedār* relative

तो *to* so; as for (see 4.2)

उम्र f *umr, umar* age

प्यारा *pyārā* dear, lovely

विदेश m *videś* foreign country; abroad

पहले *pahle* previously

मतलब m *matlab* meaning

बाल-बच्चे m.pl *bāl-bacce* children, family

अकेला *akelā* alone

मित्र m, f *mitr* friend

Pinkie Sangeeta, why weren't you in college today? Where were you?

Sangeeta I was at home; Suhas was there too. The others were out. Oh yes, Pratap was there too.

Pinkie Suhas – that handsome man? Who is he – friend or relative?

Sangeeta Not a relative, he's my very old friend.
Pinkie This friend of yours is quite a lot older ('bigger in age') than you!
Sangeeta Yes, he is older than me, but he's a very dear man.
Pinkie Is he from Delhi? Or from abroad?
Sangeeta They were in London before – I mean, there was a family with children... but now Suhas is alone.
Pinkie And Suhas is just your 'friend'?
Sangeeta Yes Pinkie, he's just my friend – my *mitra*, my 'friend'!

> **!** सुहास सिर्फ़ तुम्हारा "दोस्त" है क्या ? *Suhās sirf tumhārā 'dost' hai kyā?* Here, क्या *kyā* is colloquially thrown in at the end.

Grammar

4.1 'was' and 'were'

Unlike the present tense, the past tense of the verb होना *honā* 'to be' distinguishes gender: वह था *vah thā* 'he was', वह थी *vah thī* 'she was'.

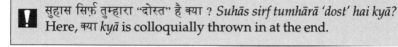

MASCULINE			FEMININE		
मैं था	*maĩ thā*	I was	मैं थी	*maĩ thī*	I was
तू था	*tū thā*	you were	तू थी	*tū thī*	you were
यह था	*yah thā*	this, he, it was	यह थी	*yah thī*	this, she, it was
वह था	*vah thā*	that, he, it was	वह थी	*vah thī*	that, she, it was
हम थे	*ham the*	we were	हम थीं	*ham thī̃*	we were
तुम थे	*tum the*	you were	तुम थीं	*tum thī̃*	you were
आप थे	*āp the*	you were	आप थीं	*āp thī̃*	you were
ये थे	*ye the*	they, these were; he was (hon.)	ये थीं	*ye thī̃*	they, these were she was (hon.)
वे थे	*ve the*	they, those were he was (hon.)	वे थीं	*ve thī̃*	they, those were she was (hon.)

मैं कल दफ़्तर में था ।	*maĩ kal daftar mẽ thā.*	Yesterday I was in the office.
चाचा जी दुकान में थे ।	*cācā jī dukān mẽ the.*	Uncle was in the shop.
माँ भी घर पर नहीं थीं ।	*mā̃ bhī ghar par nahī̃ thī̃.*	Mum too wasn't at home.
दोनों बच्चे बीमार थे ।	*donõ bacce bīmār the.*	Both children were ill.
गोलियाँ मेज़ पर थीं ।	*goliyā̃ mez par thī̃.*	The pills were on the table.

4.2 तो *to* 'so'; 'as for'

The important little word तो *to* has two separate functions: (a) as a conjunction meaning 'so', and (b) to lend emphasis to a preceding word or phrase: वे तो *ve to...* 'as for them...'. It isn't a postposition, so it doesn't affect case. Its two uses are explained separately.

(a) At the beginning of a phrase, तो *to* means 'so', or 'then':

तो क्या दुकान बंद है ?	*to kyā dukān band hai?*	So is the shop closed?
अच्छा, तो तुम लन्दन से हो ?	*acchā, to tum landan se ho?*	Ah, then you're from London?

(b) Following a word or phrase, तो *to* contrasts that preceding item to some other item in the same context:

खाना तो गरम था, पर चाय एकदम ठंडी थी ।	*khānā to garam thā, par cāy ekdam ṭhaṇḍī thī.*	The food was hot, but the tea was completely cold.
खाना अच्छा तो था, पर महँगा भी था ।	*khānā acchā to thā, par mahãgā bhī thā.*	The food was good, but it was expensive too.

Often the contrasted item or situation is only implied:

कल तो वह घर पर था ।	*kal to vah ghar par thā.*	Yesterday he was at home. ['... but today?']

कल वह घर पर तो था।	*kal vah ghar par to thā.*	Yesterday he was at home. ['... but he was busy']
कल वह तो घर पर था।	*kal vah to ghar par thā.*	Yesterday he was at home. ['... but the others?']

This second use of तो *to* usually carries a subtle nuance; it is to be understood gradually, after seeing more examples.

4.3 Comparison of adjectives

Hindi has few special adjectives corresponding to the English comparative and superlative, 'taller, tallest'. Comparisons involve just an ordinary adjective and the comparing word से *se* 'than':

संगीता राज से लम्बी है।	*Sangītā Rāj se lambī hai.*	Sangeeta is taller than Raj.
राज संगीता से मोटा है।	*Rāj Sangītā se moṭā hai.*	Raj is fatter than Sangeeta.

Comparisons can be made more specific by adding a word for 'more' (और *aur* or ज़्यादा *zyādā*) before the adjective, as in ज़्यादा लंबा *zyādā lambā* 'taller' (lit. 'more tall'). This is also done when the object of comparison is not stated:

ऋषि संगीता से ज़्यादा लंबा है। *Ṛṣi Sangītā se zyādā lambā hai.* Rishi is taller than Sangeeta.

ऋषि ज़्यादा लंबा है।	*Ṛṣi zyādā lambā hai.*	Rishi is taller.
राज ज़्यादा मोटा है।	*Rāj zyādā moṭā hai.*	Raj is fatter.

Comparisons involving the sense 'less' use the word कम *kam* 'little, less':

चाँदी सोने से कम महँगा है।	*cā̃dī sone se kam mahā̃gī hai.*	Silver is less costly than gold.
ये चीज़ें कम महँगी हैं।	*ye cīzẽ kam mahā̃gī haĩ.*	These things are less expensive.

Superlatives follow the pattern of सब से अच्छा *sab se acchā* 'best of all':

मैं सब से लंबा हूँ।	*maĩ sab se lambā hū̃.*	I am the tallest.

वह पहाड़ सब से ऊँचा है। *vah pahāṛ sab se ū̃cā hai.* That mountain is the highest.

4b Khanna ji at the office

खन्ना जी	छोटू, क्या तुमको मालूम है कि रामदास कहाँ है?
छोटू	खन्ना जी, रामदास घर पर है। उसको ज़ुकाम है।
खन्ना जी	अरे, वह कल भी बीमार था! और प्रकाश कहाँ है?
छोटू	सर, आज प्रकाश जी भी यहाँ नहीं हैं।
खन्ना जी	क्यों? क्या बात है? क्या उसको भी ज़ुकाम है?
छोटू	कल तो उनको बुख़ार था। वे शायद आज भी बीमार हैं।
खन्ना जी	या उसको काम पसंद नहीं है, शायद!
छोटू	वह बात नहीं है खन्ना जी – प्रकाश जी बहुत मेहनती आदमी हैं।
खन्ना जी	तुम अच्छे लड़के हो छोटू, लेकिन तुमको कुछ नहीं मालूम है।

Khannā jī	*Choṭū, kyā tumko mālūm hai ki Rāmdās kahā̃ hai?*
Choṭū	*Khannā jī, Rāmdās ghar par hai. usko zukām hai.*
Khannā jī	*are, vah kal bhī bīmār thā! aur Prakāś kahā̃ hai?*
Choṭū	*sar, āj Prakāś jī bhī yahā̃ nahī̃ haĩ.*
Khannā jī	*kyõ? kyā bāt hai? kyā usko bhī zukām hai?*
Choṭū	*kal to unko bukhār thā. ve śāyad āj bhī bīmār haĩ.*
Khannā jī	*yā usko kām pasand nahī̃ hai, śāyad!*
Choṭū	*vah bāt nahī̃ hai, Khannā jī – Prakāś jī bahut mehnatī ādmī haĩ.*
Khannā jī	*tum acche laṛke ho Choṭū , lekin tumko kuch nahī̃ mālūm hai.*

मालूम *mālūm* known	**बुख़ार** m *bukhār* fever
कि *ki* that	**काम** m *kām* work
ज़ुकाम m *zukām* a cold	**पसंद** *pasand* liked, pleasing
अरे *are* oh! what!	**मेहनती** *mehnatī* hardworking
कल *kal* yesterday; tomorrow	**कुछ नहीं** *kuch nahī̃* nothing

Khanna ji	Chotu, do you know where Ramdas is?
Chotu	Khanna ji, Ramdas is at home. He's got a cold.
Khanna ji	What! He was ill yesterday too! And where's Prakash?
Chotu	Sir, Prakash ji is not here today either.
Khanna ji	Why? What's the matter? Has he got a cold too?

Chotu	Yesterday he had a fever. Maybe he's ill today as well.
Khanna ji	Or he doesn't like work, maybe!
Chotu	That's not it, Khanna ji – Prakash ji's a very hardworking man.
Khanna ji	You're a good lad, Chotu, but you don't know anything.

> Chotu looks up to Prakash, and refers to him in the honorific plural as 'Prakash ji'; but Khanna is Prakash's boss, and refers to him in the singular.

Grammar

4.4 Some constructions with को *ko*

The word को *ko* 'to' appears in many constructions of the type मुझ को ज़ुकाम है *mujh ko zukām hai* 'I have a cold' (literally 'to me there is a cold'). The important thing to note here is that ज़ुकाम *zukām* 'a cold', and *not* the person suffering from it, is the subject of the verb (here, है *hai*). It is essential to understand this vital principle, because you will encounter it many times in Hindi grammar. Notice here how the verb stays the same, agreeing with masculine singular ज़ुकाम *zukām* throughout the following sentences, although the sufferer changes:

दादीजी को ज़ुकाम था।	*dādījī ko zukām thā.*	Granny had a cold.
दोनों भाइयों को ज़ुकाम था।	*donõ bhāiyõ ko zukām thā.*	Both brothers had a cold.
सौ लोगों को ज़ुकाम था।	*sau logõ ko zukām thā.*	A hundred people had a cold.

Other nouns using the same construction are:

बुख़ार *bukhār* (m) a fever	आशा *āśā* (f) hope
अफ़सोस *afsos* (m) regret	ख़ुशी *khuśī* (f) happiness

तुम को बुख़ार था।	*tum ko bukhār thā.*	You had a fever.
हम को अफ़सोस है कि तुम बीमार हो।	*ham ko afsos hai ki tum bīmar ho.*	We're sorry that you're ill.
मुझ को आशा है कि वे ठीक हैं।	*mujh ko āśā hai ki ve ṭhīk haĩ.*	I hope they're OK.
उन को ख़ुशी थी कि गाड़ी सस्ती थी।	*un ko khuśī thī ki gāṛī sastī thī.*	They were pleased the car was cheap.

The adjectives मालूम *mālūm* 'known' and पसंद *pasand* 'pleasing' also feature in this construction (translating literally as 'X is known to me', 'X is pleasing to me' etc.).

उस को समोसे पसंद हैं ।	*us ko samose pasand haĩ.*	He likes samosas.
हाँ, मुझ को मालूम है ।	*hā̃, mujh ko mālūm hai.*	Yes, I know.
क्या उस को दाल पसंद है ?	*kyā us ko dāl pasand hai?*	Does he like daal?
हम को मालूम नहीं ।	*ham ko mālūm nahī̃.*	We don't know.

In the English sentence 'Do you know where Raj is?', the core question 'Where is Raj?' is inverted to 'where Raj is'. In Hindi, the core question राज कहाँ है? *Rāj kahā̃ hai?* remains *unchanged* within the longer sentence. In each of the following three sentences, the words following कि *ki* constitute the core question.

क्या तुमको मालूम है कि राज कहाँ है ?	*kyā tumko mālūm hai ki Rāj kahā̃ hai?*	Do you know where Raj is?
क्या उसको मालूम है कि मैं कौन हूँ ?	*kyā usko mālūm hai ki maĩ kaun hū̃?*	Does he know who I am?
मुझको नहीं मालूम कि यह क्या है ।	*mujhko nahī̃ mālūm ki yah kyā hai.*	I don't know what this is.

4.4 The vocative case

The vocative (the case used when addressing someone) is the same as the oblique, except that in the plural the ending -ओ *-o* is not nasalised.

बेटे	*beṭe!*	Son!
ओ बच्चो	*o bacco!*	O, children!
भाइयो-बहिनो	*bhāiyo-bahino!*	Brothers and sisters!

EXERCISE 4a.1 Translate.

१ तुम्हारा पुराना पंखा इस नए पंखे से ज़्यादा मज़बूत था ।

२ बच्चों में से संगीता सबसे बड़ी है ।

३ क्या ऋषि राज से कम मोटा है ?

४ क्या संगीता पिंकी से ज़्यादा होशियार है ?

५ आज प्रताप घर पर है लेकिन दूसरे लोग बाहर हैं – शायद बाज़ार पर ।

1 *tumhārā purānā pankhā is nae pankhe se zyādā mazbūt thā.*
2 *baccõ mẽ se Sangītā sabse baṛī hai.*
3 *kyā Ṛṣi Rāj se kam moṭā hai?*
4 *kyā Sangītā Pinkī se zyādā hośiyār hai?*
5 *āj Pratāp ghar par hai lekin dūsre log bāhar haĩ – śāyad bāzār par.*

EXERCISE 4a.2 Translate.

1 This man is taller than that girl.
2 Was your old car better than this new car?
3 Is my sister fatter than my brother?
4 I am taller than you but you are more beautiful than me.
5 She was taller than us; she was the tallest of all.

EXERCISE 4b.1 Translate.

1 Pinkie knows that Sangeeta wasn't in college today.
2 Who doesn't know that Suhas is older than Sangeeta?
3 Sangeeta is pleased that Pinkie likes Suhas.
4 Pratap was at home today; he knows who Suhas is.
5 Pratap knows that Sangeeta likes the new white Maruti.
6 Do you know where Kamala was yesterday?
7 We're sorry that your friends are ill.
8 I don't know who that man is.

EXERCISE 4B.2 Answer the following questions, in which you are addressed as तुम *tum*.

१ तुम्हारे कमरे में कितनी कुरसियाँ हैं ?

२ क्या तुम्हारे पड़ोसी हिन्दुस्तानी हैं ?

३ क्या तुम्हारी किताब तुम्हारी मेज़ पर है ?

४ क्या तुम्हारे कपड़े साफ़ हैं ?

५ क्या तुमको मालूम है कि तुम्हारे पड़ोसी अभी कहाँ हैं ?

६ तुम्हारी तबियत कैसी है ? क्या तुमको ज़ुकाम है ?

1 *tumhāre kamre mẽ kitnī kursiyā̃ haĩ?*

2 *kyā tumhāre paṛosī hindustānī haĩ?*

3 *kyā tumhārī kitāb tumhārī mez par hai?*

4 *kya tumhāre kapṛe sāf haĩ?*

5 *kyā tumko mālūm hai ki tumhāre paṛosī abhī kahā̃ haĩ?*

6 *tumhārī tabiyat kaisī hai? kyā tumko zukām hai?*

EXERCISE 4b.3 Write a postcard as from Pratap to Mohan (मोहन *Mohan*) in Varanasi (वाराणसी *vārāṇasī*). Pratap tells Mohan his reactions to Delhi. He hopes Mohan is well; he wants to know about Mohan's family, and whether he knows where the palace (महल *mahal*) is in Varanasi. Begin प्रिय... *priy*... ('Dear...'), and end आपका प्रताप *āpkā Pratāp*.

Vocabulary

अकेला *akelā* alone
अफ़सोस ^{m} *afsos* regret
अरे *are* oh! what!
उम्र ^{f} *umr, umar* age
एकदम *ekdam* completely
और *aur* more
कम *kam* less; little
कल *kal* yesterday; tomorrow
काम ^{m} *kām* work
कालेज ^{m} *kālej* college
कि *ki* that
कुछ नहीं *kuch nahī̃* nothing
क्लास $^{m/f}$ *klās* class
खाना ^{m} *khānā* food
ख़ुशी ^{f} *khuśī* happiness, pleasure
ख़ूबसूरत *khūbsūrat* beautiful, handsome
गरम *garam* warm, hot
गोली ^{f} *golī* tablet, pill
घर पर *ghar par* at home

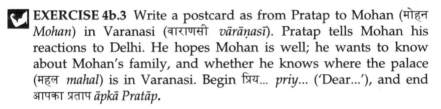

चाँदी f *cā̃dī* silver
चाचा m *cācā* paternal uncle
चाय f *cāy* tea
ज़ुकाम m *zukām* a cold
ज़्यादा *zyādā* more, very
ठंडा *ṭhaṇḍā* cold
तो *to* so, etc (see 4.2)
था, थी, थे, थीं *thā, thī, the, thī̃* was, were
दफ़्तर m *daftar* office
दाल f *dāl* daal, lentils
दुकान f *dukān* shop
दोस्त m, f *dost* friend
पड़ोसी m, f *paṛosī* neighbour
पसंद *pasand* liked, pleasing
पहले *pahle* previously
पहाड़ m *pahāṛ* hill, mountain
प्यारा *pyārā* dear, lovely
प्रिय *priy* dear
बंद *band* closed, shut
बाज़ार m *bāzār* market
बाल-बच्चे m pl *bāl-bacce* children, family
बाहर *bāhar* out; outside
बुख़ार m *bukhār* fever
मज़बूत *mazbūt* strong
मतलब m *matlab* meaning
महल m *mahal* palace
माँ f *mā̃* Ma, Mother
मालूम *mālūm* known
मित्र m *mitr* friend
मेहनती *mehnatī* hardworking
रिश्तेदार m, f *riśtedār* relative
वाराणसी f *vārāṇasī* Varanasi, Banaras
विदेश m *videś* foreign country; abroad
समोसा m *samosā* samosa
साल m *sāl* year
सोना m *sonā* gold
सौ *sau* hundred
होशियार *hośiyār* clever, intelligent

5 PLEASE SIT HERE
यहाँ बैठिए

In this unit you will learn how to

- give commands
- make requests
- talk about ownership and possession
- use more pronouns

5a Kamala's neighbour Suresh comes for lunch

कमला आइए सुरेश। खाना तैयार है, बैठिए।

सुरेश शुक्रिया। अच्छा, तो तुम अकेली नहीं हो – राज भी है। दूसरे बच्चे कहाँ हैं ?

कमला वे तो अभी बाहर हैं, खाँ मार्केट में। राज, तू बैठ। इधर मत बैठ, उधर बैठ।

राज अम्माँ, मुझको चाय दो, मुझको दूध पसंद नहीं।

कमला तू चाय मत पी, दूध पी। तू तो अभी बहुत छोटा है बेटा!

राज सुरेश अंकल, अम्माँ से कहिए कि मैं छोटा बच्चा नहीं हूँ।

सुरेश	नहीं राज, तुम तो बहुत बड़े आदमी हो ! कमला, राज साहब को चाय दो!
कमला	सुनिए सुरेश, राज बड़ा आदमी तो है, लेकिन बड़ा शैतान भी है !

Kamalā	*āie Sureś. khānā taiyār hai, baiṭhie.*
Sureś	*śukriyā. acchā, to tum akelī nahī̃ ho – Rāj bhī hai. dūsre bacce kahā̃ haĩ?*
Kamalā	*ve to abhī bāhar haĩ, khā̃ mārkeṭ mẽ. Rāj, tū baiṭh. idhar mat baiṭh, udhar baiṭh.*
Rāj	*ammā̃, mujhko cāy do, mujhko dūdh pasand nahī̃.*
Kamalā	*tū cāy mat pī, dūdh pī. tū to abhī bahut choṭā hai beṭā!*
Rāj	*Sureś ankal, ammā̃ se kahie ki maĩ choṭā baccā nahī̃ hū̃.*
Sureś	*nahī̃ Rāj, tum to bahut baṛe ādmī ho! Kamalā, Rāj sāhab ko cāy do!*
Kamalā	*sunie Sureś, Rāj baṛā ādmī to hai, lekin baṛā śaitān bhī hai!*

> **!** इधर मत बैठ, उधर बैठ *idhar mat baiṭh, udhar baiṭh* – an ideal sentence for practising the difference between dental and retroflex consonants!

(For convenience, this vocabulary listing shows commands in the forms found in the dialogue, not as infinitives.)

- **आइए** *āie* please come
- **तैयार** *taiyār* ready
- **बैठिए** *baiṭhie* please sit
- **खाँ मार्केट** m *khā̃ mārkeṭ* Khan Market (in Delhi)
- **बैठ** *baiṭh* sit
- **इधर** *idhar* here, over here
- **उधर** *udhar* there, over there
- **दो** *do* give
- **दूध** m *dūdh* milk
- **मत** *mat* don't
- **पी** *pī* drink
- **अंकल** m *ankal* uncle
- **कहिए** *kahie* please tell
- **शैतान** m *śaitān* devil

Kamala	Come, Suresh. The food is ready. Please sit.
Suresh	Thanks. Ah, you're not alone, Raj is here too. Where are the other children?
Kamala	They're out at the moment, in Khan Market. Raj, you sit. Don't sit here, sit there.
Raj	Mum, give me tea, I don't like milk.
Kamala	Don't you drink tea, drink milk. You're still very young, son!

Raj Suresh Uncle, tell Mum that I'm not a little kid.
Suresh No Raj, you're a very big fellow! Kamala, give Raj Sahib tea!
Kamala Listen Suresh, Raj is a big man, but he's a big devil too!

Grammar

5.1 The infinitive verb

The Hindi verb is listed (in dictionaries etc.) in the infinitive – बोलना *bolnā* 'to speak'. The infinitive consists of the stem बोल- *bol-* plus the infinitive ending -ना *-nā* (always written with full न, not as a conjunct).

The infinitive has a variety of grammatical uses. The stem too is the basis for many verb forms, so when you learn a new infinitive verb, find its stem form by removing the -ना *-nā* ending.

Here, in Devanagari 'alphabetical' order, are some of the most common verbs:

आना	*ānā*	to come	(से) पूछना	*pūchnā*	to ask (of)
करना	*karnā*	to do	बताना	*batānā*	to tell
(से) कहना	*kahnā*	to say (to)	बुलाना	*bulānā*	to call, invite
खाना	*khānā*	to eat	बैठना	*baiṭhnā*	to sit
चलना	*calnā*	to move, go	मारना	*mārnā*	to beat, hit
जाना	*jānā*	to go	लाना	*lānā*	to bring
देखना	*dekhnā*	to see, look	लिखना	*likhnā*	to write
देना	*denā*	to give	लेना	*lenā*	to take, receive
पढ़ना	*paṛhnā*	to read, study	सुनना	*sunnā*	to listen, hear
पीना	*pīnā*	to drink, smoke	होना	*honā*	to be, become

5.2 Commands and requests

Commands and requests convey very fully the 'politeness' hierarchy of the honorific system (1.1). As in English, they may be used with or without thc pronoun: 'speak' or 'you speak'.

तू बोल *tū bol*

The तू *tū* command consists of the verb stem alone. Its brevity accentuates its lack of formality, implying intimacy or bluntness: सुन *sun* 'Listen!'; जा *jā* 'Go!'; दे *de* 'Give!'

तुम बोलो *tum bolo*

The तुम *tum* command consists of stem plus -ओ *o*. आओ *āo* 'Come'; लिखो *likho* 'Write'; बैठो *baiṭho* 'Sit'.

आप बोलिए *ap bolie*

The आप *āp* command consists of stem plus -इए *-ie*. खाइए *khāie* 'Please eat'; कहिए *kahie* 'Please say'; पढ़िए *paṛhie* 'Please read'.

आप बोलिएगा *āp boliega*

An extra-polite variant of the आप *āp* command, to which it adds the ending -गा *-gā*. बैठिएगा *baiṭhiega* 'Please be so kind as to sit'; कल आइएगा *kal āiegā* 'Kindly come tomorrow'; आप भी एक पत्र लिखिएगा *āp bhī ek patr likhiegā* 'You also should kindly write a letter'.

बोलना *bolnā*

The infinitive too can be used as a command – often a 'deferred' one, to be acted on at some time in the future. It has no specific place in the 'honorifics' hierarchy, but it lacks the deference of an आप *āp* command and is most at home in तुम *tum* contexts.

> **!** सुनिए *sunie* 'Please listen': this is a polite way of attracting someone's attention, like 'excuse me' in English.

Four common verbs have irregular आप *āp* commands:

करना *karnā*	>	कीजिए *kījie*	please do
लेना *lenā*	>	लीजिए *lījie*	please take
देना *denā*	>	दीजिए *dījie*	please give
पीना *pīnā*	>	पीजिए *pījie*	please drink

देना *denā* and लेना *lenā* are irregular in the तुम *tum* commands also:

लेना *lenā*	>	लो *lo*	take
देना *denā*	>	दो *do*	give

The negative for commands ('don't...') is न *na*, or, more forcefully, मत *mat*. And notice that the verbs कहना *kahnā* 'to say, tell' and पूछना *pūchnā* 'to ask' use the postposition से *se* with the person addressed (see the first two examples below). There's more on this in 15.3.

मुझसे कहो ।	*mujhse kaho.*	Tell me.
पापा से न पूछो ।	*pāpā se na pūcho.*	Don't ask Papa.
वह पान मत खा !	*vah pān mat khā!*	Don't eat that paan!
यह पैसा लो ।	*yah paisā lo.*	Take this money.
ध्यान से सुनिए ।	*dhyān se sunie.*	Please listen with care.
उनका नाम लिखिएगा ।	*unkā nām likhiegā.*	Kindly write their name.
लन्दन से ख़त लिखना ।	*landan se khat likhnā.*	Write a letter from London.

> **!** One or two commands have found their way into English: 'Let's have a dekko' (a look), from देखो *dekho*; and 'shampoo', from चाँपो *cā̃po* (चाँपना *cā̃pnā* 'to rub, massage').

5b Lost keys and lost tempers

ऋषि राज, तुम्हें मालूम है कि अरुण चाचा की चाबियाँ कहाँ हैं ?

राज कौनसी चाबियाँ ? गाड़ी की चाबियाँ या घर की ?

ऋषि घर की । कल तो संगीता के कमरे में थीं, उसकी मेज़ पर । अब नहीं हैं ।

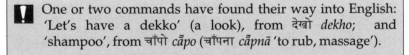

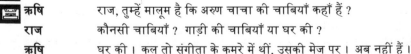

राज	तो मुझसे मत पूछो, संगीता से पूछो। मैं संगीता का नौकर हूँ क्या?
ऋषि	नहीं राज, नौकर नहीं हो, तुम तो सचमुच "राजा" हो!
राज	और इस "ऋषि" को यह भी नहीं मालूम कि घर की चाबियाँ कहाँ हैं!
अरुण	अरे बच्चो! झगड़ा मत करो! मुझे घर की चाबियाँ जल्दी दो।
ऋषि	उधर देखिए अंकल! दरवाज़े की चाबी पापा की मेज़ पर पड़ी है।

Ṛṣi	*Rāj, tumhẽ mālūm hai ki Aruṇ cācā kī cābiyā̃ kahā̃ haĩ?*
Rāj	*kaunsī cābiyā̃? gāṛī kī cābiyā̃ yā ghar kī?*
Ṛṣi	*ghar kī. kal to Sangītā ke kamre mẽ thī̃, uskī mez par. ab nahī̃ haĩ.*
Rāj	*to mujhse mat pūcho, Sangītā se pūcho. maĩ Sangītā kā naukar hū̃ kyā?*
Ṛṣi	*nahī̃ Rāj, naukar nahī̃ ho, tum to sacmuc 'rājā' ho!*
Rāj	*aur is 'ṛṣi' ko yah bhī nahī̃ mālūm ki ghar kī cābiyā̃ kahā̃ haĩ!*
Aruṇ	*are bacco! jhagṛā mat karo! mujhe ghar kī cābiyā̃ jaldī do.*
Ṛṣi	*udhar dekhie ankal! darvāze kī cābī pāpā kī mez par paṛī hai.*

तुम्हें *tumhẽ* = **तुमको** *tumko*	**ऋषि** m *ṛṣi* sage, seer
चाबी f *cābī* key	**झगड़ा** m *jhagṛā* quarrel, row;
का/की/के *kā/kī/ke* 's (apostrophe s)	**झगड़ा करना** *jhagṛā karnā* to quarrel
कौनसा/सी/से *kaunsā/sī/se* which?	**जल्दी** *jaldī* quickly
नौकर m *naukar* servant	**पड़ा** *paṛā* lying
सचमुच *sacmuc* really	**पापा** m *pāpā* Papa, Father

Rishi	Raj, do you know where Uncle Arun's keys are?
Raj	Which keys? The car keys or the house ones?
Rishi	The house ones. Yesterday they were in Sangeeta's room, on her table. They're not now.
Raj	So don't ask me, ask Sangeeta. Am I Sangeeta's servant?
Rishi	No Raj, you're not a servant, you really are a 'raja'!
Raj	And this 'rishi' [sage] doesn't even know where the house keys are!
Arun	Hey children! Don't squabble! Give me the house keys quickly.
Rishi	Look over there Uncle! The door key is lying on Papa's table.

Grammar

5.3 Possession with का *kā*

Possession is expressed through का – राम का नाम *rām kā nām*, 'Ram's name' or 'the name of Ram'. Being a postposition, it needs a preceding noun or pronoun to be in the oblique case:

बच्चे का कुत्ता	*bacce kā kuttā*	the child's dog
उन का घोड़ा	*un kā ghoṛā*	their horse

But it also agrees adjectivally with the thing possessed:

बच्चे की किताब	*bacce kī kitāb*	the child's book
उस बच्चे के खिलौने	*us bacce ke khilaune*	that child's toys

In terms of function and word order, का *kā* is equivalent to the English apostrophe 's'. When the thing possessed is in the oblique case, then का *kā* will be too:

लड़के के कमरे में	*laṛke ke kamre mẽ*	in the boy's room
लड़के की कुरसी पर	*laṛke kī kursī par*	on the boy's chair
लड़कों के कमरे में	*laṛkõ ke kamre mẽ*	in the boys' room
लड़कों के कमरों में	*larkõ ke kamrõ mẽ*	in the boys' rooms
लड़कों की कुरसियों पर	*laṛkõ kī kursiyõ par*	on the boys' chairs

उस आदमी का बेटा विद्यार्थी है।	*us ādmī kā beṭā vidyārthī hai.*	That man's son is a student.
उन लोगों के कपड़े बहुत गंदे हैं।	*un logõ ke kapṛe bahut gande haĩ.*	Those people's clothes are very dirty.
उस घर के बग़ीचे में चार लंबे पेड़ हैं।	*us ghar ke bagīce mẽ cār lambe peṛ haĩ.*	There are four tall trees in the garden of that house.
खन्ना की बहिन के कुत्ते का नाम चीकू है।	*Khannā kī bahin ke kutte kā nām Cīkū hai.*	Khanna's sister's dog's name is Chikoo.

5.4 को *ko* with the indirect and direct object

को *ko* with the indirect object

In a sentence such as 'Give the key to Raj', 'key' is the direct object and 'Raj' is the indirect object. Hindi marks the indirect object with को *ko* – राज को चाबी दो *Rāj ko cābī do.*

The pattern remains the same even if को *ko* is not translatable by 'to': मुझ को वह ख़त दो *mujh ko vah khat do*, 'Give me that letter' (='Give that letter to me'); उस को भी बताओ *us ko bhī batāo* 'Tell him too'; in these sentences the indirect objects are 'me' and 'him' respectively.

हम को गरम खाना खिलाओ।	*ham ko garam khānā khilāo.*	Serve us hot food.
धोबी को गंदे कपड़े देना।	*dhobī ko gande kapṛe denā.*	Give the dirty clothes to the dhobi.
उनको मेरा नाम मत बता !	*unko merā nām mat batā!*	Don't tell them my name!

को *ko* with the direct object

A direct object is sometimes marked with को *ko* and sometimes not; the distinction is often quite subtle – not to say elusive! Usually, direct objects such as चाय *cāy* and समोसा *samosā* in these examples take no postposition – and hence remain in the direct case:

भैया, चाय लाओ।	*bhaiyā, cāy lāo.*	Brother, bring tea.
समोसा खाओ।	*samosā khāo.*	Have ('eat') a samosa.

Here, both 'tea' and 'samosa' are perceived as generic items – there is no focus on their individuality, no *specific* cup of tea or *individual* samosa is meant. But when an object is individualised, को *ko* may be added – the effect often being similar to adding the definite article 'the' in English:

पानी पियो।	*pānī piyo.*	Drink water.
पानी को पियो।	*pānī ko piyo.*	Drink the water.
एक कुरसी लाओ।	*ek kursī lao.*	Bring a chair.
कुरसी को साफ़ करो।	*kursī ko sāf karo.*	Clean the chair.

To some extent, then, को *ko* marks a *specific* direct object. So when referring to something that's already been mentioned, को *ko* will be used:

यह किताब अच्छी है – इसको पढ़ो।	*yah kitāb acchī hai – isko paṛho.*	This book's good – read it.

The most specific thing of all is an individual, a person: so people who are verb objects (and pronouns standing for them) nearly always take को *ko*.

छोटू को मत मारना।	*Choṭū ko mat mārnā.*	Don't hit Chotu.
पिताजी को बुलाइए।	*pitājī ko bulāie.*	Call Father.
उनको जगाइए।	*unko jagāie.*	Wake them up.

5.5 Alternative forms of the oblique pronoun + को *ko*

The oblique personal pronouns + को *ko* (e.g. उसको *usko*) have alternative forms as follows:

मुझको	*mujhko*	मुझे	*mujhe*
तुझको	*tujhko*	तुझे	*tujhe*
इसको	*isko*	इसे	*ise*
उसको	*usko*	उसे	*use*
हमको	*hamko*	हमें	*hamẽ*
तुमको	*tumko*	तुम्हें	*tumhẽ*
आपको	*āpko*	(no alternative form)	
इनको	*inko*	इन्हें	*inhẽ*
उनको	*unko*	उन्हें	*unhẽ*
किसको	*kisko*	किसे	*kise*
किनको	*kinko*	किन्हें	*kinhẽ*

The two forms are completely interchangeable, although the shorter forms tend to be favoured in colloquial style, or to avoid repetitiveness if there's another को *ko* elsewhere in the sentence. In the first of the following examples, मुझे *mujhe* is preferred to मुझको *mujhko;* and in the second, हमें *hamẽ* to हमको *hamko.*

मुझे अफ़सोस है कि तुमको ज़ुकाम है ।	*mujhe afsos hai ki tumko zukām hai.*	I'm sorry that you have a cold.
हमें मालूम है कि उसको बुख़ार है ।	*hamẽ mālūm hai ki usko bukhār hai.*	We know that he has fever.

EXERCISE 5a.1 Transpose तुम *tum* commands into आप *āp* commands and vice versa. Then translate.

१ यहाँ सिग्रेट न पियो ।
२ ज़रा यहाँ ठहरो ।
३ इस कमरे में बैठो ।
४ चाय पियो, फल खाओ ।
५ मुझे ऋषि के कपड़े दो ।
६ पानी न पीजिए; काफ़ी लीजिए ।
७ आइए । बताइए, क्या हाल है?
८ गाड़ी को इधर लाइए ।
९ उधर देखिए, वह नारा पढ़िए !
१० दरवाज़े को बन्द कीजिए ।

1 *yahā̃ sigreṭ na piyo.*
2 *zarā yahā̃ ṭhaharo.*
3 *is kamre mẽ baiṭho.*
4 *cāy piyo, phal khāo.*
5 *mujhe Ṛṣi ke kapṛe do.*
6 *pānī na pījie; kāfī lījie.*
7 *āie. batāie, kyā hāl hai?*
8 *gāṛī ko idhar lāie.*
9 *udhar dekhie, vah nara paṛhie!*
10 *darvāze ko band kījie.*

EXERCISE 5a.2 Transpose the infinitive commands into तू *tū* commands. Then translate.

१ कंबलों को गंदा मत करना ।
२ खाने को मत छूना ।
३ सरल हिन्दी बोलना ।
४ किताब में मेरा नाम न लिखना ।
५ घोड़े को मत मारना !

1 *kambalõ ko gandā mat karnā.*
2 *khāne ko mat chūnā.*

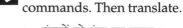

3 *saral hindī bolnā.*

4 *kitāb mẽ merā nām na likhnā.*

5 *ghoṛe ko mat mārnā!*

EXERCISE 5b.1 Rewrite the following sentences, removing को *ko* from the direct object. Then translate.

१ इन मोटे कंबलों को अलमारी में रखो ।

२ इस गरम समोसे को खाओ ।

३ उस बड़ी कुरसी को इस कमरे में लाइए ।

४ आज के अख़बार को पढ़ ।

५ चाचा जी के दरवाज़े को बन्द करना ।

1 *in moṭe kambalõ ko almārī mẽ rakho.*

2 *is garam samose ko khāo.*

3 *us baṛī kursī ko is kamre mẽ lāie.*

4 *āj ke akhbār ko paṛh.*

5 *cācā jī ke darvāze ko band karnā.*

EXERCISE 5b.2 Rewrite the following sentences, adding को *ko* to the direct object. Then translate.

१ ये नए खिलौने लो ।

२ ऋषि का पुराना कुरता पहनो ।

३ गाड़ी की चाबियाँ ढूँढ़ो ।

४ ये गंदे कपड़े धोना ।

५ यह थैला दराज़ में रखिए ।

1 *ye nae khilaune lo.*

2 *Ṛṣi kā purānā kurtā pahano.*

3 *gāṛī kī cābiyā̃ ḍhū̃ṛho.*

4 *ye gande kapṛe dhonā.*

5 *yah thailā darāz mẽ rakhie.*

EXERCISE 5b.3 Translate the questions, then answer them.

1 What is the name of Kamala's brother-in-law (देवर^m) ?
2 Is Rishi at home just now? (See Dialogue 5a.)
3 Who does not like milk?
4 Why does he not like milk?
5 Where were Sangeeta's uncle's keys yesterday?
6 Who knows where those keys are today?
7 Do you know where the Kumar family's house is?
8 In your opinion (ख़याल^m), are these questions (सवाल^m) simple?

Vocabulary

आना *ānā* to come
इधर *idhar* here, over here
उधर *udhar* there, over there
ऋषि ^m *ṛṣi* sage, seer
कंबल ^m *kambal* blanket
करना *karnā* to do
(से) कहना *kahnā* to say (to)
का/की/के *kā/kī/ke* 's (indicating possession)
काफ़ी ^f *kāfī* coffee
कुत्ता ^m *kuttā* dog
कुरता ^m *kurtā* kurta, Indian shirt
कौनसा/सी/से *kaunsā/sī/se* which?
ख़त ^m *khat* letter
ख़याल ^m *khayāl* opinion
ख़ाँ मार्केट ^m *khā̃ markeṭ* Khan Market (in Delhi)
खाना *khānā* to eat
खिलाना *khilānā* to serve, give to eat
खिलौना ^m *khilaunā* toy
घोड़ा ^m *ghoṛā* horse
चलना *calnā* to move
चाबी ^f *cābī* key
छूना *chūnā* to touch
जगाना *jagānā* to arouse from sleep
ज़रा *zarā* just, a little
जल्दी *jaldī* quickly, soon, early
जाना *jānā* to go
झगड़ा ^m *jhagṛā* quarrel, row, **झगड़ा करना** *jhagṛā karnā* to quarrel
ठहरना *ṭhaharnā* to stop, wait
ढूँढ़ना *ḍhū̃ṛnā* to look for, find
तैयार *taiyār* ready
थैला ^m *thailā* bag, cloth bag
दूध ^m *dūdh* milk
देखना *dekhnā* to see, look
देना *denā* to give
देवर ^m *devar* husband's younger brother
धोना *dhonā* to wash
धोबी ^m *dhobī* dhobi, washerman

ध्यान m *dhyān* attention; ध्यान से *dhyān se* attentively
न *na* don't (in commands)
नारा m *nārā* slogan
नौकर m *naukar* servant
पड़ा *paṛā* lying
पढ़ना *paṛhnā* to read, study
पान m *pān* paan
पानी m *pānī* water
पापा m *pāpā* Papa, Father
पीना *pīnā* to drink; to smoke
(से) पूछना *pūchnā* to ask (of)
पेड़ m *peṛ* tree
पैसा m *paisā* money; paisa (hundredth of a rupee)
फल m *phal* fruit
बंद करना *band karnā* to close, shut
बताना *batānā* to tell
बुलाना *bulānā* to call, invite
बैठना *baiṭhnā* to sit
बोलना *bolnā* to speak
भैया m *bhaiyā* brother
मत *mat* don't (with commands)
मारना *mārnā* to beat, hit
रखना *rakhnā* to put, keep
लाना *lānā* to bring
लिखना *likhnā* to write
लेना *lenā* to take, receive
शैतान m *śaitān* devil
सचमुच *sacmuc* really
सरल *saral* simple
साफ़ करना *sāf karnā* to clean
सिग्रेट f *sigreṭ* cigarette
सुनना *sunnā* to listen, hear
होना *honā* to be, become

6 WHAT DOES PRATAP DO?

प्रताप क्या करता है?

In this unit you will learn how to

- talk about regular activities
- ask what things are called in Hindi
- learn the remaining possessive pronouns
- discuss opinions and relationships

6a Suresh asks Prakash about his household

सुरेश प्रकाश, बताइए, आपका मेहमान प्रताप – वह क्या करता है ?

प्रकाश वह विद्यार्थी है। एक प्राइवेट स्कूल में हिन्दी सीखता है।

सुरेश उसका प्रोनंसियेशन बहुत साफ़ है। हिन्दी में "प्रोनंसियेशन" को क्या कहते हैं – उच्चारण !

प्रकाश हाँ, प्रताप अच्छा बोलता है। वैसे वह बहुत होनहार लड़का है।

सुरेश मालूम होता है कि संगीता उससे नफ़रत करती है; ऐसा क्यों है ?

प्रकाश मैं नहीं जानता । पर संगीता सोचती है कि प्रताप उससे प्यार करता है ।

सुरेश अच्छा ! एक बात और – राज हमेशा घर पर क्यों रहता है ? वह दिन भर क्या करता है ?

प्रकाश खेलता है, खाता है, सोता है, शरारत करता है । बच्चा है, न?

सुरेश यह अच्छी बात नहीं है कि लड़का घर पर अकेला रहता है ।

प्रकाश अरे छोड़ो इन बातों को सुरेश ! [*मन में सोचता है – "तुम इन बच्चों के बाप हो क्या ?"*]

मेहमान m	guest	**सोचना**	to think
प्राइवेट स्कूल m	private school	**प्यार** m	love
सीखना	to learn	**हमेशा**	always
प्रोनंसियेशन m	'pronunciation'	**रहना**	to stay
उच्चारण m	pronunciation	**दिन भर**	all day
अच्छा	well	**खेलना**	to play
वैसे	actually	**सोना**	to sleep
होनहार	promising	**शरारत** f	mischief
नफ़रत m	hate, dislike	**छोड़ना**	to leave
ऐसा	thus, so, like this	**मन** m	mind
जानना	to know	**बाप** m	father

Suresh Prakash, tell me, your guest Pratap – what does he do?
Prakash He's a student. He learns Hindi in a private school.
Suresh His pronunciation is very clear. What's 'pronunciation' called in Hindi – *uccāraṇ*!
Prakash Yes, Pratap speaks well. Actually he's a very promising boy.
Suresh It seems Sangeeta dislikes him. Why is it so?
Prakash I don't know. But Sangeeta thinks that Pratap loves her.
Suresh I see! One more thing – why does Raj always stay at home? What does he do all day?
Prakash He plays, eats, sleeps, makes mischief. He's a kid, isn't he?
Suresh It's not good that the boy stays alone at home.
Prakash Oh leave these things, Suresh! [Thinks to himself: 'Are you the father of these children?']

Grammar

6.1 The imperfective present tense

The imperfective tense describes regular events or habits: 'I speak Hindi', 'She lives in Delhi, 'We don't smoke'. The participle – बोलता 'speaks', from बोलना 'to speak' – is followed by हूँ / हो / है / हैं.

MASCULINE	FEMININE	
मैं बोलता हूँ	मैं बोलती हूँ	I speak
तू बोलता है	तू बोलती है	you speak
यह, वह बोलता है	यह, वह बोलती है	he, it, she speaks
हम बोलते हैं	हम बोलती हैं	we speak
तुम बोलते हो	तुम बोलती हो	you speak
आप बोलते हैं	आप बोलती हैं	you speak
ये, वे बोलते हैं	ये, वे बोलती हैं	they speak

मैं शुद्ध हिन्दी बोलता हूँ।	I speak pure Hindi.
क्या श्रीमती खन्ना पंजाबी समझती हैं ?	Does Mrs Khanna understand Panjabi?
तुम कहाँ रहते हो ?	Where do you live?
प्रताप कभी कभी शराब पीता है।	Pratap sometimes drinks.

In the negative, the auxiliary verb (हूँ / हो / है / हैं) can be dropped:

मैं सिग्रेट कभी नहीं पीता।	I never smoke.
शर्मा जी गोश्त नहीं खाते।	Sharma ji does not eat meat.
वह लखनऊ में नहीं रहती, दिल्ली में रहती है।	She doesn't live in Lucknow, she lives in Delhi.

When this happens with a feminine plural, the participle becomes nasalised, compensating for the dropped nasalised auxiliary हैं:

दादी जी गोश्त खाती हैं / नहीं खातीं।	Dadi ji eats meat / doesn't eat meat.
वे औरतें शराब पीती हैं / नहीं पीतीं।	Those women drink/ don't drink.

All these examples relate to *habitual* events. (Continuous activities, with '-ing' verbs in English (e.g. 'he is speaking'), have a separate tense: see Unit 8.) The imperfective tense is also used for ongoing states of mind:

वह सोचता है कि तुम्हारा उच्चारण अच्छा है ।	He thinks that your pronunciation is good.
मैं अक्सर अकेलापन महसूस करता हूँ ।	I often experience loneliness.

An idiomatic use of the imperfective is seen when someone who's just about to leave says अच्छा, मैं चलती हूँ 'Well, I'm off' – in which the 'leaving' is not 'habitual' at all. Similarly अभी आता हूँ 'I'm coming straightaway'.

Although expressions for time of day aren't introduced fully until 12.2, the expression कितने बजे 'at what time?' is useful in practising imperfective tenses. You can make up many sentences on the following models, using verbs such as आना 'to come', उठना 'to get up', खाना 'to eat', खेलना 'to play', जाना 'to go', and सोना 'to sleep'.

राज नौ बजे स्कूल जाता है ।	Raj goes to school at nine o'clock.
आप कितने बजे उठती हैं ?	What time do you get up?
मैं सात बजे उठती हूँ ।	I get up at seven o'clock.

Relating to the knowledge of a language, the verb आना 'to come' can be used in the imperfective construction हमें हिन्दी आती है, literally 'Hindi comes to us', i.e. 'We know Hindi'.

मुझको थोड़ी उर्दू आती है ।	I know a little Urdu.
तुमको कितनी भाषाएँ आती हैं ?	How many languages do you know?

Here's a useful way of asking the Hindi word for something:

इस लिपि को क्या कहते हैं ?	What's this script called? ('What do they call...?')
इसको देवनागरी कहते हैं ।	They call it Devanagari.

Using होता है (from होना 'to be') implies a general statement of lasting validity, whereas है alone is for a specific one-off statement.

अच्छी साड़ियाँ महँगी होती हैं।	Good saris are expensive.
हाँ, लेकिन यह साड़ी सस्ती है।	Yes, but this sari is cheap.

See also the difference of meaning between मालूम होता है and मालूम है:

मालूम होता है कि माँ नाराज़ हैं।	It seems Mother's angry.
मुझे मालूम है कि माँ नाराज़ हैं।	I know Mother's angry.

By now you're used to verb gender in the verb: masculine बोलता, feminine बोलती. When a mixture of genders is involved, agreement follows the rule given for adjectives in 2.2: if the subjects are people, then the plural verb is masculine; if they're inanimates, the verb takes its gender from the closest item.

कृष्ण और राधा खेलते हैं।	Krishna and Radha play.
क्या जूते और चप्पलें सस्ती होती हैं?	Are shoes and sandals cheap?

6.2 Possessive pronouns

As we've already seen with मेरा, तुम्हारा and आपका (3.3.), the possessive pronouns decline like adjectives – they agree with the thing possessed. An oblique pronoun + का can be written as two words or one: उसका or उस का, किसका or किस का. Here's the full list.

मैं	I	मेरा	my, mine
तू	you	तेरा	your, yours
यह	he, she, it	इसका	his, her, hers, its, of this
वह	he, she, it	उसका	his, her, hers, its, of that
हम	we	हमारा	our, ours
तुम	you	तुम्हारा	your, yours
आप	you	आपका	your, yours
ये	they	इनका	their, theirs
वे	they	उनका	their, theirs
कौन	who?	किसका	whose? (singular);
		किनका	whose? (plural)

तुम्हारा कुत्ता हमारे घर में है ।	Your dog is in our house.
तेरा पापा कहाँ है ?	Where's your father?
आपके हाथ में क्या है?	What is in your hand?
ये कपड़े किसके हैं ? मेरे तो नहीं हैं ।	Whose clothes are these? They're not mine.

Word order: look back at the points made about word order in 1.5 and 3.2, then see the difference between the following sentences:

यह मेरा दफ़्तर है ।	This is my office.
यह दफ़्तर मेरा है ।	This office is mine.

6b Pratap and Sangeeta

प्रताप संगीता, ऋषि अपने भाई से कितना बड़ा है ?

संगीता राज सबसे छोटा है – सिर्फ़ बारह साल का है । ऋषि चौदह साल का है ।

प्रताप और तुम, संगीता ? तुम्हारी उम्र कितनी है ? क्या तुम मुझसे बड़ी हो ?

संगीता मैं उन्नीस साल की हूँ । मुझे मालूम नहीं कि तुम्हारी उम्र कितनी है ।

प्रताप मैं तुम से थोड़ा बड़ा हूँ – इक्कीस साल का हूँ ।

संगीता और लंबाई में भी तुम मुझसे बड़े हो । [*व्यंग्य से*] बहुत बहुत बधाइयाँ !

प्रताप यह व्यंग्य क्यों, संगीता ? तुम मुझे क्यों नापसंद करती हो ?

संगीता कौन कहता है कि मैं तुम्हें नापसंद करती हूँ ? मैं तुम्हारे बारे में तो सोचती भी नहीं !

प्रताप तुम तो सिर्फ़ अपने बारे में सोचती हो, अपने दोस्तों के बारे में नहीं ।

संगीता अच्छा, तो तुम अपने को मेरा दोस्त समझते हो? वाह!

अपना one's own	**लंबाई** f height
बारह twelve	**व्यंग्य** m sarcasm
साल m year	**बधाई** f congratulation
चौदह fourteen	**नापसंद करना** to dislike
उन्नीस nineteen	**के बारे में** about, concerning
थोड़ा a little	**समझना** to consider, reckon
इक्कीस twenty-one	**वाह** wonderful! bravo!

Pratap	Sangeeta, how much older is Rishi than his brother?
Sangeeta	Raj is the youngest – he's only 12. Rishi is 14.
Pratap	And you, Sangeeta? What's your age? Are you older than me?
Sangeeta	I'm 19. I don't know how old you are.
Pratap	I'm a little older than you – I'm 21.
Sangeeta	And you're taller than me ('greater in height') too. [*sarcastically*] Many congratulations!
Pratap	Why this sarcasm, Sangeeta? Why do you dislike me?
Sangeeta	Who says I dislike you? I don't even think about you!
Pratap	You only think about yourself, not about your friends.
Sangeeta	I see, so you consider yourself my friend! Wonderful!

! वह बारह साल का है – ' he's 12' ('of 12 years'); का agrees with the male subject. And why isn't साल in the oblique plural, सालों? Because the 12 years constitute a *single block of time* in which the separate years are not individualised. Similarly दस दिन में 'in ten days'.

Grammar

6.3 अपना 'one's own'

अपना 'one's own' is a reflexive pronoun – it means 'my, 'your', 'her' etc. depending on the subject of the clause. Compare the following:

राज अपने कमरे में है ।	Raj is in his [own] room.
राज उसके कमरे में है ।	Raj is in his [someone else's] room.

In the first sentence, the word 'his' refers back to Raj *as the subject of the clause*; that is, the words 'Raj' and 'his' refer to the same person. In such situations, Hindi uses अपना in place of any possessive pronoun (e.g. मेरा, तेरा, उसका).

मैं संगीता को अपनी किताब देता हूँ ।	I give Sangeeta my book.
सुहास संगीता को अपनी किताब देता है ।	Suhas gives Sangeeta his book.
संगीता सुहास को अपनी किताब देती है ।	Sangeeta gives Suhas her book.
हम अपने दोस्तों को ख़त लिखते हैं ।	We write letters to our friends.
वे अपनी भाषा क्यों नहीं बोलते ?	Why don't they speak their own language?

Now compare the following sentences very carefully:

मैं अपने भाई से लंबा हूँ ।	I am taller than my brother.
मेरा भाई बहुत लंबा नहीं है ।	My brother isn't very tall.
मैं और मेरा भाई दोनों मोटे हैं ।	My brother and I are both fat.

In the first sentence, 'my' refers to 'I' as subject; so अपना is used. In the second, 'My brother' is *itself* the subject, so अपना is *not* used. Similarly अपना is *not* used in the third sentence, because मेरा भाई is part of a *joint subject* ('my brother and I') rather than being a reference to a subject.

Using the possessive and the reflexive pronouns together, e.g. मेरा अपना, gives an emphatic sense – 'my own, my very own':

यह मेरी अपनी गाड़ी है ।	This is my very own car.
हिन्दी हमारी अपनी भाषा है ।	Hindi is our own language.

In a command, 'you' will *always* be अपना, because the subject of a command is 'you':

(तुम) अपनी किताब पढ़ो ।	(You) read your book.
मुझे अपने गंदे कपड़े दो ।	Give me your dirty clothes.
अपना ख़याल/ ध्यान रखना ।	Take care of yourself.

अपना takes some getting used to. As a *general* rule, use it if you can add the word 'own' to an English possessive ('her own car', 'our own house') without changing the fundamental sense of the phrase; the main exceptions to this are with the 'joint subject', as in मैं और मेरा भाई, always linked by 'and', and in commands.

6.4 Compound postpositions

These postpositions consist of two or more words, the first of which is the possessive के (or की if used with a feminine noun, e.g. तरफ़ 'direction'). Like the one-word 'simple postpositions' (3.1), they take the oblique case.

की तरफ़	towards	घर की तरफ़	towards home
के अंदर	inside	कमरे के अंदर	inside the room

के आगे	in front of, ahead of	डाकघर के आगे	in front of the post office
के ऊपर	on top of	बस के ऊपर	on top of the bus
के नीचे	beneath, below	मेज़ के नीचे	under the table
के/से पहले	before	शुक्रवार से पहले	before Friday
के पास	near	पेड़ों के पास	near the trees
के पीछे	behind	परदे के पीछे	behind the veil
के बाद	after	इसके बाद	after this
के बारे में	about, concerning	इस बात के बारे में	about this matter
के बाहर	outside	कमरे के बाहर	outside the room
के लिए	for	बच्चों के लिए	for the children
के यहाँ	at the place of	पिंकी के यहाँ	at Pinkie's place
के सामने	facing, opposite	तेरे घर के सामने	opposite your house

Compare these two phrases, based on के लिए 'for':

उनके लिए for them	मेरे लिए for me

The first phrase, उनके लिए, features के because के is part of the possessive form उनका/उनके 'their'. But in the second phrase, मेरे लिए, no का/के is apparent; this is because there is no का/के in the possessive form मेरा 'my'. Thus when used with pronouns ('for me, for her' etc.), compound postpositions are based on the *possessive* form of the pronoun (6.2):

मैं →	मेरा →	मेरे लिए	for me
तू →	तेरा →	तेरे लिए	for you
यह →	इसका →	इसके लिए	for him/her/it
वह →	उसका →	उसके लिए	for him/her/it
हम →	हमारा →	हमारे लिए	for us
आप →	आपका →	आपके लिए	for you
तुम →	तुम्हारा →	तुम्हारे लिए	for you
कौन →	किसका →	किसके लिए	for whom?
self →	अपना →	अपने लिए	for oneself

Some more examples:

की तरफ़	towards	हमारी तरफ़	towards us
की तरह	like	मेरी तरह	like me
के पीछे	behind	मेरे पीछे	behind me
के बारे में	about	अपने बारे में	about oneself
के साथ	with	मेरे साथ	with me

6.5 Pronouns revisited

Let us revise the pronoun types encountered so far.

Direct case personal pronouns such as मैं, तू, वह came in 1.1 with the verb 'to be' and should be very familiar by now. The oblique forms मुझ, तुझ, उस etc., to which they change when followed by a postposition, came in 3.4. Then in 5.5 we saw how the 'personal pronoun + को' formula has an alternative set: मुझे, तुझे उसे etc.

'Personal pronoun + को' constructions are very common: मुझको बुख़ार है 'I have fever'. In English the subject is 'I', but in Hindi it's बुख़ार. (Remember that a verb subject *must be in the direct case.*) You may find it helpful to think in terms of two general types of construction: a 'मैं' type (मैं बीमार हूँ) and a 'मुझको' type (मुझको बुख़ार है).

Possessive pronouns (मेरा, तेरा, उसका etc.) have just been introduced in 6.2, although some had slipped in earlier. They agree with the thing possessed (not the possessor): मेरा भाई, मेरी बहिन, मेरे चाचा; so they behave just like adjectives, as in बड़ा भाई, बड़ी बहिन etc.

Possessive pronouns are replaced by अपना when the possessor is also the verb subject: 'I read my book' must be मैं अपनी किताब पढ़ता हूँ because 'I' and 'my' both refer to the same person.

We have also encountered some interrogative pronouns: कौन 'who?', किस 'whom?', किसका 'whose?', क्या 'what?', कौनसा 'which?'. And we can look forward to meeting relative pronouns ('the man who...', 'the book which...' etc.) in Unit 13.

EXERCISE 6a.1 Answer the questions (6-10 are on the dialogues).

१ आप कहाँ रहते हैं / रहती हैं ?

२ आपके घर में कितने लोग रहते हैं ?

३ हिन्दी में "प्रोनंसियेशन" को क्या कहते हैं ?

४ आप कितनी भाषाएँ बोलते हैं / बोलती हैं ?

५ क्या आपके शहर में मकान महँगे होते हैं ?

६ प्रताप किसके घर में रहता है ?

७ उस घर में कितने लोग रहते हैं ?

८ प्रताप की माँ कहाँ रहती हैं, और उनका नाम क्या है ?

९ क्या राज दिन भर काम करता है ?

१० कौन किसको नापसंद करता है ?

EXERCISE 6a.2 Translate this extract from Pratap's letter home.

प्रकाश कुमार एक बड़ी कंपनी में काम करते हैं; उनके मालिक का नाम खन्ना है। मालूम होता है खन्ना साहब बहुत बड़े आदमी हैं; प्रकाश जी उनसे डरते हैं (और शायद अपनी पत्नी कमला से भी !)। प्रकाश और कमला के दोनों बच्चे स्कूल जाते हैं; और उनकी लड़की संगीता कालेज जाती है। संगीता बहुत होशियार है लेकिन मुझसे तो ज़्यादा बात नहीं करती। मैं सोचता हूँ कि वह मुझको पसंद नहीं करती। उसकी सहेली पिंकी अक्सर यहाँ आती है; दोनों दिन भर गपशप करती हैं और ख़ूब हँसाती हैं। पिंकी खन्ना की छोटी बहिन है; वह संगीता से बड़ी है, लेकिन दोनों में से संगीता ज़्यादा ख़ूबसूरत है। वह शायद भारत की सबसे सुन्दर लड़की है !

दादीजी अक्सर मुझसे पूछती हैं कि मेरे माँ-बाप क्या करते हैं, मेरे दोस्त कौन हैं, वग़ैरह। वे राज और ऋषि को बहुत हँसाती हैं – मुझको भी ! राज को वे बहुत प्यार करती हैं; उसको "मुन्ना" या "मेरा चाँद का टुकड़ा" कहती हैं। राज को ये नाम बिलकुल पसंद नहीं हैं। पर वह चुप रहता है। दादीजी को सब लोग प्यार करते हैं।

EXERCISE 6b.1 Translate the English words, then translate the whole sentences into English.

१ प्रताप his अध्यापक से हिन्दी के बारे में अक्सर मुश्किल सवाल पूछता है।

२ दादी हम को her बचपन के बारे में बताती हैं।

३ ऋषि और his भाई their दादी के साथ बहुत हँसते हैं।

४ मुन्ना, मैं your दादी हूँ; तू मुझे क्यों नहीं your खाना खिलाता है ?

५ ऋषि, तू your काम कर; फिर मुझे my खाना खिला।

६ प्रकाश his बेटी से her सहेली के बारे में पूछता है।

७ संगीता her पिता को her सहेली के बारे में बताती है।

EXERCISE 6b.2 Translate.

They call me Rishi. Raj is my little brother; he's a bit crazy. He's not in his room at the moment, he's in my room. And I'm not in my room; I'm in his room! He doesn't know that I know that he's in my room. Here in his room there are several old newspapers, but I don't know whose they are; they're not his. Raj doesn't read books or newspapers. He plays with his friends but he doesn't talk to me. His friends are not my friends.

I like Pratap. I go to the cinema with him and we talk about films. It seems he's quite bright. He speaks good Hindi. Even his pronunciation is quite good. He doesn't speak like a foreigner.

Vocabulary

अकेलापन m loneliness
अक्सर often; usually
अच्छा well, proficiently
अपना (one's) own
इक्कीस twenty-one
उच्चारण m pronunciation
उठना to get up, rise
उन्नीस nineteen
कंपनी f company, firm
कभी कभी sometimes; **कभी नहीं** never
की तरफ़ towards
की तरह like
के अंदर inside
के आगे in front of, ahead of
के ऊपर on top of
के नीचे beneath, below
के/से पहले before
के पास near
के पीछे behind
के बाद after
के बारे में about, concerning
के बाहर outside
के यहाँ at the place of
के लिए for
के साथ with, in company of
के सामने facing, opposite
(का) ख़याल रखना to take care of, mind
ख़ूब a lot, well
गपशप f gossip
गोश्त m meat
चाँद m moon
चुप silent
चौदह fourteen
छोड़ना to leave
जानना to know
टुकड़ा m piece, bit

(से) डरना to fear
डाकघर m post-office
तेरा your (from तू)
थोड़ा a little
दिन m day; दिन भर all day
देवनागरी f Devanagari script
(का) ध्यान रखना to take care of, mind
नफ़रत f hate, dislike
नापसंद करना to dislike
प्यार m love, affection; (को/ से) प्यार करना to love
फिर then; again
बचपन m childhood
बजे o' clock
बधाई f congratulation
(से) बात/बातें करना to talk, converse
बाप m father
बारह twelve
मन m mind
महसूस करना to feel, experience
मालिक m boss
मुन्ना Munna (nickname for little boy)
मुश्किल difficult
मेहमान m guest
लंबाई f height, length
लखनऊ m Lucknow
लिपि f script
वाह (expresses admiration or scorn) wonderful!
विदेशी m, f foreigner
वैसे actually
व्यंग्य m sarcasm
शराब f alcoholic, liquor
शरारत f mischief
शुक्रवार m Friday
शुद्ध pure, unmixed
संस्कृत f Sanskrit
सहेली f girl's female friend
साड़ी f sari
साल m year
सीखना to learn
से पहले before
सोचना to think
सोना to sleep
स्टेशन m station
हँसना to laugh
हँसाना to make laugh
हमारा our, ours
हमेशा always
होनहार promising

7 FATHER USED TO TEACH URDU

पिताजी उर्दू पढ़ाते थे

In this unit you will learn how to

- talk about regular activities in the past
- express needs and wants
- use ordinal numbers – first, second
- use several colloquial expressions

7a Grandmother's childhood in Kanpur

संगीता	दादी जी, बचपन में आप लोग कानपुर में रहते थे न ?
दादी जी	हाँ बेटी, मेरे पिताजी किसी कालेज में उर्दू पढ़ाते थे। माँ भी पढ़ाती थीं।
संगीता	आपके घर में कोई अँग्रेज़ी बोलता था ?
दादी जी	हाँ, पिताजी को कोई पाँच भाषाएँ आती थीं। पर हम लोग ज़्यादातर हिन्दी बोलते थे।
संगीता	क्या आपके घर के नज़दीक कोई सिनेमा था ?
दादी जी	हाँ, हम लोग हर शनिवार को कुछ सहेलियों के साथ सिनेमा जाते थे।

संगीता अपनी सहेलियों के बारे में कुछ बताइए ।

दादी जी एक मुसलमान डाक्टर की बेटी मेरी ख़ास सहेली थी । वह मुझसे कुछ बड़ी थी ।

संगीता [*थोड़ी देर के बाद*] अच्छा दादी जी, मैं चलती हूँ । आपको कुछ चाहिए ?

दादी जी नहीं बेटी, तेरी बूढ़ी दादी को कुछ नहीं चाहिए । तू जा, अपना काम कर ।

कानपुर ^{m}	Kanpur	**हर**	every, each
किसी	obl. of **कोई**, some, a certain	**शनिवार** ^{m}	Saturday
उर्दू ^{f}	Urdu	**कुछ**	some; somewhat; something
पढ़ाना	to teach	**मुसलमान**	Muslim
कोई	anyone; some, about; any	**डाक्टर** ^{m}	doctor
के नज़दीक	near	**ख़ास**	special, particular
सिनेमा ^{m}	cinema	**देर** ^{f}	delay, a while

Sangeeta Grandma, in your childhood you people used to live in Kanpur, didn't you?

Dadi ji Yes child, my father used to teach Urdu in some college. Mother used to teach too.

Sangeeta Did anyone speak English in your home?

Dadi ji Yes, Father knew some five languages. But we mostly spoke Hindi.

Sangeeta Was there any cinema near your house?

Dadi ji Yes , we used to go to the cinema every Saturday with some friends.

Sangeeta Tell me something about your friends.

Dadi ji A Muslim doctor's daughter was my special friend. She was a bit older than me.

Sangeeta [*after a little while*] OK Grandma, I'm off. Do you need anything?

Dadi ji No, child, your old Grandma doesn't need anything. Off you go, do your work.

Grammar

7.1 The past imperfective

This tense describes regular events or habits in the past: 'She used to speak Hindi'. The participle बोलता / बोलती / बोलते 'speaks' (6.1) is followed by the auxiliary था etc.

MASCULINE	FEMININE	
मैं बोलता था	मैं बोलती थी	I used to speak
तू बोलता था	तू बोलती थी	you used to speak
यह, वह बोलता था	यह, वह बोलती थी	he, it, she used to speak
हम बोलते थे	हम बोलती थीं	we used to speak
तुम बोलते थे	तुम बोलती थीं	you used to speak
आप बोलते थे	आप बोलती थीं	you used to speak
ये, वे बोलते थे	ये, वे बोलती थीं	they used to speak

मैं तुझे ख़त लिखता था ।	I used to write you letters.
तू कभी कभी जवाब देती थी ।	You sometimes used to reply.
किताबें सस्ती होती थीं ।	Books used to be cheap.
हम दोनों बहुत-सारी किताबें पढ़ते थे ।	We both used to read lots of books.

An imperfective verb with neither present nor past auxiliary (हूँ / था) tells of an action whose timescale is indefinite; this 'routine imperfective' narrates habitual events in the past, like the English 'I would...':

रविवार को हम लंबी सैर करते ।	On Sundays we would take a long walk.
शाम को मैं अक्सर सिग्रेट पीता ।	I would often smoke in the evening.

7.2 कोई and कुछ

These two essential words have several functions. Linger on these important paragraphs!

a) As a *pronoun*, कोई means 'someone' and कुछ means 'something'. Thus the difference between the two *as pronouns* is a difference between human beings and inanimates:

ज़मीन पर कोई पड़ा था ।	There was someone lying on the ground.
ज़मीन पर कुछ पड़ा था ।	There was something lying on the ground.

b) Hence in the negative, कोई नहीं means 'nobody', and कुछ नहीं means 'nothing':

घर में कोई नहीं है ।	There's nobody in the house.
घर में कुछ नहीं है ।	There's nothing in the house.

The negative नहीं may be written separately from कोई / कुछ :

यहाँ कोई गोश्त नहीं खाता है ।	Nobody here eats meat.

c) As an *adjective* qualifying a singular 'countable' item (whether human or otherwise), कोई means 'some, a, a certain one', : कोई लड़का 'some boy', कोई गाड़ी 'some car'. As an equivalent to the English 'a', it is an alternative to एक:

डिब्बे में कोई अँग्रेज़ बैठा था ।	There was some Englishman sitting in the compartment.
कोई अख़बार फ़र्श पर पड़ी थी ।	Some newspaper was lying on the floor.

d) The oblique of कोई is किसी, both as pronoun (किसी के लिए 'for someone') and as adjective (किसी लड़के के लिए ' for some boy', किसी वजह से 'for some reason'):

किसी से कहना कि मैं यहाँ खड़ा हूँ ।	Tell someone that I'm standing (waiting) here.
यह रोटी किसी बच्चे को दो ।	Give this bread to some child.

e) In the plural, कोई and किसी both change to कुछ, qualifying a group of 'countable' items: कुछ लड़के 'some boys' (direct case), कुछ लड़कों के लिए 'for some boys' (oblique case). The word कई 'several' is partially a plural equivalent to कोई:

कुछ/कई विदेशी अच्छी हिन्दी बोलते हैं ।	Some/several foreigners speak good Hindi.
कुछ अँग्रेज़ों को सिर्फ़ अँग्रेज़ी आती है ।	Some English people only know English.

f) As an *adjective*, कुछ also means 'some', qualifying a substance or thing that is either uncountable (like 'milk'), or is a composite whose component parts aren't relevant (like 'money'): कुछ दूध 'some milk', कुछ पैसा 'some money'.

उसकी जेब में कुछ पैसा था ।	There was some money in his pocket.
कुछ दाल लीजिए न?	Take some daal, won't you?

g) कुछ is also an *adverb*, qualifying an adjective: कुछ महँगा 'rather expensive' (compare बहुत महँगा 'very expensive', and काफ़ी महँगा 'quite expensive'):

यह कपड़ा कुछ मोटा है ।	This cloth is rather coarse.
यह कुरता कुछ लंबा है ।	This kurta is a bit long.

h) कोई before a *number* means 'about, approximately': कोई दस लोग 'about ten people':

डिब्बे में कोई दस मोती पड़े थे ।	There were some ten pearls lying in the box.
शहर में कोई आठ-नौ होटल हैं ।	There are some eight or nine hotels in the town.

In this usage, कोई does not change to oblique किसी – hence कोई पाँच मिनट में 'in about five minutes'.

i) कोई and कुछ feature in several useful phrases:

हर कोई	everyone
कोई न कोई	someone or other
कोई और, और कोई	someone else
सब कछ	everything
कुछ न कछ	something or other
कुछ और, और कुछ	something else, some more

> **!** Don't confuse किसी (oblique of कोई 'someone' etc.) with किस (oblique of कौन 'who? – see 3.4) .

7.3 चाहिए 'is wanted/ needed'

The word चाहिए means 'is wanted, is needed'. The *thing wanted* becomes the grammatical subject; the person doing the wanting is in the oblique with को. This is a मुझको type of construction (see 6.5).

दादी को नया चश्मा चाहिए ।	Grandma needs new glasses.
आपको क्या चाहिए ?	What do you want/ need?
हमें रोटी चाहिए, चावल नहीं ।	We want roti (bread), not rice.

For the past, simply add था / थी / थे / थीं to चाहिए. This auxiliary agrees with the subject, i.e. the thing wanted:

हमें दो साइकिलें चाहिए थीं ।	We needed two bicycles.
मुझे इसी रंग का कपड़ा चाहिए था ।	I needed cloth of *this* colour.

Some speakers nasalize the -ए ending in the plural: मुझे पाँच कमरे चाहिएँ 'I need five rooms'.

> ! दादी को चश्मे की ज़रूरत है (literally 'to Grandma is a need of glasses') is an alternative way of saying 'Grandma needs glasses'; ज़रूरत is a feminine noun meaning 'need'. Compare ज़रूर 'of course', and ज़रूरी 'necessary, urgent'.

7b Who works where?

खन्ना जी प्रकाश, इन सब कमरों में कौन कौन काम करता है ?

प्रकाश सर, पहले और दूसरे कमरों में दफ़्तर के बड़े बाबू काम करते हैं ।

खन्ना जी और यह तीसरा कमरा किसका है ?

प्रकाश अभी तीसरे और चौथे कमरों में कोई नहीं है सर ।

खन्ना जी तो आपका कमरा कौनसा है ? पाँचवाँ ? छठा ?

प्रकाश अभी मैं छोटू के कमरे में काम करता हूँ । [*मन में सोचता है – "मुझे अलग कमरा चाहिए !"*]

खन्ना जी तीसरा कमरा ख़ाली है, उसे लेना । आपको और कोई चीज़ चाहिए ?

प्रकाश जी सर, उस कमरे में नया पंखा चाहिए । बहुत ज़रूरी है – पुराना पंखा काम नहीं करता ।

खन्ना जी गरमी का मौसम मार्च से पहले नहीं शुरू होता । पंखा बाद में लेना ।

प्रकाश जी सर ।

कौन कौन which various people?	**चाहिए** (is) needed
पहला first	**और कोई** any other
दूसरा second	**जी** yes
बाबू^{m} clerk	**ज़रूरी** necessary, urgent
तीसरा third	**गरमी**^{f} heat; summer
चौथा fourth	**मार्च**^{m} March
पाँचवाँ fifth	**शुरू होना** to begin
छठा sixth	**बाद में** later on
अलग separate, different	

Khanna ji Prakash, who works in all these rooms?
Prakash Sir, in the first and second rooms the senior clerks of the office work.
Khanna ji And whose is this third room?
Prakash There's nobody in the third and fourth rooms yet sir.
Khanna ji So which is you room? The fifth? The sixth?
Prakash At the moment I work in Ramdas's room. [*Thinks to himself: 'I need a separate room!'*]
Khanna ji The third room's vacant – take it. Do you need anything else?
Prakash Yes sir, a new fan's needed in that room. It's very urgent – the old fan doesn't work.
Khanna ji The hot weather doesn't start before March. Get a fan later on.
Prakash Yes sir.

> ! पंखा बाद में लेना – the infinitive verb लेना is here used as a 'deferred' command, i.e. one which will be acted on at some point in the future. See 5.2.

Grammar

7.4 Ordinal numbers

पहला	first	छठा	sixth
दूसरा	second	सातवाँ	seventh
तीसरा	third	आठवाँ	eighth
चौथा	fourth	नवाँ	ninth
पाँचवाँ	fifth	दसवाँ	tenth

Thereafter, simply add -वाँ to the cardinal number (Appendix 1): बारहवाँ, बीसवाँ 'twelfth, twentieth'. The ordinal numbers inflect like other adjectives, but with nasal endings -वीं, -वें; thus पाँचवीं सड़क के दसवें मकान में 'in the tenth house of the fifth road'.

Written Hindi sometimes borrows Sanskrit ordinal numbers (प्रथम 'first', द्वितीय 'second', तृतीय 'third', चतुर्थ 'fourth', पंचम 'fifth', etc.) for formal effect – rather as English can use Roman numerals in such set contexts as 'World War II' – द्वितीय महायुद्ध.

7.5 Aggregatives

Forms such as दोनों 'both, the two' indicate the total or *aggregate* number of items in a group. दोनों itself is irregular; other aggregatives simply add -ओं to the number:

तीनों बच्चे	all three children
चारों तरफ़	(on) all four sides, all around

Aggregatives can also refer to multiples of a number:

दर्जनों छात्र	dozens of students	(दर्जन	a dozen)
सैकड़ों विद्यार्थी	hundreds of students	(सैकड़ा	a hundred)
हज़ारों रुपये	thousands of rupees	(हज़ार	thousand)
लाखों औरतें	lakhs of women	(लाख	hundred thousand)
करोड़ों बच्चे	crores of children	(करोड़	ten million)

7.6 Conjunct verbs

As you have already seen, many verbs are formed by simply combining करना 'to do' with a noun or adjective.

शुरू करना	to begin	ख़त्म करना	to finish
बंद करना	to shut	साफ़ करना	to clean

These verbs are 'transitive' – that is, they can take a direct object: काम शुरू करना 'to begin work'; कमरा साफ़ करना 'to clean a room'. Many such verbs have 'intransitive' counterparts, i.e. verbs whose action is intrinsic and has no direct object: 'we start work' is transitive, with 'work' as object of 'we start', while 'work starts early today' is intransitive, with 'work' itself as subject. The distinction is not too clear in English, because the same verb often does duty for both transitive and intransitive; but in Hindi, transitive verbs using करना have intransitive equivalents using होना.

हमारी क्लास नौ बजे शुरू होती है ।	Our class begins at nine o'clock.
दरवाज़े रात को बन्द होते हैं ।	The doors are closed at night.
छुट्टियाँ अक्सर शनिवार को शुरू होती हैं ।	The holidays usually start on a Saturday.

EXERCISE 7a.1 Translate.

1 Father used to work in some office and used to get home late.
2 Some 12 students are sitting on the floor; we need some more chairs.
3 On Saturdays we used to meet some friends.
4 We don't like this cold food – we want some rice and daal.
5 Isn't there any cheap hotel here? The Taj is rather expensive!
6 'Give this money to someone else.' 'Yes, but to whom?'
7 We needed the car keys but there was nobody in the house.
8 In the evening, Grandma used to read the Ramayan and we used to watch old films.

EXERCISE 7a.2 Write ten चाहिए sentences on the model मुझे कुछ नए कपड़े चाहिए, pairing items as you like from the list.

1	I need	a good dictionary
2	you need	about ten chairs
3	they needed	a beautiful pearl
4	who (?) needs	some money
5	my friend needs	thousands of rupees
6	these students needed	today's newspapers
7	that other man needs	some hot water
8	those girls need	some more time
9	someone needed	a cigarette
10	nobody needs	a new house

EXERCISE 7a.3 Rewrite your ten sentences on the model मुझे कुछ नए कपड़ों की ज़रूरत है.

EXERCISE 7b.1 Rewrite the following sentences in the past tense, then translate them.

१ अरुण अपने बड़े भाई प्रकाश के साथ रहता है; वह किताबें लिखता है ।

२ खन्ना साहिब कहते हैं कि उनके दफ़्तर में दर्जनों लोग हैं लेकिन कोई ठीक से काम नहीं करता है ।

३ दादी जी नहीं जानती हैं कि उनके पिताजी किस कालेज में पढ़ाते थे ।

४ अध्यापक जी कहते हैं कि "कोई" और "कुछ" का फ़र्क समझना बहुत ज़रूरी है ।

५ छात्र अपने अध्यापक से हज़ारों मुश्किल सवाल पूछता है ।

६ क्या किसी को मालूम है कि संगीता का दोस्त सुहास कहाँ रहता है ?

७ किसको मालूम है कि ऋषि और राज की उम्र में कितना फ़र्क है ?

८ दादी जी सोचती हैं कि हिन्दुस्तान स्वर्ग के समान है । वे अपने बचपन के सपने बहुत देखती हैं ।

९ मालूम होता है कि प्रताप अभी दिल्ली में नहीं है शायद अपने पिताजी के यहाँ है ।

१० कुछ विद्यार्थियों के ख़याल में आठवाँ और दसवाँ सवाल सबसे मुश्किल हैं ।

EXERCISE 7b.2 Translate.

IN THE HOTEL

Boy	Come, sir. What would you like?
Khanna	I want some hot food and coffee.
Boy	Sir, the kitchen closes early on Sunday. There isn't any hot food. [leave 'any' untranslated]
Khanna	All right, give me some fruit. And clean my room tomorrow morning; it's very dirty.
Boy	Sir, tomorrow is my holiday. Please tell (कहना) someone else.
Khanna	But I need the coffee right away. Bring it and close the door.
Boy	Sir, the electricity (बिजली f) is off (बंद) at the moment. Please have ('drink') some cold water.
Khanna	This hotel is useless (बेकार); and you're useless too. I'm off.

Vocabulary

अलग separate, different	**औरत** f woman
आठ eight	**करोड़** m ten million
उर्दू f Urdu	**कानपुर** m Kanpur
और कोई any other	**किसी** oblique of **कोई**

कुछ some; somewhat; something; कुछ और something else, some more; कुछ न कुछ something or other
के नज़दीक near
के समान like, equal to
कोई anyone, someone; some, any, about; कोई और someone else; कोई न कोई someone or other; कोई नहीं no one
कौन कौन which various people
खड़ा standing, waiting
ख़त्म finished; ख़त्म करना to finish
ख़ास special, particular
गरमी f heat; summer
चतुर्थ fourth, IVth
चावल m rice
चाहिए (is) needed
चौथा fourth
छठा sixth
छुट्टी f holiday; free time
ज़मीन f ground; land
ज़रूरत f need
ज़रूरी urgent, necessary
जवाब देना to reply
जी yes
जेब f pocket
ठीक से properly; exactly
डाक्टर m doctor
डिब्बा m box; railway compartment
तरफ़ f side, direction
तीसरा third
तृतीय third, IIIrd
दर्जन f a dozen
दूर distant, far, away
दूसरा second
देर f delay, a while
द्वितीय second, IInd
नवाँ ninth
पंचम fifth, Vth
पढ़ाना to teach
पहला first
पाँचवाँ fifth
प्रथम first, Ist
फ़र्क m difference, separation
बाद में later on
बाबू m clerk
बिजली f electricity
बेकार useless
बैठा seated, sitting
महायुद्ध m great war
मार्च m March
मुसलमान m Muslim
मोती m pearl
रंग m colour
रोटी f bread; food
लाख m hundred thousand
वजह f reason, cause
शनिवार m Saturday

शाम ^f evening

शुरू करना, होना to begin

सपना ^m dream; सपना देखना to dream

सब कुछ everything

सिनेमा ^m cinema

सैकड़ा ^m a hundred

सैर ^f walk, trip; सैर करना to go for a walk, trip

स्वर्ग ^m heaven

हज़ार ^m thousand

हर each, every; हर कोई everyone

होटल ^m hotel; cafe

8 WHAT IS ARUN DOING IN LUCKNOW?

अरुण लखनऊ में क्या कर रहे हैं ?

In this unit you will learn how to

- talk about things that are happening now
- describe ownership and possession – 'to have'
- use a range of adverbs
- use dates

8a Arun in Lucknow

रफ़ीक़ अरुण, मेरे दिली दोस्त ! तुम यहाँ लखनऊ की तंग गलियों में क्या कर रहे हो ?

अरुण एक मित्र के साथ कुछ काम कर रहा हूँ; हमारी एक पुस्तक निकल रही है ।

रफ़ीक़ तो क्या तुम आजकल लखनऊ में ठहर रहे हो ?

अरुण नहीं नहीं, अभी तो दिल्ली में अपने भाई के यहाँ रह रहा हूँ ।

रफ़ीक़ तुम्हारा अपना मकान नहीं है, दिल्ली में ?

अरुण	नहीं है; पर मैं अभी सोच रहा था कि मुझे नया घर चाहिए। प्रकाश के तीन बच्चे हैं; वे मुझे बहुत तंग करते हैं।
रफ़ीक़	हाँ, तुम तो परेशान दिख रहे हो। अभी तुम्हें कोई ख़ास तकलीफ़ है?
अरुण	थोड़ी-सी थकान है, और कुछ नहीं।
रफ़ीक़	तो मेरे साथ चाय पियो। चलो, राम साहब के यहाँ चलते हैं।
अरुण	नहीं, मुझे देर हो रही है – विलंब हो रहा है; देखो, मेरे मित्र प्रेम अभी आ रहे हैं।

दिली	'of the heart', intimate	**तंग करना**	to hassle, harass
तंग	narrow	**दिखना**	to appear, seem
गली[f]	lane	**तकलीफ़**[f]	trouble, distress
पुस्तक[f]	book	**थोड़ा-सा**	a little
निकलना	to come/go out	**थकान**[f]	tiredness
आजकल	nowadays	**देर**[f], **विलंब**[m]	delay

Rafiq	Arun, my dear friend! What are you doing here in the narrow lanes of Lucknow?
Arun	I'm doing some work with a friend; a book of ours is coming out.
Rafiq	So are you staying in Lucknow nowadays?
Arun	No no, at the moment I'm living at my brother's place in Delhi.
Rafiq	You don't have your own house in Delhi?
Arun	I don't, but I was just thinking that I need a new home. Prakash has three children; they harrass me a lot.
Rafiq	Yes, you are looking hassled. Do you have any particular trouble just now?
Arun	A little tiredness, nothing else.
Rafiq	Then have tea with me. Come, we're off to Ram Sahib's.
Arun	No, I'm getting late – getting delayed; look, my friend Prem is just coming.

Grammar

8.1 The continuous tenses

Continuous tenses describe actions that are going on at the time: they are '-ing' tenses. The tense is made up of three elements: the verb stem (बोल from बोलना), plus रहा/ रही/ रहे which gives the 'continuous' sense, plus the auxiliary verb (हूँ, है, था etc.).

	MASCULINE	FEMININE	
Present	मैं बोल रहा हूँ	बोल रही हूँ	I am speaking
	तू बोल रहा है	बोल रही है	you are speaking
	यह, वह बोल रहा है	बोल रही है	he, it, she is speaking
	हम बोल रहे हैं	बोल रही हैं	we are speaking
	तुम बोल रहे हो	बोल रही हो	you are speaking
	आप बोल रहे हैं	बोल रही हैं	you are speaking
	ये, वे बोल रहे हैं	बोल रही हैं	they are speaking
Past	मैं बोल रहा था	बोल रही थी	I was speaking
	तू बोल रहा था	बोल रही थी	you were speaking
	यह, वह बोल रहा था	बोल रही थी	he, it, she was speaking
	हम बोल रहे थे	बोल रही थीं	we were speaking
	तुम बोल रहे थे	बोल रही थीं	you were speaking
	आप बोल रहे थे	बोल रही थीं	you were speaking
	ये, वे बोल रहे थे	बोल रही थीं	they were speaking

हम लोग हिन्दी सीख रहे हैं।	We are learning Hindi.
वह अपने भाई के बारे में पूछ रही है।	She's asking about her brother.
तुम कौनसी कहानी पढ़ रही हो?	Which story are you reading?
हम आज का प्रोग्राम बना रहे हैं।	We're making a plan for today.
मैं अभी घर नहीं जा रहा हूँ।	I'm not going home just yet.
मैं सोमवार को घर आ रही हूँ।	I'm coming home on Monday.
क्या आप खाना तैयार कर रहे हैं?	Are you preparing food?
तुम ग़लत नंबर मिला रहे थे!	You were ringing the wrong number!

The continuous tense is used for identification on the phone:

आप कौन बोल रही हैं?	Who is that speaking? ('Who are you speaking?')
मैं उषा बोल रही हूँ।	This is Usha speaking. ('I Usha am speaking')

8.2 Expressions for 'to have'

Hindi has no verb 'to have'. Instead, it uses the verb होना 'to be' in three different constructions, using the postpositions को, के पास and का/की/के respectively.

+ को Already seen in 4.4 — 'to have a cold' etc:

पिंकी को ज़ुकाम है ।	Pinkie has a cold.
संगीता को बुख़ार था ।	Sangeeta had a fever.

+ के पास For the possession of things, 'portable' items, time, money and so on; also for servants (!):

राज के पास बहुत खिलौने हैं ।	Raj has lots of toys.
हमारे पास समय नहीं है ।	We don't have time.
उनके पास बहुत पैसा था ।	They had lots of money.
खन्ना के पास ड्राइवर है ।	Khanna has a driver.
मेरे पास कुछ भी नहीं है ।	I have nothing at all.

+ का/ की/ के For relatives, houses, parts of the body:

राम के दो भाई हैं ।	Ram has two brothers.
कृष्ण का एक घर है ।	Krishna has one house.
शिव की तीन आंखें हैं ।	Shiva has three eyes.
प्रकाश के तीन बच्चे हैं ।	Prakash has three children.
मेरे पिता का एक अस्पताल है ।	My father owns a hospital.

Remember that some possessive pronouns – e.g. मेरा, तुम्हारा – don't contain का. Compare:

अक्षय के पाँच बच्चे हैं ।	Akshay has five children.
मेरे पाँच बच्चे हैं ।	I have five children.
शिव की तीन आँखें हैं ।	Shiva has three eyes.
मेरी सिर्फ़ एक आँख है ।	I have only one eye.

In referring to relatives, some speakers use के (rather than का or की) regardless of number and gender:

बंटी के आठ लड़कियाँ हैं ।	Bunty has eight daughters.
लक्ष्मी के एक लड़का है ।	Lakshmi has one son.

8b Khanna Sahib's coming to dinner!

प्रकाश	प्यारी, आज रात को खन्ना साहब यहाँ आ रहे हैं।
कमला	हे भगवान ! क्या उनका सारा परिवार भी आ रहा है ?
प्रकाश	हाँ। पर उनका सिर्फ़ एक बेटा है – हरीश। वह अठारह साल का है।
कमला	क्या खन्ना की छोटी बहिन नहीं आ रही है ? क्या नाम है उसका – पिंकी ?
प्रकाश	नहीं। वह तो अलग रहती है; दूसरे लोग ऊपर रहते हैं, वह नीचे रहती है।
कमला	ख़ैर, तुम जल्दी से कुछ सब्ज़ी लाना। हमारे पास कुछ भी नहीं है।
प्रकाश	गोश्त भी चाहिए न ? खन्नाजी और उनकी पत्नी दोनों गोश्त खाते हैं।
कमला	उनकी पत्नी का कोई नाम नहीं है ?
प्रकाश	मुझे क्या मालूम। खन्नाजी उन्हें हमेशा "हरीश की माँ" कहते हैं।
कमला	ख़ैर, तुम अभी बाज़ार जाओ। सारे दिन ऐश करते हो ! जाओ न !
प्रकशा	हाँ हाँ, जा रहा हूँ। मेरा सिर क्यों खा रही हो ? ऋषि, तू साथ चल।

हे Oh!
भगवान m God
अठारह eighteen
अलग separately
ऊपर above; upstairs
नीचे below; downstairs
सब्ज़ी f vegetable(s)
के पास in (our) possession
ऐश m wanton luxury; **ऐश करना** to live a life of pleasure
सिर m head; **सिर खाना** to pester
साथ along, with, in company

Prakash	Darling, tonight Khanna Sahib is coming here.
Kamala	Oh God! Is the whole family coming too?
Prakash	Yes. But he has just one son – Harish. He is 18.
Kamala	Isn't Khanna's younger sister coming? What's her name – Pinkie?
Prakash	No. She lives separately; the others live upstairs, she lives downstairs.
Kamala	Well anyway, fetch (buy, get) some vegetables quickly. We don't have anything at all.
Prakash	We need meat too, don't we? Khanna ji and his wife both eat meat.
Kamala	Doesn't his wife have a name?
Prakash	How do I know? Khanna ji always calls her 'Harish's mother'.
Kamala	Well anyway, you go to the market right now. You laze around all day! Go, won't you?

Prakash Yes, yes, I'm going. Why are you pestering me ? Rishi, you come along too.

Grammar

8.3 Some adverbial phrases

Up to this point, you have seen that the oblique case (3.2) only occurs before a postposition. An exception to this rule is with adverbial phrases such as उस दिन '[on] that day'. One may imagine that को has been dropped from such a phrase. Here are some more:

अगले महीने	next month	तीसरे पहर	in the afternoon
इस तरफ़	in this direction	दूसरे दिन	the next day
दाहिने / बायें	to the right/ left	उन दिनों	in those days
सवेरे	in the early morning	सारे दिन	all day
पिछले साल	last year	किस समय	at what time

Similarly, the destination of a 'motion' verb is usually oblique: कलकत्ते जाना 'to go to Calcutta'; उस शहर जाना, 'to go to that city'.

मैं अपने गाँव जा रहा हूँ।	I'm going to my village.
वे लोग आगरे जा रहे हैं।	They're going to Agra.

The postpositions से and पर also form adverbial phrases. से can be dropped where indicated by brackets:

बस से	by bus	ठीक तरह (से)	properly
हाथ से	by hand	ठीक से	properly, precisely
देर से	late	ज़ोर से	forcefully, loudly
अच्छी तरह (से)	well	ध्यान से	attentively
बुरी तरह (से)	badly	———	
किस तरह (से)	how?	ठीक समय पर	punctually
सावधानी से	carefully	आम तौर पर/ से	usually
जल्दी (से)	quickly	ख़ास तौर पर/ से	specially

The second part of a compound postposition (e.g. बाहर from के बाहर) can comprise an adverb:

PHRASE WITH POSTPOSITION		PHRASE WITH ADVERB	
घर के बाहर	outside the house	बाहर जाओ	go outside

कमरे के अंदर	inside the room	अंदर आओ	come inside
मेरे साथ	with me	तुम भी साथ चलो	you come along too
अलमारी के ऊपर	on top of the cupboard	ऊपर देखो	look up
कपड़े के नीचे	under the cloth	वह नीचे रहती है	she lives downstairs
दुकान के सामने	opposite the shop	वह सामने रहती है	she lives opposite
दुकान के नज़दीक	near the shop	वह नज़दीक रहता था	he lived nearby
कल के बाद	after tomorrow	दस साल बाद	ten years later

Some adverbs ending in -ए form pairs with similar adjectives:

ADJECTIVE		ADVERB	
कैसा	of what kind?	कैसे	how?
सीधा	straight	सीधे	straight
दाहिना, बायाँ	right, left	दाहिने, बायें	to the right, left

The Hindi equivalents of 'this evening, this morning' are आज शाम, आज सुबह; the pronouns यह, इस are *not* used here.

8.4 What's today's date? आज की तारीख़ क्या है ?

Dates use ordinal numbers for the first two days of the month (पहली, दूसरी 'first, second', both agreeing with feminine तारीख़ 'date'); and with cardinal numbers (तीन, चार etc.) thereafter:

पहली जनवरी	the 1st of January	तीन मार्च	the 3rd of March
दूसरी मई को	on the 2nd of May	दस जून को	on the 10th of June

Years are expressed with the word सन् 'year'. No word for 'and' stands between the hundreds and the tens: thus १९४७ is सन् उन्नीस सौ सैंतालीस '(the year) nineteen hundred [and] forty-seven'.

आज पाँच जुलाई सन् उन्नीस सौ निन्यानवे है । Today is the 5th of July 1999.

(See the appendixes for more on dates and numbers.)

8.5 Word order

A typical sentence word order is: subject, adverb, indirect object + को, direct object, verb:

SUBJECT	ADVERB	IND.OBJ.+ को	DIR.OBJ.	VERB
केशव	रोज़	हम को	फल	भेजता है ।

Keshav sends us fruit every day.

Variations on this neutral word order will emphasise a particular component:

केशव रोज़ फल हम को भेजता है ।	Keshav sends *us* fruit every day.
केशव फल हम को रोज़ भेजता है ।	Keshav sends us fruit *every day*.

So much depends on the style and context of what's being said that rules are not easily given for word order; but these last examples show that the position just before the verb often bears emphasis.

A word or phrase whose meaning is already implicit in a sentence may be thrown in as an afterthought at the end. Sentences from Dialogue 8B might have appeared as follows:

उनका सारा परिवार भी आ रहा है क्या ?	(the sentence is *implicitly* a question)
तो क्या छोटी बहिन नहीं आ रही है उनकी ?	('possession' is clear from the context)

8.6 Some colloquial usages, and pronunciation reminders

By now, you are well used to the pronouns यह, वह as singular, and ये, वे as plural. But out there in the real world, this clearcut distinction of number is not always honoured: यह and वह can both appear as plurals, even though this is not a standard grammatical use. Likewise, many people's pronunciation of यह will convince you that they're actually saying ये. Remember also that वह is usually pronounced as if spelt वो – and a few Hindi-speakers (perhaps influenced by Urdu, where *vo* is the standard form for both singular and plural) even adopt this form in writing.

Another common 'infringement' of the grammatical rules involves inconsistency in honorific levels. It's not unusual to hear someone saying आप बैठो, anomalously pairing the तुम imperative with the pronoun आप. This is perhaps felt to be a comfortable compromise between the two levels: give your addressee the benefit of the doubt by calling him or her आप, then go for a friendlier tone by switching down to the तुम imperative.

The 'royal we' is very common in Hindi: some people hardly ever use मैं, preferring हम across the board. But it has a colloquial ring, and there's nothing 'royal' about it at all. Some women use the *masculine* first person plural when referring to themselves.

A quite different effect is heard as a heated argument escalates and speakers drop progressively from high (आप) to low (तू) honorific levels! Remember that तू (and even तुम) can sound offensively blunt out of context; Hindi has a nice idiomatic verb, तू-तू मैं-मैं करना, 'to call names, trade insults'.

Hindi is spoken across a wide geographical area; its speakers include many for whom it is not a first language, and it is often heavily influenced by the grammar and vocabulary of dialects or neighbouring languages. Like most spoken languages, then, Hindi has rich internal variety. This makes Hindi-speakers very tolerant of grammatical deviance; but a non-Indian *accent* may prove much more of a block to understanding. So it's timely now to revise some pronunciation points. Many learners of Hindi need in particular to remember the following distinctions:

- between dental and retroflex consonants: दाल / डाल
- between non-aspirates and aspirates: सात / साथ
- between single and double consonants: बचा / बच्चा
- between short and long vowels: कम / काम

Also, remember the 'purity' of the vowels, particularly ए and ओ (से and सो do *not* rhyme with 'say' and 'so').

The glossary at the end of the book provides excellent pronunciation practice: read whole sequences of headwords aloud, or ask a Hindi-speaker to do so for you and repeat them afterwards. Also, practise distinguishing clearly between the two members of 'minimal pairs' (pairs of words that are identical except for one distinguishing feature) such as the following:

जाना	to go	जानना	to know
दिली	of the heart	दिल्ली	Delhi
दल	political party	दाल	daal
दाल	daal	डाल	branch
पल	moment	फल	fruit
मोटी	fat (f)	मोती	pearl
मोर	peacock	मोड़	turn, bend
सात	seven	साथ	(in) company
ताली	clapping	थाली	tray, plate of food
कम	less	काम	work
में	in	मैं	I
है	is	हैं	are

EXERCISE 8a.1 Change imperfective verbs into continuous verbs. Then translate.

१ प्रताप बहुत ध्यान से हिन्दी पढ़ता है ।
२ मैं तो अच्छा पैसा कमाता हूँ ।
३ क्या तुम गाड़ी चलाते हो ?
४ संगीता और उसका छोटा भाई सिनेमा जाते हैं ।
५ प्रताप अपने दोस्तों के साथ गोश्त खाता है ।

EXERCISE 8a.2 Translate.

1 He is preparing different food for you.
2 Tell her that she was dialling the wrong number.
3 He's coming to Delhi with his relatives tomorrow.
4 How many sisters do you have? I have two sisters.
5 All three doctors are working at that same hospital.
6 He used to dream of me but now he is dreaming of you.
7 Why are you not giving an answer to my question, Sangeeta?
8 We were talking to your neighbours about you.

EXERCISE 8a.3 Pratap phones Mohan – from Kathmandu! Supply Mohan's responses:

प्रताप नमस्ते मोहन ! मैं प्रताप बोल रहा हूँ – नेपाल से ! क्या हाल है ?

मोहन ....

प्रताप मैं यहाँ कुछ दोस्तों के साथ नेपाल की सैर कर रहा हूँ ।

मोहन ....

प्रताप नहीं, ऋषि और राज घर पर हैं, अपनी बहिन के साथ ।

मोहन ....

प्रताप अभी तो हम लोग काठमांडु में एक होटल में ठहर रहे हैं । बहुत महँगा है ।

मोहन ....

प्रताप पर यहाँ तो हमारा कोई दोस्त है नहीं – हम किसी को भी नहीं जानते नेपाल में ।

मोहन ....

प्रताप अच्छा, तो मुझे अपने रिश्तेदारों का पता दीजिए, मैं उन्हें अभी फ़ोन करता हूँ !

EXERCISE 8b.1 Translate, using *postpositions* in the first column and related *adverbs* in the second, as in the model.

	I live near Calcutta.	I live nearby.
	मैं कलकत्ते के पास रहता हूँ ।	मैं पास रहता हूँ ।
1	Sit outside the house.	Sit outside.
2	Look behind the chair.	Look back.
3	We're standing opposite the door.	The shop is opposite.
4	Come towards me.	Come this way.
5	Don't sleep under the tree.	Sleep downstairs.
6	Both brothers are with me.	You come along too.
7	Put it on top of the cupboard.	You go upstairs.
8	We live near the cycle shop.	They live nearby.

EXERCISE 8b.2 Answer the following questions.

१ आपका जन्मदिन कब है ?

२ आज की तारीख़ क्या है ?

३ कल कौनसा दिन था ?

४ क्या आपके बच्चे हैं ?

५ आपके कितने भाई और बहिनें हैं ? उनकी कितनी उम्र है ?

६ क्या आपके पास बहुत पैसा है ? क्या आपको और पैसा चाहिए ? क्यों ?

७ क्या आपका अपना घर है ? या आप दूसरे लोगों के घर में रहते हैं / रहती हैं ?

८ क्या आपको ज़ुकाम या बुख़ार है ? आपकी तबियत कैसी है ?

९ आपके ख़याल में क्या प्रताप संगीता से डरता है ?

१० तीन घंटे पहले आप क्या कर रहे थे / कर रही थीं ?

Vocabulary

अंदर inside, within
अगला next
अठारह eighteen
अलग separately
अस्पताल m hospital
आँख f eye
आगरा m Agra
आजकल nowadays
आम ordinary; **आम तौर पर** usually
ऊपर above; up; upstairs
ऐश m luxury; **ऐश करना** to live a life of pleasure
कमाना to earn
कलकत्ता m Calcutta
कहानी f story
काठमांडु m Kathmandu
के पास in (our) possession
ग़लत wrong, incorrect
गली f lane
घंटा m hour
चलाना to drive
जन्मदिन m birthday
जून m June
ज़ोर m force, strength
डाल f branch (of tree)
तंग narrow; **तंग करना** to harass
तकलीफ़ f trouble, distress
तरह f way, manner
तारीख़ m date
ताली f clapping
तू-तू मैं-मैं करना to call names
तैयार करना to prepare
थकान f tiredness
थाली f platter
थोड़ा-सा a little
दल m political party
दाहिना right (opp. of left)
दिखना to appear, seem
दिली 'of the heart', intimate
देर f delay; a while
नंबर m number
नज़दीक near, nearby
निकलना to come/go out, emerge
निन्यानवे ninety-nine
नीचे below, down, downstairs
नेपाल m Nepal

पल ^{m} moment
पहर ^{m} part of the day
पिछला last, previous
पुस्तक ^{f} book
पूरा full, complete
प्रोग्राम ^{m} programme, plan
फ़रवरी ^{f} February
बनाना to make
बाद (में) later
बायाँ left (opp. of right)
भगवान ^{m} God
भेजना to send
मई ^{f} May
महीना ^{m} month
मिलाना to dial, phone
मोड़ ^{m} turn, bend
मोर ^{m} peacock
विलंब ^{m} delay
सन् ^{m} year (of calendar or era)
सब्ज़ी ^{f} vegetable(s)
सवेरा ^{m} early morning
साथ along, with, in company
सावधानी ^{f} care
सिर ^{m} head; सिर खाना to pester
सीधा straight, straightforward;
सीधे straight; to the right
सैंतालीस forty-seven
हाथ ^{m} hand
हे Oh !

9 IN THE FUTURE
भविष्य में

In this unit you will learn how to

- use the future tense
- express assumptions – 'I suppose'
- talk about quantity
- use verbal nouns – '*speaking* is easy'

9a Dinner at home, or the cinema with Pinkie?

पिंकी	संगीता, आज रात को तुम मेरे साथ सिनेमा चलोगी ?
संगीता	मुश्किल है। तुम्हारा सारा परिवार तो हमारे यहाँ आ रहा है।
पिंकी	तो तुम घर पर बैठी रहोगी ? मेरे घर के लोग तुम्हें अच्छी तरह बोर करेंगे।
संगीता	ठीक है, आऊँगी। पर अगर ऋषि या राज माँ को बताता है तो...
पिंकी	वे किसी को क्यों बताएँगे। चुप रहेंगे। भोले-से लड़के हैं, दोनों।
संगीता	बात यह है कि... माँ को नहीं मालूम कि मैं बाहर जा रही हूँ।
पिंकी	अगर तुम मेरे साथ सिनेमा जाओगी तो उनका क्या नुक़सान होगा ?
संगीता	माँ कहती हैं... मेरा मतलब है... उन्हें मालूम है कि तुम्हारा भतीजा मेरी उम्र का है।

पिंकी	हरीश तो हमारे साथ थोड़े आएगा ! वह तो तुम्हारे माँ-बाप की दावत में जा रहा होगा ।
संगीता	फिर मुश्किल शायद कम होगी । पर माँ को क्या बताऊँगी ?

बोर करना to bore
अगर if
भोला innocent, guileless; **भोला-सा** quite innocent
नुक़सान m harm
भतीजा m nephew
थोड़े scarcely
दावत f (invitation to) a dinner

Pinkie	Sangeeta, will you come with me to the cinema tonight?
Sangeeta	It's difficult. Your whole family is coming to our place.
Pinkie	So you'll stay sitting at home? My relatives will bore you thoroughly.
Sangeeta	All right, I'll come. But if Rishi or Raj tells Mother, then...
Pinkie	Why would they tell anyone. They'll keep quiet. They're quite innocent boys, both of them.
Sangeeta	The thing is that... Mother doesn't know that I'm going out.
Pinkie	What's the harm to her if you go to the cinema with me?
Sangeeta	Mother says... I mean... she knows your nephew is my age.
Pinkie	Harish will hardly be coming with us! He'll be going to your parents' dinner party.
Sangeeta	Then maybe it'll be less difficult. But what will I tell Mother?

Grammar

9.1 The future tense

The future tense is one of the easiest. It consists of a single word, with no auxiliary (unlike the English!).

मैं बोलूँगा	बोलूँगी	I will speak
तू बोलेगा	बोलेगी	you will speak
यह, वह बोलेगा	बोलेगी	he, it, she will speak
हम बोलेंगे	बोलेंगी	we will speak
तुम बोलोगे	बोलोगी	you will speak
आप बोलेंगे	बोलेंगी	you will speak
ये, वे बोलेंगे	बोलेंगी	they will speak

The masculine endings are just -ऊँगा for मैं, -एगा for all the other singulars; -ओगे for तुम, and -एँगे for all the other plurals. Feminines follow suit, with -ई as the final vowel. The bad news is that the three very common verbs होना, लेना, देना are irregular:

मैं हूँगा, हूँगी	लूँगा, लूँगी	दूँगा, दूँगी
तू होगा, होगी	लेगा, लेगी	देगा, देगी
यह / वह होगा, होगी	लेगा, लेगी	देगा, देगी
हम होंगे, होंगी	लेंगे, लेंगी	देंगे, देंगी
तुम होगे, होगी	लोगे, लोगी	दोगे, दोगी
आप होंगे, होंगी	लेंगे, लेंगी	देंगे, देंगी
ये / वे होंगे, होंगी	लेंगे, लेंगी	देंगे, देंगी

शर्मा जी तुमको फ़ोन करेंगे ।	Sharma ji will phone you.
मैं कभी वाराणसी आऊँगा ।	I'll come to Varanasi sometime.
माँ शराब नहीं ख़रीदेंगी ।	Mother won't buy alcohol.
वह इससे ज़्यादा नहीं लेगी ।	She won't take more than this.
प्रताप तो ध्यान नहीं देगा !	Pratap won't pay attention!
पंडित जी गाना गाएँगे ।	Pandit ji will sing a song.

Verbs whose stems end in ऊ or ई shorten these in the future tense: छूना > छुएगा, पीना > पिएगा.

9.2 Future tense in the auxiliary verb

The future of the auxiliary verb होना can be used within tenses such as the continuous. Compare the following three continuous tenses:

वह जा रहा है ।	He is going.	(present auxiliary है)
वह जा रहा था ।	He was going.	(past auxiliary था)
वह जा रहा होगा ।	He will be going.	(future auxiliary होगा)

These sentences are in the present continuous, past continuous and future continuous respectively. Some more examples of the future continuous:

प्रताप अगले हफ़्ते तक दिल्ली लौट रहा होगा ।	Pratap will be returning to Delhi by next week.

अरुण की किताब थोड़े दिनों में निकल रही होगी ।	Arun's book will be coming out in a few days.
आज शाम को कमला खाना तैयार कर रही होगी ।	Kamala will be preparing food this evening.

A similar construction applies with imperfective tenses, e.g. वह जाता होगा 'he will be going (habitually)'; but such usages mostly have a special implication, as described in the next section.

9.3 'Presumptive' uses of the future

The English sentence 'That man will be our neighbour' is ambiguous: it can indicate real future time (tomorrow, next week), or it can be an assumption about the present (presumably he's our neighbour). This usage is common in Hindi, both with the simple future, होगा (as in the first example below), and with the future as auxiliary (as in the remaining examples):

वह आदमी हमारा पड़ोसी होगा ।	That man will/must be our neighbour.
बच्चे सो रहे होंगे ।	The kids will/must be sleeping.
दूसरे लोग अभी आ रहे होंगे ।	The others will/must be on their way just now.
आप उर्दू समझते होंगे ?	Presumably you understand Urdu?
शर्माजी संस्कृत जानते होंगे ।	Sharmaji will/must know Sanskrit.
वे गाड़ी का इंतज़ाम कर रहे होंगे ।	They will/must be making arrangements for a car.

9b Arun and his co-author

अरुण	प्रेम, हमारी पुस्तक छपने को तैयार है । ग्यारह सौ प्रतियाँ छप रही हैं, वाराणसी में ।
प्रेम	तो दिल्ली लौटने से पहले आप उन्हें पिक-अप करने वाराणसी जाएँगे ?
अरुण	अभी मेरे लिए उधर जाना कठिन होगा । हम उन्हें डाक से मँगवाएँगे ।
प्रेम	बुक के डिस्ट्रिब्यूशन और पब्लिसिटी का क्या होगा ?

अरुण सारी व्यवस्था यहीं हो रही है; इसीलिए मैं लखनऊ में दस दिन और रुक रहा हूँ ।

प्रेम आप सोचते हैं किताब ख़ूब बिकेगी? अच्छा-ख़ासा पैसा हाथ आएगा ?

अरुण पैसा कहाँ से हाथ आएगा, प्रेम ? अधिक से अधिक चार सौ प्रतियाँ बिकेंगी ।

प्रेम पर मेरे ख़याल से तो लोग किताब को पसंद करेंगे । "वर्थ रीडिंग" है – पढ़ने-लायक़ है !

अरुण है तो सही; परंतु आपके कहने से कुछ नहीं होगा । यदि जनता ख़रीदेगी, तो देखेंगे !

NB: Prem's English words are not given in the glossary.

छपना	to be printed	**अच्छा-ख़ासा**	really good
ग्यारह	eleven	**हाथ आना**	to come to hand
कठिन	hard, difficult	**अधिक से अधिक**	at the most
डाक ^{f}	mail, post	**लायक़**	worth (doing)
मँगवाना	to order, send for	**पसंद करना**	to like, approve
व्यवस्था ^{f}	arrangement(s)	**सही**	true, correct
रुकना	to stop, stay on	**परंतु**	but
बिकना	to be sold	**जनता** ^{f}	public, the people

Arun Prem, our book's ready for printing. 1100 copies are being printed, in Varanasi.

Prem So will you go to Varanasi to pick them up before returning to Delhi?

Arun It'll be hard for me to go there just now. We'll send for them by post.

Prem What will happen about the distribution and publicity of the book?

Arun All the organising's happening here; that's why I'm stopping in Lucknow ten days more.

Prem D'you think the book will sell well? We'll make loads of money?

Arun How ('from where') will we make money, Prem. At the most 400 copies will sell.

Prem But in *my* opinion people will like the book; it's 'worth reading' – worth reading!

Arun It is indeed; but your saying it won't effect anything. If the public buys, then we'll see!

Grammar

9.4 The emphatic ही

The word ही emphasises or restricts the word or phrase that precedes it: मैं ही 'I myself' or 'only I'; बहुत ही अच्छा 'very good indeed'. Often ही can be translated as 'only'; elsewhere the translation depends on context.

मैं हिन्दी ही बोलूँगा ।	I shall speak Hindi only.
हमारा एक ही मकान है ।	We have only one house.

In many ways, ही operates like भी (2.3): it qualifies the word or phrase *immediately preceding it*, and not being a postposition it needs no change of case.

मैं सोमवार को ही आऊँगी ।	I'll come on Monday itself.
मैं ही सोमवार को आऊँगी ।	I'll come on Monday myself.

Some pronouns coalesce with ही, giving special forms:

मुझ	+	ही	=	मुझी	उस	+	ही	=	उसी
तुझ	+	ही	=	तुझी	हम	+	ही	=	हमीं
यह	+	ही	=	यही	तुम	+	ही	=	तुम्हीं
वह	+	ही	=	वही	इन	+	ही	=	इन्हीं
इस	+	ही	=	इसी	उन	+	ही	=	उन्हीं

! वही / उसी 'that very one' also means 'the same': वही आदमी 'the same man', उसी दिन 'that same day'.

Some adverbs also coalesce with ही:

यहाँ	+	ही	=	यहीं	right here
वहाँ	+	ही	=	वहीं	right there
अब	+	ही	=	अभी	right now
सब	+	ही	=	सभी	all, absolutely all

असली हिन्दी हमीं बोलते हैं ।	It is we who speak the real Hindi.
वही गुंडा मुझसे भी पैसा माँग रहा था ।	The same lout was demanding money from me too.
हम यहीं रहेंगे, हिलेंगे ही नहीं !	We'll stay right here, we won't even move!
डाक्टर साहब, अभी आइएगा ।	Doctor, please come at once.

> ❗ Look carefully: यहीं and वहीं are different from यही and वही ! And notice also the difference in emphasis between इस लिए 'so, therefore' and इसी लिए 'for this reason', '*that's* why'.

हम यहीं रहते हैं ।	We live right here.
मैं भी यही सोचता हूँ ।	I too think the same thing.
हम वहीं जाएँगे ।	We'll go right there.
हम वही करेंगे ।	We'll do just that.

9.5 Some expressions of quantity

The word बहुत is both adjective (बहुत लोग 'many people') and adverb (बहुत बड़ा 'very big'). This can lead to ambiguities: बहुत अच्छी किताबें could theoretically mean either 'many good books' or 'very good books'. To remove this ambiguity and specify the former sense, the suffix -सा/-सी/-से can be added to the adjective:

बहुत अच्छी किताबें	very good books (adverb बहुत qualifies अच्छी)
बहुत-सी अच्छी किताबें	many good books (adjective बहुत-सी qualifies किताबें)

In a more general usage, -सा modifies or lightens the meaning of the word it's suffixed to, giving an '-ish' sense: लाल-सी रोशनी 'reddish light'; महँगे-से कपड़े 'quite expensive clothes'. Like English 'quite', its emphasis is rather ambiguous: sometimes it seems to enhance the sense of the adjective, sometimes to tone it down.

ज़्यादा and अधिक 'much, many, more' and कम 'little, few, less' are , like बहुत, both adverbs and adjectives. The sense 'too much' is expressed by बहुत ज़्यादा/अधिक, and 'too little' by बहुत कम, although the sense of 'excess' is not as specific as in these English expressions.

गरमियों में (बहुत) ज़्यादा लोग मसूरी आते हैं ।	In the summer (too) many people come to Mussoorie.
दाल में नमक बहुत ज़्यादा है ।	There's too much/a lot of salt in the daal.
वह छात्र बहुत कम काम करता है ।	That student does very little work.

Some more everyday phrases:

कम से कम at least	ज़्यादा से ज़्यादा at most
थोड़ा-बहुत a certain amount	अधिक से अधिक at most

काफ़ी quite (काफ़ी दूर, काफ़ी अच्छा); enough (काफ़ी पैसा, काफ़ी खाना)

9.6 The infinitive as verbal noun: जाना 'to go, going'

The infinitive – बोलना 'to speak' – can be used as a noun, also meaning 'speaking'.

सिग्रेट पीना मना है ।	Smoking is prohibited.
हिन्दी समझना आसान है ।	To understand Hindi is easy.
होना या न होना ।	To be or not to be.

Like any other masculine noun, this verbal noun inflects in the oblique case before a postposition: जाने से पहले, करने के बाद 'before going, after doing'. Hindi uses पर like English 'on' in पहुँचने पर 'on arriving'.

घर पहुँचने पर हमें फ़ोन करना ।	On arriving home, phone us.
मेरे जाने के बाद तुम क्या करोगे ?	What will you do after my going?
पत्र लिखने में क्या फ़ायदा है ?	What's the point in writing a letter?
चिल्लाने की (कोई) ज़रूरत नहीं है !	There's no need to shout!

The oblique infinitive expresses purpose: हम अँग्रेज़ी पढ़ाने अमरीका जा रहे हैं 'We are going to America to teach English'. The oblique infinitive may stand alone, or be followed by के लिए or को:

मैं खाना खाने किसी होटल जाऊँगी ।	I'll go to some hotel to eat.

वह कुछ ख़रीदने (के लिए) बाज़ार जा रहा है।	He's going to the market (in order) to buy something.
गाड़ी ठीक करने को कोई मिस्तरी भेजो।	Send some mechanic to fix the car.

The idiomatic English use of 'going to' as meaning 'about to' is reflected in Hindi also: मैं गाना गाने जा रहा हूँ 'I'm going to sing a song'.

> **!** Why is there no को after मिस्तरी 'mechanic', when in 5.4 we saw that a person as direct object takes को? Because the person here is not individualised – it's not a particular mechanic but कोई मिस्तरी, *any* mechanic. (मिस्तरी, incidentally, is from Portuguese 'mestre'.)

The oblique infinitive + (के) योग्य or (के) लायक़ means 'worth doing':

"टीच योरसेल्फ़ हिन्दी" पढ़ने लायक़ है;	*Teach Yourself Hindi* is worth reading;
हाँ, और उसका कैसेट सुनने योग्य है।	Yes, and its cassette is worth listening to.

In 6.1 we saw the usage मुझे हिन्दी आती है 'I know Hindi'. Similarly, आना is used with an infinitive verb as subject, meaning 'to know how to...'. Being sentence subject, the infinitive is in the direct case:

मुझे तैरना आता है।	I am able to swim, can swim.
तुम्हें गाड़ी चलाना नहीं आता है ?	You can't drive a car?
उन्हें पढ़ना तो आता है पर लिखना नहीं आता।	They can read but they can't write.

EXERCISE 9a.1 Translate.

1 The others will arrive by tomorrow morning.
2 Some day I will tell you the full story.
3 I know that he will not reply to my letters.
4 Your father must be earning good money these days.

5 They will be thinking that she must be living a life of luxury.

6 My sister will be driving my car today.

EXERCISE 9a.2 Answer the questions on Dialogue 8b:

१ क्या कमला को ख़ुशी है कि आज रात को कुछ मेहमान आ रहे हैं ? आपको कैसे मालूम है ?

२ क्या पिंकी अपने बड़े भाई के परिवार के साथ रहती है ?

३ खाना तैयार करने के लिए घर में किन चीज़ों की ज़रूरत है ?

४ प्रकाश को क्यों नहीं मालूम है कि श्रीमती खन्ना का पहला नाम क्या है ?

५ क्या कमला के ख़याल से उसका पति बहुत मेहनती आदमी है ? ऐसा कौन सोचता है ?

EXERCISE 9a.3 Answer the questions on Dialogue 9a.

१ आज शाम को प्रताप और कमला के यहाँ कौन नहीं आ रहा होगा, और क्यों ?

२ संगीता किस चीज़ से डरती है ?

३ संगीता के भाइयों के बारे में पिंकी का क्या ख़याल है ?

४ आपके ख़याल में हरीश के बारे में कमला क्या सोचती होगी ?

५ हरीश सिनेमा क्यों नहीं जाएगा ?

EXERCISE 9b.1 Translate Pratap's letter from a friend in Canada.

प्रिय प्रताप,

तुम कैसे हो ? दिल्ली में सब ठीक चल रहा है ? मैं बहुत देर के बाद यह ख़त लिख रही हूँ । तुम जानते होगे कि मैं भी हिन्दी सीखने के लिए भारत आने का प्रोग्राम बना रही हूँ । मुझे आशा है कि बहुत ध्यान से पढ़ने के बाद मैं भी तुम्हारी तरह अच्छी हिन्दी सीखूँगी । कम से कम यही तो इरादा है । हिन्दी समझना एक बात है लेकिन रवानी से बोलना दूसरी बात ! मेरी सहेली राजेश्वरी को जानते हो न ? उसकी बहिन उषा वाराणसी में रहती है । मैं उसी के साथ ठहरूँगी । उसका घर कालेज से काफ़ी दूर है; कालेज तो रामनगर में है, महाराजा के महल के नज़दीक, और उषा का घर बनारस हिन्दू विश्वविद्यालय (बी० एच० यू०) के अन्दर है । बी० एच० यू० के आस-पास बहुत-से विद्यार्थी रहते होंगे । वे रिक्शे से कालेज जाते होंगे; मैं भी उन्हीं के साथ जाऊँगी । पिताजी कहते हैं कि मेरा अकेले जाना ठीक न होगा क्योंकि वाराणसी के नौजवान बहुत गुंडागर्दी मचाते हैं और लड़कियों को तंग करते हैं । इसको "ईव-टीज़िंग" कहते हैं, न ?

कहने की ज़रूरत नहीं कि मैं भारत हवाई जहाज़ से आऊँगी । दिल्ली पहुँचने पर तुम को फ़ोन करूँगी । दिल्ली में दो-तीन दिन ठहरने के बाद मैं रेलगाड़ी से बनारस जाऊँगी । उषा मुझसे मिलने स्टेशन आएगी । गाड़ी उधर बहुत सवेरे पहुँचती है । "उषा काल" को उषा के दर्शन ! मैं उषा को नहीं जानती; उसे कैसे पहचानूँगी, समझ में नहीं आता । शायद राजेश्वरी के पास उसका कोई पुराना फ़ोटो होगा । उषा का पति विश्वविद्यालय में इतिहास का प्राध्यापक है । राजेश्वरी का कहना है कि पति-पत्नी में बहुत झगड़ा होता है । तीन बच्चे भी हैं, छोटे-बड़े । ऐसे घर में मेहमान बनना कैसा होगा, मालूम नहीं ! ख़ैर, अगर तुम्हारे पास समय होगा, तो तुम भी कभी बनारस ज़रूर आना । दिल्ली पहुंचने पर तुम्हें फ़ोन करूँगी । अपना ध्यान रखना ।

तुम्हारी गीता

EXERCISE 9b.2 Translate.

1 Will there be any special difficulty (मुश्किल f) in learning Urdu?
2 Next month our students will be going to Lucknow to study Hindi.
3 Your brother must know (use आना, 6.1) quite good Hindi by now.
4 My friends' father will come to meet me at Varanasi station.
5 There are lots of places worth seeing near Delhi.
6 We will go with you to Mussoorie to see the mountains.

EXERCISE 9b.3 Fill the gaps with the direct or oblique form of the given infinitive verb, then translate.

१ संस्कृत... आसान नहीं है; लेकिन इसे... में बहुत फ़ायदा है । (पढ़ना to study)
२ मैं फ़िल्म... जा रहा हूँ; तुम भी चलो – फ़िल्म... लायक़ होगी । (देखना to see)
३ क्या गाड़ी... आपको पसंद है ? मुझे तो गाड़ी... नहीं आता । (चलाना to drive)
४ क्या सिग्रेट... ग़लत है ? हाँ ज़रूर, और... में फ़ायदा भी क्या है ? (पीना to smoke)
५ क्या तुम तबला... यहाँ आते हो ? हाँ, मुझे तबला... बहुत पसंद है । (बजाना to play)

Vocabulary

अकेले alone	**अमरीका** m America
अगर if	**असली** real
अच्छा-ख़ासा really good	**आसान** easy
अधिक much, many, more; **अधिक से अधिक** at the most	**इंतज़ाम** m arrangement(s), organisation

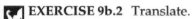

इतिहास m history
इरादा m intention
ईव-टीज़िंग f 'Eve-teasing' – sexual harrassment of girls & women
उषा f dawn
कठिन hard, difficult
कभी sometime
कम से कम at least
कमाना to earn
काल m time, period of day
के आस-पास around, in vicinity of
ख़रीदना to purchase, buy
गरमियाँ f.pl summer
ग़लत wrong
गाना1 m song
गाना2 to sing
गुंडा m lout, hooligan; गुंडागर्दी f hooliganism
ग्यारह eleven
चिल्लाना to shout
छपना to be printed
जनता f public, the people
ज़्यादा से ज़्यादा at the most
ठीक करना to put right, fix
डाक f mail, post
तबला m tabla (drum)
तैरना to swim
थोड़ा-बहुत a certain amount
थोड़े scarcely, by no means
दर्शन m vision (of), audience or auspicious meeting (with)
दावत f (invitation to) a dinner
ध्यान देना to pay attention
नमक m salt
नुक़सान m harm
नौजवान m youth, young man
पत्र m letter
परंतु but
पसंद करना to like, approve
पहचानना to recognise
पहुँचना to arrive
प्राध्यापक m lecturer
फ़ायदा m profit, advantage, point
फ़ोन करना to phone
बजाना to play (music)
बनारस m Banaras, Varanasi
बिकना to be sold
बी० एच० यू० m BHU (Banaras Hindu University)
बोर करना to bore
भतीजा m nephew
भविष्य m future
भोला innocent, guileless, simple
मँगवाना to order, send for
मचाना to create (noise etc.)
मना prohibited
मसूरी f Mussoorie
महाराजा m maharaja

(से) मिलना to meet
मिस्तरी m mechanic, artisan
यहीं right here, in this very place
रवानी f fluency
रुकना to stop, stay on
रेलगाड़ी f train
रोशनी f light
लायक़ worth (doing)
लौटना to return
वहीं right there, in that very place
विश्वविद्यालय m university
व्यवस्था f arrangement(s)
समझ f understanding; **समझ में आना** to enter the understanding, be understood
सही true, correct
हवाई जहाज़ m aeroplane
हाथ आना to come to hand
हिलना to move, stir
ही only (emphatic)

10 WHAT SHOULD I SAY?
मैं क्या बोलूँ ?

In this unit you will learn how to

- express doubts and possibilities
- make suggestions
- give gentle commands
- use conditionals: 'if...'

10a Chotu leaves a message for Prakash

छोटू हेलो, मैं छोटू बोल रहा हूँ। क्या प्रकाश जी हैं ? मैं उनका चपरासी हूँ।

कमला नहीं छोटू, बाहर हैं। आधे घंटे में आएँगे। मैं उन्हें कोई मेसेज दूँ ?

छोटू जी, आप उन्हें यह बताएँ कि खन्ना साहब उनसे बात करना चाहते हैं।

कमला कोई ज़रूरी बात है ? आख़िर हम तो आज रात को ही उनसे मिल रहे हैं।

छोटू शायद इसी बारे में खन्ना जी का कोई निवेदन हो।

कमला और तुमसे मेरा यह निवेदन है, छोटू, कि तुम अपनी बात ख़त्म करो। मेरे पास समय नहीं है।

छोटू मैडम, बहुत ज़रूरी है कि प्रकाश जी ख़ुद खन्ना साहब से बात करें।

कमला बताऊँगी उनको। तुम खन्ना साहब से कहो कि यहाँ आठ बजे आएँ।

चपरासी m	peon, orderly	**आख़िर**	after all
आधा m	half	**बारे में**	about, concerning
मेसेज m	'message'	**निवेदन** m	request
चाहना	to want, wish	**ख़ुद**	oneself (himself)

Chotu Hello, this is Chotu here. Is Prakash ji there? I'm his peon.

Kamala No Chotu, he's out. He'll come in half an hour. Should I give him some message?

Chotu Yes, please tell him (this,) that Khanna Sahib wants to talk to him.

Kamala Is it something urgent? After all we're meeting him just tonight.

Chotu Perhaps that's what Khanna ji might have some request about.

Kamala And my request to you, Chotu, is that you finish what you have to say. I have no time.

Chotu Madam, it's very important that Prakash ji phone Khanna Sahib himself.

Kamala I'll tell him. You tell Khanna Sahib that they should come here at eight.

Grammar

10.1 The subjunctive

The subjunctive is a 'mood' or form of the verb whose action is uncertain, speculative, desired, or suggested: 'I may speak, might speak, should speak' etc. To form the Hindi subjunctive, simply take the future verb, e.g. बोलूँगा, and remove the -गा/ -गी/ -गे ending, leaving बोलूँ. Masculine and feminine forms are identical; and all plural forms except तुम are identical, ending in -एँ.

मैं बोलूँ	I may speak	हम बोलें	we may speak
तू बोले	you may speak	तुम बोलो	you may speak
—		आप बोलें	you may speak
यह, वह बोले	he, she, it may speak	ये, वे बोलें	they may speak

मैं कुछ बोलूँ ?	May/should I say something?
हम भी चलें ?	May/should we go too?
आप यहीं रहें ।	You should stay right here. Please stay right here.

This last example shows how the 'suggestive' implication of the second-person subjunctive (तुम रहो, आप रहें) can also be interpreted as a mild command. Indeed the तुम form of the subjunctive – रहो, बोलो, जाओ – is identical with the imperative. The negative for subjunctives is न. Some more examples:

अपने जूते यहाँ उतारें / उतारिए ।	Please take your shoes off here.
अपना पता यहाँ लिखें / लिखिए ।	Please write your address here.
मंदिर के अंदर फ़ोटो न खींचो ।	Don't take photos inside the temple.
आप से निवेदन है कि आप बैठे रहें ।	You are requested to remain seated.

This last sentence means literally 'there is a request of you that you remain seated'. This is a common formula: an opening clause indicates the existence of a hope, wish, expectation, possibility, request, etc., while the second clause (introduced by कि 'that') spells out the detail of that wish etc. with a subjunctive verb:

मुझे आशा थी कि वह पत्र लिखे ।	I hoped he/she might write a letter.
हमें उम्मीद है कि इलाज लंबा न हो ।	We hope the treatment won't be long.
छोटू से कहो कि वह चाय लाए ।	Tell Chotu to bring tea ('that he should bring tea').
संभव है कि ट्रेन देर से पहुँचे ।	It's possible that the train may arrive late.
असंभव है कि वे ऐसी भूल करें ।	It's impossible that they would make such a mistake.
बहुत ज़रूरी है कि तुम कल रात तक लौटो ।	It's vital that you return by tomorrow evening.

By now you'll be getting a feel for the uncertain, speculative, 'maybe' senses of the subjunctive. Equivalent sentences in the future tense show a more clearcut expectation, a more confident hope:

मुझे विश्वास था कि वह पत्र लिखेगा ।	I was confident that he would write a letter.
हमें यक़ीन है कि इलाज लंबा नहीं होगा ।	We are sure that the treatment won't be long.

10.2 The subjunctive in the auxiliary verb

As with the future tense (9.2), the subjunctive of the auxiliary verb होना can appear within tenses such as the continuous and the imperfective. Compare the following:

राज सो रहा होगा ।	Raj will/must be sleeping.
राज सो रहा हो ।	Raj may be sleeping.
उषा यहाँ रहती होगी ।	Usha will/must be living here.
उषा वाराणसी में रहती हो ।	Usha may be living in Varanasi.

10.3 The verb चाहना

चाहना means 'to want, to wish'. It is used with a direct infinitive verb as follows:

पिताजी घर जाना चाहते हैं ।	Father wants to go home.
मैं उर्दू भी सीखना चाहता हूँ ।	I want to learn Urdu too.
उर्वशी मुझसे मिलना नहीं चाहती ।	Urvashi doesn't want to meet me.

This construction only applies when the subject of the 'wanting' and the subject of the 'doing' are *one and the same* – 'Father' in the first example. But if Father wants *someone else* to do something, the change of subject calls for a more complex construction: 'Father wishes that I should go home', with the second verb in the subjunctive.

पिताजी चाहते हैं कि मैं घर जाऊँ ।	Father wants me to go home.
उर्वशी चाहती है कि मैं दूर रहूँ ।	Urvashi wants me to keep away.

चाहना also means 'to like, love, be fond of':

सब लोग तुम्हें बहुत चाहते हैं ।	Everyone's very fond of you.
मजनूँ लैला को बहुत चाहता था ।	Majnu loved Laila very much.

> **!** Don't confuse these uses of चाहना with the quite separate चाहिए construction (7.3).

10b Sangeeta's dilemma

संगीता	ऋषि, अगर मैं आज रात को पिंकी से मिलने जाऊँ तो तुम अम्माँ को नहीं बताओगे न ?
ऋषि	तुम बाहर जा रही हो ? पर अम्माँ चाहती हैं कि तुम यहीं घर पर ही रहो।
संगीता	हाँ, मालूम है । पर घर में तो बड़ी बोरियत होगी । तुम्हीं बताओ – रहूँ कि जाऊँ ?
ऋषि	मामला कुछ टेढ़ा है ! मैं पिताजी से पूछूँ कि उनका क्या ख़याल है ? तुम उनकी सलाह लो ।
संगीता	हाँ पूछो न, देखें पिताजी क्या कहते हैं । पर अगर वे सो रहे हों तो उन्हें मत जगाना ।
ऋषि	थोड़ी देर पहले तो बाहर जानेवाले थे । अम्माँ कह रही थीं कि पिताजी सब्ज़ी लाएँ ।
कमला	[*दूर से*] ऋषि ! ओ ऋषि ! राज से कहो कि वह दूधवाले को बुलाए ।
ऋषि	[*संगीता से*] राज तो दूध पीनेवाला बच्चा है ही – दूधवाले को क्यों नहीं बुलाएगा !

बोरियत f boredom	**मामला** m matter, affair
कि or	**टेढ़ा** twisted, complex

Sangeeta	Rishi, if I go to meet Pinkie tonight you won't tell Mum will you?
Rishi	You're going out? But Mum wants you to stay here.
Sangeeta	Yes I know. But it will be very boring at home. You tell me – should I stay or go?
Rishi	It's a rather tricky matter! Should I ask Father what he thinks? Take his advice.

Sangeeta Yes, ask won't you, let's see what Father says. But if he's sleeping don't wake him.

Rishi A little while ago he was about to go out. Mum was saying that he should get vegetables.

Kamala [*from a distance*] Rishi! Oh Rishi! Tell Raj to call the milkman.

Rishi [*to Sangeeta*] Raj *is* a milk-drinking kid – why wouldn't he call the milkman!

Grammar

10.4 Conditional sentences (1)

You've already seen some conditional sentences, for example in Dialogue 9a. There are two clauses: an 'if' clause beginning अगर, and a 'then' clause beginning तो.

In 'if' sentences referring to future events, the verb choice for the अगर clause is between imperfective, subjunctive and future, usually with a future verb in the तो clause. The perceived likelihood of the condition being fulfilled varies accordingly:

अगर पानी पड़ता है तो हम अंदर रहेंगे ।	If it rains, we'll stay inside. (*imperfective*: neutral forecast)
अगर पानी पड़ेगा तो हम अंदर रहेंगे ।	If it rains, we'll stay inside. (*future:* rain likely)
अगर पानी पड़े तो हम अंदर रहेंगे ।	Should it rain, we'll stay inside. (*subjunctive*: rain less likely)

The following examples show imperatives in the तो clause; यदि 'if' is a Sanskritic synonym for अगर.

यदि जाना चाहते हो तो अभी जाओ ।	If you wish to go, go now.
अगर तू ख़ाली हो तो मेरे साथ चल ।	If you're free, come with me.

Tenses such as the continuous may also appear in an अगर clause:

अगर वह सो रही हो तो उसे जगाना ।	Wake her if she's sleeping.
अगर राम आ रहा है तो मैं भी आऊँगा ।	If Ram's coming I'll come too.

In English, 'then' is optional in an 'if' sentence ('if she comes [then] I'll tell her'); but in Hindi अगर can be dropped, while तो is essential.

दादी कहती हैं, (अगर) पानी पड़े तो बाहर मत जाना ।	Grandma says, if it rains, don't go out.

10.5 The suffix -वाला

The suffix वाला / वाली / वाले relates a person to the noun it adjoins: दूधवाला 'milkman', दिल्लीवाली 'woman from Delhi', गाँववाले 'villagers'. The initial noun may be in the oblique: रिक्शेवाला 'rickshaw driver'.

पुलिसवाले को नाराज़ मत करना ।	Don't displease the policeman.
कुछ पैसेवाले तो बड़े कंजूस होते हैं ।	Some rich folk are very mean.
हिन्दीवालों को अपनी भाषा पर गर्व है ।	Hindi-speakers are proud of their language.

Suffixed to an adverb, वाला forms an adjective – ऊपरवाला कमरा 'upstairs room', पासवाली दुकान 'nearby shop'; or a noun – ऊपरवाला 'God' (the one up above).

मुझे बीचवाली तस्वीर पसंद है ।	I like the middle picture.
सब कुछ ऊपरवाले के हाथ में है ।	Everything's in God's hand(s).
कौनसी गाड़ी हमारी है ? यह-वाली ।	Which car is ours? This one.

Suffixed to an oblique infinitive verb, वाला refers to that verb's action, either as noun (हिन्दी बोलनेवाला 'Hindi-speaker', शहर के रहनेवाले 'townspeople') or adjective (आनेवाला कल 'tomorrow', आनेवाले हफ़्ते में 'in the coming week').

सिग्रेट पीनेवालो, बाहर बैठो !	Cigarette smokers, sit outside!
मुझे झूठ बोलनेवाले बच्चों से नफ़रत है !	I hate children who tell lies!
आप कहाँ के रहनेवाले हैं ?	Where are you from?

The same construction can mean 'about to...' – जानेवाला 'about to go'.

दुकान बंद होनेवाली है ।	The shop's about to close.
हम अभी फ़ोन करनेवाले थे ।	We were just about to phone.
वह अभी जानेवाली थी ।	She was just about to go.

EXERCISE 10a.1 Fill the gap with a subjunctive, using the verb indicated. Then translate.

१ क्या मैं भी तुम्हारे साथ ... , या यहीं घर पर ... ? (जाना; रहना)
२ अगर मौसम ख़राब न... तो शायद वे लोग शाम तक गाँव... । (होना; पहुँचना)
३ उचित है कि वह तुम्हारे आने से पहले घर को ख़ाली... । (करना)
४ ज़रूरी नहीं है कि हम किसी की सलाह... या किसी की बात... । (लेना; सुनना)
५ उससे कहो कि वह आज रात तक जवाब... और अपनी ज़िम्मेदारी न... । (देना; भूलना)
६ आपसे निवेदन है कि आप इलाज के पैसे अभी... । (देना)

EXERCISE 10a.2 Transpose imperative to चाहना + subjunctive on the pattern shown. Then translate the new sentence.

आप अभी घर जाइए । → मैं चाहता हूँ कि आप अभी घर जाएँ ।
I want you to go home right now.

१	आप तुरंत जवाब दीजिए ।	(मैं चाहता हूँ कि...)
२	तुम चुप रहो ।	(मैं चाहता हूँ कि...)
३	गाय को न मारो ।	(मैं चाहता हूँ कि...)
४	सीढ़ियों पर न बैठो ।	(मैं चाहता हूँ कि...)
५	मेरा हाथ पकड़ !	(मैं चाहता हूँ कि...)
६	आज की संस्कृत की क्लास पढ़ाइए ।	(मैं चाहता हूँ कि...)

EXERCISE 10a.3 Complete the sentence with an appropriate clause. Then translate.

१ अगर आप ख़ाली हों तो ....
२ यदि आपको असुविधा न हो तो अवश्य ....
३ अगर तुम उनसे मिलना चाहती हो तो ....
४ यदि यह काम सचमुच बहुत ही कठिन है तो ....
५ अगर पुलिस आएगी तो ....
६ .... तो आप किसी दोस्त की सलाह लें ।
७ .... तो वह तुम पर ज़रूर गुस्से होगा ।
८ .... तो आप अभी भारत न जाएँ ।
९ .... तो बहुत बुरा होगा ।
१० .... तो मैं भी तुम्हारे साथ जाऊँगी ।

EXERCISE 10b.1 Translate Kamala's note to Prakash.

प्रकाश – खन्ना जी चाहते हैं कि तुम उन्हें फ़ोन करो। भूलो मत – शायद आज रात के बारे में कोई ज़रूरी बात हो। मैं अभी सब्ज़ीवाले के पास जा रही हूँ। मेरे कहने पर भी तुम सब्ज़ी नहीं लाते हो – भूलने में तो माहिर हो। उसके बाद थोड़ी देर के लिए सुरेश से मिलने जाऊँगी। गाड़ी तो तुम्हारे पास है इसलिए मैं बाज़ार आटो से जाऊँगी। दुकानों से चावल वग़ैरह चाहिए – तुम लाना। नए काँटे, चम्मच, छुरियाँ भी चाहिए। सब चीज़ों की लिस्ट सोनेवाले कमरे की मेज़ पर पड़ी है। अब की बार किसी चीज़ को मत भूलना। सारी चीज़ें तुम मार्केट-वाली दुकान से लेना; गली-वाली दुकान पर मत जाना, वहाँ तो दाम बहुत ऊँचे होते हैं। तुमसे क्या कहूँ? तुम तो किसी चीज़ की सही क़ीमत भी नहीं जानते! ठीक से ख़रीदारी करना भी नहीं आता तुम्हें।

मैं तो डेढ़ घंटे में आऊँगी। अगर तुम पहले घर लौटोगे (मतलब – इससे पहले कि मैं लौटूँ) तो बैठनेवाले कमरे को साफ़ करो। नहीं तो बाद में करना; पर करना तो सही। मैं बार-बार तुम्हारी माँ से कहती हूँ कि वे सफ़ाई के काम में हाथ बँटाएँ मगर मेरी बात कौन सुनता है। तुम्हारी माँ तो दिन भर मक्खियाँ मारती हैं। पता नहीं इस घर में सब लोग इतने कामचोर क्यों होते हैं। काम करनेवाली मैं ही हूँ। समझ में नहीं आ रहा कि मैं इतना लंबा नोट क्यों लिख रही हूँ। मेरे पास वक़्त भी कहाँ है? जल्दी में हूँ, मुझे देर हो रही है। क०

EXERCISE 10b.2 Answer the questions on Kamala's note.

१ आपके ख़याल से कमला क्यों नाराज़ है?
२ क्या खन्ना जी चाहते थे कि प्रकाश उन्हें वापस फ़ोन करे?
३ आज इतनी ख़रीदारी क्यों हो रही है?
४ सब्ज़ी ख़रीदने के बाद कमला किससे मिलने जाएगी?
५ अगर प्रकाश जल्दी घर वापस आए तो वह क्या करे?
६ कौनसी दुकान गली-वाली दुकान से ज़्यादा सस्ती है?
७ प्रकाश को कैसे पता चलेगा कि घर में किन चीज़ों की ज़रूरत है?
८ कमला क्यों चाहती है कि दादी जी घर की सफ़ाई करें?
९ कमला की बातें कौन सुनता है?
१० क्या कमला सोचती है कि दादी जी घर में बहुत मदद देती हैं?

EXERCISE 10b.3 Translate.

1 Kamala wants Prakash to do some shopping for tonight's dinner.
2 Nobody knows why everything in the nearby shop is so expensive.
3 It's possible that Pratap may return from Nepal by tonight.
4 For some reason, even Sangeeta wants Pratap to come home soon.
5 If Pratap's train is late, someone might go to meet him at the station.
6 If Pratap brings something for Sangeeta, what will she say?

Vocabulary

अब की बार this time
अवश्य certainly
असंभव impossible
आख़िर after all
आटो m auto-rickshaw
आधा m half
इतना so (as in 'so big'), so much
इलाज m treatment, cure
उचित proper, appropriate
उतारना to take down, take off
उम्मीद f hope
ऊँचा high
कंजूस miserly, mean
काँटा m fork
कामचोर work-shy, lazy
कि or
ख़रीदारी f buying, shopping
ख़ाली करना to vacate
खींचना to draw; take (photo)
ख़ुद oneself
गर्व m pride
गाय f cow
गुस्से angry
चपरासी m peon, orderly
चम्मच m spoon
चाहना to want, wish, be fond of
छुरी f knife
ज़िम्मेदारी f responsibility
झूठ m lie
टेढ़ा twisted, complex
डेढ़ one and a half
तुरंत immediately
दाम m price
नहीं तो otherwise
निवेदन m request
नोट m note
पकड़ना to catch, grab, hold
पड़ना to fall
पता m address; **पता नहीं** don't know, no idea; **पता होना** to know, be aware
पानी पड़ना to rain

पुलिस ^{f} (used in singular) police
बार ^{f} time, occasion; बार बार time and again
बारे में about, concerning
बोरियत ^{f} boredom
भारी heavy
भूल ^{f} mistake; भूल करना to make a mistake
भूलना to forget, err
मंदिर ^{m} temple
मक्खी ^{f} fly; मक्खियाँ मारना to 'kill flies', laze about
मगर but
मदद ^{f} help; मदद देना to help
मामला ^{m} matter, affair
माहिर expert, skilled
यक़ीन ^{m} confidence, faith
यदि if
रिक्शा ^{m} rickshaw
लिस्ट ^{f} list
वक़्त ^{m} time
वापस back; वापस आना to come back
विश्वास ^{m} belief, confidence
संभव possible
सफ़ाई ^{f} cleaning
सलाह ^{f} advice
सीढ़ी ^{f} stair, staircase
हफ़्ता ^{m} week
हाथ बँटाना to lend a hand

11 PRATAP HAS COME BACK

प्रताप वापस आया है

In this unit you will learn how to

- describe past events
- distinguish regular actions from one-off events

11a Pratap rejoins his Hindi class

शर्मा जी अरे प्रताप ! तुम तो बहुत दिनों के बाद क्लास में आए हो ! क्या तुम बाहर गए थे ?

प्रताप जी हाँ, मैं काठमांडू गया था । माफ़ कीजिएगा । अभी कल रात को ही दिल्ली लौटा ।

शर्मा जी माफ़ी माँगने की कोई ज़रूरत नहीं है; पर तुम नेपाल में क्या कर रहे थे ?

प्रताप मैं कुछ दोस्तों के साथ ट्रेकिंग करने गया था, पर आख़िर में हम काठमांडू में ही रहे ।

शर्मा जी क्यों ? क्या हुआ ? कोई दुर्घटना तो नहीं हुई ?

प्रताप जी नहीं; मेरे पिताजी मुझसे मिलने नेपाल आए थे, इसलिए मैं उनके साथ उनके कुछ दोस्तों से मिलने गया ।

शर्मा जी अब मैं समझा । तो सुनो प्रताप, नेपाल में तुम कुछ हिन्दी बोले ?

प्रताप जी हाँ, उधर बहुत-से लोग हिन्दी बोलते हैं । मैं अपनी हिन्दी नहीं भूला हूँ !

शमा जी और क्या तुम्हारे पिताजी भी तुम्हारे साथ दिल्ली वापस आए हैं ?

प्रताप जी हाँ, हम साथ साथ आए । वे तो डिफ़ेंस कालोनी में किसी दोस्त से मिलना चाहते हैं ।

माफ़ करना	to forgive, excuse	**आख़िर में**	in the end
माफ़ी f	forgiveness	**दुर्घटना** f	accident
ट्रेकिंग f	'trekking'	**साथ साथ**	together

Sharma ji Oh Pratap! You've come to class after a long time! Did you go away?

Pratap Yes, I'd gone to Kathmandu. I'm sorry. I returned to Delhi just yesterday night.

Sharma ji There's no need to apologise; but what were you doing in Nepal?

Pratap I'd gone to do some trekking with some friends, but in the end we stayed in Kathmandu.

Sharma ji Why? What happened? There wasn't an accident was there?

Pratap No, my father had come to meet me, so I went with him to see some friends of his.

Sharma ji Now I understand. So listen Pratap, did you speak some Hindi in Nepal?

Pratap Yes, lots of people speak Hindi there. I haven't forgotten my Hindi!

Sharma ji And has your father come back to Delhi with you too?

Pratap Yes, we came together. He wants to meet some friend in Defence Colony.

Grammar

11.1 Transitivity

Intransitive verbs are those which do not take a direct object: they describe a change of state (e.g. a motion or movement) – 'He arrived'; 'We'll go to India'; 'She got up' – rather than an action done *to* something. (In English we can't say 'He arrived the house' or 'We'll go India', because these verbs are intransitive.)

A transitive verb is one that *can* take a direct object – it describes an action done to something: 'I drank the water'; 'Sweep the floor!'; 'We'll write a letter'. Such verbs are still transitive even when there's no object expressed: 'I drank'; 'Sweep!'; 'We'll write'.

In the perfective tenses – 'I spoke, have spoken, had spoken' – most *intransitive* verbs in Hindi take a construction in which the verb agrees with the subject, as in other tenses met earlier; these are introduced in 11.2 below. (लाना 'to bring', though transitive, shares this construction.) But most *transitive* verbs follow a quite distinctive construction, introduced in 11.3. The two constructions are then brought together in 11.4. Each section has its own dialogue.

11.2 Perfective tenses – intransitive verbs

The perfective tenses refer to *completed* actions: 'I rose, I have risen, I had risen'. The participle consists of stem + -आ, -ए, -ई, ईं; thus उठा, उठे, उठी, उठीं.

The Hindi equivalents of the auxiliary 'have' and 'had' in these tenses are हूँ and था respectively: मैं उठा हूँ, मैं उठा था. The tense मैं उठा था 'I had risen', can also refer to a relatively remote past, with the sense 'I rose [some time ago]'.

	MASCULINE	FEMININE	
मैं	उठा, उठा हूँ, उठा था	उठी, उठी हूँ, उठी थी	I rose, have risen, had risen
तू	उठा, उठा है, उठा था	उठी, उठी है, उठी थी	you rose, have risen, had risen
यह/वह	उठा, उठा है, उठा था	उठी, उठी है, उठी थी	he/it/she rose, has risen, had risen
हम	उठे, उठे हैं, उठे थे	उठीं, उठी हैं, उठी थीं	we rose, have risen, had risen
तुम	उठे, उठे हो, उठे थे	उठीं, उठी हो, उठी थीं	you rose, have risen, had risen
आप	उठे, उठे हैं, उठे थे	उठीं, उठी हैं, उठी थीं	you rose, have risen, had risen
ये/वे	उठे, उठे हैं, उठे थे	उठीं, उठी हैं, उठी थीं	they rose, have risen, had risen

Verbs whose stems end in a vowel (e.g. आ- from आना 'to come') insert a य between the stem and the masculine singular participle ending (giving आया), and optionally elsewhere:

आना – आया, आई, आईं, आए (optionally आयी, आयीं, आये)

(The verbs जाना and होना have irregular perfectives:

जाना –	गया, गए, गई, गईं	(optionally गये, गयी, गयीं)
होना –	हुआ, हुए, हुई, हुईं	

> **!** हुआ means 'happened' and describes an *action*; था means 'was' and describes a *state*.

This construction *only applies with intransitive verbs*, such as घूमना 'to roam, tour'; ठहरना 'to stay, wait'; चलना 'to move'; निकलना 'to emerge'; पड़ना 'to fall, befall'; पहुँचना 'to arrive'; बजना 'to resound, chime'; भूलना 'to forget'; मिलना 'to meet'; रहना 'to stay, remain'; रोना 'to weep'; लौटना 'to return'; होना 'to occur'; and, as noted earlier, लाना 'to bring'.

क्या हुआ ?	What happened?
माली लौटा ।	The gardener returned.
लड़कियाँ कल पहुँचीं ।	The girls arrived yesterday.
लड़के ख़ूब रोये ।	The boys cried a lot.
क्या तुम मेरी दवा भी लाए ?	Did you bring my medicine too?

कुछ नहीं हुआ है ।	Nothing has happened.
क्या पिताजी लौटे हैं ?	Has Father returned?
तुम घर पहुँचे हो ।	You have reached home.
मैं भी कई बार रोया हूँ ।	I too have cried several times.
ऋषि आपकी दवा लाया है ।	Rishi has brought your medicine.

क्या कोई दुर्घटना हुई थी ?	Had some accident happened?
हम लोग दस बजे तक लौटे थे ।	We had returned by 10 o'clock.
माताजी परसों पहुँची थीं ।	Mother had arrived the day before yesterday.
दोनों औरतें रोई थीं ।	Both women had cried.
वह उसे कल ही लाया था ।	He'd brought it *yesterday*.

11b What Pratap did in Nepal

शर्मा जी तो यह बताओ प्रताप, नेपाल में तुमने नेपाली भाषा सीखी ?

प्रताप मैंने कोई बीस-पच्चीस शब्द सीखे, इससे ज़्यादा नहीं ।

शर्मा जी और क्या तुमने कुछ ख़रीदा ? कोई उपहार या भेंट ?

प्रताप जी हाँ, मैंने कुछ तिब्बती ज़ेवर ख़रीदे, और दो चाँदी की मूर्तियाँ भी ख़रीदीं ।

शर्मा जी काठमांडू में तुमने कुछ फ़ोटो खींचे ?

प्रताप फ़ोटो खींचने का इरादा तो था, पर नेपाल पहुँचने पर मैंने अपना कैमरा बेचा ! मजबूरी थी ।

शर्मा जी तुमने ऐसा क्यों किया ? पैसे की इतनी भारी आवश्यकता थी क्या ?

प्रताप हाँ, क्योंकि पिताजी ने मुझसे चार हज़ार रुपए उधार लिए थे, कुछ तोहफ़े ख़रीदने के लिए ।

नेपाली Nepali	**कैमरा** m camera
बीस twenty	**बेचना** to sell
पच्चीस twenty-five	**मजबूरी** f compulsion
शब्द m word	**आवश्यकता** f necessity
उपहार m present, gift	**रुपया** m rupee; money
भेंट f gift, presentation	**उधार** m loan; **उधार लेना** to borrow
तिब्बती Tibetan	**तोहफ़ा** m a present
ज़ेवर m (item of) jewellery	
फ़ोटो m photograph	

Sharma ji So tell me Pratap, did you learn the Nepali language in Nepal?

Pratap I learnt some 20 or 25 words, not more than this.

Sharma ji And did you buy anything? Some present or gift?

Pratap Yes, I bought some Tibetan jewellery, and I also bought two silver images.

Sharma ji Did you take some photos in Kathmandu?

Pratap I intended to take pictures, but I sold my camera on arriving in Nepal. I had no choice.

Sharma ji Why did you do such a thing? Did you need money so badly?

Pratap Yes, because Father had borrowed 4000 rupees from me, to buy some presents.

Grammar

11.3 Perfective tenses – transitive verbs

The perfective tenses of transitive verbs have a unique construction, still based on a participle comprising stem + -आ, -ए, -ई, -ईं. The following example uses the transitive verb लिखना ' to write':

लड़के ने पाँच चिट्ठियाँ लिखीं । The boy wrote five letters.

For the English subject 'the boy', Hindi has लड़के ने, in which the 'agentive' postposition ने is an untranslatable word indicating the agent or 'doer' of the action. The verb लिखीं agrees with the चिट्ठियाँ 'letters' – feminine plural. See how the verb agreement changes through the following sequence:

लड़के ने एक चिट्ठी लिखी । The boy wrote one letter.
(लिखी agrees with चिट्ठी fem. singular)

लड़के ने दो चिट्ठियाँ लिखीं। The boy wrote two letters.
(लिखीं agrees with चिट्ठियाँ fem. plural)

लड़के ने एक पत्र लिखा । The boy wrote one letter.
(लिखा agrees with पत्र masc. singular)

लड़के ने पाँच पत्र लिखे । The boy wrote five letters.
(लिखे agrees with पत्र masc. plural)

Agreement also applies to the *auxiliary* verb (e.g. in सुना है, सुना था):

राम ने दस प्याले ख़रीदे हैं । Ram has bought ten cups.
(ख़रीदे हैं agrees with प्याले masc. plural)

लड़की ने कई गीत गाए हैं । The girl has sung several songs.
(गाए हैं agrees with गीत masc. plural)

चोरों ने खिड़की तोड़ी थी । The thieves had broken a window.
(तोड़ी थी = खिड़की fem. singular)

तुमने चिट्ठियाँ कहाँ रखी हैं ? Where have you put the letters?
(रखी हैं agrees with चिट्ठियाँ fem. plural)

मैंने कई किताबें पढ़ी थीं । I had read several books.
(पढ़ी थीं agrees with किताबें fem. plural)

If no direct object is expressed, or if the direct object takes the postposition को, the verb is invariably in the masculine singular:

लड़की ने ध्यान से सुना ।	The girl listened carefully. (no object expressed)
लड़की ने दोनों गीतों को सुना ।	The girl listened to both the songs.
लड़कियों ने चिट्ठी को पढ़ा था ।	The girls had read the letter.

> **!** Not sure when to use को with a direct object? See 5.4.

A few verbs that normally follow the intransitive construction (11.2) switch to the transitive construction when a direct object is expressed. Examples include समझना 'to understand':

हम समझे ।	We understood. (no object expressed)
हमने तुम्हारी बात नहीं समझी ।	We didn't understand your point.

> **!** In the Glossary, verbs that take the ने construction are marked with a capital 'N' (करना^{N}); verbs that *sometimes* take it are marked with a lower-case 'n' (समझना^{n}); verbs that *never* take it are unmarked (आना). This is an important aid, because transitivity is not a completely reliable indicator of which verbs take ने.

Some common verbs have irregular perfective participles:

करना	किया	किए	की	कीं
लेना	लिया	लिए	ली	लीं
देना	दिया	दिए	दी	दीं
पीना	पिया	पिए	पी	पीं

There's one more thing to learn for this rather demanding construction – a special set of pronouns used with ने, some of which differ from the usual oblique pronouns (3.4):

मैं	मैंने	हम	हमने	कौन	किसने (singular)
तू	तूने	तुम	तुमने	कौन	किन्होंने (plural)
यह	इसने	ये	इन्होंने	कोई	किसीने
वह	उसने	वे	उन्होंने		
		आप	आपने		

11c Pratap phones home

प्रताप	हलो माँ, मैं प्रताप बोल रहा हूँ ।
अनीता	प्रताप ! तुमने कई हफ़्तों से फोन नहीं किया, फ़ैक्स नहीं भेजा ! क्या हुआ ?
प्रताप	मैं नेपाल में घूमने गया था । वहाँ से मैं आपके लिए कुछ सुन्दर चीज़ें लाया हूँ माँ !
अनीता	हाँ, लाए होगे, और तुम्हें ख़ूब मज़ा भी आया होगा ! पर तुम्हारी हिन्दी की पढ़ाई... ?
प्रताप	अभी क्लास में ग्यारहवाँ पाठ चल रहा है । मेरे नेपाल जाने से पहले हम तीसरा पाठ कर रहे थे ।
अनीता	तो तुम बहुत पीछे छूटे होगे । या तुमने नेपाल में भी अपना पढ़ाई जारी रखी ?
प्रताप	जारी तो रखी, लेकिन ज़्यादा काम नहीं किया क्योंकि मैंने पिताजी के साथ कई दिन गुज़ारे ।
अनीता	अच्छा, वह भी वहाँ आया था ! मैंने सोचा था कि वह लखनऊ में होगा, अपने घर में ।

फ़ैक्स^{m}	fax	**पीछे**	behind
घूमना	to travel for pleasure, tour	**छूटना**	to be left, fall back
मज़ा^{m}	fun, pleasure, enjoyment	**जारी**	current, continuing; **जारी रखना** to maintain
पढ़ाई^{f}	studies, studying		
पाठ^{m}	lesson, chapter	**गुज़ारना**	to spend (time)

Pratap	Hello Mum, this is Pratap speaking.
Anita	Pratap! You haven't phoned or sent a fax for several weeks. What happened?
Pratap	I went travelling in Nepal. I've brought some lovely things for you from there, Mum!
Anita	Yes, you must have, and you must have had a great time too! But your Hindi studies...?
Pratap	Just now the eleventh lesson's going on; before I went to Nepal we were doing the third lesson.
Anita	Then you must have fallen far behind. Or did you keep your studies going in Nepal too?
Pratap	Yes I did, but I didn't do a lot of work because I spent several days with Father.
Anita	Oh, he came there too! I'd thought he must be in Lucknow, at his home.

Grammar

11.4 More on perfective verbs

Dialogue 11c uses perfective tenses of both transitive and intransitive verbs. It includes examples of the perfective with a future-tense auxiliary (होगा), yielding the sense 'will have done, must have done' etc. (see 9.2. and 9.3 for parallels in the imperfective and continuous tenses). The auxiliary may also appear in the subjunctive (हो), giving the sense 'may have done' etc. Here then is the full set of perfective possibilities:

उन्होंने फ़ैक्स भेजा ।	They sent a fax.
उन्होंने फ़ैक्स भेजा है ।	They have sent a fax.
उन्होंने फ़ैक्स भेजा था ।	They had sent a fax.
उन्होंने फ़ैक्स भेजा होगा ।	They will/must have sent a fax.
उन्होंने फ़ैक्स भेजा हो ।	They may have sent a fax.

Finally, here are some more examples of perfective tenses. Make sure you understand the agreement of each verb. When you've done this, you have mastered a really essential construction.

नई किताब सन् २००० तक निकली होगी । The new book will have come out by 2000.

मुमकिन है कि दादाजी न पहुँचे हों।	It's possible that Grandpa may not have arrived.
दोनों लड़कियाँ ऊपरवाले कमरे में सोईं।	Both girls slept in the upstairs room.
उसने उनके मीठे शब्दों को सुना।	He/she listened to their sweet words.
हमने उन्हें भूत की कहानी सुनाई थी।	We had told them a ghost story.
रात को हमें नींद नहीं आई।	We didn't sleep at night. ('sleep didn't come')
हमने एक अच्छी-सी फ़िल्म देखी।	We saw quite a good film.
धोबी ने हमारे सारे कपड़े धोए हैं।	The dhobi has washed all our clothes.
मेरी कुरसी किसने ली ? किसी लड़के ने।	Who took my chair? Some boy.
गीता अपना सामान लाई है।	Gita has brought her luggage.
संगीता ने कमरा ख़ाली पाया।	Sangeeta found the room empty.

> ! Remember that the verb लाना 'to bring', though transitive, does *not* take the ने construction.

EXERCISE 11a.1 Translate.

१ लड़कियाँ कल सुबह बनारस पहुँचीं। / पहुँची हैं, पहुँची थीं, पहुँची होंगी, पहुँची हों
२ आज वे देर तक सोईं। / सोई हैं, सोई थीं, सोई होंगी, सोई हों
३ वे तीन बार गंगा देखने घाट पर गईं। / गई हैं, गई थीं, गई होंगी, गई हों
४ दोपहर को वे कुछ दोस्तों से मिलीं। / मिली हैं, मिली थीं, मिली होंगी, मिली हों
५ उन्हें बहुत आनंद आया। / आया है, आया था, आया होगा, आया हो

EXERCISE 11a.2 Translate.

1 My sons went to India. / have been, had been, will have been, may have been
2 They toured (घूमना) for two weeks. / have toured, had toured, will have toured, may have toured

3 They stayed in cheap hotels. / have stayed, had stayed, must have stayed, may have stayed

4 They spoke (बोलना) a little Hindi. /have spoken, had spoken, must have spoken, may have spoken

5 They had quite a good time. /have had, had had, must have had, may have had

EXERCISE 11b.1 Translate.

१ पापा ने पेट की दवा ख़रीदी । / ख़रीदी है, ख़रीदी थी, ख़रीदी होगी, ख़रीदी हो

२ उन्होंने सही क़ीमत दी । / दी है, दी थी, दी होगी, दी हो

३ दुकानदार ने ज़्यादा माँगा । / माँगा है, माँगा था, माँगा होगा, माँगा हो

४ पापा ने शिकायत की । / की है, की थी, की होगी, की हो

५ माँ ने तमाशे को देखा । / देखा है, देखा था, देखा होगा, देखा हो

EXERCISE 11b.2 Translate.

1 The dhobi washed both saris. / has washed, had washed, will have washed, may have washed

2 He only gave one sari back. / has given, had given, will have given, may have given

3 His wife wore (पहनना) the other. / has worn, had worn, will have worn, may have worn

4 We saw her at someone's wedding. / have seen, had seen, will have seen, may have seen

5 They apologised. / have apologised, had apologised, will have apologised, may have apologised

EXERCISE 11c.1 Add को to the direct object. Then translate.

MODEL: उसने खिड़की खोली । → उसने खिड़की को खोला ।
He/she opened the window.

१ दुकानदार ने पापा की शिकायत सुनी थी ।

२ पर उसने पापा की बातें नहीं मानीं ।

३ माँ ने दुकानदार की बाँह पकड़ी ।

४ पापा ने अपने पैसे वापस लिए होंगे क्योंकि ...

५ ... दुकानदार ने अपनी भारी-सी लाठी उठाई ।

EXERCISE 11c.2 Remove को from the direct object. Then translate.

MODEL: उसने दोनों किताबों को पढ़ा । → उसने दोनों किताबें पढ़ीं ।
He/she read both books.

१ मैंने अपने सारे कपड़ों को उतारा ।

२ डाक्टर ने अपनी सिग्रेट को ख़त्म किया और उँगलियों को गिलास में धोया ।

३ फिर उन्होंने दराज़ में से अपनी किताब को निकाला ...

४ ...और अपने चश्मे को नाक पर सीधा किया ।

५ तब उन्होंने अपनी आँखों को बंद किया और दो प्रसिद्ध फ़िल्मी गीतों को सुनाया ।

EXERCISE 11c.3 Write (or make up) a diary entry for any recent day. (Say what time you got up, what you had for breakfast, where you went, whom you met, etc. Pay careful attention to which verbs take the ने construction and which do not.)

Vocabulary

आख़िर में	in the end, after all	**गीत** m	song
आनंद m	joy, enjoyment; **आनंद आना** to feel enjoyment	**गुज़ारना**	to spend (time)
आवश्यकता f	necessity	**घाट** m	(steps at) riverbank
उँगली f	finger	**घूमना**	to tour, roam
उठाना	to pick up	**चोर** m	thief
उधार m	loan; **उधार लेना** to borrow	**छूटना**	to be left, fall back
उपहार m	present, gift	**जारी**	current, continuing; **जारी रखना** to maintain
कब	when?	**ज़ेवर** m	(piece of) jewellery
क़ीमत f	price, value, cost	**ट्रेकिंग** f	'trekking'
कैमरा m	camera	**तमाशा** m	spectacle, show
खोलना	to open	**तिब्बती**	Tibetan
गंगा f	Ganges	**तोड़ना**	to break
गिलास m	tumbler (glass or metal)	**तोहफ़ा** m	a present
		दवा f	medicine

दादा m paternal grandfather
दुकानदार m shopkeeper
दुर्घटना f accident
देर तक until late
दोपहर f noon, afternoon
नाक f nose
नींद f sleep; नींद आना to feel sleepy
पच्चीस twenty-five
पढ़ाई f studies, studying
परसों the day before yesterday; the day after tomorrow
पहनना to put on, wear
पाठ m lesson, chapter
पाना to find, obtain
पीछे behind
पेट m stomach
प्याला m cup
प्रसिद्ध famous
फ़िल्म f film
फ़िल्मी film-related, film-style
फ़ैक्स m fax
फ़ोटो m photograph
बजना to resound, chime
बाँह f (upper) arm
बीस twenty
बेचना to sell
भूत m ghost
भेंट f gift, presentation
मजबूरी f compulsion
मज़ा m fun, pleasure, enjoyment; मज़ा आना to enjoy, have fun
मानना to accept, believe
माफ़ करना to forgive, excuse
माफ़ी f forgiveness; माफ़ी माँगना to apologise
माली m gardener
मीठा sweet
मुमकिन possible
रोना to weep, cry
लाठी f lathi, stick
वापस लेना to take back
शब्द m word
शिकायत f complaint; शिकायत करना to complain
साथ साथ together
सुनाना to relate, tell, recite

12 ASK HIM AND TELL ME
उनसे पूछकर मुझे बता दो

In this unit you will learn how to

- link verbs in sequence
- tell the time in detail
- talk about ability to do things
- express nuance in verb actions

12a Khanna phones Prakash

खन्ना	प्रकाश, मैं खन्ना बोल रहा हूँ। यह बताइए – आज रात के डिनर में आपकी बेटी रहेगी ?
प्रकाश	अभी "गृह मंत्री" से पूछकर बताऊँगा। कृपा करके एक मिनट होल्ड कीजिएगा सर। [*आवाज़ धीमी करके*] कमला, खन्ना साहब पूछ रहे हैं कि क्या संगीता होगी आज रात को ?
कमला	[*ऊँची आवाज़ में*] ऐसा क्यों पूछ रहे हैं ? संगीता से उन्हें क्या लेना-देना !
प्रकाश	पता नहीं खन्ना साहब के मन में क्या बात होगी। अभी पूछकर बताऊँगा।
कमला	हाँ पूछो तो सही – पर उनसे इतनी ज़्यादा जी-हुज़ूरी मत करना !
प्रकाश	वे मेरे मालिक हैं कि नहीं ? तुम चाहती हो कि मैं पानी में रहकर मगर से वैर करूँ ? [*आवाज़ मीठी करके*] खन्ना साहब, कोई ख़ास बात थी ?
खन्ना	हमारा बेटा हरीश है न ? हम ज़रा सोच रहे थे... ख़ैर, कोई बात नहीं !

डिनर m	dinner	**धीमा**	low, faint
गृह मंत्री m,f	Home Minister (wife)	**लेना-देना** m	dealings, connection
कृपा करके	kindly, please	**जी-हुज़ूरी** f	sycophancy, flattery
मिनट m	minute	**कि**	or
होल्ड करना	to hold (phone line)	**मगर** m	crocodile
आवाज़ f	voice, sound	**वैर** m	hostility

Khanna	Prakash, it's Khanna speaking. Tell me this – will your daughter be at tonight's dinner?
Prakash	I'll just ask the 'Home Minister' and tell you. Kindly hold a moment sir. [*lowering his voice*] Kamala, Khanna Sahib's asking if Sangeeta will be there tonight.
Kamala	[*in a high voice*] Why is he asking such a thing? What business does he have with Sangeeta!
Prakash	I don't know what must be in Khanna Sahib's mind. I'll just ask and tell you.
Kamala	Yes, do ask – but don't be such a yes-man to him!
Prakash	Is he my boss or not? Do you want me to antagonise the crocodile while living in the water? [*sweetening his voice*] Khanna Sahib, was there anything in particular?
Khanna	You know our son Harish? We were just thinking... Well anyway, never mind!

> **!** वे मेरे मालिक हैं कि नहीं ? Note this use of कि for 'or' between a simple pair of alternatives. चाय लेंगे कि काफ़ी ?

Grammar

12.1 जाकर 'having gone, after going'

जाकर (verb stem + कर) means literally 'having gone' or 'after going'. It's often used for the first of two verbs describing a sequence of events, where English might use two main verbs linked by 'and' – 'She opened the door and came in'. खोलकर means 'having opened' or 'after opening' – दरवाज़ा खोलकर वह कमरे में आई. This form is called the 'conjunctive particle' or the 'absolutive' – technical names for a beautifully simple grammatical device!

उधर बैठकर आराम करो ।	Sit over there and rest.
हम अपने दोस्तों से मिलकर गपशप करते थे ।	We used to meet our friends and chat.
काफ़ी पीकर मैंने सीग्रेट भी पी ।	After drinking coffee I had a cigarette too.
वह टैक्सी बुलाकर सीधे घर गई ।	She called a taxi and went straight home.

Colloquially, -कर can be replaced by -के, giving जाके, खोलके etc. Note that करना has करके *only*.

हाथ धोके खा !	Wash your hands before eating!
मैं उन्हें फ़ोन करके बताऊँगा।	I'll phone them and tell them.
सड़क को पार करके बायें मुड़ना।	After crossing the road turn left.

The conjunctive particle is independent of the main verb: it has no impact on the surrounding grammar. In the first example below, बैठना is intransitive, but the main verb is खाना, which is transitive and takes ने; in the second example, बनाना is transitive, but the main verb is लाना, which does *not* take ने.

उसने फ़र्श पर बैठकर आम खाया।	He/she sat on the floor and ate a mango.
छोटू चाय बनाके लाया।	Chotu made tea and brought it.

Thus the conjunctive particle phrase is a bit like a parenthesis, insulated from the main clause: उसने (फ़र्श पर बैठकर) आम खाया; छोटू चाय (बनाके) लाया.

> **!** The subject of the conjunctive particle is usually the same as the subject of the main verb.

Some conjunctive particles function as adverbs:

उसने हँसकर कहा, "तुम पागल हो!"।	He/she said laughingly, 'You're crazy!'
माली दौड़कर पहुँचा।	The gardener arrived running.
मेहरबानी करके / कृपा करके	kindly, please

The following phrases are also based on conjunctive particles:

को छोड़कर	apart from, except for	(से) होकर	via
जान-बूझकर	deliberately	भूलकर भी	even by mistake

मुझको छोड़कर कोई नहीं बोला।	Nobody spoke apart from me.
गाड़ी आगरे से होकर ग्वालियर जाती है।	The train goes via Agra to Gwalior.
तुम हमें जान-बूझकर चिढ़ाती हो !	You irritate us on purpose!
वहाँ भूलकर भी न जाना !	Don't even *think* of going there!

12.2 What's the time?

Telling the time involves the following vocabulary:

बजना	to chime, resound	डेढ़	one and a half
पौन, पौना	three-quarters	ढाई	two and a half
सवा	one and a quarter	साढ़े	plus a half (with three and upwards)

कितने बजे हैं? / क्या बजा है ? / क्या टाइम हुआ ? What's the time?				
पौन बजा है	एक बजा है	सवा बजा है	डेढ़ बजा है	पौने दो बजे हैं
It's... 12.45	1 o'clock	1 .15	1.30	1.45
दो बजे हैं	सवा दो बजे हैं	ढाई बजे हैं	पौने तीन बजे हैं	साढ़े तीन बजे हैं
It's...2 o'clock	2.15	2.30	2.45	3.30

Saying 'at' a particular time involves the oblique form बजे (used adverbially – see 8.3):

एक बजे आओ ।	Come at one o'clock.
हम लोग डेढ़ बजे पहुँचेंगे ।	We'll arrive at 1.30.

Minutes *before* and *after* the hour are expressed by बजने में and बजकर respectively. बजना also features in other tenses and expressions:

सात बजनें में दस मिनट हैं ।	It's ten to seven.
आठ बजकर बीस मिनट हैं ।	It's twenty past eight.
गाड़ी पहुँची सात बजने में दस मिनट पर ।	The train arrived at ten to seven.
भारत में रात के नौ बज रहे हैं ।	It's just nine at night in India. (nine is striking)
सुबह के दस बजनेवाले हैं ।	It's nearly ten in the morning. (ten's about to strike)
ठीक ग्यारह बजने पर गाड़ी छूटेगी ।	The train will depart at eleven on the dot.

Traditional Indian timekeeping divided the day into eight three-hour 'watches' called पहर (Sanskrit प्रहर). The word survives in the following expressions:

दोपहर	noon, early afternoon
तीसरे पहर	in the afternoon
आठों पहर	all day long (आठों 'all eight' – see 7.5)

12b Dinner preparations

कमला ओ अरुण, ज़रा प्रताप के कमरे में जाकर एक कुरसी ले आना। उधर रख देना।

अरुण जी, अवश्य, तुरंत ला दूँगा। कोई विशेष कुरसी चाहिए?

कमला कोई भी लाओ। तब सुरेश को फ़ोन करके उनसे पूछना कि क्या वे भी डिनर में आ सकते हैं।

अरुण उन्हें बुलाने की आवश्यकता नहीं है भाभीजी, यदि उन्हें अवकाश हो तो आ ही जाएँगे।

कमला और तुम भी रहोगे, अरुण? तुमसे मिलकर खन्ना जी ख़ुश हो जाएँगे।

अरुण खेद की बात है कि मैं नहीं रुक सकता। अपने प्रकाशक के यहाँ भोजन करने जा रहा हूँ।

कमला तो तुम खन्ना साहब से मिलना नहीं चाहते? बाद में पछताओगे!

अरुण मैं तो उनसे मिल चुका हूँ। एक मित्र के विवाह में हमारी भेंट हुई थी। अद्भुत आदमी हैं।

विशेष	particular	**भोजन** m	food
सकना	to be able	**भोजन करना**	to dine, eat
आवश्यकता f	necessity	**चुकना**	to have already done
भाभी f	elder brother's wife	**विवाह** m	marriage
अवकाश m	leisure, free time	**भेंट** f	meeting, encounter
खेद m	regret	**अद्भुत**	remarkable
प्रकाशक m	publisher		

Kamala Oh Arun, just go into Pratap's room and bring a chair. Put it over there.

Arun Yes of course, I'll fetch it immediately. Do you require any particular chair?

Kamala Bring any one. Then phone Suresh and ask him if he can come to the dinner too.

Arun It's not necessary to invite him, sister-in-law; if he's at leisure he's sure to turn up.

Kamala And will you stay too, Arun? Khanna ji will be pleased to meet you.

Arun Regrettably I cannot stay. I'm going to dine at my publisher's.

Kamala So you don't want to meet Khanna ji? You'll regret it later!

Arun I've met him already. We met at a friend's wedding. He's a remarkable man.

Grammar

12.3 सकना, पाना, चुकना

These three verbs are used with the stem of a preceding verb (खाना 'to eat' in our example) to give the senses shown:

खा सकना	to be able to eat
खा पाना	to manage to eat
खा चुकना	to have already eaten, finished eating

वह खा सकती है।	She can eat.
क्या तुम कल आ सकते हो ?	Can you come tomorrow?
वह तेरे साथ नहीं जा सकेगी।	She won't be able to go with you.

मैं पूरे सेब को नहीं खा पाया।	I couldn't eat the whole apple.
तुम उसकी हिन्दी समझ पाओगे ?	You'll manage to understand his Hindi?
"ढ़" को ठीक से बोल पाना मुश्किल है।	It's difficult to manage to say '*ṛha*' correctly.

हम खाना खा चुके हैं।	We have already eaten.
धोबी कपड़े धो चुका होगा।	The dhobi will have finished washing the clothes.
चाय पी चुके हो? हाँ, पी चुका हूँ।	Had your tea? Yes, finished it.

As some of the examples show, these constructions *don't* take ने.

क्या संगीता ने वह काम ख़त्म किया है ?	Has Sangeeta finished that work? (ने with करना)
नहीं, वह उसे ख़त्म नहीं कर पाई।	No, she didn't manage to finish it. (no ने with कर पाना)

And चुकना is rarely used in the negative.

क्या संगीता नाश्ता कर चुकी है ?	Has Sangeeta already had breakfast?
नहीं, उसने नाश्ता नहीं किया है।	No, she hasn't had breakfast. (चुकना dropped in negative)

> **!** The verb stem cannot be left out in this usage: सकना / पाना / चुकना do not stand alone.

12.4 Compound verbs (1)

'Compound verbs' operate like सकना: verb stem + auxiliary verb. In a compound verb, the auxiliary loses its own primary meaning, but lends a certain shade of meaning to the main verb. For example, while बैठना means 'to sit', बैठ जाना means 'to sit down'.

The nuance they express is often very subtle and their function is best absorbed gradually from examples, though their grammatical structure is easy enough.

The ने construction applies only when both the main verb and the auxiliary verb are ने verbs. Three auxiliaries are introduced here: जाना, लेना, देना; others follow in 17.3.

जाना gives a sense of completeness, finality, or change of state.

आना	to come	आ जाना	to arrive
खाना	to eat	खा जाना	to eat up
पीना	to drink	पी जाना	to drink up
बैठना	to sit	बैठ जाना	to sit down
समझना	to understand	समझ जाना	to realise
सोना	to sleep	सो जाना	to go to sleep
होना	to be	हो जाना	to become

सीता रामायण को अंत तक सुन गई ।	Sita listened to the Ramayan right to the end.
छोटू आधी बोतल पी गया था ।	Chotu had consumed half the bottle.
पुलिस साढ़े दस बजे आ गई ।	The police turned up at half past ten.
दुकानें सात बजे बंद हो जाती हैं ।	The shops close (become closed) at seven o'clock.
तुम मेरी तकलीफ़ समझ गए होगे ।	You must have realised my distress.

With a few verbs that can be either intransitive or transitive (बदलना to change, खोना to lose/ be lost), using जाना as auxiliary specifies *intransitive* usage.

उनका नंबर बदल गया होगा।	Their number must have changed.
मोती खो गए।	The pearls got lost.

लेना suggests that the benefit of an action flows *towards* the doer		**देना** suggests that the benefit of an action flows *away from* the doer	
कविता पढ़ लो।	Read the poem to yourself.	कविता पढ़ दो।	Read the poem out.
यह पता लिख लो।	Take a note of this address.	वह पता लिख दो।	Write out that address.
थैला रख लो।	Keep the bag.	थैला रख दो।	Put the bag down.

The 'benefit-towards-the-doer' implication of लेना may imply a sense of achievement – मैंने सारा काम कर लिया है 'I've done all the work' (and it's a relief to have finished it!).

The following examples show how compounds can colour meaning. Being concerned with the *manner* in which a thing happens or is done, they're mostly used with completed actions and imperatives – much less with negated verbs, conjunctive particles (12.1), continuous tenses (8), or statements that are hypothetical or speculative. This is because an event that hasn't taken place at all cannot have taken place in a particular manner, and compound verbs express *manner* above all.

मैं थोड़ी उर्दू भी बोल लेता हूँ।	I (can) also speak a little Urdu.
रेडियो पर समाचार सुन लें ?	Shall we have a listen to the news on the radio?
मेरी जेब में से चाबी ले लो।	Take the key from my pocket.
अपना पैसा रख लो, भैया।	Keep your money, brother.
हमने नई गाड़ी ख़रीद ली है।	We have bought a new car.
पत्र पढ़के इसे पापा को दे दो।	Read the letter and give it to Father.
मिठाइयाँ बच्चों में बाँट दीजिए।	Distribute the sweets among the children.

माँ ने हमें सारी कहानी सुना दी ।	Mother related the whole story to us.
मैंने तेरा सामान रिक्शे पर रख दिया ।	I put your luggage onto the rickshaw.
हमने पुरानी गाड़ी को बेच दिया है ।	We have sold the old car.

12.5 Verbs in combination

These work similarly to compound verbs (12.4), the difference being that here, each of the two verbs adds its own meaning to the overall expression. आना or जाना are the usual auxiliaries, and hence the ने construction is not involved.

लौट आना	to come back	लौट जाना	to go back
ले आना	to bring	ले जाना	to take away
निकल आना	to come out	निकल जाना	to go out

Slightly different to these is चला जाना 'to go one's way': चला is a participle, not a stem, and must agree with the subject – लक्ष्मी चली गई 'Lakshmi went away'. चला आना 'to come up, approach' is also found.

हम होली से पहले भारत लौट जाएँगे ।	We'll go back to India before Holi.
इस बदमाश को ले जाओ ।	Take this rogue away.
मुझे यहाँ खड़ा देखकर वह चली गई ।	Seeing me standing here she went away.

EXERCISE 12a.1 Make single sentences of the following pairs, using a conjunctive particle. Then translate.

MODEL: वह कमरे में आया । उसने चाय पी । > उसने कमरे में आकर चाय पी ।
He/she came into the room and had tea.

१ संगीता घर गई । उसने किसी दोस्त को फोन किया ।

२ ऋषि ने अपनी किताब खोली । उसने दो-तीन कहानियाँ पढ़ीं ।

३ कमला ने अपना काम ख़त्म किया । वह तुरंत बाहर गई ।

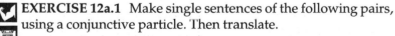

४ हम छोटू के यहाँ जाएँगे । हम खाना बनाएँगे ।

५ खन्ना जी डिब्बे में आए । उन्होंने ऊपरवाली बर्थ पर अपना सामान रखा ।

EXERCISE 12a.2 Replace the 'infinitive + के बाद' with a conjunctive particle. Then translate.

MODEL: घर जाने के बाद हम रेडियो सुनेंगे । > घर जाकर हम रेडियो सुनेंगे ।
After going/when we go home we'll listen to the radio.

१ आज सुबह नहाने के बाद तूने साबुन को कहाँ रखा ?

२ परीक्षा देने के बाद प्रताप और उसके साथी कम से कम दो हफ़्ते तक आराम करेंगे ।

३ अपनी डिगरी पास करने के बाद तुम क्या करना चाहते हो ?

४ लन्दन वापस आने के बाद उसने भारत के बारे में कई पुस्तकें लिखीं ।

५ शाम को दफ़्तर से लौटने के बाद प्रकाश कभी कभी बाज़ार में सैर करते हैं ।

EXERCISE 12b.1 Translate.

1 What's the time? It's half past seven. I've already had breakfast.
2 I usually arrive at half-past eight, but today I couldn't come until a quarter to nine.
3 I have lunch (दोपहर का खाना) between 1.30 and 2.30.
4 Will the students come at exactly eleven o' clock? No, they'll turn up by a quarter past.
5 By a quarter to one in the morning I managed to finish my studies.

EXERCISE 12b.2 Complete the replies, using the compound verb given in brackets:

१ आप हिन्दी बोलते हैं ? हाँ, ... (बोल लेना)

२ क्या उसने काम ख़त्म कर लिया है ? नहीं, ... (कर सकना)

३ क्या बच्चे सो रहे हैं ? हाँ, वे तो हमेशा सात बजे... (सो जाना)

४ क्या संगीता ने खाना खा लिया है ? हाँ, वह आधे से ज़्यादा ... (खा चुकना)

५ दुकान अभी बंद नहीं हुई ? क्यों ? वह तो चार बजे ... (बंद हो जाना)

Vocabulary

अंत m end
अद्भुत remarkable
अवकाश m leisure, free time
आठों पहर all day long
आम m mango
आराम करना to rest
आवाज़ f voice, sound
आवश्यकता f necessity
कविता f poem; poetry
कि or
कृपा f kindness, grace; कृपा करके kindly, please
खेद m regret
खोना to lose
गृह मंत्री m, f Home Minister
ग्वालियर m Gwalior
चला आना to come back; चला जाना to go one's way
चिढ़ाना to irritate, tease
चुकना (after verb stem) to have already done
(को) छोड़कर apart from, except for
जान-बूझकर deliberately
जी-हुज़ूरी f sycophancy, flattery
टैक्सी f taxi
डिगरी f degree
डिनर m dinner
ढाई two and a half
तीसरे पहर in the afternoon
दौड़ना to run
धीमा low, faint
नहाना to bathe, wash
नाश्ता m breakfast
पछताना to regret, repent
परीक्षा f examination, परीक्षा देना to take (sit) an exam
पाना (after verb stem) to manage to
पार करना to cross
पास करना to pass (exam etc.)
पौन, पौना three-quarters
प्रकाशक m publisher
बदमाश m villain, rogue
बदलना to change
बर्थ m berth
बाँटना to divide
बोतल f bottle
भाभी f elder brother's wife
भूलकर भी even by mistake
भेंट f meeting, encounter
भोजन m food; भोजन करना to dine
मगर m crocodile
मिठाई f sweet, sweet dish
मिनट m minute
मुड़ना to turn
मेहरबानी करके kindly, please
रेडियो m radio
ले आना to bring; ले जाना to take away

लेना-देना ^m^ dealings, connection

विवाह ^m^ marriage

विशेष particular

वैर ^m^ hostility

सकना (after verb stem) to be able

समाचार ^m^ news

सवा one and a quarter, plus a quarter

साढ़े plus a half

सात seven

साथी ^m^ companion, friend

साबुन ^m^ soap

सेब ^m^ apple

(से) होकर via

होली ^f^ Holi, springtime festival of colours

होल्ड करना to hold (phone line)

13 THOSE WHO KNOW
जो जानते हैं

In this unit you will learn how to

- use relative clauses: 'the day when...', 'the one who...'
- express compulsion: 'I should, must...'
- talk about availability: 'to get'

13a Pratap practises his Hindi with Rishi

ऋषि जब तुम नेपाल से लौटे तब तुम्हारी माँ ने क्या कहा फोन पर ?

प्रताप उन्होंने कहा कि आगे चलकर मुझे बहुत मेहनत करनी पड़ेगी ।

ऋषि जब तक तुम हमारे यहाँ रहोगे तब तक तुम्हें हिन्दी ही बोलनी चाहिए ।

प्रताप हाँ, जब से भारत आया हूँ तब से मैं हिन्दी ही बोल रहा हूँ ।

ऋषि और जैसे ही तुम लन्दन लौटोगे वैसे ही अपनी हिन्दी को भूल जाओगे !

प्रताप नहीं, जब तक मैं हिन्दी ठीक से नहीं सीखूँगा तब तक मुझे अपनी पढ़ाई को जारी रखना है ।

ऋषि लंदन वापस जाकर तुमको कुछ हिन्दी-बोलनेवाले दोस्तों से मिलकर बात करनी चाहिए ।

प्रताप यही करूँगा । और आज तो "जब"-वाले वाक्यों का अच्छा अभ्यास हुआ है !

जब... तब when... then

आगे later, ahead; **आगे चलकर** in future, from now on

मेहनत^{f} hard work

जब तक... तब तक for as long as... for that long

चाहिए should, ought to

जब से... तब से since the time when... since then

जैसे ही... वैसे ही as soon as ... then

जब तक नहीं... तब तक until... until then

अभ्यास^{m} practice

Rishi	What did your mother say on the phone when you returned from Nepal?
Pratap	She said that from now on I'd have to work very hard.
Rishi	As long as you stay with us you should speak only Hindi.
Pratap	Yes, since I came ('have come') to India I've been speaking only Hindi.
Rishi	And as soon as you go back to London you'll forget your Hindi!
Pratap	No, until I learn Hindi properly I must keep my studies going.
Rishi	After going back to London you should meet some Hindi-speaking friends and talk.
Pratap	I'll do just that ('this'). And today I've had good practice of '*jab*'-type sentences!

Grammar

13.1 जब... तब, 'when... then' (Relative clauses 1)

Hindi has several 'relative-correlative' constructions – structures for building sentences such as 'When the train comes, I'll go' or 'The person who wrote this is a fool', in which two adjacent statements are related to one another as paired clauses.

We deal first with relative-correlative expressions for time: जब... तब 'when... then'; further structures come in 13.3 and 14.4-7. Relative pronouns and adverbs all begin with a 'ज-', whereas interrogatives such as कब 'when?' begin with a 'क-'. (By contrast, English 'w' words such as 'when' are both relative and interrogative.)

The Hindi construction uses a balanced pair of clauses: '*When* the train comes, *then* I will go'. जब 'when' introduces the relative clause, and तब 'then' introduces the correlative clause.

जब गाड़ी आएगी तब मैं जाऊँगा ।	When the train comes I'll go.
जब घंटी बजती है तब हम काम ख़त्म करते हैं ।	When the bell rings we stop work.
जब मैं कहूँगा तब आना ।	Come when I tell you. ('When I say, come then.')

तब is often replaced by तो, because the correlative is often a *consequence* of the relative:

जब कुत्ता भौंकता है तो छोटू डर जाता है ।	When the dog barks Chotu gets scared.
जब बारिश होती है तो मैं बाहर नहीं जाता ।	When it rains I don't go out.

Among emphatic forms are जब भी 'whenever', and तभी 'at that very time, instantly'. Other relative-correlative pairs are:

जब से 'since (the time) when...' तब से 'since then':

जब से तू आई है तब से मैंने काम ही नहीं किया है ।	Since you came I haven't worked at all.
जब से मैंने छाता ख़रीद लिया तब से पानी नहीं पड़ा ।	Since I bought myself an umbrella it hasn't rained.

जब तक 'as long as, by the time that...' तब तक 'by then':

जब तक वह रहेगा तब तक मैं ख़ुश रहूँगी ।	As long as he stays I'll remain happy.
जब तक मैं पहुँचा तब तक वह जा चुकी थी ।	By the time I arrived she had already gone.

जब तक... न/ नहीं 'until...' तब तक 'until then':

जब तक मैं न कहूँ तब तक तुम यहीं रहोगे ।	You'll stay right here until I say ('as long as I don't say').
जब तक वे नहीं खाएँगे तब तक मैं भी भूखा रहूँगा ।	Until they eat I too will go hungry.

ज्योंही / जैसे ही 'as soon as...' त्योंही / वैसे ही 'at that moment, then'

ज्योंही मैंने घंटी बजाई त्योंही बस चल दी ।	As soon as I rang the bell, the bus set off.
जैसे ही वह बैठ गया वैसे ही बत्ती बंद हो गई ।	As soon as he sat down the light went out.

In both English and Hindi, the clause order can be reversed ('I haven't worked at all since you came', etc.); but it's best to stick to the जब... तब order until the construction becomes fully clear. The reversing of clauses is looked at in 14.8.

13.2 Infinitive + चाहिए, 'should, ought'

The sense 'should, ought' is expressed with the infinite verb + चाहिए. चाहिए means 'is wanted/needed' (and is an old form of the passive). The person under compulsion takes को. In past contexts, the auxiliary था is added.

मुझको अंदर जाना चाहिए।	I should go inside.
हमको चलना चाहिए।	We should set off.
तुमको भी आना चाहिए था।	You should have come too.

If there's a direct object, the infinitive (and any auxiliary) agrees with it:

उनको हिन्दी सीखनी चाहिए।	They should learn Hindi. (हिन्दी fem. singular)
हमको ये काम ख़त्म करने चाहिए।	We should finish these jobs. (ये काम masc. plural)
तुम्हें दो चिट्ठियाँ लिखनी चाहिए थीं।	You should have written two letters. (दो चिट्ठियाँ fem. plural)

But if the direct object takes को, then the verb stays in the -ना form, with auxiliary also invariable as था. (This may remind you of a similar rule relating to the ने construction – see 11.3.)

तुम्हें इस किताब को पढ़ना चाहिए।	You should read this book.
उन्हें बच्चों को नहीं मारना चाहिए।	They shouldn't hit the children.
हमें घंटी को बजाना चाहिए था।	We should have rung the bell.

With intransitive verbs such as होना and रहना, the infinitive can agree with a subject (without को being involved):

आम पक्के होने चाहिए।	The mangoes should be ripe.
चाय गरम रहनी चाहिए।	The tea should remain hot.

This usage without को usually involves inanimate objects; they are not under the 'moral' or pragmatic kind of compulsion that rests on a *person* (with को... चाहिए), as the following pair of sentences shows:

मौसम अच्छा होना चाहिए ।	The weather should be good. (no को; no moral implication)
बच्चों को चुप रहना चाहिए ।	Children should keep quiet. (with को and moral implication)

> **!** Unsure when to use को with a direct object? See 5.4.

Notice the difference in meaning between (a) चाहिए with a noun, 'is wanted/needed' (7.3) and (b) चाहिए with a verb, 'should/ought'. Different again is the straightforward meaning of चाहना as 'to want', which can be used either (c) with a noun or (d) with an infinitive verb in the direct case (e.g. पीना). Here's the full set.

(a)	मुझे चाय चाहिए ।	I want/need tea.
(b)	मुझे चाय पीनी चाहिए ।	I should drink tea.
(c)	मैं बियर चाहता हूँ ।	I want beer.
(d)	मैं बियर पीना चाहता हूँ ।	I want to drink beer.

13.3 Infinitive + होना / पड़ना, 'I am to, must'

The infinitive verb + होना or पड़ना is used in a parallel construction to that of चाहिए, with the same rules of agreement, but meaning 'have to' rather than 'should'.

Using होना gives a relatively mild sense of 'compulsion', as in describing tasks that are to be done *as a matter of course*:

आज मुझे दिल्ली जाना है;	Today I have to go to Delhi;
तुमको भी आना होगा ।	you'll have to come too.
वहाँ जाकर हमें कुछ चीज़ें ख़रीदनी हैं...	When we go there we have to buy some things...
और उन चीज़ों को घर लाना होगा ।	and we'll have to bring those things home.

These sentences could be translated 'I am to... you are to', etc. – it's a sense of programmed events rather than forced compulsion. Again, the sense can be of simple intention:

तुम्हें हाथ धोने हैं ?	Like to wash your hands?
कल हमें आराम करना था ।	Yesterday we were to rest.

Using पड़ना implies an *external* compulsion – one that's beyond the control of the individual. In the perfective (पड़ा), such compulsion is often *unplanned* or *unwelcome*:

बारिश की वजह से हमें छाता ख़रीदना पड़ा ।	Because of the rain we had to buy an umbrella.
गाड़ी छूट चुकी थी इसलिए उन्हें बस पकड़नी पड़ी ।	The train had already left so they had to catch a bus.
धोबी बीमार था इसलिए हमें गंदे कपड़े पहनने पड़े ।	The dhobi was ill so we had to wear dirty clothes.

Here, incidentally, we see an almost literal sense of पड़ना as 'to fall':

ख़त का जवाब मुझे देना पड़ा ।	It fell to me to answer the letter.

The imperfective (पड़ता है / पड़ता था) indicates *habitual* or *regular* compulsion:

हमें हर हफ़्ते इलाहाबाद जाना पड़ता है ।	We have to go to Allahabad every week.
हमें गुरु जी के लिए खाना बनाना पड़ता था ।	We used to have to cook for guru ji.
उन दिनों हमें सब कुछ हाथ से करना पड़ता था ।	In those days we had to do everything by hand.

The future (पड़ेगा) is parallel to होगा, but with stronger compulsion:

हमें दो टैक्सियाँ लेनी पड़ेंगी ।	We will have to get two taxis.
उन्हें बहुत काम करना पड़ेगा ।	They'll have to do a lot of work.
कलकत्ते जा रहे हो ? तुम्हें बँगला सीखनी पड़ेगी !	Going to Calcutta? You'll have to learn Bengali!

तुमको जाना चाहिए ।	You should go. (*moral* compulsion)
तुमको जाना है ।	You are to go. (*neutral* compulsion)
तुमको जाना पड़ेगा ।	You will have to go. (strong *external* compulsion)

13b At the dinner

खन्ना जी [*धीमी आवाज़ में*] जो लड़का कोने में बैठा है, वह तुम्हारा कौन लगता है राज ?

राज अंकल, वह हमारा रिश्तेदार नहीं है । वह लन्दन से आया है, हिन्दी सीखने के लिए ।

सुरेश जिन लोगों को असली हिन्दी सीखनी हो, उन्हें दिल्ली में नहीं रहना चाहिए ।

कमला ऐसा क्यों कहते हैं सुरेश ? कौनसी ऐसी बात है जो दिल्ली में नहीं मिलती है?

सुरेश इधर हमारे पंजाबी भाइयों ने हमारी हिन्दी भाषा को बरबाद कर दिया है ।

प्रकाश [*खन्ना की ओर नज़र डालकर*] अरे नहीं, बिलकुल नहीं ! हिन्दी को पंजाबियों की बहुत बड़ी देन है !

ऋषि हाँ, सही बात है; और हिन्दी और पंजाबी बहुत मिलती-जुलती हैं अंकल !

खन्ना जी जो चीज़ें मिलती-जुलती हैं, उनमें भी अनबन हो सकती है ऋषि ।

कमला हाँ ऋषि, तुम राज से मिलते हो, पर लड़ने में तुम्हें देर नहीं लगती ! [*सब हँसते हैं*]

कोना m corner	डालना to throw
लगना to be related, attached; to be expended (of time)	देन f contribution, gift
इधर recently, latterly	मिलना-जुलना to resemble
बरबाद करना to ruin	अनबन f discord
नज़र f glance, look	लड़ना to fight, quarrel

Khanna ji [*In a low voice*] What relation to you is that boy who's sitting in the corner, Raj?

Raj Uncle, he's not a relative of ours. He's come from London to learn Hindi.

Suresh People who want to learn the real Hindi shouldn't stay in Delhi.

Kamala Why do you say that Suresh? What is there that one can't get in Delhi?

Suresh Our Panjabi 'brothers' have ruined our Hindi language of late.

Prakash [*throwing a glance at Khanna*] Oh no, not at all! The Panjabis have [made] a huge contribution to Hindi.

Rishi Yes, it's true; and Hindi and Panjabi are very much alike, uncle!

Khanna ji Even things that are alike can have discord between them Rishi.

Kamala Yes Rishi, you look like Raj, but it doesn't take long for you to fight! [*all laugh*]

> ! इधर applies to both *time* ('recently') and *space* ('over here').

Grammar

13.4 जो... वह – 'the one who ...' (Relative clauses 2)

जो means '(the one) who/which'. It is both singular and plural.

जो आदमी बाहर खड़ा है	the man who is standing outside
जो बोलता है	he who speaks
जो खिलौने मैंने तुझे दिए	the toys I gave you

Such relative clauses are paired with correlative clauses, on the pattern of जब... तब (13.1); the correlative here is वह / वे. The जो clause defines an item about which something *further* is said in the correlative clause.

जो आदमी बाहर खड़ा है वह विदेशी है।	The man who is standing outside is a foreigner.
जो बोलता है वह नहीं जानता।	He who speaks, does not know.
जो खिलौने मैंने तुझे दिए वे कहाँ हैं?	Where are the toys I gave you?

Many such Hindi sentences are ordered quite differently from their English equivalents. 'Where are the toys I gave you?' becomes 'the toys that I gave you, where are they?' in the Hindi clause order. (Possible variations are discussed in 14.8.)

जो has the oblique forms जिस, जिसने (singular), and जिन, जिन्होंने (plural); these sit in parallel to उस, उसने and किस, किसने etc.

जिस बूढ़े ने हमारा घर ख़रीदा वह मर गया है।	The old man who bought our house has died.
जिनको अपने दोस्तों से लड़ना हो उनकी क़िस्मत बुरी है।	Those who have to fight their friends are unfortunate.
जिस दिन उनकी शादी हुई उसी दिन मेरा तलाक़ हो गया।	The very day they married I got divorced.

In जिस बूढ़े ने हमारा घर ख़रीदा वह मर गया है, the relative is oblique (जिस बूढ़े) because of the postposition ने; but the correlative is direct (वह) because it's the subject of the verb मर गया है. Thus the relative and correlative pronouns match the grammar *of their respective clauses.* Test this principle in the following examples:

जो किताब मेज़ पर पड़ी है उसे पढ़ लेना।	Read the book that's lying on the table.
जिसने यह लिखा था वह मूर्ख होगा।	The person who wrote this must be a fool.
जो लोग 'खन्ना' कहलाते हैं वे पंजाबी होते हैं।	People who are called 'Khanna' are Panjabis.
जिन दोस्तों को हमने बुलाया था वे नहीं आ सकते।	The friends we invited cannot come.

जो फ़िल्म मैंने देखी, उसका हीरो बहुत बदसूरत है ।	The hero of the film I saw is very ugly.
जिस जवान लड़की से तुमने बातें कीं वह कौन है ?	Who is the young girl you talked to?

जो कोई means 'anyone, whoever'; जो भी, 'whoever, anyone at all, whichever', is more emphatic. जो कुछ is 'whatever':

आपके पास जो कुछ हो, उसे दे देना ।	Give whatever you have.
गुरु जो भी बोलता है उसे उसका शिष्य लिख लेता है ।	Whatever the guru says, his disciple takes down.

When relating to a subject that's hypothetical or indefinite in some way, such pronouns often take a subjunctive verb.

जो कोई सोचता हो कि हिन्दी आसान है उसका विचार ग़लत है ।	Anyone who may think Hindi is easy has the wrong idea.

Occasionally one sees the old correlative pronoun सो – especially in aphorisms and old saws:

जो हो सो हो ।	What is to be will be.

13.5 मिलना 'to be available' ('to get')

मिलना means 'to be received, obtained, found', and it's the usual way of expressing 'to get'. The item received ('your fax' in the first example) is the grammatical subject, and the receiver takes को.

माँ को तुम्हारा फ़ैक्स मिला ।	Mum received your fax.
बेचारे छोटू को क्या मिलेगा ?	What will poor Chotu get?
इस होटल में कमरा मिल जाएगा ।	[You'll] get a room in this hotel.

The last example shows how मिलना can mean 'to be available' without necessarily specifying the receiver.

The same मिलना construction using को can also mean 'to meet' when an encounter between people is *unplanned*:

कल हम को सीता मिली ।	Yesterday we met Sita (by chance).

But when 'We met Sita' refers to a *planned* encounter, 'we' becomes the subject, and Sita takes से.

कल हम सीता से मिले ।	Yesterday we met Sita (intentionally).

मिलना also means 'to resemble'; in such senses it can link with जुलना 'to be joined' to form मिलना-जुलना. And finally: मिलकर or मिल-जुलकर ('having met and joined') has the idiomatic sense 'together'.

उषा तुमसे बहुत मिलती-जुलती है ।	Usha looks very much like you.
हम सब मिल-जुलकर यह काम करेंगे ।	We'll all do this work together.

13.6 लगना 'how does it strike you?' (do you like?)

लगना means 'to be attached, applied, stuck': टिकट लिफ़ाफ़े पर लगी थी 'the stamp was affixed to the envelope'. It also means 'to strike' in describing an experience or reaction; the experiencer takes को.

दिल्ली आपको कैसी लगती है ?	How do you like Delhi (how does Delhi strike you)?
यह शहर मुझे बहुत अच्छा लगता है ।	I like this city very much.
यहाँ मेरा मन / दिल लगता है ।	I feel at home here.
डाकू को दो गोलियाँ लगीं ।	The bandit was hit by two bullets.
हमारे जवानों को चोट लगी ।	Our soldiers got injured.
हमें डर लग रहा है ।	We're feeling afraid.
तुम्हें ठंड / गरमी लग रही होगी ।	You must be feeling cold / hot.
मुझे प्यास / भूख लगी है ।	I'm feeling thirsty / hungry.
उन्हें बहुत बुरा लगा ।	They felt very bad, aggrieved.

लगना also means 'to seem, appear'; and 'to catch' (of fire or illness).

तेरी कहानी थोड़ी अजीब लगती है ।	Your story seems a little odd.
यह वाक्य ठीक नहीं लगता ।	This sentence doesn't seem right.
ऊपरवाले कमरे में आग लग गई ।	Fire broke out in the upstairs room.
बेचारे को ज़ुकाम लग गया है ।	The poor fellow's caught a cold.

लगना also means 'to be taken, be expended (of time)'. The action that's done takes an infinitive + में, and the unit of time (minutes, days) is the subject: 'in making tea five minutes are taken':

चाय बनाने में पाँच मिनट लगते हैं।	Making tea takes five minutes.
घर पहुँचने में एक घंटा लगेगा।	It will take one hour to get home.
उसका ख़त पढ़ने में मुझे २५ मिनट लगे।	It took me 25 minutes to read his letter.

This sense of 'being expended' also applies to money:

गाड़ी को ठीक करने में रु० ५०० लगेंगे।	It'll cost Rs. 500 to fix the car.

Finally, लगना can indicate a blood relationship: अरुण संगीता का चाचा लगता है, 'Arun is Sangeeta's uncle' ('is related to Sangeeta as uncle').

EXERCISE 13a.1 Complete the replies using a चाहिए construction. Then translate the replies.

MODEL: क्या मैं भी लखनऊ जाऊँ? हाँ, आपको जाना चाहिए।
Yes, you should go.

१ क्या हम चाय तैयार कर दें? हाँ, हमको...
२ बच्चों को कौन खाना खिलाएगा? पापा को ही...
३ क्या मेरी सहेली हिन्दुस्तानी कपड़े पहने? जी नहीं, उसको...
४ क्या मुझे ताज होटल में कमरा मिल जाएगा? हाँ, तुम्हें...
५ परीक्षाओं के बाद हम थोड़ा आराम करें? हाँ, हमें...
६ मैं उसकी जेब से थोड़ा पैसा लूँ? नहीं, तुमको...

EXERCISE 13a.2 Replace चाहिए constructions with पड़ना in the future tense; then translate the new version.

१ तुझे मेरी सहेली की सलाह लेनी चाहिए।
२ मुझे रोज़ पढ़ाई का काम करना चाहिए।
३ माँ कहती हैं कि मुझे हर हफ़्ते उन्हें चिट्ठी लिखनी चाहिए।
४ अगर चोरी का डर है तो हमें एक ताला ख़रीदना चाहिए।
५ अगर चावल न मिले तो तुम्हें रोटी खानी चाहिए।
६ हमें कम से कम दो भाषाएँ सीखनी चाहिए।

EXERCISE 13a.3 Complete the sentences with an appropriate clause. Then translate.

१ जैसे ही वह कमरे में आया ....
२ जब तक मुझे उधार का पैसा नहीं मिलेगा ....
३ जब आपको फ़ुरसत हो ....
४ ज्योंही मुझे महसूस हुआ कि उसे यह जगह अच्छी नहीं लगती ....
५ .... तब हम अवश्य मिलेंगे ।
६ .... तब तक वह तुम्हें माफ़ नहीं करेगा ।
७ .... तब से मुझे उसकी एक भी चिट्ठी नहीं मिली ।
८ .... तभी हम तुम्हें तुम्हारा पैसा वापस देंगे ।

EXERCISE 13b.1 Translate. (Begin by establishing a जो clause – '*the shop which* I showed you, in it...'; '*the books which* you need, them you will find', etc.)

1 You can get foreign clothes in the shop that I showed you.
2 You will find the books you need on that table.
3 Did you get the letter that I sent you?
4 Those who get the chance should meet again next year.
5 The children we saw yesterday are my friend's children.
6 The man who looks like my brother is my uncle.
7 The lock we bought in Khan Market is quite strong.
8 You should learn the sentences you wrote yesterday.
9 People who smoke should stay outside.

EXERCISE 13b.2 Answer the questions on Dialogues 13a (1-4) and 13b (5-8):

१ प्रताप की माँ ने उससे कब कहा कि उसको मेहनत करनी पड़ेगी ?
२ जब से प्रताप भारत आया है तब से वह क्या कर रहा है ?
३ जब प्रताप लन्दन जाएगा तब उसे किन लोगों से मिलना चाहिए ?
४ आज प्रताप को ऋषि से बात करने से क्या फ़ायदा मिला ?
५ जो लड़का कोने में बैठा है, उसके बारे में कौन पूछ रहा है ?
६ क्या सुरेश संगीता का भाई लगता है ?
७ जिस दिन यह डिनर हुआ, उस दिन अरुण को कहाँ जाना था ? (12b देखें)
८ अंत में कमला विषय को क्यों बदलना चाहती है ?

EXERCISE 13b.3 Write six sentences of advice to travellers in India, using चाहिए constructions (13.2); then rewrite them substituting subjunctive verbs (10.1).

MODEL: आप को इलाहाबाद ज़रूर जाना चाहिए। > आप इलाहाबाद ज़रूर जाएँ।

Vocabulary

अजीब strange, odd
अनबन f discord
अभ्यास m practice
आग f fire
आगे later, ahead; **आगे चलकर** in future, from now on
इधर recently, latterly
इलाहाबाद m Allahabad
कहलाना to be called, named
क़िस्मत f fate
की वजह से because of
कोना m corner
गुरु m teacher, guru
गोली f bullet
घंटी f bell
चल देना to set off
चाहिए (with infinitive) should
चोट f hurt, injury
चोट लगना to get hurt
चोरी f theft, robbery
छाता m umbrella
जगह f place
जब... तब when.. then
जब तक... तब तक for as long as... for that long
जब तक नहीं... तब तक until... until then
जब से... तब से since the time when... since then
जवान adj/m young, youthful; soldier
जैसे ही... वैसे ही as soon as ... then
जो who/which, the one who/which
जो कुछ whatever
जो कोई whoever
जो भी whoever, whatever
टिकट m/f ticket; stamp
ठंड f cold
डर m fear
डाकू m dacoit, bandit
डालना to throw
तलाक़ m divorce; **तलाक़ होना** to become divorced
ताला m lock
दिल लगना to feel at home

देन ^{f} contribution, gift
नज़र ^{f} glance, look
पक्का ripe
प्यास ^{f} thirst; प्यास लगना thirst to strike – to feel thirsty
फ़ुरसत ^{f} leisure, free time
बँगला ^{f} Bengali (language)
बत्ती ^{f} light, lamp
बदसूरत ugly
बरबाद करना to ruin
बारिश ^{f} rain; बारिश होना to rain
बियर ^{m} beer
बेचारा $^{adj/\ m}$ poor, wretched, helpless; poor fellow
भूख ^{f} hunger; भूख लगना hunger to strike – to feel hungry
भूखा hungry
भौंकना to bark
मन लगना to feel at home
मरना to die
मिलना to be available; to resemble; मिलना-जुलना to resemble; मिल-जुलकर together, jointly
मूर्ख ^{m} fool
मेहनत ^{f} hard work
रोज़ every day, daily
लगना to strike; to appeal; to seem; to catch (of fire, illness); to be related, attached; to be expended (of time, money)
लड़ना to fight, quarrel
लिफ़ाफ़ा ^{m} envelope
वाक्य ^{m} sentence
विचार ^{m} thought, idea, opinion
विषय ^{m} subject
शादी ^{f} marriage, wedding, X की शादी Y से होना X to marry Y
शिष्य ^{m} disciple
सो he, she, it (archaic)
हीरो ^{m} 'hero', male film-star

14 THIS WAS BOUGHT IN KATHMANDU

यह तो काठमांडु में ख़रीदा गया

In this unit you will learn how to

- use the passive: 'this was bought'
- use 'to begin' and 'to allow'
- use the remaining relative constructions

14a Sangeeta gets touchy

सुरेश	तुम्हें ये नेपाली ज़ेवर कहाँ से मिले, संगीता ? बहुत बढ़िया हैं ।
संगीता	ये तो काठमांडु से ही लाए गए थे, अंकल ! इधर सब लोग इस तरह के ज़ेवर पहनने लगे हैं ।
सुरेश	अच्छे लगते हैं । अच्छा एक बात बताओ – कल की दावत में हरीश क्यों नहीं आया ?
संगीता	पता नहीं । उसे बुलाया तो गया था । शायद उसके पिता ने उसे आने नहीं दिया ।
सुरेश	पर मुझे तो बताया गया था कि खन्ना साहब चाहते थे कि तुम दोनों...
संगीता	रहने दो, अंकल ! ये ऊल-जलूल बातें हैं ! दूरदर्शन पर ख़बरें देखी जाएँ ?

सुरेश अरे, बड़ों से ऐसी बातें की जाती हैं ?

संगीता माफ़ कीजिए, अंकल, मुझसे गुस्ताख़ी हो गई – पर मुझसे तो हरीश का चेहरा देखा नहीं जाता ।

कमला [*अन्दर आकर*] क्यों सुरेश, आपको क्या हो गया? बहुत नाराज़ लग रहे हैं !

सुरेश हाँ, मैं अभी तुम्हारी बेटी से हरीश के बारे में कुछ पूछने लगा था कि वह तू-तू मैं-मैं करने लगी !

बढ़िया (inv.) nice, of good quality
लगना (with obl. infinitive) to start, to begin to
देना (with obl. infinitive) to allow to, let
ऊल-जलूल silly, pointless
दूरदर्शन m television; Doordarshan (national TV network)
ख़बर f news
गुस्ताख़ी f rudeness, impertinence
चेहरा m face, features
कि when (suddenly)

Suresh Where did you get this Nepali jewellery, Sangeeta? It's really nice.
Sangeeta It was brought from Kathmandu itself, Uncle! Recently everyone's started wearing this kind of jewellery.
Suresh It looks good. Now tell me one thing – why didn't Harish come to last night's dinner?
Sangeeta No idea. He *was* invited. Maybe his father didn't let him come.
Suresh But I'd been told that Khanna Sahib wanted you two to...
Sangeeta Let it be, uncle! This is silly talk! Shall we watch the TV news?
Suresh What, is that how one talks to one's elders?
Sangeeta Sorry, uncle, I was rude – but I can't stand Harish's face.
Kamala [*coming in*] Why Suresh, what's happened to you? You're looking very cross!
Suresh Yes, I'd just started asking your daughter something about Harish when she suddenly started being abusive!

Grammar

14.1 बोला जाना 'to be spoken' – the passive

The active verb 'to speak' is बोलना; the passive verb 'to be spoken' is बोला जाना. Thus the Hindi passive consists of *perfective* participle (e.g. बोला, लिखा, बनाया) +the auxiliary verb जाना. Both parts agree with the subject.

हिन्दी कई प्रदेशों में बोली जाती है ।	Hindi is spoken in many states.
यह कपड़ा जयपुर में बनाया जाता है ।	This cloth is made in Jaipur.
बहुत-से ऐसे पत्र लिखे जाते हैं ।	Many such letters are written.

The passive can be used with any tense, and with compound verbs (12.4).

संस्कृत प्राचीन काल में बोली जाती थी ।	Sanskrit was spoken in ancient times.
यह लेख जून में लिखा गया ।	This article was written in June.
दो नए पुल बनाए जाएँगे ।	Two new bridges will be built.
भूखों को खाना दिया जा रहा है ।	The hungry are being fed.
चाय अभी लाई जाए ।	Tea should be brought *now*.
बिजली बन्द कर दी गई थी ।	The electricity had been cut off.

> **!** बिजली बन्द कर दी गई थी – a complex verb phrase!
>
> बन्द 'closed'
> बन्द करना 'to close'
> बन्द कर देना compound verb
> बन्द कर दिया जाना passive infinitive
> बन्द कर दिया गया था remote past (11.2)
> बन्द कर दी गई थी agreement with fem. subject बिजली

Adding को to the subject makes the passive verb revert to masculine singular:

सड़कें साफ़ की गईं > सड़कों को साफ़ किया गया ।	The roads were cleaned.
किताब पढ़ी गई > किताब को पढ़ा गया ।	The book was read.

This process is similar to that in both ने (11.3) and चाहिए (13.2):

मैंने किताब पढ़ी	> मैंने किताब को पढ़ा ।	I read the book.
हमें किताब पढ़नी चाहिए	> हमें किताब को पढ़ना चाहिए ।	We should read the book.

Some more passive examples with को –

मच्छरों को मारा गया ।	The mosquitoes were killed.
उनको इसके बारे में बताया जाएगा ।	They will be told about this.
हमें पाकिस्तान भेजा जा रहा है ।	We're being sent to Pakistan.
बिजली को बन्द कर दिया गया था ।	The electricity had been cut off.

What is the passive *for*? A passive verb tends to focus attention on the *action done* rather than the 'doer' or 'agent' of the action, who is often not mentioned at all. When mentioned, the agent takes the postposition से or, in a more formal style, के द्वारा.

यह काम किसी और से किया जाए ।	This work should be done by someone else.
ताज महल शाहजहाँ के द्वारा बनाया गया था ।	The Taj Mahal was built by Shah Jahan.

Even some intransitive verbs can be used in the passive: बैठा जाए ? 'Shall we sit?' (lit. 'shall it be sat [by us]?'). In this construction, the perfective participle for जाना is जाया, not गया.

बाज़ार जाया जाए ?	Shall we go to the market?
चला जाए ?	Shall we be off?

The passive with से (not के द्वारा) can imply inability or unwillingness to do something:

यह खाना मुझसे खाया नहीं जाता ।	I can't (bear to) eat this food.
इतनी गरमी में हमसे सोया नहीं गया ।	We couldn't sleep in such heat.
मुझसे न रहा गया ।	I couldn't contain myself.

> Participle + जाना gives a *passive* verb, e.g. बोला जाना 'to be spoken'; but stem + जाना gives a *compound* verb, e.g. बोल जाना 'to speak out' (12.4).

14.2 Transitivity and the passive

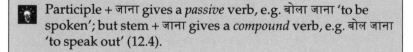

The concept of transitivity, met in 11.1, needs revisiting here. Hindi makes a greater distinction between transitive and intransitive verbs than English does, as the following example of active (not passive) verbs shows:

INTRANSITIVE	TRANSITIVE
टूटना to break	तोड़ना to break
बोतल टूटती है ।	वह बोतल को तोड़ता है ।
The bottle breaks.	He breaks the bottle.

The English verb 'to break' covers both what happens to the bottle (an intransitive action) and what the person does to the bottle (a transitive action); but Hindi has two separate verbs. Sometimes the only way an intransitive action can be expressed in English is with a passive verb: 'this cloth *is made* in Jaipur' – it would be odd to say 'this cloth comes into being in Jaipur', an intransitive equivalent. Hindi, on the other hand, can express similar meanings through the transitive verb बनाना used in the passive (like 'is made') and the intransitive verb बनना used in the active (like 'comes into being'):

यह कपड़ा जयपुर में बनाया जाता है ।	This cloth is made in Jaipur.
यह कपड़ा जयपुर में बनता है ।	This cloth is made in Jaipur.

The same applies with many other such pairs, such as transitive बेचना 'to sell' and intransitive बिकना 'to be sold':

यहाँ किताबें बेची जाती हैं ।	Books are sold here.
यहाँ किताबें बिकती हैं ।	Books are sold here.

The former sentence (passive transitive बेचा जाना) focuses attention on the *act of selling*, while the latter (active intransitive बिकना) focuses on a more general sense of books being available. Such nuances depend greatly on the context of the sentence.

इधर मकान बनाए जाएँगे / बनेंगे ।	Houses will be built here.
कपड़े नदी में धोए जाते हैं / धुलते हैं ।	Clothes are washed in the river.
काम शुरू किया गया / शुरू हुआ ।	Work was begun / began.

14.3 पानी पड़ने लगा 'it began raining' – to begin to

The oblique infinitive + लगना means 'to begin to'. लगना does *not* take ने; and it's only rarely used in the negative.

बारिश होने लगी ।	It began to rain.
बच्चे तालियाँ बजाने लगे ।	The children began to clap.
माँ मेरा नाम चिल्लाने लगीं ।	Mother began calling my name.
हमें प्यास लगने लगी ।	We began feeling thirsty.
मुझे महसूस होने लगा कि यह पाठ तो कभी ख़त्म नहीं होगा ।	It began to feel to me that this chapter would never end.

Another way to express 'to begin to' is with a *direct* infinitive + शुरू करना, e.g. लिखना शुरू करना 'to begin to write'. This often implies a greater sense of planned action or deliberate purpose than the लगना usage, and so isn't normally used with spontaneous, unplanned sensations like thirst, or natural actions like rain falling.

पिछले साल मैंने लिखना शुरू किया ।	Last year I took up writing.
हम उर्दू सीखना शुरू करेंगे ।	We'll start learning Urdu.

! लगना as 'to begin' takes *oblique* infinitive: but शुरू करना takes *direct* infinitive.

14.4 मुझे जाने दो ! 'let me go!' – to allow

The oblique infinitive + देना means 'to allow to, to let'. देना *does* take ने, and the perfective verb agrees with a direct object (unless marked with को) – see agreement with गाड़ी in the first example:

चाचाजी ने मुझे अपनी गाड़ी चलाने दी ।	Uncle let me drive his car.
पिताजी ने बच्चे को मिठाइयाँ खाने दीं ।	Father let the child eat the sweets.
बिल्ली को मक्खन न खाने देना ।	Don't let the cat eat the butter.
अरे, रहने दो ! बारिश होने दो !	Oh, let it be! Let it rain!

14b Arun's book

प्रकाश तुम्हारी किताब की क्या ख़बर है अरुण ? ख़ूब बिक रही होगी ?

अरुण जितनी प्रतियाँ बिकनी चाहिए उतनी नहीं बिकी हैं । बहुत निराशा हुई ।

प्रकाश तो जिस तरह की किताबें आम लोगों को पसंद हैं, उस तरह की क्यों नहीं लिखते ?

अरुण नहीं साहब, ऐसा घटिया साहित्य मुझसे लिखा नहीं जाएगा !

प्रकाश तब तो तुम्हें सफल लेखक बनने के सपने को भूलना होगा ।

अरुण आपके विचार में, आर्थिक सफलता प्राप्त करने से ही कोई व्यक्ति सफल हो जाता है क्या ?

प्रकाश मेरे ख़याल से तुम्हें प्रेम की कहानियाँ लिखनी चाहिए, तब पढ़नेवाले ख़ुश हो जाएँगे ।

अरुण जैसी कहानियाँ तुम्हें पसंद हैं, वैसी कहानियाँ जनता के मन को भ्रष्ट कर देती हैं, प्रकाश ।

प्रकाश किताब पढ़ने से किसका मन कभी भ्रष्ट हो गया ? सभी तरह का साहित्य चलता है, लेखक महोदय !

जितना... उतना	as much as...	**सफलता** f	success
निराशा f	disappointment, despair	**प्राप्त करना**	to obtain, attain
घटिया (inv.)	inferior, low grade	**व्यक्ति** m	person, individual
साहित्य m	literature	**प्रेम** m	love
सफल	successful	**भ्रष्ट**	corrupted; **भ्रष्ट करना** to corrupt
लेखक m	writer	**महोदय**	gentleman; sir
आर्थिक	financial		

Prakash What's the news of your book, Arun? Must be selling well?

Arun Not as many copies have sold as should have done. I'm very disappointed.

Prakash Then why don't you write the kind of books that ordinary people like?

Arun No sir, I couldn't bring myself to write such inferior literature!

Prakash Then you'd better forget the dream of becoming a successful writer.

Arun In your opinion, does an individual become succesful merely by acquiring financial success?

Prakash In my opinion you should write love stories, then the readers will be happy.

Arun Stories of the kind you like corrupt the mind of the public, Prakash.

Prakash Whose mind ever got corrupted by reading a book? Every kind of literature has its place, Mr Writer sir!

Grammar

14.5 जितना... उतना 'as much as' (Relative clauses 3)

Our third foray into relative-correlative constructions deals with जितना... उतना 'as much... that much':

जितना तुमको चाहिए, उतना लो ।	Take as much as you want.
उनकी जितनी ज़मीन है उतनी ही हमारी भी है ।	We have just as much land as they do.
जितने लोग हिन्दी बोलते हैं, उतने बँगला नहीं बोलते।	Not as many people speak Bengali as speak Hindi.
जितनी अच्छी पुरानी फ़िल्में थीं उतनी अच्छी नई फ़िल्में नहीं हैं ।	The new films aren't as good as the old films were.
भारत की जितनी आबादी है उतनी पाकिस्तान की नहीं है ।	Pakistan's population is not as big as India's.

14.6 जैसा... वैसा 'as... so' (Relative clauses 4)

This relative-correlative pair describes likeness of *kind* and *manner*. Firstly, they are adjectival (describing a *thing*):

जैसा बाप वैसा बेटा ।	Like father, like son.
जैसी दाल हमें चाहिए वैसी यहाँ नहीं मिलती ।	The kind of daal we need isn't available here.
जैसा महीन काम वह करता है वैसा और कोई नहीं कर पाता ।	Nobody else can achieve the delicate work that he does.

Secondly, they are adverbial (describing an *action*):

जैसा तुम चाहो वैसा ही करो ।	Do just you like.
देवनागरी जैसी लिखी जाती वैसी ही पढ़ी भी जाती है ।	Devanagari is read just as it's written.

जिस तरह का... उस तरह का is an alternative for the adjectival type:

जिस तरह के लोग उस इलाक़े में रहते हैं, उस तरह के लोग चोरी नहीं करते !	People of the kind who live in that area don't steal!

And similarly जिस तरह (से)... उस तरह (से) is an alternative for the adverbial type:

जिस तरह से तू भूतों से डरता है उसी तरह से मैं तुझसे डरता हूँ ।	I fear you just as you fear ghosts.

14.7 जहाँ... वहाँ 'where... there' (Relative clauses 5)

Our final relative-correlative context relates to *place*; and जहाँ भी means 'wherever'.

जहाँ मैं रहता हूँ वहाँ कोई उर्दू नहीं जानता ।	Where I live nobody knows Urdu.
जहाँ नदी या तालाब हो वहाँ आबादी भी होगी ।	Where there's a river or a pond there will also be habitation.
वह हीरो जहाँ भी जाता है वहाँ भीड़ लगती है ।	Wherever that film-star goes a crowd gathers.
जहाँ फूल है वहाँ काँटा भी होगा ।	Where there's a flower there will also be a thorn.

जिधर... उधर 'whither... thither' is a close parallel to जहाँ... वहाँ (and relates to इधर 'here, over here', उधर 'there, over there', and किधर 'whereabouts?'):

जिधर से तू आया है, उधर वापस जा !	Go back where you came from!

14.8 Clause reversal (Relative clauses 6)

Relative-correlative constructions were introduced in 13.1, 13.4, and 14.4-6. Revise those sections before continuing.

The relative-correlative sentences seen so far have had the relative clause first and the correlative clause second. Hindi, like English, also uses other patterns. The two clauses may often be reversed, as is shown in the following pairs of sentences, prefaced by relevant section numbers (possible variations in the English are not shown):

13.1 जब तक बिजली नहीं आएगी तब तक हमें ठंडे पानी से नहाना पड़ेगा ।
हमें तब तक ठंडे पानी से नहाना पड़ेगा जब तक बिजली नहीं आएगी ।
We'll have to bathe in cold water until the electricity comes.

13.4 जिस लड़के ने यह प्याला तोड़ दिया उसको बुलाओ ।
उस लड़के को बुलाओ जिसने यह प्याला तोड़ दिया ।
Call the boy who broke this cup.

14.4 जितना खाना बन चुका हो उतना खिला दो ।
उतना खाना खिला दो जितना बन चुका हो ।
Serve however much food is already prepared.

14.5 जैसा मौक़ा आज मिला है वैसा दुबारा नहीं मिलेगा ।
वैसा मौक़ा दुबारा नहीं मिलेगा जैसा आज मिला है ।
An opportunity such has arisen today won't come again.

14.6 जहाँ हमारी पहली मुलाक़ात हुई थी हम वहीं चलें ।
हम वहीं चलें जहाँ हमारी पहली मुलाक़ात हुई थी ।
Let's go to the place where we first met.

Some relative clauses use mixed pairs of pronouns rather than the formal relative-correlative pairs introduced earlier:

14.4 जितने लोग पार्टी में आए थे, सभी शादी-शुदा थे । However many people (all the people who) had come to the party, all of them were married.

14.6 जिस तरह का खाना हमें चाहिए था, वह तो नहीं मिलेगा ।
We won't get the kind of food we wanted.

A relative clause may be used as a parenthesis within a sentence, or as an afterthought:

प्रताप (जो लन्दन से है) कई महीनों से हमारे यहाँ रह रहा है ।
Pratap (who is from London) has been staying at our place for several months.

अनीता हर हफ़्ते फ़ोन करती है – जो प्रताप को कुछ बुरा लगता होगा ।
Anita phones every week – which must rather annoy Pratap.

Some speakers add कि to a relative pronoun such as जो; this does not affect meaning.

कुछ बोलनेवाले तो "जो" के बाद "कि" भी जोड़ देते हैं, जो कि वाक्य के अर्थ में कोई परिवर्तन नहीं लाता है ।

Some speakers add 'कि' after 'जो', which does not bring any alteration to the meaning of the sentence.

EXERCISE 14a.1 Rewrite the following in the passive, omitting any reference to an 'agent'. Then translate the passive version.

MODEL: हमने ये समोसे कल रात बनाए थे । → ये समोसे कल रात बनाए गए ।

These samosas were made last night.

१ तमिल तो दक्षिण भारत में बोलते हैं ।
२ हम सारी तैयारियाँ ६ बजे तक करेंगे ।
३ यह चिट्ठी मैं हवाई डाक से भेजूँगा ।
४ इस विश्वविद्यालय में कुछ लोग संस्कृत भी पढ़ते हैं ।
५ मंदिर में फोटो नहीं खींचना चाहिए ।
६ हमें ज़िन्दगी को थोड़ा और सरल बनाना चाहिए ।

EXERCISE 14a.2 Translate.

1 The newest houses were built just last year.
2 All the letters had been put in one big envelope.
3 It was said in the newspaper that the thieves had been caught.
4 Several strange books have been written about Indian languages.
5 Sangeeta began thinking that Sunday would never come.
6 It started to rain, so Kamala didn't let Raj go out.
7 When the children began to feel hungry I let them eat.
8 We were told that the guests had begun to arrive.
9 Don't let anyone come in until I tell you.
10 In future, people who don't work will not be given any money.

EXERCISE 14a.3 Write a brief third-person account, in Hindi, of Dialogue 14a.

EXERCISE 14b.1 Complete the sentence with an appropriate clause. Then translate.

१ मेरे जितने दोस्त हैं, ...

२ तुम जितने ध्यान से पढ़ोगे, ...

३ जितनी अच्छी यह नई किताब है, ...

४ जहाँ हम लोग रहते हैं, ...

५ .... जहाँ बहुत कम लोग जाते हों ।

६ .... वहाँ अमीर लोगों की आबादी ज़रूर होगी ।

७ .... उतने ही हमारे पास भी हैं ।

८ .... उतना बड़ा लखनऊ नहीं है ।

EXERCISE 14b.2 Translate the following extract from Pratap's letter to his mother.

कल मुझे कमला और प्रकाश कुमार के डिनर में बुलाया गया । बहुत ही शानदार डिनर था । हमें जितना खाना खिलाया गया, उतना मैंने कभी नहीं खाया है ! जब कमला जी मुझे तीसरी बार और खाना देने लगीं तो मैं "बस! बस!" कहने लगा, पर उन्होंने ध्यान नहीं दिया । गोश्त, सब्ज़ी, दाल, रोटी, चावल, चटनी – इतना ज़्यादा खाना तैयार किया गया था कि मैं बता नहीं सकता ! जैसा हिन्दुस्तानी खाना लन्दन में मिलता है, वैसा नहीं था; यहाँ तो हर चीज़ एकदम ताज़ी थी, और जितनी ताज़ी थी, उतनी ही स्वादिष्ट ! मिठाई तो किसी दुकान से लाई गई थी, पर मिठाई को छोड़कर हर चीज़ घर में ही बनाई गई थी । खाना बनाने में तो कमला जी माहिर हैं ।

लेकिन तुम अपने मन में पूछ रही होगी, डिनर में कौन कौन आया था ? मैं बताता हूँ । अपनी पढ़ाई की वजह से मैं तो देर से पहुँचा । मेरे पहुँचने पर मुझे कमरे के एक कोने में बिठाया गया । खन्ना जी को सबों के बीच में बिठाया गया, और उनकी बग़ल में उनकी पत्नी, जो मुझे बहुत अच्छी लगीं । उनके लड़के को भी बुलाया गया था, पर किसी वजह से वह नहीं आया । संगीता अपनी सहेली पिंकी (खन्ना जी की छोटी बहिन) के साथ फ़िल्म देखने गई थी; वे लोग फ़िल्म के ख़त्म होने पर क़रीब ग्यारह बजे घर आ गईं और जितना खाना बचा था, खा लिया । (फ़िल्म थी "हम आपके हैं कौन", जो कई साल पहले बनाई गई थी; संगीता तो उसे कम से कम चार-पाँच बार देख चुकी होगी, उसे फिर से क्यों देखना चाहती थी, मेरी समझ में नहीं आता ।) सुरेश भी आए थे; कमला जी ने उन्हें अपने पास बिठा लिया । अरुण तो किसी दोस्त से मिलने गए थे इसलिए वे तो "अनुपस्थित" थे । उन्हें इस प्रकार के शब्द बहुत पसंद हैं – अपनी बोली में वे इतने संस्कृत के शब्द लाद देते हैं कि मुझसे तो उनकी आधी बातें समझी नहीं जातीं ।

डिनर के दौरान हिन्दी के बारे में बहुत-सी दिलचस्प बातें कही गईं। सुरेश ने कहा कि दिल्ली की हिन्दी भ्रष्ट हो गई है, पंजाबी ज़बान के कारण। (शर्माजी भी क्लास में कह रहे थे कि पंजाबी लोग ज़्यादातर "मैंने जाना है" कहते हैं, जो कि ग़लत प्रयोग है – "मुझे जाना है" ही सही है।) पर जब सुरेश ने यह बात कही तो प्रकाश जी ने ऐसे आँखें दिखाईं कि सुरेश बेचारे चुप हो गए। बात यह है न, कि खन्ना जी ख़ुद पंजाबी हैं; और उनके सामने प्रकाश एकदम दब जाते हैं – भीगी बिल्ली की तरह ! अंत में कमला जी ने विषय बदलकर ऋषि और राज के बारे में कोई मज़ाक़ किया तो सब लोग हँसने लगे। पर बाद में कमला जी ने सुरेश को ख़ूब डाँटा होगा !

श्रीमती खन्ना बहुत अच्छी महिला हैं। भाषाओं के बारे में बहुत जानती भी हैं। जब मैंने उनसे पूछा कि "राजस्थान" में "थ" क्यों है जब कि "पाकिस्तान" में "त" ही है तो उन्होंने यह कहकर बात को समझा दिया कि "स्थान" तो संस्कृत का शब्द है जब कि "स्तान" फ़ारसी का है। दोनों शब्दों का वही अर्थ है – "जगह"। तो शब्दों के भी परिवार होते हैं ! पर कुमार परिवार की तरह नहीं। बिलकुल नहीं !

Vocabulary

अनुपस्थित absent	**(के) द्वारा** by, by means of
अमीर rich, wealthy	**के बीच में** in the middle of
अर्थ m meaning	**ख़बर** f news; information
आँखें दिखाना to look angrily	**गुस्ताख़ी** f rudeness, impertinence
आबादी f population, settlement	**घटिया** (inv.) inferior, lowgrade
आर्थिक financial	**चटनी** f chutney
इलाक़ा m area	**चेहरा** m face, features
ऊल-जलूल silly, pointless	**चोरी करना** to steal
क़रीब about, roughly	**जब कि** while
काँटा m thorn; fork	**ज़बान** f language, tongue
कारण m reason, cause	**जहाँ... वहाँ** where... there
कि when suddenly	**जितना... उतना** as much as...
किधर where? whither?	**जिधर... उधर** whither... thither
की बग़ल में next to	**जैसा... वैसा** as... so
के कारण because of	**जोड़ना** to add

डाँटना to scold
तमिल f Tamil
ताज़ा fresh
तालाब m pond
तालियाँ बजाना to clap
दक्षिण m south
दबना to yield, cower
दिलचस्प interesting
दुबारा again, a second time
दूरदर्शन m television; Doordarshan (national TV network)
देना (with obl.inf.) to allow to, let
धुलना to be washed
नदी f river
निराशा f disappointment, despair
परिवर्तन m alteration
पाकिस्तान m Pakistan
पुल m bridge
प्रकार m manner, way, type, kind
प्रदेश m state, province
प्रयोग m use, usage
प्राचीन ancient
प्राप्त करना to obtain, attain
प्रेम m love
फ़ारसी f Persian
फूल m flower
बचा saved, left
बढ़िया (inv.) nice, of good quality
बस enough! that's all!
बिठाना to make sit
बिल्ली f cat
बोली f speech, dialect
भीगा wet; भीगी बिल्ली f 'wet cat', timid creature
भ्रष्ट corrupted; भ्रष्ट करना to corrupt
मक्खन m butter
मच्छर m mosquito
मज़ाक़ m joke
महसूस होना to be felt, experienced
महिला f lady
महीन fine, delicate
महोदय m gentleman, sir
मुलाक़ात f meeting, encounter
मौक़ा m chance, opportunity
राजस्थान m Rajasthan
लगना (with obl. inf.) to begin to
लादना to load
लेख m article (written)
लेखक m writer
व्यक्ति m person, individual
शादी-शुदा (inv.) married
शानदार magnificent
सफल successful
सफलता f success
साहित्य m literature
स्वादिष्ट tasty
हवाई डाक f airmail

15 GO ON LEARNING HINDI!

हिन्दी सीखते जाओ !

In this unit you will learn how to

- use new ways of describing habitual actions
- use reflexive pronouns – 'I myself'

15a Pratap's 'new peacock'

दादी जी तुम कब से हिन्दी सीख रहे हो प्रताप ?

प्रताप मैं तीन साल से सीख रहा हूँ। शुरू में मैं एक ईवनिंग क्लास में सीखा करता था।

दादी जी तुमने किससे सीखी ? तुम्हारा उच्चारण तो बहुत साफ़ है।

प्रताप हमारे लन्दन-वाले अध्यापक यू० पी० से थे। वे कहते थे कि हिन्दी बोलते जाओ, बोलते जाओ...

दादी जी और तुम्हें हमारी हिन्दी भाषा पसंद है बेटे ?

प्रताप जिस दिन मैंने हिन्दी सीखना शुरू किया, उसी दिन से मेरे जीवन में एक नया मोर आया।

दादी जी	[*ख़ूब हँसकर*] अरे "मोर" नहीं बेटे, "मोड़" ! "एक नया मोड़" !
प्रताप	[*झेंपकर*] माफ़ कीजिए दादीजी, ऐसी उच्चारण की ग़लतियाँ मुझसे हमेशा हुआ करती हैं !
दादी जी	कोई बात नहीं, हिन्दी सीखते जाओ, सीखते जाओ ! जीते रहो, बेटे ।

कब से	since when?	**जीवन** m	life
शुरू m	beginning	**झेंपना**	to be embarrassed
ईवनिंग क्लास f	'evening class'	**ग़लती** f	mistake
यू० पी० m	UP (Uttar Pradesh)	**जीते रहो**	bless you ('stay living')

Dadi ji	Since when have you been learning Hindi, Pratap?
Pratap	I've been learning for three years. In the beginning I used to study in an evening class.
Dadi ji	Whom did you learn from? Your pronunciation is very clear.
Pratap	Our London teacher was from UP. He used to say 'Go on talking Hindi, go on talking...'.
Dadi ji	And you like our Hindi language, child?
Pratap	From the very day I began learning Hindi, my life took a new peacock.
Dadi ji	[*laughing loudly*] Oh, not *mor* ['peacock'] child, *moṛ*! ['turn'] ! 'A new turn'!
Pratap	[*abashed*] Sorry Dadi ji, I'm always making these mistakes in pronunciation!
Dadi ji	Never mind, go on learning Hindi, go on learning! Bless you, son.

Grammar

15.1 करता रहना/जाना 'to go on doing'

An imperfective participle + रहना means 'to keep on doing': वह काम करती रही 'she went on working'. The participle agrees with the subject.

हम लोग रात भर काम करते रहे ।	We went on working all night.
वह शराबी है न? शराब पीता रहेगा ।	He's a drunk isn't he? He'll go on drinking.
अगर दिन भर पढ़ते रहोगे तो थक जाओगे ।	If you go on reading all day you'll get tired.

An imperfective participle + जाना also means 'to keep on doing', but suggests a *progressive* action, as if heading for some kind of culmination: किराया बढ़ता गया 'the rent went on increasing'.

भिखारी चपातियाँ खाता जा रहा है।	The beggar is going on eating chapatties.
यात्री रिक्शे पर सामान लादता गया।	The traveller went on loading stuff onto the rickshaw.
सलमान साहब उपन्यास लिखते जाएँगे।	Salman Sahib will go on writing novels.

15.2 किया करना 'to do habitually'

A perfective participle + करना means 'to do something habitually': वह सोमवार को फ़िल्में देखा करती है 'she makes a habit of seeing films on Mondays'. The participle is invariable in -आ (masculine singular).

वह हमें गालियाँ दिया करती है।	She's forever calling us names.
हर हफ़्ते मुझे एक पत्र लिखा करो।	Write me a letter every week.
ब्राह्मण गंगा में स्नान किया करते हैं।	Brahmins bathe in the Ganges.
गुरु जी पेड़ के नीचे बैठकर पढ़ाया करते थे।	Guru ji used to teach sitting under a tree.

The construction can even be used with intransitive verbs like होना (using the participle हुआ), जाना (using the participle जाया) and आना:

१ अगस्त को एक आम छुट्टी हुआ करती थी।	There used to be a public holiday on 1 August.
हम लोग समुद्र के किनारे जाया करते थे।	We used to go to the seaside.
मैं विश्वविद्यालय पैदल जाया करती हूँ।	I go to the university on foot.
कभी कभी हमारे यहाँ आया करो, न ?	Come to our place from time to time, won't you?

15.3 से revisited

The postposition से has such a variety of uses that it's worth bringing them together here. We've already seen the following:

from	मैं दिल्ली से आ रही हूँ।	I'm coming from Delhi.
by	मैं ट्रेन से आऊँगी।	I'll come by train.
with	मैंने अपने पैसे से टिकट ख़रीदा।	I bought a ticket with my own money.
than	राजधानी दूसरी गाड़ियों से महँगी है।	The Rajdhani is more expensive than other trains.
because of, with	यात्री ठंड से काँपने लगे।	The passengers began shivering with cold.

> **!** For 'in company with', use के साथ (not से): हम आपके साथ चलेंगे 'We'll go with you'.

Added to a noun, से forms an adverb, on the same pattern as the English 'with difficulty':

मुश्किल से	with difficulty
आसानी से	easily, with ease
आराम से	comfortably
ख़ुशी से	happily
देर से	late

A more formal style of adverb is based on the noun रूप 'form':

औपचारिक रूप से	formally
अनौपचारिक रूप से	informally
व्यक्तिगत रूप से	individually

Several common verbs take से –

इनकार करना वह लड़की मेरे यहाँ आने से इनकार कर रही है!
to refuse That girl is refusing to come to my place!

कहना मैंने उससे कहा कि दूसरे लोग भी होंगे।
to say I told her that others would be there too.

डरना वह मेरी माँ से डरती होगी।
to fear She must be afraid of my mother.

नफ़रत करना	या शायद वह मुझसे नफ़रत करती है ।
to hate	Or perhaps she hates me.
नाराज़ होना	मुमकिन है कि वह मुझसे नाराज़ हो ।
to be displeased	It's possible that she's angry with me.
पूछना	मैं उसकी सहेली से उसके बारे में पूछूँ ?
to ask, enquire	Should I ask her friend about her?
प्यार करना / होना	मैं उससे प्यार करता हूँ, मगर उसको मुझसे प्यार नहीं है !
to love	I love her, but she has no love for me!
बातें करना	इसके बारे में किससे बातें करूँ ?
to converse	Who can I talk to about this?
मिलना	मेरे दोस्त तो मुझसे मिलना भी नहीं चाहते ।
to meet	My friends don't even want to meet me.
माँगना	तो किससे मदद माँगूँ ?
to demand, ask for	So whom should I ask for help?
लड़ना	उसका बड़ा भाई मुझसे लड़ना चाहता है ।
to fight	Her elder brother wants to fight me.
शादी करना	प्यारी, क्या तू मुझसे शादी करेगी ?
to marry	Beloved, will you marry me?
शिकायत करना	हे भगवान, वह मेरी पत्नी से शिकायत करने गई है ।
to complain	O God, she's gone to complain to my wife.

> **!** Such verbs stand *without* से if the sense of connection is implicit rather than explicit: हम उनसे मिलेंगे 'We'll meet them', but फिर मिलेंगे '[We'll] meet again', 'See [you] later'.

से also means 'since': कब से ? कल से 'Since when? Since yesterday'. Describing a situation which still exists in the present, a present-tense verb is used:

हम लोग सोमवार से यहाँ हैं।	We've been here since Monday.

तुम कब से लखनऊ में रह रहे हो ?	Since when have you been living in Lucknow?
हम लोग चार साल से सितार सीख रहे हैं।	We've been learning the sitar for four years.

15b Harish at his father's office

हरीश छोटू, एक मजाक सुनोगे ? दो शराबी आधीरात को आपस में बातें कर रहे हैं। पहला शराबी दूसरे शराबी से पूछता है, "भैया, रात को सूरज क्यों नहीं निकलता है ?"। दूसरा शराबी क्या जवाब देता है, जानते हो ?

छोटू [*जंभाई लेकर*] आप बताइए, तो देखेंगे।

हरीश दूसरा शराबी कहता है, "निकलता तो है, लेकिन इतने घने अँधेरे में दिखाई नहीं देता !"।

छोटू [*बत्तीसी दिखाकर*] वाह ! वाह ! कितना बढ़िया मज़ाक़ है ! "इतने घने अँधेरे में दिखाई नहीं देता"। वाह !

हरीश अच्छा छोटू, पिताजी भी दिखाई नहीं दे रहे हैं। बाहर गए हैं क्या?

छोटू हाँ, खन्ना जी अचानक किसी से मिलने गए हैं। परेशान-से लग रहे थे।

हरीश क्या पिता जी ख़ुद गाड़ी चला रहे थे ?

छोटू जी नहीं। खन्ना-जी जैसे बड़े लोग गाड़ी स्वयं क्यों चलाएँगे ! उनके पास ड्राइवर तो है।

हरीश पिता जी का कहना था कि आज सिवाय चौकीदार के, सब लोग छुट्टी पर होंगे।

छोटू पर हमारे जैसे ग़रीब आदमियों को छुट्टी कब मिलती है भैया ? इधर तो हमारी हालत बहुत ख़राब है।

हरीश अगर तुम तरक़्क़ी करना चाहते हो तो पिताजी से ख़ुद बात कर लो। वे अपने आप तो कुछ नहीं करेंगे तुम्हारे लिए।

छोटू मैं उनसे कुछ कहना चाहता था, मगर मारे डर के मैं कुछ कह नहीं पाया।

हरीश अरे छोटू, डरपोक मत बनो तुम !

आधीरात f midnight	**जंभाई** f yawn; **जंभाई लेना** to yawn
आपस में between themselves	**घना** thick, dense
सूरज m sun	**अँधेरा** m darkness

बत्तीसी f	set of 32 – the teeth;	**चौकीदार** m	watchman
बत्तीसी दिखाना	to grin broadly	**जैसा**	like, such as
दिखाई देना	to be visible, appear	**ग़रीब**	poor
अचानक	suddenly, unexpectedly	**हालत** f	state, condition
-सा	-like, -ish	**तरक़्क़ी** f	progress, advancement
स्वयं	oneself	**अपने आप**	of one's own accord
ड्राइवर m	driver	**के मारे**	on account of, through
के सिवाय	apart from	**डरपोक**	timid

Harish Chotu, will you listen to a joke? Two drunks are talking together at midnight. The first drunk asks the second drunk, 'Brother, why doesn't the sun come out at night?' Do you know what the second drunk replies?

Chotu [*yawning*] You tell me and we'll see.

Harish The second drunk says, 'It *does* come out, but it's not visible in such deep darkness!'

Chotu [*grinning broadly*] Wah! Wonderful! What a fine joke! 'It's not visible in such deep darkness.' Wonderful!

Harish OK Chotu, Father's not to be seen anywhere either. Has he gone out?

Chotu Yes, Khanna ji has suddenly gone out to meet someone. He was looking a bit worried.

Harish Was Father driving the car himself?

Chotu No. Important people like Khanna ji don't drive themselves! He has a driver after all.

Harish Father was saying that everyone except the watchman would be on holiday today.

Chotu But when do poor people like us get a holiday, brother? We're in a very bad state here.

Harish If you want to make progress (be promoted), talk to Father yourself. He won't do anything of his own accord.

Chotu I wanted to say something to him, but I was afraid to speak.

Harish Oh Chotu, don't be a wimp!

> **!** 'I wanted to...': such past contexts take चाहना in the imperfective (चाहता था), because they describe an ongoing state of mind rather than a specific action.

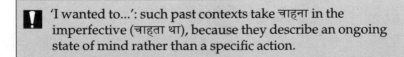

Grammar

15.4 जैसा 'like'

जैसा is a postposition meaning 'like'. Like the possessive का (5.3), it agrees adjectivally with a subject noun or pronoun, while also putting a preceding noun or pronoun into the oblique:

मुझ जैसे लोग काम नहीं करते ।	People like me don't work.
तेरे हाथ किसी कोमल फूल जैसे हैं ।	Your hands are like some soft flower.

An alternative structure is based on a possessive pronoun – उनके जैसे 'like them', हमारे जैसे 'like us'.

मेरे जैसे आदमी के बारे में कौन परवाह करता है ?	Who cares about a man like me?
छोटू के जैसे मूर्ख मत बनो ।	Don't be a fool like Chotu.

The adverb जैसे (कि) means 'as, just as'; and with a subjunctive verb, 'as though'.

जैसे तुम्हें बताया जा चुका है, नल का पानी पीने लायक़ नहीं है ।	As you've already been told, the tap water isn't drinkable.
वह हँसने लगी जैसे कि पागल हो ।	She started laughing as though she were mad.

15.5 -सा '-ish, -like'

-सा/-सी/-से is suffixed to adjectives to moderate their sense a little:

मेरा गोरा-सा चेहरा और लाल-सी नाक	my palish face and reddish nose
तेरे भोले-से सवाल	your rather innocent questions

As in English 'rather', -सा can emphasise a quality while ostensibly moderating it:

छोटी-सी चिड़िया	a tiny little bird
बहुत-से नेता	lots of leaders (politicians)

-सा can also be suffixed to a noun+ possessive:

नेता का-सा घमंड	arrogance like a politician's
बंदर की-सी पूंछ	a tail like a monkey's

It can also be suffixed to various parts of the verb:

औरत बैठ-सी गई ।	The woman kind of sat down.
सपने में मैं उड़-सा रहा था ।	In the dream I was as if flying.

It takes a regular oblique case when required:

उस घने-से जंगल में	in that quite dense jungle
ठंडे से पानी में	in the coldish water

-सा is also an element of the word कौनसा 'which'; similarly, कोई-सा means 'any one (out of a range of choices)':

कोई-सी किताब ले लो ।	Take any book.
कौनसी लूँ ?	Which one should I take?

And finally, एक-सा means 'similar':

एक-सी चीज़ें	similar things
हमारे घर एक-से हैं ।	Our houses are similar.

15.6 Inverted postpositions

Some compound postpositions may optionally be inverted without affecting the sense.

के बिना	पैसे के बिना, बिना पैसे के	without money
के बजाय	फल के बजाय, बजाय फल के	instead of fruit
के मारे	डर के मारे, मारे डर के	on account of fear
के सिवा	आपके सिवा, सिवा आपके	apart from you

15.7 Reflexive pronouns

ख़ुद means 'myself', 'yourself' etc., depending on the subject; आप and स्वयं (pronounced *svayam*) are more formal equivalents.

वह ख़ुद गाड़ी नहीं चलाता ।	He doesn't drive the car himself.
मैंने यह फ़ोटो ख़ुद खींचा ।	I took this photo myself.
पंडित जी स्वयं ही आएँगे ।	Pandit ji will come in person.

Oblique cases usually involve अपने को or अपने आप को –

अमित अपने को बड़ा आदमी समझता है ।	Amit considers himself a big shot.
डाकू अपने आप को मारने लगा ।	The bandit began beating himself.

अपने आप also means 'of one's own accord'; आपस में means 'between themselves, among themselves'.

पहिया अपने आप घूमने लगा ।	The wheel began turning of its own accord.
लड़के आपस में फुसफुसाने लगे ।	The boys began whispering amongst themselves.

EXERCISE 15a.1 Fill the gaps in the 'imperfective + रहना / जाना' constructions. Then translate.

१ हम दिन भर काम करते .... ।

२ बेचारी छात्रा दस दिन तक पढ़ती .... ।

३ आप ध्यान से काम .... रहिए, तभी सफल होंगे ।

४ सरकार की शक्ति बढ़ती .... , यहाँ तक कि हमें देश को छोड़ना पड़ा ।

५ बादल और भी घने होते .... , फिर दस दिन तक बर्फ़ गिरती .... ।

EXERCISE 15a.2 Rewrite using the 'perfective + करना' construction. Then translate.

१ पिताजी एक मशहूर सरकारी अख़बार चलाते थे ।

२ वह बदमाश अपने बच्चों को मारता है ।

३ सच है कि किसी ज़माने में हमारे भी कई नौकर होते थे ।

४ शाम को दादीजी हमेशा मंदिर जाती हैं ।

५ हमारे पड़ोसी हमें अक्सर धोखा देते हैं ।

EXERCISE 15a.3 Complete the sentence using an appropriate clause. Then translate.

१ जैसा आपने कहा था, वैसा ही ....

२ जैसी फ़िल्में आजकल बन रही हैं, ...

३ जिस तरह की नौकरी मैं करती हूँ ....

४ .... उस तरह के मकान पुराने शहर में नहीं मिलते ।

५ .... वैसा मौक़ा तुम्हें दुबारा नहीं मिलनेवाला है ।

EXERCISE 15b.1 Translate.

1 People like him don't get a job easily.
2 As dozens of people had already told me, the man had gone mad.
3 He slept as though he had not slept for several weeks.
4 We have been living in this country since 1947.
5 Since the accident happened he has not driven the car.
6 You should complain to the doctor if the medicine doesn't work.
7 I wanted to talk to the boss but I was too afraid to say anything.
8 You'll have to fetch the newspapers yourself today because the paper boy is sick.

EXERCISE 15b.2 Answer the questions on Dialogues 15a and 15b.

१ प्रताप कितने साल से हिन्दी पढ़ रहा है ? और आप ? आपने हिन्दी सीखना कब शुरू किया ?

२ जो आदमी प्रताप को लंदन में हिन्दी पढ़ाया करता था, वह कहाँ से था ?

३ क्या प्रताप कभी कभी उच्चारण की गलतियाँ किया करता है ? कोई उदाहरण दीजिए ।

४ क्या प्रताप के पास असल में कोई मोर है ?

५ क्या दादी जी सोचती हैं कि प्रताप को अपनी हिन्दी की पढ़ाई को छोड़ देना चाहिए ?

६ छोटू को कैसे मालूम है कि खन्ना जी स्वयं गाड़ी नहीं चला रहे हैं ?

७ हरीश क्यों सोचता है कि आज शायद उसके पिताजी गाड़ी चला रहे होंगे ?

८ किन लोगों की हालत ख़राब है ? आपके ख़याल से उनके पास किस तरह की समस्याएँ होंगी?

९ अगर छोटू को तरक़्क़ी करनी हो तो उसे क्या करना चाहिए ?

१० आपके ख़याल से क्या खन्ना जी छोटू के बारे में परवाह करते हैं ?

EXERCISE 15b.3 Write (or make up) a diary entry describing a recent day in your life.

Vocabulary

अँधेरा m darkness
अगस्त m August
अचानक suddenly, unexpectedly
अनौपचारिक रूप से informally
अपने आप of one's own accord, oneself
असल में really, in reality
आधीरात m midnight
आपस में between/among themselves
आसानी से easily
(से) इनकार करना to refuse (to)
उड़ना to fly
उदाहरण m example
उपन्यास m novel
औपचारिक रूप से formally
कब से since when
कभी कभी sometimes
काँपना to shiver, tremble
किनारा m edge, shore
किराया m rent, fare
के बजाय instead of
के बिना without
के मारे on account of, through
के सिवा, सिवाय apart from
ग़रीब poor
ग़लती f mistake
गाली f abuse, swearing; गाली देना to abuse, swear at
गोरा adj/m pale, fair; white person
घना dense, thick
घमंड m pride, arrogance
चपाती f chapati
चौकीदार m watchman
जंगल m jungle, scrub
जँभाई f yawn; जंभाई लेना to yawn
ज़माना m period, age, time
जीते रहो bless you ('stay living')
जीना to live, be alive
जीवन m life
जैसा like, such as
जैसे कि as if, as though
झेंपना to be embarrassed
ट्रेन f train
डरपोक timid
ड्राइवर m driver
तरक़्क़ी f progress, advancement
थकना to be tired

दिखाई देना to be visible, appear
देर से late
देश m country
धोखा m trick, deceipt; धोखा देना to trick, deceive
नल m pipe, tap
नेता m leader, politician
नौकरी f job, employment, service
पंडित m pandit
परवाह करना to care
पहिया m wheel
पूँछ f tail
पैदल on foot, walking
फुसफुसाना to whisper
बंदर m monkey
बढ़ना to increase, grow
बत्तीसी f set of 32 – the teeth; बत्तीसी दिखाना to grin broadly
बर्फ़ f snow, ice
बादल m cloud
ब्राह्मण m Brahmin
भिखारी m beggar
मशहूर famous
यात्री m traveller, passenger
यू० पी० m UP (Uttar Pradesh)
राजधानी f 'the capital' – name of some Delhi express trains
रात भर all night
व्यक्तिगत रूप से personally
शक्ति f power
शराबी m drunkard
शुरू m beginning
सच true
समस्या f problem
समुद्र m sea, ocean
सरकार f government; सरकारी governmental
-सा -like, -ish
सितार m sitar
सूरज m sun
स्नान करना to bathe (esp. ritually)
स्वयं oneself
हालत f state, condition

16 HE WAS PRAISING YOU
वह तुम्हारी तारीफ़ कर रहा था

In this unit you will learn how to

- use conjunct verbs
- use emphasis through repetition of words
- use echo words and 'either/or' choices

16a Chotu misses his chance

छोटू	साहब, आपका बेटा हरीश जो है न, वह बड़ा होनहार लड़का लगता है ।
खन्ना	वह तुम्हारी भी बहुत तारीफ़ कर रहा था । उल्लू कहीं का !
छोटू	उसकी शादी कब हो जाएगी सर ? अगले महीने वह २० साल का होनेवाला है ।
खन्ना	अरे तुमने उसकी उम्र भी मालूम कर ली है ?
छोटू	जिस महीने हरीश का जन्म हुआ, उसी महीने मेरे पिताजी का देहान्त हो गया । इस लिए...
खन्ना	अच्छा, इसी लिए तुम्हें ये सारी बातें याद रहती हैं ।

छोटू	हाँ साहब । खन्ना जी, कल जो है, मैंने आपसे एक बात कहने की कोशिश की थी मगर...
खन्ना	तंग मत किया करो छोटू । अभी मुझे एक ज़रूरी मीटिंग का इंतज़ाम करना है ।

तारीफ़ f praise; **की तारीफ़ करना** to praise
उल्लू m 'owl' – stupid person
कहीं का (derogative) complete, utter
मालूम करना to find out, ascertain
देहान्त m death; **का देहान्त होना** to die
इस लिए so
इसी लिए that's why
याद रहना to be remembered
की कोशिश करना to try
मीटिंग f meeting
इंतज़ाम m arrangement; **का इंतज़ाम करना** to arrange

Chotu	Sahib, you know your son Harish – he seems a very promising boy.
Khanna	He was praising you a lot too. Silly fool!
Chotu	When will he get married sir? He's about to turn 20 next month.
Khanna	What, you've even found out his age?
Chotu	The very month Harish was born, my father died. So...
Khanna	Oh I see, *that's* why you remember all these things.
Chotu	Yes sahib. Khanna ji, yesterday, you know, I tried to say something to you but...
Khanna	Don't always be bothering (me) Chotu. Right now I've got to arrange an important meeting.

> जो है underlines an item for special focus, establishing a subject before going into details: लखनऊ की यह तहज़ीब जो है, वह तो सारी दुनिया में मशहूर है 'This Lucknow culture – it's famous the world over.'

Grammar

16.1 Conjunct verbs with करना / होना

FIRST TYPE. Conjunct verbs of the first type were introduced in 7.6: they're based on adjective + करना (साफ़ करना to clean, to 'make clean') or noun + करना (शुरू करना to start, to 'make a start').

Intransitive equivalents take होना instead of करना. We may call the noun component a 'base noun'.

छोटू को अपनी साइकिल ठीक करनी है ।	Chotu has to fix his bike.
दुकानदार दाम को कम करनेवाला नहीं है ।	The shopkeeper isn't about to lower the price.
कार्यक्रम ५ बजे शुरू हुआ / होगा ।	The programme began / will begin at 5 o'clock.

SECOND TYPE. In the second type, the base noun is 'possessed' by the verb's object, using का/की/के; thus मैं राम की मदद करूँगा 'I'll help Ram' (literally 'I'll do Ram's help'; मदद is 'possessed' by राम). Try making up examples of your own based on the following:

With *masculine* base nouns:

का इंतज़ाम करना	to arrange
का इंतज़ार करना	to wait for
का इस्तेमाल करना	to use
का पीछा करना	to follow

With *feminine* base nouns:

की तलाश करना	to look for
की देखभाल करना	to look after
की निंदा करना	to blame, speak ill of
की तारीफ़ करना	to praise

In the passive, the subject of a conjunct verb is the base noun itself:

नए घर की तलाश की जाएगी ।	A new house will be sought. (तलाश subject)
पुलिस का इंतज़ार किया जाए ।	(We'd) better wait for the police. (इंतज़ार subject)

Similarly, a conjunct verb in a ने construction agrees with its own base noun:

राम ने बच्चों की देखभाल की ।	Ram looked after the children. (की agrees with देखभाल)

उमा ने कंप्यूटर का इस्तेमाल किया ।	Uma used a computer. (किया agrees with इस्तेमाल)
मैंने दूसरी ट्रेन का इंतज़ार किया ।	I waited for the next train. (किया agrees with इंतज़ार)

The conjunct verb की कोशिश करना 'to try' often follows an infinitive verb, which must be in the oblique because of the की postposition: समझने की कोशिश करो 'try to understand'.

मैंने फ़ोन करने की कोशिश की ।	I tried to telephone.
समय पर आने की कोशिश करो ।	Try to come on time.
उन्होंने अन्दर आने की कोशिश की ।	They tried to come in.

! Practise substituting other verbs for फ़ोन करना in the first of these examples; this is an extremely useful formula.

A few verbs of the second type can drop their possessive का/की/के, thus becoming first-type verbs: तलाश करना 'to search for'. Just occasionally, a base noun even sprouts a -ना ending and thus generates a verb: किसी को तलाशना 'to search for someone'.

कोई नया घर तलाश करें ।	Let's look for some new house.
मैं तुझे दस साल तक तलाशता रहा ।	I went on searching for you for ten years.

Intransitive conjunct verbs are very common in describing events and processes. Remember that the subject of the verb is the event itself – जन्म^{m} 'birth', शादी^{f} 'marriage', etc.:

पिताजी का जन्म सन् १९१५ में हुआ था ।	Father was born in 1915. (जन्म ^{m} 'birth')
छोटू की शादी अभी नहीं हुई ।	Chotu isn't married yet. (शादी ^{f} 'marriage')
अनीता का तलाक़ कब हुआ ? ।	When did Anita get divorced? (तलाक़ ^{m} 'divorce')
ओम का देहान्त हो गया है ।	Om has passed away. (देहान्त ^{m} 'demise')

नई इमारत का उद्घाटन हुआ ।	The new building was opened. (उद्घाटन m 'inauguration')

16.2 Other conjunct verbs

करना and होना are the most common makers of conjunct verbs, but they're not the only ones. For example, the range of possibilities having याद 'memory' as base noun includes:

याद करना	to remember, learn by memory; to think of, summon (e.g. an employee)
याद होना	to be remembered
याद आना	to be recalled, come to mind, be missed
याद दिलाना	to remind
याद रखना	to keep in mind, not to forget
याद रहना	to remain remembered

पाठ १६ को ठीक से याद करो ।	Learn lesson 16 properly.
खन्ना जी तुम्हें याद कर रहे हैं ।	Khanna ji wants you to go to him ('is remembering you').
मुझे तेरा चेहरा याद है ।	I remember your face.
मुझे अभी याद आया है कि श्रीमती खन्ना का नाम उमा है ।	I just remembered that Mrs Khanna's name is Uma.
उन्हें कल शाम की याद दिला दो ।	Remind them about tomorrow evening.
जो मैंने तुम्हें बताया, उसे याद रखना ।	Bear in mind what I told you.
प्यारे, तुम सदा याद रहोगे ।	Beloved, I'll always remember you.

The meaning of most conjunct verbs can be deduced easily enough, but some are quite idiomatic. For example, दिखाई देना/पड़ना means 'to be/become visible, to be seen' and its partner सुनाई देना/पड़ना means 'to be/become audible, to be heard'. Neither takes the ने construction!

गली में एक पुरानी गाड़ी दिखाई पड़ी ।	An old car came into view in the alley.
रात को खाँसने की आवाज़ सुनाई देती थी ।	At night the sound of coughing could be heard.

16b Khanna's anxiety about Harish

उमा	क्या हुआ मेरे पति-देव? आज तो तुम कहीं ज़्यादा परेशान लग रहे हो ।
खन्ना	कहीं हरीश की शादी का इंतज़ाम हो जाए तो... बस, यही चिंता है ।
उमा	इसमें चिंता-विंता की क्या बात है ? तुम्हें नहीं मालूम कि उसे संगीता कुमार से प्यार है ?
खन्ना	प्यार-व्यार तो हो सकता है, पर ज़रा सोचो, कहीं प्यार से ही शादी बनती है किसी की ?
उमा	अरे तुम्हारा सोचने का ढंग तो बिलकुल बूढ़ों का जैसा है ।
खन्ना	ज़िंदगी में अहम चीज़ है पैसा । संगीता के पास क्या है ? न पैसा न पेशा ।
उमा	दुनिया में तरह तरह के लोग हैं; सबों की अपनी अपनी जगह होती है ।
खन्ना	मगर गुज़ारे के साधन भी होने चाहिए – चाहे कोई काम करे चाहे चोरी !

पति-देव m 'respected husband'
कहीं ज़्यादा particularly
चिंता f anxiety, concern
चिंता-विंता f anxiety etc.
प्यार-वार m love and all that
ढंग m way, manner
ज़िंदगी f life
अहम important
न... न neither... nor
पेशा m profession
दुनिया f world
तरह तरह का of various kinds
गुज़ारा m livelihood, subsistence
साधन m means
चाहे...चाहे whether... or

Uma	What's up, my dear husband? You're looking particularly worried today.
Khanna	If Harish's marriage could just be fixed somehow... that's all I'm worried about.
Uma	What's there to worry about? Don't you know he loves Sangeeta Kumar?

Khanna	There may be love and all that, but just think, does love alone make anyone's marriage?
Uma	Oh really, your way of thinking is just like the old folks'.
Khanna	The important thing in life is money. What does Sangeeta have? Neither money nor profession.
Uma	There are many kinds of people in the world; everyone has (his or) her own place.
Khanna	But there should be a means of livelihood too – whether one works or steals!

> तुम्हारा सोचने का ढंग – here तुम्हारा agrees with ढंग, not with सोचने.

Grammar

16.3 कहीं 'somewhere'

कहीं means 'anywhere' or 'somewhere', कहीं और 'somewhere else', कहीं नहीं 'nowhere', सब कहीं 'everywhere', कहीं भी 'anywhere at all', कहीं न कहीं 'somewhere or other'. A versatile little word! Less literal senses include:

somehow, by some means:

कहीं पैसे मिल जाएँ तो समस्या हल हो जाएगी ।

If somehow we get the money, the problem will be solved

considerably, very much:

दूसरा मकान कहीं ज्यादा महँगा था ।

The other house was much dearer.

let it not be that, lest (+ न + subjunctive):

मैं डर रहा था कि कहीं मेरी पत्नी न आ जाए ।

I was afraid lest my wife turn up.

is it possible that ? (rhetorical question):

कहीं कोई इनसान अपने बच्चे को मारेगा ?

Would a human being ever beat his own child?

कहीं का ('of somewhere', hence 'of dubious origin') sharpens the edge of an insult or derogatory label:

बदमाश कहीं का !

Wretched scoundrel!

16.4 Repetition of words

Repeating a word may indicate distribution ('one rupee each') or separation ('sit separately'):

हरेक लड़के को एक एक रुपया दो ।	Give each boy one rupee.
तुम दोनों अलग अलग बैठो ।	You two sit separately from each other.
हरेक प्रयोग के तीन तीन उदाहरण हैं ।	There are three examples of each usage.

Or it may indicate variety and diversity:

हमने तरह तरह के जानवर देखे ।	We saw various different kinds of animals.
भारत में आम कहाँ कहाँ मिलते हैं ?	Where in India can you get mangoes?
शादी में तुम्हें कौन कौन मिला ?	Which various people did you meet at the wedding?

Repetition of an adjective or adverb lends it emphasis:

हमें साफ़ साफ़ बताओ ।	Tell us plainly.
बहुत बहुत धन्यवाद ।	Thank you very much indeed.
बड़ी बड़ी आँखें	great big eyes
गरम गरम चाय	piping hot tea

16.5 Echo words

An 'echo word' echoes another word and generalises its sense. Thus चाय-वाय means 'tea etc., tea or something similar', as in चाय-वाय पियो 'Have some tea or something', in which -वाय echoes चाय. Echo words usually begin with व-, but not always; they can be formed quite creatively, often with a dismissive or disdainful sense.

हमें कोई पेंसिल-वेंसिल दो ।	Give us a pencil or something.
हमें किसी तरह की माला-वाला नहीं चाहिए ।	We don't want any kind of garland or anything.
मुझे किसी मीटिंग-शीटिंग में नहीं जाना है ।	I won't go to any meeting or anything of the kind.

Some echo pairings are an established part of Hindi vocabulary:

गप	gossip	गप-शप	chit-chat, tittle-tattle
ठीक	all right	ठीक-ठाक	fine, in good shape
भीड़	crowd	भीड़-भाड़	hustle and bustle

A further type consists of two words of similar meaning:

नौकर-चाकर	servants, etc.	(both words mean ' servant')
मिलना-जुलना	to mix, associate	(both words mean 'to join')
जान-बूझकर	deliberately	('knowing and understanding')

16.6 या तो... या; न... न; चाहे... चाहे

'Either... or' is या (तो)... या.

सिग्रेट को या तो पी लो या मुझे पीने दो ।	Either smoke the cigarette yourself or let me smoke it.
कसूर या तो तेरा है या मेरा ।	The fault is either yours or mine.

'Neither... nor' is न... न.

छोटू न आलसी है न बेवकूफ़ ।	Chotu is neither lazy nor stupid.
हम न प्याज़ खाते हैं न लहसुन ।	We eat neither onions nor garlic.

'Whether... or' is चाहे... चाहे / या.

खाना चाहे अच्छा हो चाहे ख़राब	whether the food's good or bad
चाहे मर्द हो या औरत	whether man or woman

चाहे alone means 'no matter whether'; and the formula चाहे... क्यों न हो means 'no matter how/what'.

चाहे जो भी हो, तुम्हें नदी को पार करना होगा ।

No matter what happens, you'll have to cross the river.

चाहे वह कितना बड़ा आदमी क्यों न हो, मैं उससे नहीं मिलूँगा ।

No matter how important a man he may be, I won't meet him.

यह समस्या कितनी ही कठिन क्यों न हो, उसका हल निकाला ही जाएगा ।

No matter how hard this problem may be, it shall be solved.

EXERCISE 16a.1 Answer the questions as fully as possible.

१ क्या आपको साइकिल ठीक करना आता है ?

२ आप सुबह को कितने बजे अपना पढ़ाई का काम शुरू करते / करती हैं ?

३ आप किस तरह की फ़िल्में पसंद करते / करती हैं ?

४ जब आप निबंध वग़ैरह लिखते / लिखती हैं तो क्या आप कंप्यूटर का इस्तेमाल करते / करती हैं ?

५ क्या आपने कभी हिन्दी में ई-मेल (ई-पत्र) भेजने की कोशिश की है ?

६ क्या आपकी शादी हो गई है ?

७ क्या आज शाम को किसी दोस्त या सहेली से आपकी मुलाक़ात होगी ?

८ जिस कमरे में आप अभी बैठे / बैठी हैं, वहाँ क्या क्या दिखाई दे रहा है ?

९ आप हिन्दी के नए शब्दों को कैसे याद करते / करती हैं ?

१० क्या आपको याद है कि आज से ठीक एक साल पहले आप क्या कर रहे थे / कर रही थीं ?

EXERCISE 16a.2 Translate.

1 We've been told that we'll have to wait for the other passengers.
2 The luggage has been loaded on the train but nobody has made any arrangements for our food.
3 It seems that some passenger has passed away.
4 Please follow those other passengers; we'll look after your children.
5 I tried to phone a friend but the phone wasn't working.
6 They can't use the computer today because there's no electricity.
7 Don't blame the people who work here, it's not their fault.
8 I married the man I met at the station.

EXERCISE 16a.3 Write a third-person account of Dialogues 15b and 16a.

EXERCISE 16b.1 Complete the sentence with an appropriate clause. Then translate.

१ जहाँ मैं पैदा हुआ, ...

२ जहाँ जंगली जानवर रहते हैं, ...

३ जहाँ भी तुम बैठना चाहते हो, ...

४ .... मेरी शादी वहीं हुई थी ।

५ .... वहाँ बिजली का इस्तेमाल नहीं किया जाता है ।

६ .... तब तक उनके पिता का देहान्त हो चुका था ।

EXERCISE 16b.2 Translate, bringing out the meaning of any repeated words and echo words.

१ भारत में तुम कहाँ कहाँ घूमे और क्या क्या देखा ?

२ बचपन में उसके तरह तरह के अनुभव रहे होंगे ।

३ सब लोग अपने अपने विचारों में डूब गए थे ।

४ गरम गरम चाय पीकर हम सभी अपने अपने कमरे में चले गए ।

५ कुलियों को बीस बीस रुपये देना ।

६ कहो राजू, ठीक-ठाक हो ? कुछ चाय-वाय लोगे ?

८ मैं किसी मीटिंग-शीटिंग में जाकर अपना समय क्यों गँवाऊँ ?

EXERCISE 16b.3 Translate.

1 We should give them ten rupees each, so that they can get some tea or something.
2 Whom [which various people] did you encounter in Pakistan?
3 Remember that you shouldn't have any food or anything in such dirty places.
4 You should all take one tablet every day after eating your food.
5 I have neither money nor time, so you'll have to look after the guests yourself.

Vocabulary

अनुभव m experience
अहम important
आलसी lazy
इंतज़ाम m arrangement; **का इंतज़ाम करना** to arrange
इंतज़ार m wait, waiting; **का इंतज़ार करना** to wait for
इनसान m human being, person
इमारत f building
इस लिए so
इसी लिए that's why
इस्तेमाल m use; **का इस्तेमाल करना** to use
ई-पत्र m e-mail

ई-मेल m e-mail
उदाहरण m example
उद्घाटन m inauguration
उल्लू m 'owl' – stupid person
कंप्यूटर m computer
कम करना to reduce
कसूर m fault, error
कहीं somewhere; somehow; कहीं और somewhere else; कहीं का downright, utter (see 16.3); कहीं ज़्यादा particularly; कहीं न कहीं somewhere or other; कहीं नहीं nowhere; कहीं भी anywhere at all
कार्यक्रम m programme
कुली m porter
कोशिश f attempt; की कोशिश करना to try
खाँसना to cough
गँवाना to waste, squander
गप f, गपशप f gossip
गुज़ारा m livelihood, subsistence
चाहे... चाहे whether... or
चिंता f anxiety
जंगली wild
जन्म m birth; का जन्म होना to be born
जानवर m animal
ज़िंदगी f life
डूबना to be immersed, drown
ढंग m way, manner
तरह तरह का of various kinds
तलाश f search; की तलाश करना to search for
तलाशना to search for
तहज़ीब f refinement, culture
तारीफ़ f praise; की तारीफ़ करना to praise
दुनिया f world
देखभाल f supervision, care; की देखभाल करना to take care of
देहान्त m death, demise; का देहान्त होना to die
न... न neither... nor
निंदा f blame, speaking ill; की निंदा करना to blame
निकालना to extract, bring out
निबंध m essay
नौकर-चाकर m servants etc.
पति-देव m 'respected husband'
(का) पीछा करना to follow
पेंसिल f pencil
पेशा m profession
प्याज़ m onion
प्रयोग m use, usage; का प्रयोग करना to use
बेवक़ूफ़ stupid
मदद f help; की मदद करना to help
मर्द m man, male
माला f garland
मालूम करना to ascertain

मीटिंग ^f^ meeting

या तो... या either... or

याद ^f^ memory; **याद आना** to be recalled, come to mind, be missed; **याद करना** to remember, learn by memory; to think of, summon (e.g. an employee); **याद दिलाना** to remind; **याद रखना** to keep in mind, not to forget; **याद रहना /होना** to be remembered

लहसुन ^m^ garlic

सदा always, ever

सवारी ^f^ rider, passenger

साधन ^m^ means

सुनाई देना/पड़ना to be heard, be audible

हरेक each, every

हल ^m^ solution; **हल होना** to be solved

17 IF YOU WEREN'T SO STUBBORN...

अगर तुम इतनी ज़िद्दी न होतीं...

In this unit you will learn how to

- use a fuller range of conditional sentences
- express the sense 'although...'
- express nuance through new compound verbs
- distinguish formal and informal styles of vocabulary

17a Sangeeta angers Prakash

प्रकाश संगीता बेटी, अगर मैं तुम्हारी शादी की बातचीत शुरू करता तो तुम्हें कैसा लगता ?

संगीता अगर बातचीत खन्ना से होती तो मैं भाग जाती यहाँ से । मुझे हरीश से सख़्त नफ़रत है !

प्रकाश तुम इतनी ज़िद्दी न होतीं तो बात बन जाती । हरीश का नाम मैंने कब लिया था ?

संगीता अगर हरीश नहीं है तो कौन है पापा, जिसे तुम मेरा "जीवन-साथी" बनाना चाहते हो ?

प्रकाश	कल मैंने प्रताप की माँ को लंदन में फ़ोन किया था। वे कहती हैं कि प्रताप राज़ी हो जाएगा।
संगीता	प्रताप ! वह तो इतना बदसूरत है और... अरे पापा, मज़ाक मत करना !
प्रकाश	हालाँकि प्रताप सुंदर तो नहीं है, फिर भी वह बड़ा होनहार लड़का है।
संगीता	होनहार मेरा सिर !
प्रकाश	ऐसी बातें मुझसे क्यों सुनी जाएँगी – और अपनी बेटी के मुँह से !

बातचीत [f] conversation; negotiation over marriage
भागना to run away, flee
ज़िद्दी obstinate, stubborn
बात बनना an aim to be achieved, to go well
का नाम लेना to mention
राज़ी agreeable, content
हालाँकि although
फिर भी even so
मेरा सिर 'my foot!'
मुँह [m] mouth, face

Prakash	Sangeeta (my) daughter, how would it be if I began marriage negotiations for you ?
Sangeeta	If the negotiations were with Khanna I'd run away from here. I detest Harish.
Prakash	If you weren't so stubborn we'd get somewhere. When did I mention Harish?
Sangeeta	If it's not Harish, who is that you want to make my 'life partner', Papa?
Prakash	Yesterday I phoned Pratap's mother in London. She says that Pratap would agree.
Sangeeta	Pratap! He's so ugly, and... oh Papa, don't joke!
Prakash	Although Pratap isn't handsome, he's a promising boy.
Sangeeta	Promising, my foot!
Prakash	Why should I listen to such things – and from my own daughter!

Grammar

17.1 Conditional sentences (2)

In 10.4 we saw how conditional sentences can use an imperfective, subjunctive or future verb in the अगर clause. Another possibility is a *perfective* verb, such as आया, मिला, or हुआ; thus अगर राम आया तो क्या तुम उससे मिलोगी? 'If Ram comes, will you meet him?' Using the perfective makes the अगर clause a given, a supposition – 'supposing Ram came...'.

अगर कुछ गरम पानी बाक़ी रहा तो मैं भी नहा लूँगा ।	If there's any hot water left I'll bathe too.
अगर तुम्हें छात्रवृत्ति मिली तो भारत जाओ ।	If you get the scholarship, go to India.
यदि मेरी योजना सफल हुई तो आपका भी लाभ होगा ।	If my plan succeeds you'll benefit too.

A condition that remains unfulfilled or hypothetical (e.g. 'if I were rich') uses the imperfective participle *without* auxiliary (e.g. होता, *without* था) in both clauses; the femine plural is nasalised. This construction is so unambiguously conditional that the अगर/यदि is often dropped.

(यदि) तुम मुझे बुलाते तो मैं ज़रूर आता ।	If you called me I would certainly come.
(अगर) मैं कवि होता तो तेरे बारे में कविता लिखता ।	If I were a poet I'd write poetry about you.
(अगर) सीता जी विदेश जातीं तो ज़्यादा पैसे कमातीं ।	If Sita ji went abroad she'd earn more.

The time frame here is unspecific: the first example could also mean 'If you had called me I would certainly have come'. When a specifically *past* time frame is needed, unfulfilled conditions can take a perfective participle + होता (e.g. बुलाया होता) in the अगर clause; the तो clause usually has an imperfective participle alone (आता).

(अगर) तुम १० बजे आए होते तो उनसे बात कर पाते ।	If you'd come at 10 o'clock you'd have been able to talk to them.
(अगर) टिकट मिली होती तो हम भी तुम्हारे साथ आते ।	If we'd received the ticket we would have come with you too.
(अगर) वह ध्यान से पढ़ी होती तो उसे डिगरी मिल जाती ।	If she'd studied attentively she would have got the degree.

Other tenses, such as the continuous, may also appear in an अगर clause:

अगर वह सो रही होती तो उसे जगाना ठीक नहीं होता।	It wouldn't have been right to wake her if she'd been asleep.

Because they tell of situations which no longer have the potential to be fulfilled, such sentences are sometimes called 'counter-to-fact', 'contrafactuals', or 'impossible conditions'.

17.2 हालाँकि 'Although'

'Although' sentences have two clauses, the first introduced by हालाँकि 'although', the second by फिर भी or तो भी 'even so'.

हालाँकि वह ग़रीब है, फिर भी वह काफ़ी ख़ुश लगता है।
Although he's poor, he seems quite happy.

हालाँकि उसकी हालत ख़राब है, फिर भी वह ठीक हो जाएगा।
Although his condition is bad, he'll get better.

हालाँकि उसे बुलाया गया था, फिर भी वह नहीं आई।
Although she was called, she didn't come.

हालाँकि मज़दूरों ने हड़ताल कर दी, फिर भी मालिक पर कोई असर नहीं पड़ा।
Although the workers went on strike, it had no effect on the boss.

Formal Hindi uses the Sanskritic यद्यपि... तथापि.

यद्यपि संतोष की पुस्तक शीघ्र ही प्रकाशित हुई, तथापि ये प्रकाशक से संतुष्ट नहीं हैं।
Although Santosh's book was published very quickly, he is not satisfied with the publisher.

यद्यपि उनकी स्थिति गंभीर है, तथापि वे सुधर जाएँगे।
Although their situation is grave, they will improve.

17b Sangeeta angers Kamala

कमला बेटी तुम अपने बाप को बहुत नाराज़ कर बैठीं। तुम्हारी बातें सुनकर उनसे रहा नहीं गया।

संगीता मैंने बस इतना कहा कि न हरीश से शादी करूँगी न प्रताप से, तो पिताजी बिगड़ उठे।

कमला लेकिन संगू, किसी से तो शादी करनी ही होगी तुम्हें!

संगीता	क्यों माँ ? जिस तरह तुम फँस गईं, उसी तरह मुझे भी फँस जाना है क्या ?
कमला	तुमसे कौन बात करे । कोई अच्छी-सी बात भी कहे तो तुम लड़ने लगती हो ।
सुरेश	[*कमरे में आकर*] यह क्या महाभारत मच रहा है ?
संगीता	अंकल मैंने माँ से कितनी दफ़ा कह रखा है कि शादी नहीं करूँगी मगर वे तो मानतीं नहीं ।
कमला	सुरेश, यह लड़की मेरे सारे सपने तोड़ डालना चाहती है !
सुरेश	ओ कमला, किसके सभी सपने पूरे होते हैं ?

बिगड़ना to go wrong, get angry
मचना to break out, be caused
फँसना to be stuck, caught, snared
दफ़ा f time, occasion
महाभारत m India's mythical epic war

Kamala	Daughter, you've gone and made your father very angry. He was beside himself at what you said.
Sangeeta	All I said was that I won't marry either Harish or Pratap, and Father went mad.
Kamala	But Sangoo, you'll have to marry someone!
Sangeeta	Why Mum? Must I get trapped the same way you did?
Kamala	Who could talk to you. Even if someone talks nicely to you, you start fighting.
Suresh	[*coming into the room*] What's this Mahabharata breaking out?
Sangeeta	Uncle, I've told Mum so many times that I won't marry, but she won't accept (it).
Kamala	Suresh, this girl wants to shatter all my dreams.
Suresh	O Kamala, who has all their dreams fulfilled?

Grammar

17.3 Compound verbs (2)

Compound verbs using the auxiliaries जाना, लेना and देना were introduced in 12.4. It is now time to look at some more auxiliaries. Remember that ने constructions apply only when main verb and auxiliary *both* take ने.

डालना indicates that an action is done vigorously, decisively, violently, or recklessly:

गुंडों ने मेरे कुरते को फाड़ डाला।	The ruffians tore my kurta apart.
दंगे के दिन उन्होंने तीन आदमियों को मार डाला।	On the day of the riot they killed three men.
दवा पीने से तबियत ठीक हो जाएगी – पी डालो !	Taking the medicine will make you better – drink it down!

बैठना implies that an action was done foolishly or stubbornly:

ओहो ! छोटू क्या कर बैठा है ?	Oho! What's Chotu gone and done?
जो भी मन में आया, उमा वही कह बैठी।	Uma blurted out whatever came into her mind.
उस दिन हम सचमुच ग़लती कर बैठे।	That day we really blundered.

पड़ना adds a sense of suddenness or change of state. Its literal sense 'to fall' sometimes shows through in a sense of *downward* movement:

ज्योंही गाड़ी रुकी त्योंही हम उतर पड़े।	We got down as soon as the train stopped.
मैं रो पड़ा मगर तू हँस पड़ी।	I burst into tears but you burst out laughing.
अचानक ऐसा हुआ कि तीन अजनबी डिब्बे में घुस पड़े।	Suddenly it happened that three strangers burst into the compartment.

उठना suggests the inception of an action or feeling. Its literal sense 'to rise' sometimes shows through in a sense of *upward* movement:

हड़ताल की ख़बर सुनकर पिताजी बिगड़ उठे।	Hearing news of the strike Father lost his temper.
लकड़ियों का ढेर जल उठा।	The pile of logs burst into flames.
जब तुम बाँसुरी बजाने लगे तो बूढ़े नाच उठे।	When you began playing the flute the old men broke into a dance.

रखना – the basic sense of 'to keep, maintain' can imply a firmness of action, or one whose results or implications might last over time:

सुनो, चाबी मैंने पुलिस को दे रखी है – उनसे लेकर दरवाज़ा खोल लेना।	Listen, I've given the key to the police; get (it) from them and open the door.
हमने उसको साफ़ कह रखा है कि हम नहीं जाएँगे, मगर वह मानता ही नहीं।	We've told him clearly that we won't go, but he just won't accept (it).
हमने एक अच्छा-सा घर देख रखा है।	We've seen, got our eye on, a pretty good house.

17.4 The vocabulary of Hindi

Like all languages, Hindi inherits vocabulary from a variety of sources. This contributes to its flexibility and richness. Different contexts need different styles of vocabulary: formal Hindi uses many Sanskrit loanwords, whereas colloquial Hindi admits a freer mix of words from Sanskrit, Persian, English and Portuguese. (Some Persian loanwords come from Arabic and Turkish.) The name 'Hindi' is itself Persian. It's important to be aware of these different 'registers' in order to be able to hit the right tone: heavily Sanskritised Hindi, for example, may sound comically over-formal in everyday speech, just as saying 'One desires a residence in relative proximity to the terminus' would sound odd when telling someone that you wanted a house quite near the station. Yet some speakers (like Arun in dialogue 12b) do favour a Sanskritised style, even in conversation.

The main stylistic choice, then, is between a formal-sounding word (usually Sanskritic) and an informal, colloquial synonym (often Persian). Here are some common synonyms or near-synonyms.

PERSO-ARABIC	SANSKRIT	
अख़बार m	**समाचार-पत्र** m	newspaper
अगर	**यदि**	if
अफ़सोस m	**खेद** m	regret
आख़िर m	**अन्त** m	end

PERSO-ARABIC	SANSKRIT	
आम	साधारण	ordinary
उम्मीद f	आशा f	hope
किताब f	पुस्तक f	book
ख़त m	पत्र m	letter
ख़त्म	समाप्त	finished
ख़बर f	समाचार f	news
खाना m	भोजन m	food
ख़ास	विशेष	special
ख़ूबसूरत	सुन्दर	beautiful
गोश्त m	माँस m	meat
ज़बान f	भाषा f	language
ज़रूर	अवश्य	of course, certainly
ज़रूरत f	आवश्यकता f	need, necessity
जवाब m	उत्तर m	reply
ज़्यादा	अधिक	more
तकलीफ़ f	कष्ट m	trouble
दोस्त m	मित्र m	friend
नामुमकिन	असंभव	impossible
फ़र्क m	भेद m, अंतर m	difference
फ़ायदा m	लाभ m	profit, advantage
फ़ुरसत f	अवकाश m	leisure time
मुमकिन	संभव	possible
मुलाक़ात f	भेंट f	meeting
मुश्किल	कठिन	difficult
मुसाफ़िर m	यात्री m	traveller
मेहरबानी f	कृपा f	kindness
लेकिन, मगर	परंतु, किंतु	but
वक़्त m	समय f	time
वजह f	कारण m	reason, cause
शादी f	विवाह m	marriage

PERSO-ARABIC	SANSKRIT	
शुक्रिया	**धन्यवाद**	thank you
शुरू m	**आरंभ** m	beginning
सफ़र m	**यात्रा** f	journey
सवाल m	**प्रश्न** m	question
साल m	**वर्ष** m	year
हफ़्ता m	**सप्ताह** m	week

English words are also used very commonly in Hindi – as favoured by Prem in dialogue 9b. In cities like Delhi and Bombay, words such as क़लम, घड़ी, प्याला, बायाँ, दाहिना are losing ground to their English equivalents – पेन, वॉच, कप, लेफ़्ट, राइट. Helped by the rapid expansion of satellite television, Hindi is now absorbing English words faster than ever. The influence of English even extends into Hindi idiom (e.g. दूसरे शब्दों में 'in other words') and, occasionally, syntax; but such matters are beyond the scope of this book. The positive side of this is that learners of Hindi can feel free to use an English word for which they don't know the Hindi – इसमें कोई "प्रॉब्लम" नहीं है!

> **!** Recognising source languages: only Sanskrit loanwords contain ज्ञ, ण, ष, क्ष, ः (*avagraha*); only words inherited from Persian contain क़, ख़, ग़.

The facility of basing innumerable verbs on करना greatly aids the take-up of loanwords, and even such unexpected items as की लुक-आफ़्टर करना 'to look after' (with feminine gender following देखभाल) are not uncommon in informal speech.

Some words which seem familiar from English are far from being loanwords: the intransitive verb कटना 'to be cut' and its transitive equivalent काटना 'to cut' derive from Sanskrit – evidence of the ancient links between Indo-European languages. By the same token, English has borrowed numerous words from Hindi: words such as लूटना, ठग and खाट are not derived from 'to loot', 'thug' 'cot', but are the *sources* of these English words.

Although many English words are widely understood in India, this comprehension depends on their following *Indian* pronunciation.

The phonetic nature of the Devanagari script prepares the learner for this, as Hindi spellings reflect Indian pronunciations of English words.

Some Hindi-speakers find initial conjuncts such as the 'sk' in स्कूल easier to pronounce if an initial vowel is added: forms such as इस्कूल, इस्टेशन are sometimes heard (but are rare in writing).

EXERCISE 17a.1 Translate.

1 If you had gone by plane you would have arrived by now.
2 Although I tried to stop them, they did not pay attention to my advice.
3 If Delhi weren't so far from here I'd come to see you straightaway.
4 If I'd known how bad his state was I wouldn't have told him the truth.
5 If the hero weren't so popular, nobody would come to see such a film.
6 Although she knew my grandfather well, she suggested we invite him.
7 If you'd told me how serious the problem was I would not have wasted my time.
8 Although I said that this was not my fault, he still complained.

EXERCISE 17a.2 Rewrite, using a हालांकि construction. Then translate the new version.

१ कोशिश करने पर भी मैं काम को पूरा नहीं कर पाया ।
२ मैं रात भर तलाश करती रही, पर वह पुराना पत्र नहीं मिला ।
३ मैंने रस्सी को काटने की बहुत कोशिश की मगर वह कटी नहीं ।
४ हमारे शिकायत करने पर भी कोई परवाह नहीं करता ।

EXERCISE 17a.3 Write a new Dialogue 16a (between Chotu and Khanna ji) as Chotu would have liked it to go.

EXERCISE 17b.1 Answer the questions on Dialogues 16b (1-4) and 17a (5-8).

१ खन्ना जी को किस बात की चिंता है ?
२ क्या उमा भी इस बात के बारे में परेशान है ? इसका कारण क्या है ?
३ खन्ना जी क्यों सोचते हैं कि हरीश को संगीता से शादी नहीं करनी चाहिए ?
४ शादी के मामले में आप किनके विचारों से सहमत हैं – खन्ना के या उमा के ? क्यों ?

५ क्या संगीता हरीश से इतना प्यार करती है जितना हरीश उससे करता है ?

६ प्रकाश क्यों कहता है कि संगीता ज़िद्दी है ?

७ क्या प्रकाश अनीता से बात कर चुका है ? क्या उनकी बातचीत रूबरू हुई थी ?

८ अगर आप प्रताप की जगह होते/ होतीं, तो क्या आप संगीता की गुस्ताख़ी को माफ़ करते / करतीं? क्यों/ क्यों नहीं?

EXERCISE 17b.2 Rewrite the following, using compound verbs as indicated; then translate.

१ एक साल के अन्दर मैंने पूरे सात लेख लिखे । [+ डालना]

२ उसने जो पैसे बड़ी मेहनत करके कमाये थे, सब को गँवाया है । [+ देना]

३ अरे, तुम किस तरह की पागल बातें बोले ? [+ बैठना]

४ मेरे बेटे ने गुस्से में अपने सबसे क़ीमती कपड़ों को फाड़ा । [+ डालना]

५ समाचार को सुनकर छोटू हँसा [+ उठना] लेकिन दूसरे लोग रोए । [+ पड़ना]

६ पुलिस ने कहा [+ रखना] है कि बेचारा खिड़की से गिरा था । [+ पड़ना]

७ जैसे ही दूसरे लोग आए [+ जाना], हमने काम आरंभ किया । [+ देना]

८ जिसने हमारे दोस्त को मारा [+ डालना], उससे हम रूबरू बात करें । [+ लेना]

EXERCISE 17b.3 Write five Hindi sentences using Perso-Arabic vocabulary from the list in 17.4, then rewrite them in a more formal register using synonyms from the Sanskrit list.

Vocabulary

अंतर m difference
अजनबी m stranger
असर m effect, impact; **असर पड़ना** to have an effect
आख़िर m end
आरंभ m beginning
उतरना to get down, alight
उत्तर m reply
उबलना to boil, rage
ओहो oho! oh no!
कटना to be cut
कवि m poet
कष्ट m trouble, distress
काटना to cut

किंतु but
क़ीमती costly, valuable
ख़बर f news
खाट f bedstead, 'cot'
गंभीर serious, profound
गुस्सा m anger; angry
घड़ी f wristwatch
घुसना to enter (forcibly, or uninvited)
छात्रवृत्ति f scholarship
जलना to burn
ज़िद्दी obstinate, stubborn
ठग m swindler, robber
ढीला loose
ढेर m pile, heap
तथापि nevertheless, even so
दंगा m riot
दफ़ा f time, occasion
दिमाग़ m mind, brain
नाचना to dance
(का) नाम लेना to mention
नामुमकिन impossible
निहायत extremely
प्रकाशित published
प्रश्न m question
फँसना to be stuck, caught, snared
फाड़ना to tear
फिर भी even so
बरदाश्त करना to tolerate, endure
बाँसुरी f bamboo flute
बाक़ी remaining, left
बात बनना an aim to be achieved, to go well
बातचीत f conversation, negotiation
बिगड़ना to go wrong, get angry
भागना to run away, flee
भेद m difference
मचना to break out, be caused
मज़दूर m worker, labourer
महाभारत m India's mythical epic war
माँस m meat
मुँह m mouth, face
मुसाफ़िर m traveller
मेरा सिर 'my foot!'
यद्यपि although
यात्रा f journey, travel
योजना f plan, scheme
रस्सी f string, cord
राज़ी agreeable, content
रूबरू face to face
रोकना to stop
लकड़ी f wood; stick
लाभ m profit, advantage
लूटना to loot, steal, pillage
लोकप्रिय popular
वर्ष m year
वापस मिलना to be got back
शीघ्र soon, quickly

शूटिंग f 'shooting', filming
संतुष्ट satisfied
संतोष m satisfaction
सप्ताह m week
सफ़र m journey, travel
समाचार-पत्र m newspaper
समाप्त finished, concluded
सहमत in agreement
साधारण ordinary
सुझाव m suggestion; सुझाव देना to make a suggestion
सुधरना to improve, be put right
हड़ताल f strike, lockout; हड़ताल करना to strike
हालाँकि although

18 A LOVE THAT WON'T BE STOPPED

ऐसा प्यार जो रोके भी नहीं रुकता

In this unit you will learn how to

- use participles for several new functions
- distinguish transitive and intransitive verbs
- usc causative verbs – to 'get something done'

18a Sangeeta confides in Suresh

सुरेश तुम हाथों में सिर थामे क्यों बैठी हो संगीता ? तुम्हें क्या तकलीफ़ है ?

संगीता माँ की ज़िद सुनते सुनते मैं तंग आ गई हूँ अंकल । वे किसी छुटभैये से मेरी शादी करने पर तुली हुई हैं । और बिना मेरी राय पूछे ।

सुरेश ज़ाहिर है कि तुम्हारा दिल किसी और से लगा हुआ है । मैंने अभी तुम्हें किसी आदमी से बातें करते हुए सुना है फ़ोन पर । कौन था ?

संगीता वही था जिससे मुझे प्यार है । या तो उसी से शादी करूँगी, या करूँगी ही नहीं – दुनिया चाहे माने या न माने ।

सुरेश वह अधेड़ उम्र का शख़्स तो नहीं है, जिसे मैंने परसों-नरसों प्रताप के साथ बग़ीचे में टहलता हुआ देखा ? वह सुहास ?

संगीता हाँ, वही । और मैं तो जी ही नहीं सकती उसके बिना । वह अभी यहाँ आ रहा है, मुझसे मिलने । उसके आते ही हम दोनों साथ भाग निकलेंगे ।

सुरेश अरे तुम क्या पागल इरादा बना बैठी हो ? किसी अजनबी से इस तरह इश्क़ लड़ाते हुए तुम्हें शर्म नहीं आती ?

संगीता इसमें शर्म की क्या बात है ? अगर सुहास अजनबी भी होता तो भी मैं उससे प्यार करती । लेकिन जिसके बेटे को इस घर में रहते कोई आठ महीने हुए हैं, उसे अजनबी कैसे कहा जा सकता है ?

सुरेश इसी घर में ? तुम्हारा कहने का मतलब.... प्रताप ? संगू, तुम क्या कह रही हो ?

संगीता [*ठंडी साँस भरकर*] हाँ, सुहास प्रताप का पिता है ।

सुरेश अब बात समझ में आ रही है कुछ कुछ ! जो नेपाली ज़ेवर तुम पहने हुए थीं उस दिन, वे सुहास के दिए हुए थे, न कि प्रताप के ! मगर... मगर... जिसकी शादी किसी और से हो चुकी है उससे तुम कैसे शादी करोगी, संगू ?

संगीता सुहास शादी-शुदा नहीं है, तलाक़-शुदा है । अनीता को छोड़े हुए उसे पूरे चार साल हो गए हैं ।

सुरेश तो क्या तुम्हारे बेचारे माँ-बाप को इन सारी प्रेम-कहानियों की कुछ ख़बर है ?

संगीता [*उठकर, बाहर देखती हुई*] घर छोड़ते वक़्त मैं उन्हें सब कुछ समझा दूँगी । सब कुछ समझा दूँगी... [*बाहर से रुकती हुई टैक्सी की आवाज़ सुनाई देती है*]

थामना to hold, support

ज़िद f obstinacy

तंग आना to be fed up

छुटभैया m a nobody, someone of no importance

X **की शादी** Y **से करना** to marry X to Y

तुलना to be determined (to, **पर**)

राय f opinion

ज़ाहिर clear, evident

अधेड़ middle aged

शख़्स m individual, fellow

नरसों three days ago/ahead

टहलना to stroll

इश्क़ m romantic love; **इश्क़ लड़ाना** to have an affair

शर्म f shame; **शर्म आना** to feel ashamed

साँस f sigh; **ठंडी साँस भरना** to heave a deep sigh

न कि and not

तलाक़-शुदा divorced

समझाना to explain

Suresh Why are you sitting holding your head in your hands, Sangeeta? What's your trouble?

Sangeeta I'm fed up listening constantly to Mum's obstinacy, Uncle. She's determined to marry me to some nobody. And without asking my opinion!

Suresh It's clear that you're in love with someone else. I just heard you talking to some man on the phone. Who was it?

Sangeeta It was the person I'm in love with. I'll either marry him, or won't marry at all – whether the world accepts it or not!

Suresh It's not that middle-aged fellow I saw strolling in the garden with Pratap two or three days ago? That Suhas?

Sangeeta Yes, him. And I cannot *live* without him. He's just coming here to meet me. As soon as he arrives we'll elope together.

Suresh Oh no, what mad scheme have you gone and made up? Aren't you ashamed, carrying on with some stranger like this?

Sangeeta What's shameful about it? Even if Suhas were a stranger I'd still love him. But how can someone whose son has been living in this house for some eight months be called a stranger?

Suresh In this house? You mean to say... Pratap? Sangoo, what are you saying?

Sangeeta [*heaving a deep sigh*] Yes, Suhas is Pratap's father.

Suresh Now I'm beginning to understand the thing a little! That Nepali jewellery you were wearing that day was given by Suhas, not by Pratap! But... but... how will you marry someone who's already married to someone else, Sangoo?

Sangeeta Suhas isn't married, he's divorced. It's a full four years since he left Anita.

Suresh So are your poor parents aware of all these love stories at all?

Sangeeta [*getting up, looking out*] As I leave home I'll explain everything to them. I'll explain everything... [*the sound of a stopping taxi is heard from outside*]

Grammar

18.1 Participles

In English, participles like 'passing, passed' can either be part of a main verb ('the days are passing, the days have passed'), or can have a subsidiary role to the main verb, acting adverbially ('the days seem short in passing' or adjectivally 'I remember passed days'). A similar process applies in Hindi, using the imperfective and perfective participles (बीतता, बीता) in a number of constructions.

Sometimes the participle may take the auxiliary हुआ, whose slight effect is to confirm the *ongoing* quality of an imperfective (बीतता हुआ 'passing'), or the *completed* quality of a perfective (बीता हुआ 'passed').

Adding हुआ can resolve ambiguity. The basic sentence खिलौना टूटा था can mean either 'the toy was broken' (a state) or 'the toy had broken' (a past action). The former sense is specified by adding हुआ (खिलौना टूटा हुआ था), and the latter sense is specified by using a compound verb (खिलौना टूट गया था).

Used as an adjective, the participle (+ auxiliary) agrees with the noun it qualifies:

IMPERFECTIVE		PERFECTIVE	
बीतते (हुए) दिन	passing days	बीते (हुए) दिन	passed days
जलती (हुई) कार	a burning car	जली (हुई) कार	a burned car
हँसते (हुए) लड़के	laughing boys	फटी (हुई) किताबें	torn books

पुलिस ने भागते हुए चोर को पकड़ा ।	The police caught the absconding thief.
माँ ने रोती हुई लड़की को गोद में उठा लिया ।	Mother took up the crying girl into her lap.
वह रेडियो सुनता हुआ आदमी कौन है ?	Who is that man listening to the radio?
हमने कोई लड़की सड़क पर बैठी हुई देखी ।	We saw some girl sitting ('seated') on the road.
पलंग पर कुछ कपड़े पड़े हुए थे ।	There were some clothes lying ('fallen') on the bed.
वह रेशम की बनी हुई साड़ी सबसे सुन्दर है ।	That sari made of silk is the loveliest.

The perfective participle usages just shown describe a *state* that results from a previous *action*: the girl *had sat down* on the road (action) and consequently was now 'sitting' there (state); the clothes *had fallen* onto the bed (action) and consequently were now 'lying' there (state).

Used as an adverb, the participle (+ auxiliary) has an invariable -ए ending:

चिड़िया आकाश में उड़ते हुए दिखाई दी ।	The bird appeared flying in the sky.
हमने भूत को चलते-फिरते देखा ।	We saw the ghost wandering about.

मैंने उन्हें आपकी तारीफ़ करते सुना है।	I have heard them praising you.
माँ अपना सामान पकड़े हुए खड़ी थीं।	Mother was standing holding her luggage.
धोबी इस्तरी को लिए हुए आया था।	The dhobi had come bringing ('taking') the iron.
वह सलवार क़मीज़ पहने हुए थी।	She was wearing a salwar-qamiz.

> **!** खड़ा 'standing' is an adjective rather than a verb participle; but it behaves just like बैठा 'sitting, seated', पड़ा 'lying, fallen', लेटा 'lying, reclined' etc. Like these participles, it can take an auxiliary – खड़ा हुआ (like बैठा हुआ and पड़ा हुआ).

Participle constructions based on these principles are many and various. Here are some of the most important ones:

a) A participle is repeated (without हुआ) when an action is repeated over time:

दिन भर खेलते खेलते बच्चे थक गए।	Playing all day the children got tired.
इंतज़ार करते करते वह बेचैन हो रही थी।	Waiting constantly she was becoming restless.
बस्ती में घूमते घूमते हम ऊब गए।	We got bored wandering around the settlement.

Or when an action runs in parallel to that of the main verb:

टी०वी० को देखते देखते मैं इस्तरी कर रहा था।	While watching TV, I was doing the ironing.
गाड़ी की मरम्मत करते करते मिस्तरी गाना गाता रहा।	While repairing the car the mechanic went on singing.
हिन्दी सीखते सीखते हम हँसी-मज़ाक भी कम नहीं करते।	While learning Hindi we have plenty of laughs too.

Or to stress that the main-verb action happened *just* as the subsidiary action was done:

घर पहुँचते पहुँचते मेरे मन में तरह तरह की शंकाएँ पैदा हुईं ।

Arriving home, many kinds of doubts arose in my mind.

निबंध ख़त्म करते करते मुझे महसूस होने लगा कि मैंने ग़लत विषय चुना है ।

As I finished the essay I began to feel that I'd chosen the wrong subject.

b) A repeated imperfective participle in -ए followed by बचना 'to escape, survive' describes a narrow escape:

साइकिल से टकराकर वह गिरते गिरते बचा ।	Colliding with the bicycle, he nearly fell.
पुल से गिरकर वह डूबते डूबते बची ।	Falling from the bridge she narrowly escaped drowning.

c) An imperfective participle in -ए followed by समय or वक़्त means 'at the time of doing':

घर जाते समय हमसे मिलना ।	Meet us on your way home.
मरते वक़्त लोगों को बचपन के दिन याद आते हैं ।	At the time of dying, people remember their childhood days.

d) An imperfective participle in -ए followed by ही means 'immediately on doing', 'as soon as':

होटल पहुँचते ही हमने खाना खा लिया ।	We had our meal as soon as we reached the hotel.
पत्र पाते ही मैंने उत्तर लिख डाला ।	Immediately on receiving the letter I dashed off a reply.

In the two examples above, the main verb and the participle share a single subject. But when two separate entities are involved, the participle may be 'possessed' (using का) by one of them:

ख़त के आते ही मैंने जवाब लिख डाला ।	As soon as the letter came I dashed off a reply.

आपके स्वीकार करते ही दूसरों को भी बुलाया जाएगा।	As soon as you accept, the others will be invited too.

e) To indicate the passage of time *since a completed event took place*, the perfective participle is used as follows, with the unit of time as grammatical subject:

मेरे कुत्ते को मरे हुए सिर्फ़ एक महीना हुआ है।	It's only one month since my dog died.
श्रुति को ग्वालियर गए दो हफ़्ते हो गए हैं।	It's two weeks since Shruti went to Gwalior.

f) To indicate the passage of time *since a current situation began*, the imperfective participle is used as follows:

मुझे उर्दू सीखते हुए आठ महीने हुए हैं।	I've been learning Urdu for eight months.
लंदन में रहते हुए हमें एक साल हुआ है।	We've been living in London for one year.

g) बिना + perfective participle in -ए (e.g. **किए**) means 'without doing':

वह बिना बोले घास काटने लगा।	Without speaking he began to cut the grass.
बिना सोचे कुछ मत करना।	Don't do anything without thinking.

h) Both participles can be 'possessed' like nouns:

मेरा कहा कोई नहीं मानता।	Nobody accepts what I say ('my utterance').
यह लेख मेरा लिखा हुआ है।	This article was written by me.
रवि के रहते तू कुछ नहीं कर सकती।	You can't do anything while Ravi's around.
मेरे जीते जी यह घर बेचा नहीं जाएगा।	As long as I'm alive this house won't be sold.

i) A pairing of related transitive and intransitive verbs indicates the failure of an attempt (in the intransitive verb) despite someone's trying (in the transitive, 'possessed' by the person making the attempt):

हमारे बचाए वह नहीं बची ।	She didn't survive, despite our trying to save her.
ड्राइवर के रोके भी कार रुक नहीं पाई ।	Despite the driver's trying to stop it the car couldn't stop.
छोटू के उड़ाते भी वह पतंग तो उड़ने का नाम नहीं लेती ।	For all Chotu's attempts, that kite just refuses to fly.

18b A happy ending

NB: all the quotations in this dialogue are from classic film songs.

[सुहास और संगीता बैठक के एक कोने में सटे हुए बैठे हैं । प्रताप, सुरेश, और कुमार परिवार के सारे सदस्य भी पास बैठे हुए हैं – सिवाय प्रकाश के, जो तेज़ कदमों से बैठक को माप रहा है ।]

प्रकाश [*झट से ऐनक उतारके*] यह शादी नहीं हो सकती ! मेरे जीते जी यह शादी नहीं होगी !

दादी जी बेटे, थोड़ी दया से काम लो ! संगू के लिए किसी अच्छे-से लड़के की तलाश

	थी, तो यह सुहास टपक पड़ा ! बड़ा नेक आदमी है, और अच्छे स्वभाव का भी लगता है । इसमें क्या कमी है ? और प्यार जो है...
ऋषि	कमाल है, यहाँ सब लोग फ़िल्मी डॉयलॉग झाड़ने लगे हैं ! [*गाते हुए*] "कभी कभी मेरे दिल में ख़याल आता है... कि जैसे तुझको बनाया गया है मेरे लिए..."
सुरेश	कमला, ज़रा चाय बनवा दो न, सबों के लिए ?
कमला	ऐसे वक़्त में आपको चाय पीने-पिलवाने की कैसे सूझ सकती ?
ऋषि	"... तू सब से पहले सितारों में बस रही थी कहीं... तुझे ज़मीं पे बुलाया गया है मेरे लिए... कभी कभी..."
संगीता	अरे चुप भी करो ऋषि !
सुहास	प्रताप, टैक्सीवाले को कहलवा दो कि वह चला जाए ।
सुरेश	हाँ, टैक्सी को तो बाद में वापस बुलवाया जा सकता है । या आपका यहीं रुकने का इरादा है सुहास ?
कमला	[*सुरेश की बात को काटकर*] सुहास जी, आगे चलकर आप कहाँ रहने की सोच रहे हैं ?
सुहास	कमला जी, मेरा लखनऊ में एक अच्छा-सा घर है । और जैसे ही मेरा लन्दन-वाला घर बिक जाएगा वैसे ही एक नया घर बनवा लूँगा, यहीं दिल्ली में ही आपके इस घर के सामने...
ऋषि	[*एक नया गीत छेड़ते हुए*] "तेरे घर के सामने इक घर बनाऊँगा, तेरे घर के सामने दुनिया बसाऊँगा , तेरे..."
प्रकाश	ऋषि चुप कर । बहुत हो गया । [*सुहास की ओर मुड़कर, त्योरी चढ़ाते हुए*] आपका धंधा क्या है ? आपके गुज़ारे के साधन...?
सुहास	मैं नर्तक हूँ । मेरे लन्दन में रहते समय, जो भारतीय मूल के परिवार वहाँ बस गए हैं, वे मुझसे अपने बच्चों को कथक सिखवाते थे । अब तो मुझे भारत में ही यही काम करने के लिए बुलवाया गया है । श्रावण से स्थायी रूप से इस देश में बसा हुआ हूँ ।
ऋषि	[*फिर से गीत बदलकर*] "सावन का महीना, पवन करे सोर... जियरा रे झूमे ऐसे जैसे बनमा नाचे मोर..."
प्रकाश	[*कमला के कान में फुसफुसाते हुए*] इस साले नचवैये से तुम हमारी इकलौती बेटी की शादी करवाओगी क्या ? हमीं को नाच नचा रहा है यह ! [*सुहास की ओर बढ़ते हुए*] तो सुहास, आपको किसने यहाँ बुलाया है, दिल्ली की छोकरियों को नाच-वाच कराने के लिए ?

सुहास सरकारी नौकरी है । स्वयं प्रधान मंत्री ने मुझे यह नौकरी दिलवाई थी, यानी उन्होंने ही मुझे सुझाव दिया था कि मैं इस नौकरी के लिए अर्ज़ी दूँ ।

प्रकाश [*बड़े आश्चर्य से, खुले दिल से मुस्कराते हुए*] अच्छा ! तो नृत्य की दुनिया में आप काफ़ी जाने-पहचाने होंगे । अच्छा-सा वेतन भी मिलता होगा ! [*कमला से, कान में*] संगीता की माँ, बंगाली मार्केट से बढ़िया-सी मिठाई तुरंत मँगवाओ – लड्डू, जलेबियाँ...। [*सुहास से, बड़ी आत्मीयता से*] तो कहिए जनाब, क्या चलेगा ? चाय लेंगे ? नहीं नहीं, चाय का वक़्त निकल गया । बियर लेंगे कि ह्विस्की ?

अरुण [*अपने आप से*] ऐसा प्रतीत होता है कि हमारी पारिवारिक परिस्थितियों में एक आश्चर्यजनक परिवर्तन शीघ्र ही आनेवाला है ।

सुहास [*उठ खड़े होकर*] जो भी संगीता लेगी, वही लूँगा । [*संगीता की तरफ़ मुड़ते हुए*] संगू, तुम ही नहीं, तुम्हारे सारे घरवाले भी लाजवाब हैं !

ऋषि और राज [*हाथ में हाथ मिलाए, नाचते हुए, एक चौथा गीत छेड़कर*] "चौदहवीं का चाँद हो, या आफ़ताब हो; जो भी हो तुम – ख़ुदा की क़सम, लाजवाब हो..." ।

प्रकाश [*सुहास को गले लगाते हुए*] आओ सुहास बेटे !

सुहास और संगीता [*एक साथ, प्रकाश से*] पिताजी ! पिताजी !

प्रताप [*सुहास से*] पिताजी ! तुम्हारे सारे सपने पूरे हो रहे हैं ! ख़ुदा की क़सम, यह तो बड़ा कामयाब दिन निकला !

सुरेश कामयाब मेरा सिर ! यह डॉयलॉग बहुत लंबा हो रहा है । मैं तो चलता हूँ ।

दादी जी फ़िल्मी गाने क्या मुझे नहीं आते ? [*झूमती हुई, मस्त आवाज़ में गाने लगती हैं*] "अच्छा तो हम चलते हैं ! फिर कब मिलोगे ? जब तुम कहोगे ....." [*सब लोग हँसते हँसते लोट-पोट हो जाते हैं*]

बैठक f sitting room
सदस्य m member
पास nearby
तेज़ quick, rapid
क़दम m step, pace
मापना to measure, cover
झट से suddenly, briskly
ऐनक f spectacles
के जीते जी during the lifetime of
दया f compassion
स्वभाव m nature, disposition
टपकना to appear (unexpectedly), drop in
नेक good, virtuous, decent
कमी f lack, want
कमाल m miracle, wonder
डॉयलॉग m dialogue
झाड़ना to spout, pour out
बनवाना to cause to be made
सूझना to occur to the mind; **की [बात] सूझना** [an idea] to occur
सितारा m star
बसना to dwell, settle, inhabit
ज़मीं f (usually **ज़मीन**) f land, earth
पे (=पर) on, to
चुप करना to be quiet, shut up
कहलवाना to send word
बुलवाना to cause to be called
बात काटना to interrupt
आगे चलकर later on, in the future
की [बात] सोचना to think of doing, intend to do
छेड़ना to stir up, start up
इक (=एक) a, one
बसाना to settle, found
तयोरी f brow; **त्योरी चढ़ाना** to frown, scowl
धंधा m work, occupation
नर्तक m dancer
मूल m origin
कथक m kathak, a North Indian dance style
सिखवाना to cause to be taught
श्रावण m Shravan, a monsoon month (July–August)
स्थायी रूप से permanently
सावन m = **श्रावण**
पवन m wind
करे (dialect) = **करता/करती है**
सोर m **(=शोर)** noise, tumult (poetic)
जियरा m soul, heart (poetic)
झूमना to sway (in pleasure); **झूमे** (dialect) = **झूमता है**

बन m forest, wood, jungle; **बनमा** (dialect) = **बन में**
नाचना to dance; **नाचे** (dialect) = **नाचता है**
कान m ear
साला m, adj wife's brother; term of abuse
नचवैया m dancer (derogatory)
इकलौता sole, only (child)
नाच m dance; **नाच नचाना** to lead one a fine dance
छोकरी f young girl, lass
प्रधान मंत्री m prime minister
दिलवाना to cause to be given
यानी that is to say
अर्ज़ी f application; **अर्ज़ी देना** to apply
आश्चर्य m surprise
खुला open
मुस्कराना to smile
नृत्य m dance
जाना-पहचाना recognised, known
वेतन m pay, salary
आत्मीयता से cordially
जनाब sir
ह्विस्की f whisky
प्रतीत होना to appear, seem
पारिवारिक familial
परिस्थिति(याँ) f circumstance(s)
आश्चर्यजनक astonishing
लाजवाब beyond compare
हाथ मिलाना to join hands
चौदहवीं 14th (day of lunar month – full moon day)
आफ़ताब m sun
ख़ुदा m God; **ख़ुदा की क़सम** by God
क़सम f oath
गला m throat, neck; **गले लगाना** to embrace
मस्त blithely joyful, delighted
कामयाब successful
लोट-पोट rolling, helpless (with laughter)

[*Suhas and Sangeeta are sitting close in a corner of the sitting room. Pratap, Suresh, and all the members of the Kumar family are also sitting nearby – except Prakash, who is pacing rapidly up and down the room.*]

Prakash [*whipping his glasses off*] This marriage cannot take place! As long as I'm alive this marriage will not happen!

Dadi ji Son, have a little compassion! We were looking for a suitable boy for Sangoo, and this Suhas turns up! He's a very decent man, and seems kind-hearted. What is there lacking in him? And this thing called love...

Rishi How amazing, everyone's started spouting film dialogues here. [*singing*] 'At times I fancy in my heart... that just as you were made for me...'

Suresh Kamala, just get tea made for everybody, won't you?

Kamala How could you think of drinking and offering tea at such a time?

Rishi '... You first were dwelling somewhere 'midst the stars... you were called to earth for me...at times...'

Sangeeta Oh do be quiet, Rishi!

Suhas Pratap, have word sent to the taxi driver that he should go.

Suresh Yes, the taxi can be called back later. Or is it your intention to stop here, Suhas?

Kamala [*interrupting Suresh*] Suhas ji, where are thinking of living in the future?

Suhas Kamala ji, I have a pretty good house in Lucknow. And as soon as my London house sells I'll get a house built for myself right here in Delhi, opposite this house of yours...

Rishi [*launching into a new song*] 'Opposite your house I'll build a house, opposite your house I'll found a world, opposite ...'

Prakash Rishi, shut up. That's quite enough. [*turning towards Suhas, scowling*] What's your trade? Your means of livelihood...?

Suhas I'm a dancer. While I was living in London, the families of Indian origin who have settled there used to get their children taught kathak by me. Now I've been called to do the same work in India. I've been permanently settled in this country since Shravan.

Rishi [*changing songs again*] 'In Shravan's month the wind makes moan... my heart's a-sway like peacocks dancing in the wood...'

Prakash [*whispering in Kamala's ear*] Are you going to marry off our only daughter to this bloody dancer fellow? It's us he's leading a fine dance. [*moving towards Suhas*] So Suhas, who has invited you here to set the young girls of Delhi dancing and prancing?

Suhas It's a government position. The Prime Minister himself had the job given me, that is to say he himself suggested to me that I apply for it.

Prakash [*in great surprise, smiling open-heartedly*] Really! So you must be quite well-known in the world of dance ! And you must be getting a good salary too! [*to Kamala, in her ear*] Sangeeta's mother, have some quality sweets fetched from Bengali Market straightaway – laddus, jalebis... [*to Suhas, very cordially*] Well my dear sir, what'll it be? Will you have tea? No, no, the time for tea has passed – will you have beer, or whisky?

Arun [*to himself*] It appears that an astonishing transformation is about to occur imminently in our familial circumstances.

Suhas [*standing up*] I'll have whatever Sangeeta will have. [*turning towards Sangeeta*] Sangoo, not just you, your whole family's beyond compare!

Rishi & Raj [*dancing with hands joined, beginning a fourth song*] 'Are you a waxing moon, or a solar glare; whate'er you are – God's oath! – you are beyond compare...'

Prakash [*embracing Suhas*] Come Suhas, my son!

Suhas & Sangeeta [*together, to Prakash*] Father! Father!

Pratap [*to Suhas*] Father! All your dreams are being fulfilled! God's oath, this has turned out to be a very successful day!

Suresh Successful, my foot! This dialogue is getting very long. Me, I'm leaving.

Dadi ji [You think that] I can't sing film songs? [*swaying happily, she starts singing in a blithe voice*] 'Well then, I'm leaving. When'll we meet? Whene'er you say...' [*everybody rolls around in helpless laughter*]

> **!** The film lyrics quoted in this dialogue have a poetic register (hence the slightly purple translations): Persian words like आफ़ताब 'sun', dialect forms such as करे (= करता है) and Sanskrit words like पवन 'wind' would be out of place in everyday speech. Arun's speech is, typically, excessively Sanskritised.

Grammar

18.2 Intransitive and transitive verbs

In 14.2 we looked at the operation of intransitive and transitive verbs and saw that Hindi maintains a more crucial difference between the two than English does. For example, the Hindi equivalent of the sentence 'The gardener cut his finger' (माली की उँगली कट गई 'the gardener's finger became cut') will use intransitive

कटना 'to be cut', since using transitive काटना (माली ने अपनी उँगली को काटा, काट दिया) would imply that the cutting was deliberate. In this section, we look at the formal relationships between certain intransitive and transitive verbs.

You will have noticed that transitive verbs are often formed by lengthening the stem of the intransitive:

INTRANSITIVE		TRANSITIVE	
बनना	to be made	बनाना	to make
उठना	to rise	उठाना	to raise
पहुँचना	to arrive	पहुँचाना	to convey
बचना	to escape	बचाना	to save
लगना	to adhere	लगाना	to affix, apply
समझना	to understand	समझाना	to explain

Other transitives are formed by lengthening the non-final syllable:

कटना	to be cut	काटना	to cut
निकलना	to emerge	निकालना	to extract
मरना	to die	मारना	to kill, beat
लदना	to be loaded	लादना	to load

This change is sometimes accompanied by a change to the first syllable. (A semi-vowel, usually ल, is added to a stem ending in a long vowel, as with सोना 'to sleep'.)

ऊ > उ	घूमना	to go round	घुमाना	to make go round
ए > इ	लेटना	to lie down	लिटाना	to lay down
ऐ > इ	बैठना	to sit	बिठाना	to seat
ओ > उ	सोना	to sleep	सुलाना	to make sleep

Other intransitive-transitives pairs are formed by vowel changes as shown here – sometimes with a change of consonant also:

उ > ओ	धुलना	to be washed	धोना	to wash
ऊ > ओ	टूटना	to be broken	तोड़ना	to break
इ > ए	बिकना	to be sold	बेचना	to sell
ई > ए	दीखना	to be visible	देखना	to see

Lengthening of the stem also occurs in the second of two related transitive verbs:

TRANSITIVE 1		TRANSITIVE 2	
खाना	to eat	खिलाना	to serve (food)
बोलना	to speak	बुलाना	to call
देखना	to see	दिखाना	to show
सुनना	to hear	सुनाना	to recite, make hear

Thus some verbs fall into a three-way series: intransitive, plus two successive transitives:

टूटना	to be broken	तोड़ना	to break	तुड़ाना	to have broken
दिखना	to appear	देखना	to see	दिखाना	to show

18.3 Causative verbs

A further extension of the pattern shown in 18.2 is the causative verb, whose stem ends in -वा-. Thus लिखवाना means 'to cause to be written', 'to have written (by somebody)'. That 'somebody', when specified, takes से. Causatives are not always listed independently in dictionaries.

हम घर बनवा रहे हैं।	We're having a house built.
हमने बच्चों को हिन्दी सिखवाई है।	We've had Hindi taught to the children.
हमें दर्ज़ी से कुछ कुरते सिलवाने हैं।	We have to get some kurtas sewn by the tailor.
लखपति ने अपनी कविता का अनुवाद करवाया।	The millionaire had his poetry translated.
किसी से डाक्टर को बुलवा लो।	Get someone to call the doctor. (lit. 'Get the doctor called by someone'.)

EXERCISE 18a.1 Answer the questions.

१ इस शहर (या गाँव) में रहते हुए आपको कितने दिन हुए हैं ?

२ जिस कमरे में आप बैठे हुए / बैठी हुई हैं, उसका वर्णन कीजिए ।

३ आज आप कैसे कपड़े पहने हुए हैं ?

४ बिना भारत गए क्या हिन्दी सीखना संभव है ?

५ पैसा जोड़ते जोड़ते जो लोग लाखों रुपये कमाते हैं, उनको क्या कहा जाता है ?

६ इस किताब को छपे हुए कितने साल हुए हैं ?

७ क्या आप नहाते समय गाना गाते / गाती हैं ? किस तरह का गाना ?

८ क्या इन सवालों के जवाब लिखते लिखते आप थक गए / गई हैं ?

EXERCISE 18a.2 Fill the gaps with the appropriate participle. Then translate.

१ अपने दोस्तों का इंतज़ार ......[करना]...... हम ऊबने लगे ।

२ फ़र्श पर ......[पड़ना]......कपड़ों को उठाओ और उन्हें उस......[टूटना]...... कुरसी पर रख दो ।

३ लखनऊ में ......[रहना]......मुझे सात महीने ......[होना]......हैं ।

४ वह ......[गाना]...... लड़की कौन है ? उसे गाना ......[सीखना]......कितने साल हुए हैं ?

५ इस स्कूल में ......[पढ़ना]......बच्चे लोग तो काम करने का नाम नहीं लेते ।

६ अंकल के ......[पहुँचना]......ही सारे घरवाले चुप हो गए ।

EXERCISE 18b.1 Translate.

1 If you get thirsty, please have the teaboy called and have yourself some tea made.
2 If you can't understand the story, get it translated into English by someone.
3 Pandit ji says we should have the children taught Sanskrit words, and not Urdu words.
4 Without saying anything she closed the book and put it in the cupboard.
5 While complaining to the neighbours I was learning Hindi from them.
6 Watching television I began to realise that many people mix a lot of English words in their Hindi.
7 The broken toys were lying on the floor.
8 As soon as my friend got home I told her what had happened.

EXERCISE 18b.2 Translate.

आप शायद जानना चाहेंगे कि आगे चलकर कुमार परिवार में क्या क्या हुआ। बहुत लंबी कहानी है; किसी दिन हम इसके बारे में विस्तार से लिखेंगे। फ़िलहाल मैं आपको बस इतना बताऊँ कि सबों की ज़िन्दगी बड़ी ख़ुशी से बीती (सिवाय बेचारे सुरेश की)। कहने की ज़रूरत नहीं कि संगीता और सुहास की शादी हो गई, और बहुत धूमधाम से; आजकल वे दिल्ली में ही रह रहे हैं, और लखनऊ-वाला घर तो लन्दन से आए हुए कुछ हिन्दी के विद्यार्थियों को किराये पर दे दिया गया है। अगर आप कभी अपने को दिल्ली में पाएँ, तो खाँ मार्केट की किसी दुकान में जाकर आपको संगीता और सुहास ख़रीदारी करते हुए दिखाई देंगे – हमेशा एक साथ, हमेशा मुस्कराते हुए, हमेशा ख़ुश। संगीता को बच्चा भी होनेवाला है। परिवार में एक तकलीफ़ यह हुई कि दादीजी की तबियत कुछ समय के लिए ठीक नहीं रही; दो तीन महीनों तक उनको लेकर बहुत चिंता रही। पर अब तो वे सुधर गई हैं।

आपको यह जानकर ख़ुशी होगी कि दफ़्तर में प्रकाश की तरक़्क़ी हो रही है, जिसका एक नतीजा यह है कि वह छोटू की मदद भी कर पा रहा है; अभी छोटू गाड़ी चलाना सीख रहा है – वह प्रकाश का ड्राइवर बनेगा। अरुण और प्रेम की दूसरी किताब गरम गरम समोसों की तरह बिक रही है; लगता है कि अंत में उन्होंने प्रकाश की सलाह को स्वीकार कर लिया होगा, क्योंकि उनकी यह दूसरी किताब एक प्रेम कहानी है – "दास्तान दो दिलों की", जिस में संगीता की पूरी कहानी विस्तार से बताई गई है। संभव है कि इसकी फ़िल्म भी बनेगी, बाद में।

राज और ऋषि के बीच जो वैर था वह धीरे धीरे ख़त्म हो जा रहा है, दोनों में एक दोस्ती-सी बन रही है – हालांकि कभी कभी वह पुराना युद्ध फिर से मच भी जाता है। सुरेश के विषय में क्या कहा जाए; कई कारणों से उसे तो बहुत दुःख उठाना पड़ा है, और ज़िंदगी से ऊबकर वह शराब कुछ ज़्यादा पीने लगा है। पहले तो वह किसी होटल में काम कर रहा था, पर उसके ज़्यादा पीने की वजह से उसकी नौकरी ख़त्म हो गई है। ख़ुदा जाने, आगे क्या होगा उसका। खन्ना साहब कुछ समय के लिए लन्दन जानेवाले हैं, काम के सिलसिले में, और उमा को भी लन्दन में ही अच्छी-सी नौकरी मिल गई है। हरीश तो अमेरिका के किसी विश्वविद्यालय में बी० ए० करने जाएगा, जबकि पिंकी की शादी एक अँग्रेज़ से होनेवाली है। और प्रताप ? उसकी आगे की कहानी काफ़ी दिलचस्प है (अगर अरुण इस समय यहाँ होता तो कहता कि "अद्भुत है !")। हाँ, प्रताप की ज़िन्दगी में क्या क्या हो जाता है, यह सुनकर आपको आश्चर्य होगा; पर उसकी कहानी तो किसी दूसरी किताब में बताई जाएगी !

EXERCISE 18b.3 Translate.

दोस्तो, आप अभी इस किताब का अठारहवाँ पाठ ख़त्म कर रहे हैं – आपने बहुत मेहनत से काम किया है । रास्ता कुछ लंबा था; आपके साथ चलना मुझे बहुत अच्छा लगा । मुझे आशा है कि भविष्य में आपकी हिन्दी की पढ़ाई जारी रहेगी । यह किताब तो ख़त्म हो रही है, लेकिन पढ़ाई के रास्ते का कोई अंत नहीं है । आपके मन में यह प्रश्न उठ सकता है कि आगे कैसे पढ़ना चाहिए ? मेरा पहला सुझाव यह है कि आप एकाध अच्छे-से शब्दकोश को ज़रूर ख़रीद लें, जिससे कि किताबों और अख़बारों को पढ़ना थोड़ा आसान हो जाएगा । आर० एस० मेकग्रेगर (R.S.McGregor) की "Hindi-English Dictionary", जो आक्सफ़र्ड युनिवर्सिटी प्रेस से प्रकाशित हुई है, बहुत ही अच्छी है; यह शब्दकोश आक्सफ़र्ड से भी छपा है और दिल्ली से भी, इसलिए आसानी से मिलना चाहिए । इसके अलावा हरदेव बाहरी के कई शब्दकोश भी बहुत बढ़िया हैं । इन किताबों को अपने पास रखें । आपको सरल कहानियों को पढ़ने में ज़्यादा मुश्किल नहीं होनी चाहिए । मेरा दूसरा सुझाव यह है कि आप हिन्दी फ़िल्में देखा करें, जिससे कि आपको आम बातचीत को सुनने और समझने का अभ्यास हो जाए । और अगर हो सके तो आप भारत जाने की कोशिश करें – या किसी दूसरे देश में जहाँ हिन्दी भाषा बोली जाती है; तब तो हरेक हिन्दी-बोलनेवाला आपका अध्यापक बन जाएगा, चाहे पंडित हो, चाहे ट्रेन का मुसाफ़िर, चाहे दुकानदार ! जो भी हो, मुझे पूरा विश्वास है कि आपको हिन्दी सीखने और बोलने में बहुत आनंद आएगा । नमस्ते ।

Vocabulary

अधेड़ middle aged

अनुवाद m translation

अर्ज़ी f application

आकाश m sky

आत्मीयता से cordially

आफ़ताब m sun, solar glow

आश्चर्य m surprise; **आश्चर्यजनक** astonishing

इक (=एक) a, one

इकलौता sole, only (child)

इश्क़ m romantic love; **इश्क़ लड़ाना** to have an affair

इस्तरी f clothes iron; ironing

उड़ाना to make fly; to indulge

ऊबना to be bored

एकाध one or two, a couple (of)

कथक m kathak, a North Indian dance style

क़दम ^{m} step, pace
कमाल ^{m} miracle, wonder
कमी ^{f} lack, want
करे (dialect) = करता/करती है
क़सम ^{f} oath
कहलवाना to send word
कान ^{m} ear
ख़ुदा ^{m} God; ख़ुदा की क़सम by God; ख़ुदा जाने God knows
खुला open
गला ^{m} throat, neck; गला लगाना to embrace
गिरना to fall
गोद ^{f} lap, embrace
घास ^{f} grass
घुमाना to make go round
चुनना to choose
चुप करना to be quiet, shut up
चौदहवीं 14th (day of lunar month – full moon day)
छुटभैया ^{m} a nobody, someone of no importance
छेड़ना to stir up, start up
छोकरी ^{f} young girl, lass
जनाब sir
ज़मीं ^{f} (also ज़मीन ^{f}) land, earth
जाना-पहचाना recognised, known
ज़ाहिर clear, evident
ज़िद ^{f} obstinacy
जियरा ^{m} (poetic) soul, heart
झट से suddenly, briskly
झाड़ना to spout, pour out
झूमना to sway (in pleasure); झूमे (dialect) = झूमता है
टकराना to collide
टपकना to drop in, appear unexpectedly
टहलना to stroll
टूटना to break, be broken
डॉयलॉग ^{m} dialogue
तंग आना to be fed up
तलाक़-शुदा divorced
तुड़ाना to cause to be broken
तुलना to be determined (to, पर)
तेज़ quick, rapid
थामना to hold, support
दया ^{f} compassion
दर्ज़ी ^{m} tailor
दास्तान ^{f} tale
दिलवाना to cause to be given
दीखना to appear, be visible, seem
दुःख ^{m} grief, pain, suffering
धंधा ^{m} work, occupation
धूमधाम ^{m} pomp, show
न कि and not
नचवैया ^{m} dancer (derogatory)
नरसों three days ago/ahead
नर्तक ^{m} dancer
नाच ^{m} dance; नाच नचाना to lead (someone) a fine dance

नाचना to dance; नाचे (dialect) = नाचता है

नृत्य m dance

नेक good, virtuous, decent

पतंग f kite (toy)

परिस्थिति(याँ) f circumstance(s)

पवन m wind

पहुँचाना to convey, deliver

पारिवारिक familial

पास nearby (adverb)

पे (=पर) on, to

पैदा होना to be born, produced

प्रतीत होना to appear, seem

प्रधान मंत्री m prime minister

फिरना to turn, move

फ़िलहाल in the meantime

बचना to escape, survive

बचाना to rescue, save

बन m forest, wood, jungle; बनमा (dialect) = बन में

बसना to dwell, settle, inhabit

बसाना to settle, found

बस्ती f settlement, slum

बात काटना to interrupt

की [बात] सोचना to think of doing, intend to do

बीतना to pass (of time)

बेचैन restless

बैठक f sitting room

मरम्मत f repair; की मरम्मत करना to repair, set right

मस्त blithely joyful, delighted

मापना to measure, cover

मिलाना to join (e.g. hands); to mix

मुस्कराना to smile

मूल m origin

यानी that is to say

राय f opinion

रेशम m silk

लखपति m rich man, 'millionaire'

लगाना to apply, affix

लदना to be loaded

लाजवाब beyond compare

लिटाना to make lie down

लेटना to lie, recline

लोट-पोट rolling, helpless (with laughter)

वर्णन m description; का वर्णन करना to describe

विस्तार से at length, in detail

वेतन m pay, salary

शंका f doubt, suspicion

शख़्स m individual, fellow

शर्म f shame; शर्म आना to feel ashamed

शादी; X की शादी Y से करना to marry X to Y

श्रावण m Shravan, a monsoon month (July–August)

सदस्य m member

समझाना to explain; to talk (someone) round; to console
सलवार क़मीज़ f salwar qameez
साँस f sigh; **ठंडी साँस भरना** to heave a deep sigh
साला m, adj wife's brother; term of abuse
सावन m = **श्रावण**, monsoon month (July–August)
सितारा m star
सिलवाना to cause to be sewn
सिलसिला m connection; **के सिलसिले में** in connection with
सुलाना to make sleep
सूझना to occur to the mind
सोर m (=**शोर** m) noise, tumult
स्थायी रूप से permanently
स्वभाव m nature, disposition
स्वीकार करना to accept
हँसी-मज़ाक m laughter, fun, joking
हाथ मिलाना to join hands
ह्विस्की f whisky

APPENDIXES

Appendix 1: Numbers

Try learning the numbers *horizontally* as progressions of tens, as well as *vertically* as progressions of units.

0 शून्य				
1 एक	11 ग्यारह	21 इक्कीस	31 इकत्तीस	41 इकतालीस
2 दो	12 बारह	22 बाईस	32 बत्तीस	42 बयालीस
3 तीन	13 तेरह	23 तेईस	33 तैंतीस	43 तैंतालीस
4 चार	14 चौदह	24 चौबीस	34 चौंतीस	44 चवालीस
5 पाँच	15 पंद्रह	25 पच्चीस	35 पैंतीस	45 पैंतालीस
6 छह, छै, छः	16 सोलह	26 छब्बीस	36 छत्तीस	46 छियालीस
7 सात	17 सत्रह	27 सत्ताईस	37 सैंतीस	47 सैंतालीस
8 आठ	18 अठारह	28 अट्ठाईस	38 अड़तीस	48 अड़तालीस
9 नौ	19 उन्नीस	29 उनतीस	39 उनतालीस	49 उनचास
10 दस	20 बीस	30 तीस	40 चालीस	50 पचास

51 इक्यावन	61 इकसठ	71 इकहत्तर	81 इक्यासी	91 इक्यानवे
52 बावन	62 बासठ	72 बहत्तर	82 बयासी	92 बानवे
53 तिरपन	63 तिरसठ	73 तिहत्तर	83 तिरासी	93 तिरानवे
54 चौवन	64 चौंसठ	74 चौहत्तर	84 चौरासी	94 चौरानवे
55 पचपन	65 पैंसठ	75 पचहत्तर	85 पचासी	95 पचानवे
56 छप्पन	66 छियासठ	76 छिहत्तर	86 छियासी	96 छियानवे
57 सत्तावन	67 सरसठ	77 सतहत्तर	87 सत्तासी	97 सत्तानवे
58 अट्ठावन	68 अड़सठ	78 अठहत्तर	88 अट्ठासी	98 अट्ठानवे
59 उनसठ	69 उनहत्तर	79 उन्यासी	89 नवासी	99 निन्यानवे
60 साठ	70 सत्तर	80 अस्सी	90 नब्बे	100 सौ

Numbers featuring 'hundreds' are expressed without the 'and' that appears in English: दो सौ तीन 'two hundred and three'.

Higher numerals are divided by commas to indicate groups of thousands (हज़ार), hundred thousands (लाख, 'lakh'), ten million (करोड़, 'crore'):

100,000 = 1 लाख

100,00,000 = 100 लाख = 1 करोड़ (10,000,000)

२,९२,३०,६३७ दो करोड़ बानवे लाख तीस हज़ार छह सौ सैंतीस (29,230,637)

The term प्रतिशत 'percent' is used before the measured item just like any other 'quantity' word: दस किलो चावल '10 kilos of rice'; दस प्रतिशत लोग '10 percent of the people'.

'Divided by' is बटे 'over' (from बँटना or बटना 'to be divided'), as in address formulae like '17/4 सत्रह बटे चार' ('house 17 in block 4').

Appendix 2: Money and shopping

The rupee (रुपया) consists of 100 paisa (पैसा). Sums of money are quoted in the usual decimal system, preceded by the abbreviation रु० for रुपया; in English this is rendered 'Re.' in the singular, 'Rs' in the plural. Thus रु० ४२.५० is Rs 42.50.

यह कितने का है ?	How much is this?
इसका दाम क्या है ?	What's the price of this?
यह किताब एक सौ साठ रुपये की है ।	This book costs Rs 160.
कुल मिलाकर कितना हुआ ?	How much is that altogether?
डेढ़ सौ रुपये में कितना कपड़ा मिलेगा ?	How much cloth will I get for Rs 150?
केले तुम कैसे दे रहे हो ?	What's the rate for bananas?
बहुत महँगा है, भाव कुछ कम कर देना ।	It's very expensive, bring the rate down a bit.
मेरे पास खुले पैसे नहीं हैं ।	I don't have change.

Appendix 3: The calendar

The western calendar is used for everyday events, but religious and ceremonial events follow the Hindu calendar; this is based on lunar months but solar years, and a 'leap month' (मलमास) added after every 30th month makes up for the discrepancy. Each month is divided into a 'bright' or 'waxing' fortnight (शुक्ल पक्ष) and a 'dark' or 'waning' fortnight (कृष्ण पक्ष or बदी). Although calendars vary, the new year is often celebrated as beginning on the first day of the dark fortnight of the month चैत.

This wheel shows the months in Hindi (outer part of dark circle) and Sanskrit (inner part); all are masculine. English month names ending in -ई are feminine, the rest masculine.

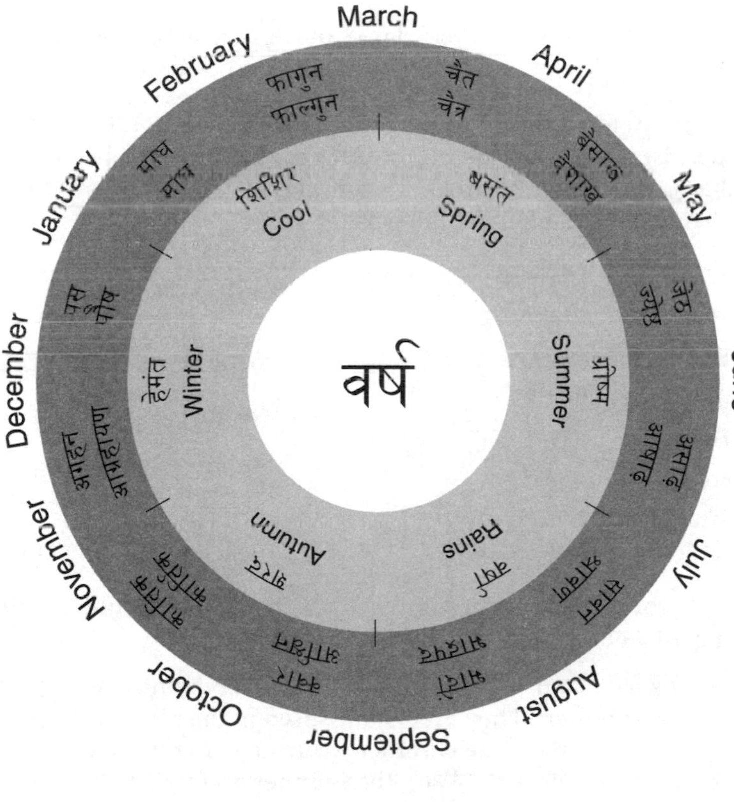

Numerous dating systems other than the western system are used in India. The commonest, विक्रम संवत् ('VS') dates from the era (संवत्) of King Vikramaditya, which began in 57–58 CE. To convert VS to CE, subtract 58 if the VS date falls between the second half of पूस and the first half of फागुन (inclusive); otherwise subtract 57. Vikram dates are usually identified by the word संवत्, while dates in the Christian calendar are preceded by सन् (or ईसवी सन् 'Christian era'); thus संवत २००४ = ईसवी सन् १९४७.

Examples of dates expressed according to the Vikram calendar are:

माघ शक्ल पक्ष १२ संवत् २००९	12th day of the bright fortnight of Magh, VS (Vikram Samvat) 2009 (= CE 1952)
आश्विन बदी ३ संवत् १७६८	3rd day of the dark fortnight of Ashwin, VS 1768 (= CE 1711)

Many Hindu festivals are named after the Sanskrit month: राम नवमी, Rama's birthday, is on चैत शुक्ल पक्ष ९ (the ninth day of the bright half of Chait), and जन्माष्टमी, Krishna's birthday, is on भादों कृष्ण पक्ष (the eighth day of the dark half of Bhadon).

The days of the week are:

Monday	सोमवार
Tuesday	मंगलवार
Wednesday	बुधवार
Thursday	गुरुवार, बृहस्पतिवार
Friday	शुक्रवार
Saturday	शनिवार
Sunday	रविवार, इतवार

The 'वार' component, meaning 'day', can be dropped colloquially, leaving सोम, मंगल, बुध etc.

The nouns जाड़ा and सरदी ('cold') are used for 'winter', and गरमी ('heat') for 'summer'. They are usually used in the plural (जाड़ों में 'in the winter, गरमियों में 'in the summer'), but stay singular when used with other nouns (गरमी की छुट्टियाँ 'the summer holidays').

Appendix 4: Kinship terms

The Indian family tree identifies relationships much more precisely than the English equivalent. First cousins are called चचेरा भाई/बहिन (paternal), ममेरा भाई/बहिन (maternal). These are distinguished from सगा भाई / सगी बहिन 'real brother/sister'.

The word साला, 'brother-in-law', doubles as a term of abuse: to call someone साला is to imply carnal knowledge of that person's sister. The word has become so common colloquially that it is even used as an adjective. This usage is sometimes extended into adjectival territory, when साला qualifies a noun.

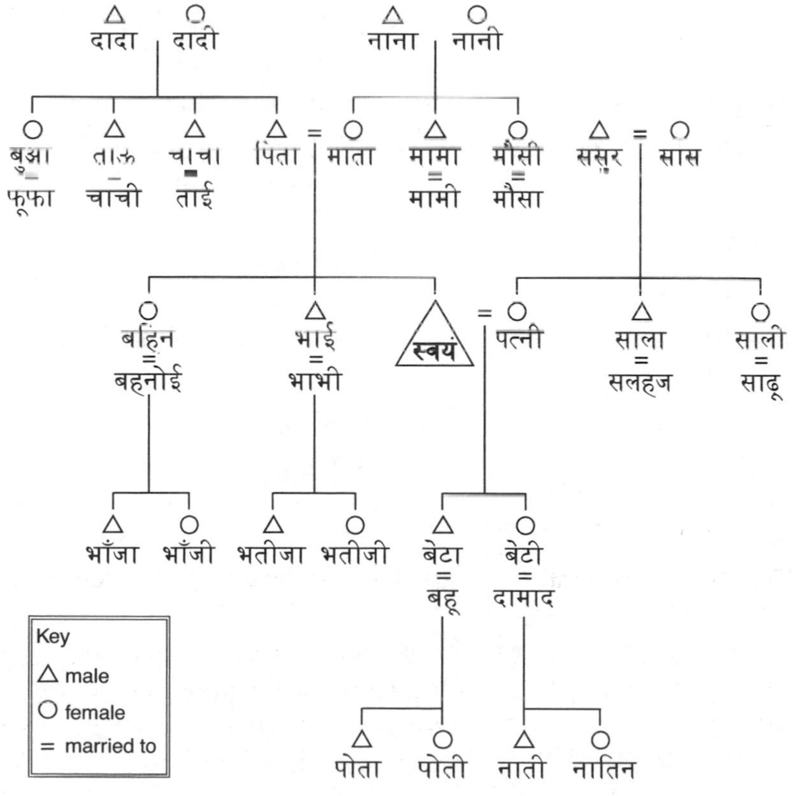

Appendix 5: Body and health

ख़ून^{m}, रक्त^{m} blood
गरदन^{f} neck
गर्भ^{m} womb
गाल^{m} cheek
घुटना^{m} knee
चमड़ी^{f} skin
छाती^{f}, सीना^{m} chest
जीभ^{f} tongue
जोड़^{m} joint
टाँग^{f} leg
त्वचा^{f} skin
दाँत^{m} tooth
नाख़ून^{m} nail
पसीना^{m} (आना) sweat
पाँव^{m}, पैर^{m} foot
पाँव की उँगली^{f} toe
पीठ^{f} back
फेफड़ा^{m} lung
बाँह^{f} arm
माथा^{m} forehead
शरीर^{m} body
हड्डी^{f} bone

इलाज^{m} treatment, cure
उलटी^{f} (होना, करना) vomiting
कब्ज़^{f} constipation
कमज़ोर weak
कमज़ोरी^{f} weakness
क़ै^{f} (आना, होना, करना) vomiting, nausea
गर्भ^{m} होना to be pregnant
खाँसी^{f} (आना) cough
चेचक^{f}, शीतला^{f} smallpox
टट्टी^{f} (करना) faeces, stool
तंदुरुस्त healthy, fit
तंदुरुस्ती^{f}, सेहत^{f}, स्वास्थ्य^{m} health
दर्द^{m} (होना, करना) pain
दस्त^{m} (आना) diarrhoea
पचना to be digested
पेशाब^{m} (करना) urine
बवासीर^{f} piles
मरीज़$^{m, f}$, रोगी$^{m, f}$ patient
मलेरिया^{m} malaria
सुई^{f} (लगाना) injection, 'needle'
हैज़ा^{m} cholera

उसे गर्भ है।	She is pregnant.
उसे दस्त आते हैं।	He/she's got diarrhoea.
मुझे क़ै हो गई।	I vomited.
कल उसे उलटी हुई।	He/she vomited yesterday.
उन्हें कब्ज़ है।	They're constipated.
मुझे खाँसी आती है।	I have a cough.

मेरा गला ख़राब है ।	I have a sore throat.
उन्हें चोट लगी ।	They got hurt, injured.
मुझे चक्कर आ रहा है ।	I'm feeling dizzy.
हम उसे डाक्टर को दिखाएँगे ।	We'll take him/her to the doctor.
दवा खाओ/पिओ ।	Take/drink the medicine.
मुझे मच्छर/कुत्ते ने काटा है ।	A mosquito/dog has bitten me.
मेरा गला बैठ गया है ।	I am hoarse.
मेरे सिर में दर्द है ।	I have a headache.
मेरे जोड़ दर्द कर रहे हैं ।	My joints are hurting.
उबला पानी पिया करो ।	Always drink boiled water.
शौचालय/टॉयलेट किधर है ?	Where's the loo?

Appendix 6: Letterwriting

प्रिय सुरेश	Dear Suresh
आदरणीय महोदय/महोदया	Dear ('respected') sir/madam
सादर नमस्ते ।	Respectful greeting (opening phrase)
सप्रेम नमस्ते ।	Affectionate greeting (opening phrase)
आप सपरिवार सकुशल होंगे ।	I hope you and your family are well.
तुम्हारा ख़त पढ़कर ख़ुशी हुई ।	I was pleased to read your letter.
आपका १ मई का पत्र मिला ।	I received your letter of 1 May.
प्रकाश की ओर से प्यार ।	Prakash sends his love.
रवि से मेरी नमस्ते कहना ।	Say hello to Ravi.
बच्चों को प्यार ।	Love to the children.
दीवाली की शुभकामनाएँ ।	Best wishes for Diwali.
शेष कुशल है ।	Everything else is all right, auspicious.
पत्र का उत्तर जल्दी दें ।	Reply soon.
आपकी कमला	Yours, Kamala
भवदीय	Yours sincerely (भवदीया fem. writer).
पुनश्च	postscript

Appendix 7: Summary of verb tenses and constructions

References are to the relevant paragraphs.

IMPERFECTIVE	PERFECTIVE	CONTINUOUS
बोलता speaks	बोला spoke	बोल रहा speaking
	वह बोला he spoke	
वह बोलता है 6.1 he speaks	वह बोला है 11.2 he has spoken	वह बोल रहा है 8.1 he is speaking
वह बोलता था 7.1 he used to speak	वह बोला था 11.2 he had spoken	वह बोल रहा था 8.1 he was speaking
वह बोलता होगा 9.2 he will/must speak	वह बोला होगा 11.4 .... have spoken	वह बोल रहा होगा 9.2 .... be speaking
वह बोलता हो 9.3 he may speak, be speaking	वह बोला हो 11.4 .... have spoken	वह बोल रहा हो 10.2 .... be speaking

वह बोलेगी	she will speak 9.1
वह बोले	he/she may speak 10.1
हिन्दी बोली जाती है	Hindi is spoken 14.1
वह बोलती जाती है	she goes on speaking 15.1
वह बोलती रहती है	she continues speaking 15.1
वह बोला करती है	she speaks habitually 15.2
उसे बोलना चाहिए	he/she should speak 13.2
उसे बोलना है	he/she is to speak 13.3
उसे बोलना पड़ता है	he/she has to speak (habitually) 13.3
उसे बोलना पड़ा	he/she had to speak (unexpectedly) 13.3
उसे बोलना पड़ेगा	he/she will *have* to speak 13.3

अगर वह बोले(गी)	if she speaks 10.4
अगर वह बोली	if she spoke, speaks 17.1
अगर वह बोलती	if she spoke, had spoken 17.1
अगर वह बोली होती	if she had spoken 17.1
वह बोल सकती है	she can speak 12.3
वह बोल नहीं पाई	she didn't manage to speak 12.3
उसे बोलना आता है	he/she knows how to speak 9.6
वह बोल चुकी है	she has already spoken 12.3
वह बोलने लगी	she began speaking 14.3
उसने बोलना शुरू किया	he/she began to speak 14.3
उसे बोलने दो	let him/her speak 14.4
वह बोलना चाहती है	she wants to speak 10.3
बोलकर	having spoken 12.1
वह बोलनेवाली है	she is about to speak 10.5
बोल, बोलो, बोलिए(गा), बोलना	speak! 5.2

KEY TO EXERCISES

Pronunciation key

You may like to refer to this key while listening to the sounds and words at the beginning of the cassette.

Vowels

अ *a*	अब *ab*	सब *sab*
आ *ā*	आप *āp*	का *kā*
इ *i*	इस *is*	कि *ki*
ई *ī*	ई-मेल *ī-mel*	की *kī*
उ *u*	उस *us*	पुलिस *pulis*
ऊ *ū*	ऊपर *ūpar*	तू *tū*
ऋ *ṛ*	ऋषि *ṛṣi*	कृपा *kṛpā*
ए *e*	एक *ek*	के *ke*
ऐ *ai*	ऐसा *aisā*	पैसा *paisā*
ओ *o*	ओर *or*	बोलो *bolo*
औ *au*	और *aur*	चौदह *caudah*

Nasalised vowels

अँ *ã*	हँसी *hãsī*	महँगा *mahãgā*
आँ *ā̃*	हाँ *hā̃*	पाँच *pā̃c*
ईं *ī̃*	ईंट *ī̃ṭ*	आईं *āī̃*
उँ *ũ*	उँगली *ũglī*	मुँह *mũh*
एँ *ẽ*	में *mẽ*	सड़कें *saṛkẽ*
ऐं *aĩ*	मैं *maĩ*	हैं *haĩ*
ओं *õ*	होंठ *hõṭh*	दोस्तों *dostõ*

Consonants

क *ka*	कल *kal*	स्कूल *skūl*
क़ *qa*	क़ीमत *qīmat*	बाक़ी *bāqī*
ख *kha*	खाना *khānā*	रखो *rakho*
ख़ *kha*	ख़याल *khayāl*	सख़्त *sakht*
ग *ga*	गाना *gānā*	लगा *lagā*
ग़ *ga*	ग़लत *galat*	बग़ीचा *bagīcā*
घ *gha*	घर *ghar*	माघ *māgh*
च *ca*	चाबी *cābī*	चाचा *cācā*
छ *cha*	छात्र *chātr*	कुछ *kuch*
ज *ja*	जो *jo*	आज *āj*
ज़ *za*	ज़रूर *zarūr*	नज़र *nazar*
झ *jha*	झूठ *jhūṭh*	समझ *samajh*
ट *ṭa*	टेढ़ा *ṭeṛhā*	मार्केट *mārkeṭ*
ठ *ṭha*	ठीक *ṭhīk*	पाठ *pāṭh*
ड *ḍa*	डर *ḍar*	अंडा *aṇḍa*
ड़ *ṛa*	बड़ी *baṛī*	भीड़ *bhīṛ*
ढ *ḍha*	ढाई *ḍhāī*	ढंग *ḍhang*
ढ़ *ṛha*	पढ़ाई *paṛhāī*	डेढ़ *ḍeṛh*
ण *ṇa*	कारण *kāraṇ*	रामायण *rāmāyaṇ*
त *ta*	तीन *tīn*	सात *sāt*
थ *tha*	था *thā*	साथ *sāth*
द *da*	दो *do*	विदेश *videś*
ध *dha*	धो *dho*	आधा *ādhā*
न *na*	नाक *nāk*	निकलना *nikalnā*
प *pa*	पंजाबी *panjābī*	ऊपर *ūpar*
फ *pha*	फिर *phir*	सफल *saphal*
फ़ *fa*	फ़्लैट *flaiṭ*	साफ़ *sāf*
ब *ba*	बीस *bīs*	अब *ab*
भ *bha*	भारत *bhārat*	अभी *abhī*
म *ma*	माँ *mā̃*	धीमा *dhīmā*

य *ya*	यह *yah*	समय *samay*
र *ra*	रात *rāt*	चार *cār*
ल *la*	लाल *lāl*	कल *kal*
व *va*	वह *vah*	रवि *ravi*
श *śa*	शाबाश *śābāś*	आशा *āśā*
ष *ṣa*	भाषा *bhāṣā*	ऋषि *ṛṣi*
स *sa*	सरल *saral*	दस *das*
ह *ha*	हिन्दी *hindī*	वाह *vāh*

Doubled consonants

अममाँ *ammā̃*, अस्सी *assī*, उत्तर *uttar*, उन्नीस *unnīs*, उम्मीद *ummīd*, उल्लू *ullū*, कुत्ता *kuttā*, गुस्सा *gussā*, चप्पल *cappal*, चम्मच *cammac*, ज़िद्दी *ziddī*, दिल्ली *dillī*, पच्चीस *paccīs*, बत्ती *battī*, रस्सी *rassī*.

1a

१	है	*hai*	That man is Panjabi.
२	हैं	*haĩ*	Are these men Pakistani?
३	है	*hai*	Raj, you're not a good boy.
४	हूँ, हूँ	*hū̃, hū̃*	I'm not German, I'm Russian.
५	हैं, है	*haĩ, hai*	We are not Hindus, but this man is Hindu.
६	हो, हूँ	*ho, hū̃*	Peter, are you English? No, I'm German.
७	हो, हैं	*ho, haĩ*	Are you both English? No, we're American.
८	है, हैं	*hai, haĩ*	Sushila is Gujarati, but Sushil and Ravi are both Panjabi.
९	हैं, हूँ	*haĩ, hū̃*	Are you Pratap? Yes, I'm Pratap.
१०	हैं, हैं	*haĩ, haĩ*	Are those two men German? No, they're English.

1b

Sunday, 15 January
Kamala and Prakash Kumar are very nice people. There are three children – one girl, Sangeeta, and two boys, Rishi and Raj. Sangeeta is very beautiful. Rishi is big [older], Raj is little [younger]. Dadi ji is old but very nice. The house is clean and the garden is very beautiful. My room is quite big. There's one bed, two cupboards

(both empty), one small table, two chairs. There isn't a fan, but the room is airy. There is a white Maruti car and two or three old bikes.

2a.1

१ शर्मा जी अध्यापक हैं। *śarmā jī adhyāpak haĩ.*

२ पाँच छात्र और नौ छात्राएँ हैं। *pā̃c chātr aur nau chātrāẽ haĩ.*

३ जी नहीं, यह काफ़ी महँगी किताब है। *jī nahī̃, yah kāfī mahā̃gī kitāb hai.*

४ जी नहीं, शब्दकोश बहुत सस्ते हैं। *jī nahī̃, śabdkoś bahut saste haĩ.*

५ रामायण बहुत मोटी किताब है। *rāmāyaṇ bahut moṭī kitāb hai.*

2a.2

Monday 16 January; New Delhi
Everything is OK here. Sharma ji is a good man, but he's quite strict too. We are 14 students. The other students are mostly English, German or American. There are also two Japanese girls. Both are very thin! Delhi is beautiful but the air isn't clean – it's very dirty. The pollution is very bad. But today the weather is all right. How's the weather there? Pratap

2b.1

१ संगीता लंबी है; ऋषि भी लंबा है। *Sangītā lambī hai; Ṛṣi bhī lambā hai.*

२ अध्यापक सख़्त हैं; वे पागल भी हैं। *adhyāpak sakht hai; ve pāgal bhī haĩ.*

३ नया पंखा सस्ता है; और वह अच्छा भी है। *nayā pankhā sastā hai; aur vah acchā bhī hai.*

४ ये जूते गंदे हैं; चप्पलें भी गंदी हैं। *ye jute gande haĩ; cappalẽ bhī gandī haĩ.*

५ वह लड़की मोटी है; वह सुंदर भी है। *vah laṛkī moṭī hai; vah sundar bhī hai.*

६ ये अख़बार अच्छे हैं; ये सस्ते भी हैं। *ye akhbār acche haĩ; ye saste bhī haĩ.*

2b.2

१ ये बच्चे अच्छे नहीं हैं, बीमार हैं। *ye bacce acche nahī̃ haĩ, bīmār haĩ.*

२ हम लंबे नहीं हैं, छोटे हैं। *ham lambe nahī̃ haĩ, choṭe haĩ.*

३ वे किताबें कैसी हैं? क्या वे अच्छी हैं? *ve kitābẽ kaisī haĩ? kyā ve acchī haĩ?*

४ वे मेज़ें साफ़ नहीं हैं, बहुत गंदी हैं। *ve mezẽ sāf nahī̃ haĩ, bahut gandī haĩ.*

५ ये नए अख़बार बहुत अच्छे नहीं हैं। *ye nae akhbār bahut acche nahī̃ haĩ.*

६ ये शब्दकोश सस्ते हैं। हाँ, और काफ़ी अच्छे भी हैं। *ye śabdkoś saste haĩ. hā̃, aur kāfī acche bhī haĩ.*

3a.1

१ प्रताप बिलकुल ठीक है । *Pratāp bilkul ṭhīk hai.*

२ कुमार परिवार में छह लोग हैं – कमला और प्रकाश, दादी जी, संगीता, ऋषि, और राज । *Kumār parivār mẽ chah log haĩ – Kamalā aur Prakāś, Dādī jī, Sangītā, Ṛṣi, aur Rāj.*

३ मकान में दस कमरे हैं । एक कमरा छोटा है, दूसरे बड़े हैं । *makān mẽ das kamre haĩ. ek kamrā choṭā hai, dūsre baṛe haĩ.*

४ सारे कमरों में नया सामान है । *sāre kamrõ mẽ nayā sāmān hai.*

५ पंखा मेज़ पर है । वह नया है । *pankhā mez par hai. vah nayā hai.*

६ जी नहीं, दरी भी नई है । वह फ़र्श पर है । *jī nahī̃, darī bhī naī hai. vah farś par hai.*

3a.2 (sample answer)

मेरा कमरा काफ़ी सुन्दर है । कमरा बहुत बड़ा नहीं है, लेकिन हवादार है । यहाँ दो पलंग, एक छोटी मेज़ और कई कुरसियाँ हैं । दीवारों पर अच्छी तस्वीरें हैं, और खिड़कियों पर परदे हैं । ये परदे नए नहीं हैं, काफ़ी पुराने हैं । फ़र्श पर एक छोटी हिन्दुस्तानी दरी है । मेज़ पर दो पंखे हैं; एक बहुत पुराना है लेकिन दूसरा नया है । अलमारियों में बहुत-सारा सामान है; यह मेरा नहीं है !

merā kamrā kāfī sundar hai. kamrā bahut baṛā nahī̃ hai, lekin havādār hai. yahā̃ do palang, ek choṭī mez aur kaī kursiyā̃ haĩ. dīvarõ par acchī tasvīrẽ haĩ, aur khiṛkiyõ par parde haĩ. ye parde nae nahī̃ haĩ, kāfī purāne haĩ. farś par ek choṭī hindustānī darī hai. mez par do pankhe haĩ; ek bahut purānā hai lekin dūsrā nayā hai. almāriyõ mẽ bahut-sārā sāmān hai; yah merā nahī̃ hai !

3b.1

१	यह बड़ा कमरा	इस बड़े कमरे में	लड़के इस बड़े कमरे में हैं ।
२	वे काली कुरसियाँ	उन काली कुरसियों पर	कपड़े उन काली कुरसियों पर हैं ।
३	यह गंदा फ़र्श	इस गंदे फ़र्श पर	इस गंदे फ़र्श पर (एक) दरी है ।
४	ये पुरानी मेज़ें	इन पुरानी मेज़ों पर	किताबें इन पुरानी मेज़ों पर हैं ।
५	वह बड़ा बग़ीचा	उस बड़े बग़ीचे में	उस बड़े बग़ीचे में (एक) गाड़ी है ।
६	ये नए कमरे	इन नए कमरों में	क्या इन नए कमरों में पंखे हैं ?

७	पुराना शहर	पुराने शहर से	वे लड़कियाँ पुराने शहर से हैं।
८	यह छोटा गाँव	इस छोटे गाँव से	क्या वह लड़का इस छोटे गाँव से है?
९	यह साफ़ रसोईघर	इस साफ़ रसोईघर में	इस साफ़ रसोईघर में (एक) मेज़ है।
१०	वे लंबे लड़के	उन लंबे लड़कों से	यह चिट्ठी उन लंबे लड़कों से है।

1	*yah baṛā kamrā*	*is baṛe kamre mẽ*	*laṛke is baṛe kamre mẽ haĩ.*
2	*ve kālī kursiyā̃*	*un kālī kursiyõ par*	*kapṛe un kālī kursiyõ par haĩ.*
3	*yah gandā farś*	*is gande farś par*	*is gande farś par (ek) darī hai.*
4	*ye purānī mezẽ*	*in purānī mezõ par*	*kitābẽ in purānī mezõ par haĩ.*
5	*vah baṛā bagīcā*	*us baṛe bagīce mẽ*	*us baṛe bagīce mẽ (ek) gāṛī hai.*
6	*ye nae kamre*	*in nae kamrõ mẽ*	*kyā in nae kamrõ mẽ pankhe haĩ?*
7	*purānā śahar*	*purāne śahar se*	*ve laṛkiyā̃ purāne śahar se haĩ.*
8	*yah choṭā gā̃v*	*is choṭe gā̃v se*	*kyā vah laṛkā is choṭe gā̃v se hai?*
9	*yah sāf rasoīghar*	*is sāf rasoīghar mẽ*	*is sāf rasoīghar mẽ (ek) mez hai.*
10	*ve lambe laṛke*	*un lambe laṛkõ se*	*yah ciṭṭhī un lambe laṛkõ se hai.*

3b.2 (sample answer)

ऋषि	माता जी, मेरी नई किताब कहाँ है?
कमला	शायद उस छोटी मेज़ पर है, बड़े कमरे में?
ऋषि	नहीं, बड़े कमरे में नहीं है। वहाँ सिर्फ़ मेरा शब्दकोश है।
कमला	अच्छा। और क्या वह तुम्हारी दराज़ में भी नहीं है?
ऋषि	नहीं माता जी, मेरी दराज़ में बहुत सामान है, लेकिन किताबें नहीं हैं!
कमला	रसोईघर में एक नई किताब है।
ऋषि	हाँ, लेकिन वह किताब मेरी नहीं है।

Ṛṣi	*mātā jī, merī naī kitāb kahā̃ hai?*
Kamalā	*śāyad us choṭī mez par hai, baṛe kamre mẽ?*
Ṛṣi	*nahī̃, baṛe kamre mẽ nahī̃ hai. vahā̃ sirf merā śabdkoś hai.*
Kamalā	*acchā. aur kyā vah tumhārī darāz mẽ bhī nahī̃ hai?*
Ṛṣi	*nahī̃ mātā jī, merī darāz mẽ bahut sāmān hai, lekin kitābẽ nahī̃ haĩ!*
Kamalā	*rasoīghar mẽ ek naī kitāb hai.*
Ṛṣi	*hā̃, lekin vah kitāb merī nahī̃ hai.*

4a.1

1 Your old fan was stronger than this new fan.
2 Sangeeta is the biggest of the children.

3 Is Rishi less fat than Raj?
4 Is Sangeeta cleverer than Pinkie?
5 Today Pratap is at home but the others are out – perhaps at the market.

4a.2 (ज़्यादा *zyādā* may be replaced with और *aur*, or omitted.)

१ यह आदमी उस लड़की से ज़्यादा लंबा है । *yah ādmī us ādmī se zyādā lambā hai.*

२ क्या तुम्हारी पुरानी गाड़ी इस नई गाड़ी से ज़्यादा अच्छी थी ? *kyā tumhārī purānī gāṛī is naī gāṛī se zyādā acchī hai?*

३ क्या मेरी बहिन मेरे भाई से ज़्यादा मोटी है ? *kyā merī bahin mere bhāī se zyādā moṭī hai?*

४ मैं तुमसे ज़्यादा लंबा/लंबी हूँ लेकिन तुम मुझसे ज़्यादा सुंदर हो । *maĩ tumse zyādā lambā/lambī hū̃ lekin tum mujhse zyādā sundar ho.*

५ वह हम से ज़्यादा लंबी थी; वह तो सबसे लंबी थी । *vah ham se zyādā lambī thī; vah to sabse lambī thī.*

4b.1

१ पिंकी को मालूम है कि संगीता आज कालेज में नहीं थी । *Pinkī ko mālūm hai ki Sangītā āj kālej mẽ nahī̃ thī.*

२ किसको मालूम नहीं कि सुहास संगीता से बड़ा है ? *kisko mālūm nahī̃ ki Suhās Sangītā se baṛā hai?*

३ संगीता को ख़ुशी है कि पिंकी को सुहास पसंद है । *Sangītā ko khuśī hai ki Pinkī ko Suhās pasand hai.*

४ प्रताप आज घर पर था; उसको मालूम है कि सुहास कौन है । *Pratāp āj ghar par thā; usko mālūm hai ki Suhās kaun hai.*

५ प्रताप को मालूम है कि संगीता को नई सफ़ेद मारुति पसंद है । *Pratāp ko mālūm hai ki Sangītā ko naī safed Māruti pasand hai.*

६ क्या आपको मालूम है कि कमला कल कहाँ थी ? *kyā āpko mālūm hai ki Kamalā kal kahā̃ thī?*

७ हमको अफ़सोस है कि तुम्हारे दोस्त बीमार हैं । *hamko afsos hai ki tumhāre dost bīmār haĩ.*

८ मुझको मालूम नहीं कि वह आदमी कौन है । *mujhko mālūm nahī̃ ki vah ādmī kaun hai.*

4b.2 (sample answers)

१ मेरे कमरे में चार कुरसियाँ हैं । *mere kamre mẽ cār kursiyā̃ haĩ.*

२ जी नहीं, मेरे पड़ोसी हिन्दुस्तानी नहीं हैं, पाकिस्तानी हैं । *jī nahī̃, mere paṛosī hindustānī nahī̃ haĩ, pākistānī haĩ.*

३ जी हाँ, मेरी किताब मेरी मेज़ पर है। *jī hā̃, merī kitāb merī mez par hai.*

४ हाँ ज़रूर ! मेरे सारे कपड़े बहुत साफ़ हैं ! और तुम्हारे ? *hā̃ zarūr! mere sāre kapṛe bahut sāf haĩ! aur tumhāre?*

५ जी हाँ, मुझको मालूम है कि मेरे पड़ोसी अभी घर पर हैं। *jī hā̃, mujhko mālūm hai ki mere paṛosī abhī ghar par haĩ.*

६ मेरी तबियत ठीक नहीं है। मुझको ज़ुकाम है। *merī tabiyat ṭhīk nahī̃ hai. mujhko zukām hai.*

4b.3 (sample answer)

प्रिय मोहन,

नमस्ते। आप कैसे हैं ? मुझको आशा है कि आप ठीक हैं। यहाँ दिल्ली में तो सब ठीक है। यह शहर मुझको बहुत पसंद है, लेकिन प्रदूषण बहुत ख़राब है। वाराणसी कैसी है ? क्या वहाँ भी प्रदूषण है ? वाराणसी में एक पुराना महल है – क्या आपको मालूम है कि वह कहाँ है ? क्या आप लोग वाराणसी से हैं ? आपके कितने भाई और बहिनें हैं ?

आपका प्रताप

priy Mohan,

namaste. āp kaise haĩ? mujhko āśā hai ki āp ṭhīk haĩ. yahā̃ dillī mẽ to sab ṭhīk hai. yah śahar mujhko bahut pasand hai, lekin pradūṣaṇ bahut kharāb hai. vārāṇasī kaisī hai? kyā vahā̃ bhī pradūṣaṇ hai? vārāṇasī mẽ ek purānā mahal hai – kyā āpko mālūm hai ki vah kahā̃ hai? kyā āp log vārāṇasī se haĩ? āpke kitne bhāī aur bahinẽ haĩ?

āpkā Pratāp

5a.1

१ यहाँ सिग्रेट न पीजिए। *yahā̃ sigreṭ na pījie.*
Please don't smoke here.

२ ज़रा यहाँ ठहरिए। *zarā yahā̃ ṭhaharie.*
Just wait here please.

३ इस कमरे में बैठिए। *is kamre mẽ baiṭhie.*
Please sit in this room.

४ चाय पीजिए, फल खाइए। *cāy pījie, phal khāie.*
Please have some tea, eat some fruit.

५ मुझे ऋषि के कपड़े दीजिए। *mujhe Ṛṣi ke kapṛe dījie.*
Please give me Rishi's clothes.

६ पानी न पियो; काफ़ी लो। *pānī na piyo; kāfī lo.*
Don't drink water; take some coffee.

७ आओ। बताओ, क्या हाल है? *āo. batāo, kyā hāl hai?*
Come. Tell me, how's things?

८ गाड़ी को इधर लाओ। *gāṛī ko idhar lāo.*
Bring the car over here.

९ उधर देखो, वह नारा पढ़ो! *udhar dekho, vah nārā paṛho!*
Look over there, read that slogan!

१० दरवाज़े को बन्द करो। *darvāze ko band karo.*
Close the door.

5a.2

१	... कर। *kar*	Don't dirty the blankets.
२	... छू। *chū*	Don't touch the food.
३	... बोल। *bol*	Speak simple Hindi.
४	... लिख। *likh*	Don't write my name in the book.
५	... मार! *mār*	Don't beat the horse!

5b.1

१ ये मोटे कंबल अलमारी में रखो। *ye moṭe kambal almārī mẽ rakho.*
Put these thick blankets in the cupboard.

२ यह गरम समोसा खाओ। *yah garam samosā khāo.*
Eat this hot samosa.

३ वह बड़ी कुरसी इस कमरे में लाइए। *vah baṛī kursī is kamre mẽ lāie.*
Please bring that big chair into this room.

४ आज का अख़बार पढ़। *āj kā akhbār paṛh.*
Read today's newspaper.

५ चाचा जी का दरवाज़ा बन्द करना। *cācā jī kā darvāzā band karnā.*
Close Uncle's door.

5b.2

१ इन नए खिलौनों को लो। *in nae khilaunõ ko lo.*
Take these new toys.

२ ऋषि के पुराने कुरते को पहनो। *Ṛṣi ke purāne kurte ko pahno.*
Wear Rishi's old kurta.

३ गाड़ी की चाबियों को ढूँढ़ो। *gāṛī kī cābiyõ ko ḍhū̃ṛho.*
Find the car keys.

४ इन गंदे कपड़ों को धोना। *in gande kapṛõ ko dhonā.*
Wash these dirty clothes.

५ इस थैले को दराज़ में रखिए। *is thaile ko darāz mẽ rakhie.*
Put this bag in the drawer.

5b.3

१ कमला के देवर का नाम क्या है? कमला के देवर का नाम अरुण है। *Kamalā ke devar kā nām kyā hai? Kamalā ke devar kā nām Aruṇ hai.*

२ क्या ऋषि अभी घर पर है? जी नहीं, वह अभी खाँ मार्केट में है। *kyā Ṛṣi abhī ghar par hai? jī nahī̃, vah abhī khā̃ mārkeṭ mẽ hai.*

३ किसको दूध पसंद नहीं है? राज को दूध पसंद नहीं है। *kisko dūdh pasand nahī̃ hai? Rāj ko dūdh pasand nahī̃ hai.*

४ उसको दूध क्यों नहीं पसंद है? क्योंकि वह छोटा बच्चा नहीं है। *usko dūdh kyõ nahī̃ pasand hai? kyõki vah choṭā baccā nahī̃ hai.*

५ कल संगीता के चाचा की चाबियाँ कहाँ थीं? दरवाज़े की चाबी तो प्रकाश की मेज़ पर पड़ी थी। *kal Sangītā ke cācā kī cābiyā̃ kahā̃ thī̃? darvāze kī cābī to Prakāś kī mez par paṛī thī.*

६ किसको मालूम है कि आज वे चाबियाँ कहाँ हैं? ऋषि को मालूम है कि चाबियाँ कहाँ हैं। *kisko mālūm hai ki āj ve cābiyā̃ kahā̃ haī̃? Ṛṣi ko mālūm hai ki cābiyā̃ kahā̃ haī̃.*

७ क्या आपको मालूम है कि कुमार परिवार का घर कहाँ है? जी हाँ, मुझको मालूम है कि वह दिल्ली में है। *kyā āpko mālūm hai ki Kumār parivār kā ghar kahā̃ hai? jī hā̃, mujhko mālūm hai ki vah dillī mẽ hai.*

८ आपके ख़याल में क्या ये सवाल सरल हैं? जी हाँ, मेरे ख़याल में तो ये सवाल बहुत सरल हैं! *āpke khyāl mẽ kyā ye savāl saral haī̃? jī hā̃, mere khyāl mẽ to ye savāl bahut saral haī̃!*

6a.1 (1-5 are sample answers)

१ मैं लन्दन में रहता/रहती हूँ।

२ मेरे घर में सिर्फ़ दो लोग रहते हैं। एक कुत्ता भी है।

३ हिन्दी में "प्रोनंसियेशन" को "उच्चारण" कहते हैं।

४ मैं चार भाषाएँ बोलता/बोलती हूँ। इनमें से हिन्दी भी एक है।

५ जी हाँ, लन्दन में मकान बहुत ज़्यादा महँगे होते हैं।

६ प्रताप अभी प्रकाश और कमला के मकान में रहता है, दिल्ली में।

७ उस घर में सात लोग रहते हैं।

८ प्रताप की माँ लन्दन में रहती हैं। उनका नाम अनीता है।

९ जी नहीं, राज तो काम नहीं करता – वह खेलता है, खाता है, सोता है और शरारत करता है।

१० संगीता प्रताप को नापसंद करती है (प्रताप के ख़याल से)।

6a.2

Prakash Kumar works in a big company; his boss's name is Khanna. It seems that Mr Khanna is a big shot; Prakash ji is afraid of him (and perhaps of his (own) wife Kamala as well!). Prakash and Kamala's two sons go to school; and their daughter Sangeeta goes to college. Sangeeta is very clever but she doesn't talk to me much. I think she doesn't like me. Her friend Pinkie comes here often; the two of them chat all day and laugh a lot. Pinkie is Khanna's younger sister; she's older than Sangeeta, but Sangeeta is the more beautiful of the two of them. She is perhaps the most beautiful girl in India!

Dadi ji often asks me what my parents do, who my friends are, and so on. She makes Rishi and Raj laugh a lot – and me too! She's very fond of Raj; she calls him 'Munna' ('little one') or 'my piece-of-the-moon'. Raj doesn't like these names one bit. But he keeps quiet. Everybody loves Dadi ji.

6b.1

1 अपने – Pratap often asks his teacher difficult questions about Hindi.

2 अपने – Dadi tells us about her childhood.

3 उसका; अपनी – Rishi and his brother laugh with their grandmother a lot.

4 तेरी; अपना – Little one, I'm your grandmother; why don't you give me your food to eat?

5 अपना; मेरा – Rishi, you do your work; then give me my food.

6 अपनी; उसकी – Prakash asks his daughter about her friend.

7 अपने; अपनी – Sangeeta tells her father about her friend.

6b.2

मुझे ऋषि कहते हैं। राज मेरा छोटा भाई है; वह थोड़ा पागल है। वह अभी अपने कमरे में नहीं है, वह मेरे कमरे में है। और मैं अपने कमरे में नहीं हूँ, मैं उसके कमरे में हूँ! उसको नहीं मालूम कि मुझे मालूम है कि वह मेरे कमरे में है। इधर उसके कमरे में कई पुराने अख़बार हैं, लेकिन मैं नहीं जानता कि वे किसके हैं; उसके तो नहीं हैं। राज तो किताबें या अख़बार नहीं पढ़ता। वह अपने दोस्तों के साथ खेलता है पर मुझसे बात नहीं करता। उसके दोस्त मेरे दोस्त नहीं हैं।

मुझे प्रताप पसंद है। मैं उसके साथ सिनेमा जाता हूँ और हम फ़िल्मों के बारे में बातें करते हैं। मालूम होता है कि वह काफ़ी होशियार है। वह अच्छी हिन्दी बोलता है। उसका उच्चारण भी काफ़ी अच्छा है। वह विदेशी की तरह नहीं बोलता।

7a.1

१ पिताजी किसी दफ़्तर में काम करते थे और देर से घर पहुँचते थे।

२ कोई १२ विद्यार्थी फ़र्श पर बैठे हैं; हमें कुछ और कुरसियाँ चाहिए।

३ शनिवार को हम कुछ दोस्तों से मिलते थे।

४ हमको यह ठंडा खाना पसंद नहीं – हमें कुछ चावल दाल चाहिए।

५ क्या यहाँ कोई सस्ता होटल नहीं है? ताज तो कुछ महँगा है!

६ "यह पैसा किसी और को देना!" "हाँ, पर किसको?"

७ हमें गाड़ी की चाबियों की ज़रूरत थी लेकिन घर में कोई नहीं था।

८ शाम को, दादीजी रामायण पढ़ती थीं और हम लोग पुरानी फ़िल्में देखते थे।

7a.2 and 7a.3 (sample answers)

१ उन्हें कुछ गरम पानी चाहिए था। उन्हें कुछ गरम पानी की ज़रूरत थी।

२ मुझे कुछ पैसा चाहिए। मुझे कुछ पैसे की ज़रूरत है।

३ तुम्हें कुछ और समय चाहिए। तुम्हें कुछ और समय की ज़रूरत है।

४ मेरे दोस्त को एक अच्छा शब्दकोश चाहिए। मेरे दोस्त को एक अच्छे शब्दकोश की ज़रूरत है।

५ उन लड़कियों को नया घर चाहिए। उन लड़कियों को नए घर की ज़रूरत है।

६ किसी को एक सुन्दर मोती चाहिए था। किसी को एक सुन्दर मोती की ज़रूरत थी।

७ किसको आज के अख़बार चाहिए ? किसको आज के अख़बारों की ज़रूरत है ?

८ इन विद्यार्थियों को कोई दस कुरसियाँ चाहिए थे । इन विद्यार्थियों को कोई दस कुरसियों की ज़रूरत थी ।

९ सिग्रेट किसी को नहीं चाहिए । किसी को सिग्रेट की ज़रूरत नहीं है ।

१० उस दूसरे आदमी को हज़ारों रुपए चाहिए । उस दूसरे आदमी को हज़ारों रुपयों की ज़रूरत है ।

7b.1

१ अरुण अपने बड़े भाई प्रकाश के साथ रहता था; वह किताबें लिखता था । Arun lived with his elder brother Prakash; he used to write books.

२ खन्ना साहिब कहते थे कि उनके दफ़्तर में दर्जनों लोग थे लेकिन कोई ठीक से काम नहीं करता था । Khanna Sahib used to say that dozens of people used to work in his office but nobody worked properly.

३ दादी जी नहीं जानती थीं कि उनके पिताजी किस कालेज में पढ़ाते थे । Dadi ji didn't know which college her father used to teach in.

४ अध्यापक जी कहते थे कि "कोई" और "कुछ" का फ़र्क समझना बहुत ज़रूरी था । The teacher used to say that it was very important to understand the difference between *koī* and *kuch*.

५ छात्र अपने अध्यापक से हज़ारों मुश्किल सवाल पूछता था । The student used to ask his teacher thousands of difficult questions.

६ क्या किसी को मालूम था कि संगीता का दोस्त सुहास कहाँ रहता था ? Did anyone know where Sangeeta's friend Suhas lived?

७ किसको मालूम था कि ऋषि और राज की उम्र में कितना फ़र्क था ? Who knew how much age difference there was between Rishi and Raj?

८ दादी जी सोचती थीं कि हिन्दुस्तान स्वर्ग के समान था । वे अपने बचपन के सपने बहुत देखती थीं । Dadi ji used to think that India was like paradise. She used to dream of her childhood a lot.

९ मालूम होता था कि प्रताप अभी दिल्ली में नहीं था; शायद वह अपने पिताजी के यहाँ था । It seemed that Pratap wasn't still in Delhi; perhaps he was at his father's place.

१० कुछ विद्यार्थियों के ख़याल में आठवाँ और दसवाँ सवाल सबसे मुश्किल थे । In the opinion of some students the eighth and tenth questions were the most difficult.

7b.2 होटल में

लड़का आइए साहब। आपको क्या चाहिए ?

खन्ना मुझे कुछ गरम खाना और काफ़ी चाहिए।

लड़का सर, रविवार को रसोईघर जल्दी बंद होता है। गरम खाना नहीं है।

खन्ना अच्छा, तो मुझे कुछ फल दो। और कल सुबह मेरे कमरे को साफ़ करना; बहुत गंदा है।

लड़का सर, कल तो मेरी छुट्टी है। किसी और से कहिएगा।

खन्ना पर काफ़ी तो अभी चाहिए। उसे लाओ और दरवाज़ा बंद करो।

लड़का सर, अभी तो बिजली बंद है। कुछ ठंडा पानी पीजिए।

खन्ना यह होटल बेकार है; तुम भी बेकार हो। मैं चलता हूँ।

8a.1

१ प्रताप बहुत ध्यान से हिन्दी पढ़ रहा है।
Pratap is studying Hindi very attentively.

२ मैं तो अच्छा पैसा कमा रहा हूँ।
I, at least, am earning good money.

३ क्या तुम गाड़ी चला रहे हो ?
Are you driving the car?

४ संगीता और उसका छोटा भाई सिनेमा जा रहे हैं।
Sangeeta and her younger brother are going to the cinema.

५ प्रताप अपने दोस्तों के साथ गोश्त खा रहा है।
Pratap is eating meat with his friends.

8a.2

१ तुम्हारे लिए वह अलग खाना तैयार कर रहा है।

२ उसको बताओ कि वह ग़लत नंबर मिला रही थी।

३ वह कल अपने रिश्तेदारों के साथ दिल्ली आ रहा है।

४ आपकी कितनी बहिनें हैं? मेरी दो बहिनें हैं।

५ तीनों डाक्टर उसी अस्पताल पर काम कर रहे हैं।

६ वह पहले मेरा सपना देखता था पर अब तो वह तुम्हारा सपना देख रहा है।

७ तुम मेरे सवाल का जवाब क्यों नहीं दे रही हो संगीता ?

८ हम लोग तुम्हारे पड़ोसियों से तुम्हारे बारे में बात कर रहे थे।

8a.3 (sample answer; only Mohan's lines are given here)

मैं ठीक हूँ। पर आप नेपाल में क्या कर रहे हैं?

क्या ऋषि और राज भी आपके साथ सैर कर रहे हैं ?

आप लोग नेपाल में कहाँ ठहर रहे हैं ?

होटल तो हमेशा महँगे होते हैं। किसी दोस्त के यहाँ ठहरिए।

मेरे कई रिश्तेदार काठमांडु में रहते हैं। उनसे मिलिए।

8b.1

१ मकान के बाहर बैठो। बाहर बैठो।

२ कुरसी के पीछे देखो। पीछे देखो।

३ हम दरवाज़े के सामने खड़े हैं। दुकान सामने है।

४ मेरी तरफ़ आओ। इस तरफ़ आओ।

५ पेड़ के नीचे मत सोना। नीचे सोना।

६ दोनों भाई मेरे साथ हैं। तुम भी साथ चलो।

७ उसे अलमारी के ऊपर रखो। तुम ऊपर जाओ।

८ हम लोग साइकिल की दुकान के पास रहते हैं। वे लोग पास रहते हैं।

8b.2 (sample answers)

१ मेरा जन्मदिन १५ जनवरी को है।

२ आज की तारीख़ है रविवार, दस अक्तूबर, सन् उन्नीस सौ निन्यानवे।

३ कल तो शनिवार था – नौ अक्तूबर।

४ जी हाँ, मेरे दो बच्चे हैं। दोनों लड़के हैं।

५ मेरी दो बहिनें हैं; एक छप्पन साल की है, दूसरी बावन या तिरपन साल की। हमारा कोई भाई नहीं है।

६ बिलकुल नहीं। मैं अध्यापक हूँ, इसलिए ग़रीब हूँ। मुझे पैसा ज़रूर चाहिए – सब लोगों की तरह – लेकिन किसी ख़ास काम के लिए नहीं।

७ मेरा अपना घर है। छोटा है, लेकिन मुझे बहुत पसंद है।

८ अभी तो मुझे कोई भी तकलीफ़ नहीं है; मेरी तबियत बहुत अच्छी है, शुक्रिया।

९ मेरे ख़याल से वह संगीता से नहीं डरता; शायद उससे प्यार करता है। पर किसी वजह से संगीता उससे बात भी नहीं करती।

१० तीन घंटे पहले मैं ... यह किताब पढ़ रहा था !

9a.1

१ दूसरे लोग कल सुबह तक पहुँचेंगे ।

२ किसी दिन मैं आपको पूरी कहानी बताऊँगा/बताऊँगी ।

३ मुझे मालूम है कि वह मेरी चिट्ठियों का जवाब नहीं देगा ।

४ आजकल तुम्हारे पिताजी अच्छा पैसा कमा रहे होंगे ।

५ वे सोच रहे होंगे कि वह ऐश की ज़िन्दगी बिता रहे होगे/होंगी ।

६ आज मेरी बहिन मेरी गाड़ी चला रही होगी ।

9a.2

१ जी नहीं, कमला को ख़ुशी नहीं है । हमको मालूम है क्योंकि वह कहती है "हे भगवान !" ।

२ जी नहीं, पिंकी का एक अलग घर है ।

३ घर में सब्ज़ी और गोश्त की ज़रूरत है ।

४ क्योंकि खन्ना जी अपनी पत्नी को हमेशा "हरीश की माँ" कहते हैं ।

५ कमला सोचती है कि उसका पति दिन भर ऐश करता है । छोटू ही कहता है कि प्रकाश मेहनती हैं ।

9a.3

१ आज शाम को संगीता और पिंकी दावत में नहीं आएँगी । वे दोनों सिनेमा जा रही हैं ।

२ उसको डर है कि शायद ऋषि या राज माँ को बताएगा कि वह सिनेमा जा रही है ।

३ पिंकी का ख़याल है कि दोनों लड़के भोले-से हैं; वह सोचती है कि वे चुप रहेंगे, किसी से कुछ नहीं कहेंगे ।

४ कमला सोचती होगी कि शायद हरीश संगीता को तंग करेगा ।

५ क्योंकि वह अपने माँ-बाप के साथ कुमार परिवार की दावत में जा रहा होगा ।

9b.1

Dear Pratap,

How are you? Is everything going OK in Delhi? I'm writing this letter after a long time. You must be aware that I too am planning to come to India to study Hindi. I hope that like you, I'll learn good Hindi, after studying very hard. At least this is the intention. To understand Hindi is one thing but to speak it fluently is something different! You know my friend Rajeshwari don't you? Her sister

Usha lives in Varanasi. It's her I'll stay with. Her house is quite far from the college; the college is in Ramnagar, near the Maharaja's palace, and Usha's house is inside Banaras Hindu University (BHU). Lots of students must be living in the vicinity of BHU. They must go to college by rickshaw; I'll go with them too. Father says that it wouldn't be all right for me to go alone because the Varanasi youths get up to a lot of loutish behaviour and hassle girls. They call this 'Eve-teasing', don't they?

Needless to say, I'll come to India by plane. On reaching Delhi I'll phone you. After staying in Delhi for two or three days I'll go to Banaras by train. Usha will come to meet me at the station. The train gets there very early in the morning. A meeting with 'Usha' [the name means 'dawn'] at dawn! I don't know Usha; how I'll recognise her I've no idea. Maybe Rajeshwari will have some old photo of her. Usha's husband is a history lecturer in the university. Rajeshwari says that the two of them, husband and wife, fight a lot. There are also three kids of various ages. I don't know what it'll be like being a guest in such a household! Anyway, if you have the time, you too be sure to come to Banaras sometime. When I reach Delhi I'll phone you. Take care of yourself.

Yours, Geeta.

9b.2

१ क्या उर्दू सीखने में कोई ख़ास मुश्किल होगी ?

२ अगले महीने हमारे विद्यार्थी हिन्दी सीखने लखनऊ जा रहे होंगे ।

३ अब तक तुम्हारे भाई को हिन्दी अच्छी तरह आती होगी ।

४ मेरे दोस्तों के पिता जी मुझसे मिलने वाराणसी के स्टेशन आएँगे ।

५ दिल्ली के आस-पास बहुत-सी देखने-लायक़ जगहें हैं ।

६ हम पहाड़ों को देखने आपके साथ मसूरी चलेंगे ।

9b.3

१	पढ़ना	पढ़ने	Studying Sanskrit isn't easy; but there's a lot of advantage in studying it.
२	देखने	देखने	I'm going to see a film; you come too – the film will be worth seeing.
३	चलाना	चलाना	Do you like driving? I can't (don't know how to) drive.

४	पीना	पीने	Is it wrong to smoke? Yes of course, and what's the point in smoking?
५	बजाने	बजाना	Do you come here to play tabla? Yes, I'm very fond of playing tabla.

10a.1

१	जाऊँ	रहूँ	Should I go with you, or should I stay right here at home?
२	हों	पहुँचें	If the weather isn't bad, they may reach the village by evening.
३	करे		It's right that he should vacate the house before you come.
४	लें	सुनें	It's not necessary for us to take anyone's advice or listen to what anyone says.
५	दे	भूले	Tell him he should reply by tonight and not forget his responsibility.
६	दें		You are requested to pay for the treatment straightaway.

10a.2

१ कि... आप तुरंत जवाब दें। I want you to answer immediately.

२ कि... तुम चुप रहो। I want you to keep quiet.

३ कि... तुम गाय को न मारो। I don't want you to hit the cow. ('I want you not to...')

४ कि... तुम सीढ़ियों पर न बैठो। I don't want you to sit on the stairs. ('I want you not to...')

५ कि... तू मेरा हाथ पकड़े। I want you to hold my hand!

६ कि... आप आज की संस्कृत की क्लास पढ़ाएँ। I want you to teach today's Sanskrit class.

10a.3 (sample answers)

१ अगर आप ख़ाली हों तो ज़रा इन काग़ज़ों पर नज़र डालिए। If you're free, just cast a glance over these papers.

२ यदि आपको असुविधा न हो तो अवश्य हमारे साथ चलें। If not inconvenient, certainly come with us.

३ अगर तुम उनसे मिलना चाहती हो तो ८ बजे तक यहाँ आओ। If you want to meet them, come here by 8 o'clock.

४ यदि यह काम सचमुच बहुत ही कठिन हो तो आप किसी से कहें कि वह आपकी मदद करे। If this work is really very hard, ask someone to help you.

५ अगर पुलिस आएगी तो हमें जल्दी ही बताना। If the police come, tell us quickly.

६ अगर आप इसके बारे में परेशान हों तो किसी दोस्त की सलाह लें। If you're worried about this, take advice from some friend.

७ अगर तुम फ़ोटो खींचोगे तो वह तुम पर ज़रूर गुस्से होगा। If you take a photo he'll certainly be angry with you.

८ अगर आपकी तबियत ठीक नहीं है तो आप अभी भारत न जाएँ। If your health isn't good you shouldn't go to India just now.

९ अगर तू मेरी बात नहीं मानती तो बहुत बुरा होगा। It'll be very bad if you don't accept what I say.

१० अगर मुझे फ़ुरसत हो तो मैं भी तुम्हारे साथ जाऊँगा। I'll come with you too if I'm free.

10b.1

Prakash – Khanna ji wants you to phone him. Don't forget – it might be something important about tonight. I'm just going to the vegetable seller. Even when I tell you, you don't bring vegetables – you're expert at forgetting. After that I'll go to see Suresh for a bit. You've got the car so I'll go to the market by auto. We need rice etc. from the shops – you bring it. We also need new forks, spoons and knives. There's a list of everything lying on the table in the bedroom. Don't forget anything this time. Get everything from the shop in the market; don't go to the shop in the lane, the prices there are very high. What can I say to you? You don't even know the proper price for anything! You don't even know how to do the shopping properly.

I'll be back in an hour and a half. If you get home first (I mean – before I do), clean the sitting room. Otherwise do it later; but do it for sure. Time and again I tell your mother that she should lend a hand with the cleaning work, but who listens to me. Your mother just swats flies [idles about] all day. I've no idea why everyone in this house is so work shy. I'm the only one who works. I don't understand why I'm writing such a long note. Do I even have the time? I'm in a hurry, I'm getting late. K.

10b.2

१ मेरे ख़याल से कमला नाराज़ है क्योंकि वह नहीं चाहती कि खन्ना परिवार खाना खाने आए ।

२ हाँ, खन्ना जी चाहते हैं कि प्रकाश उन्हें फ़ोन करें ।

३ ख़रीदारी इसीलिए हो रही है कि बहुत लोग डिनर में आ रहे हैं और घर में खाना नहीं है ।

४ कमला कहती है कि वह अपने दोस्त सुरेश से मिलने जाएगी ।

५ अगर वह पहले घर आए तो वह बैठने-वाले कमरे को साफ़ करे ।

६ बाज़ार-वाली दुकान सस्ती है ।

७ चीज़ों की लिस्ट मेज़ पर पड़ी है ।

८ क्योंकि घर का सारा काम कमला ही करती है ।

९ कमला सोचती है कि उसकी बातें कोई नहीं सुनता । पर प्रकाश तो ज़रूर सुनता है क्योंकि वह कमला से बहुत डरता होगा ।

१० नहीं, वह सोचती है कि दादी जी सिर्फ़ मक्खियाँ मारती हैं ।

10b.3

१ कमला चाहती है कि आज रात के डिनर के लिए प्रकाश कुछ दुकानदारी करे ।

२ किसी को नहीं मालूम है कि पासवाली दुकान में हर चीज़ इतनी महँगी क्यों है ।

३ संभव है कि प्रताप आज रात तक नेपाल से लौटे ।

४ किसी वजह से संगीता भी चाहती है कि प्रताप जल्दी ही घर वापस आए ।

५ अगर प्रताप की गाड़ी देर से पहुँचेगी तो शायद कोई उससे मिलने स्टेशन पर जाएगा ।

६ अगर प्रताप संगीता के लिए कोई चीज़ लाता है तो वह क्या कहेगी ?

11a.1

1 The girls arrived in Banaras yesterday morning. / have arrived, had, will have, may have

2 They slept late last night. / have slept, had, will have, may have

3 They went to the ghat three times to see the Ganges. / have gone, had, will have, may have

4 In the afternoon they met some friends. / have met, had, will have, may have
5 They enjoyed it a lot. / have enjoyed, had, will have, may have

11a.2

१ मेरे लड़के भारत गए। / गए हैं, गए थे, गए होंगे, गए हों

२ वे दो हफ़्ते के लिए घूमे। / घूमे हैं, घूमे थे, घूमे होंगे, घूमे हों

३ वे सस्ते होटलों में रहे। / रहे हैं, रहे थे, रहे होंगे, रहे हों

४ वे थोड़ी हिन्दी बोले। / बोले हैं, बोले थे, बोले होंगे, बोले हों

५ उन्हें काफ़ी मज़ा आया। / आया है, आया था, आया होगा, आया हो

11b.1

1 Papa bought stomach medicine. / has bought, had, will have, may have
2 He paid the correct price. / has paid, had, will have, may have
3 The shopkeeper demanded more. / has demanded, had, will have, may have
4 Papa complained. / has complained, had, will have, may have
5 Ma watched the goings-on./ has watched, had, will have, may have

11b.2

१ धोबी ने दोनों साड़ियाँ धोईं। / धोई हैं, धोई थीं, धोई होंगी, धोई हों

२ उसने एक ही साड़ी वापस दी। / दी है, दी थी, दी होगी, दी हो

३ उसकी पत्नी ने दूसरी पहनी। / पहनी है, पहनी थी, पहनी होगी, पहनी हो

४ हमने उसे किसी की शादी में देखा। / देखा है, देखा था, देखा होगा, देखा हो

५ उन्होंने माफ़ी माँगी। / माँगी है, माँगी थी, माँगी होगी, माँगी हो

11c.1

१ दुकानदार ने पापा की शिकायत को सुना था। The shopkeeper had listened to Papa's complaint.

२ पर उसने पापा की बातों को नहीं माना। But he didn't accept the things Papa said.

३ माँ ने दुकानदार की बाँह को पकड़ा । Ma grabbed the shopkeeper's arm.

४ पापा ने अपने पैसों को वापस लिया होगा क्योंकि... Papa must have taken his money back because...

५ ...दुकानदार ने अपनी भारी-सी लाठी को उठाया । ...the shopkeeper picked up his stout stick.

11c.2

१ मैंने अपने सारे कपड़े उतारे । I took off all my clothes.

२ डाक्टर ने अपनी सिग्रेट ख़त्म की और उँगलियाँ गिलास में धोईं । The doctor finished his cigarette and washed his fingers in a glass.

३ फिर उन्होंने दराज़ में से अपनी किताब निकाली... Then he took his book out from the drawer...

४ ...और अपना चश्मा नाक पर सीधा किया । ... and straightened the specs on his nose.

५ तब उन्होंने अपनी आँखें बंद कीं और दो प्रसिद्ध फ़िल्मी गीत सुनाए । Then he closed his eyes and sang two famous film songs.

11c.3 (sample answer)

आज मैं सात बजे उठा । नाश्ते में मैने रोटी खाई और चाय पी । आठ बजे मैंने दफ़्तर जाने के लिए बस पकड़ी । काम करने का मन मुझे बिलकुल नहीं था, क्योंकि मुझे बहुत थकान थी । इसलिए मैंने बहुत कम काम किया । कई दोस्तों को फ़ोन किया । उनमें से एक ने कहा कि "शाम को क्यों न मिलें ?" । इसलिए शाम को घर लौटने के बाद मैं उससे मिलने उसके घर गया । हमने उसके यहाँ थोड़ी देर के लिए बातें कीं, फिर एक पासवाले होटल में गए । वहाँ हम ने दाल-रोटी खाई । खाना इतना अच्छा तो नहीं था, पर सस्ता था । फिर ग्यारह बजे मैं घर वापस आया । बस, यही था मेरा दिन का प्रोग्राम ।

12a.1

१ संगीता ने घर जाकर किसी दोस्त को फ़ोन किया । Sangeeta went home and phoned some friend.

२ ऋषि ने अपनी किताब खोलकर दो-तीन कहानियाँ पढ़ीं । Rishi opened his book and read two or three stories.

३ कमला अपना काम ख़त्म करके तुरंत बाहर गई । Immediately after finishing her work Kamala went out.

४ हम छोटू के यहाँ जाकर खाना बनाएँगे। We'll go to Chotu's place and cook.

५ खन्ना जी ने डिब्बे में आकर ऊपरवाले बर्थ पर अपना सामान रखा। Coming into the compartment, Khanna ji put his luggage on the upper berth.

12a.2

१ आज सुबह नहाकर तूने साबुन को कहाँ रखा ? Where did you put the soap after bathing this morning?

२ परीक्षा देकर प्रताप और उसके साथी कम से कम दो हफ़्ते तक आराम करेंगे। After taking the exam, Pratap and his companions will rest for at least two weeks.

३ अपनी डिगरी पास करके तुम क्या करना चाहते हो ? What do you want to do after passing your degree?

४ लन्दन वापस आकर उसने भारत के बारे में कई पुस्तकें लिखीं। Returning to London, he/she wrote several books about India.

५ शाम को दफ़्तर से लौटकर प्रकाश कभी कभी बाज़ार में सैर करता है। Prakash sometimes goes for a stroll in the market after coming home from work in the evening.

12b.1

१ कितने बजे हैं ? साढ़े सात बजे हैं। मैं नाश्ता कर चुका हूँ।

२ मैं अक्सर साढ़े आठ बजे पहुँचता हूँ, पर आज मैं पौने नौ से पहले नहीं पहुँच पाया।

३ मैं दोपहर का खाना डेढ़ और ढाई बजे के बीच खा लेता हूँ।

४ क्या विद्यार्थी ठीक ग्यारह बजे पहुँचेंगे ? नहीं, वे तो सवा ग्यारह तक आ जाएँगे।

५ सुबह के पौने एक बजे तक मैं अपना पढ़ाई का काम ख़त्म कर पाया।

12b.2

१ हाँ, बोले लेता हूँ।

२ नहीं, वह उसे ख़त्म नहीं कर सका।

३ हाँ, वे तो हमेशा सात बजे सो जाते हैं।

४ हाँ, वह आधे से ज़्यादा खा चुकी है।

५ क्यों, वह तो चार बजे बंद हो गई थी।

13a.1

१ हाँ, हमको चाय तैयार कर देनी चाहिए। Yes, we should prepare tea.

२ पापा को ही बच्चों को खाना खिलाना चाहिए। *Papa* should feed the kids.

३ जी नहीं, उसको हिन्दुस्तानी कपड़े नहीं पहनने चाहिए। No, she shouldn't wear Indian clothes.

४ हाँ, तुम्हें कमरा मिल जाना चाहिए। Yes, you should get a room.

५ हाँ, हमें थोड़ा आराम करना चाहिए। Yes, we should rest a little.

६ नहीं, तुमको उसकी जेब से पैसा नहीं लेना चाहिए। No, you should not take money from his/her pocket.

13a.2

१ तुझे मेरी सहेली की सलाह लेनी पड़ेगी। You will have to take my friend's advice.

२ मुझे रोज़ पढ़ाई का काम करना पड़ेगा। I will have to study everyday.

३ माँ कहती हैं कि मुझे हर हफ़्ते उन्हें चिट्ठी लिखनी पड़ेगी। Mother says I will have to write her a letter every day.

४ अगर चोरी का डर है तो हमें एक ताला ख़रीदना पड़ेगा। If there's a risk of theft we will have to buy a lock.

५ अगर चावल न मिले तो तुम्हें रोटी खानी पड़ेगी। If rice isn't available you will have to eat roti.

६ हमें कम से कम दो भाषाएँ सीखनी पड़ेंगी। We will have to learn at least two languages.

13a.3 (sample answer)

१ जैसे ही वह कमरे में आया वैसे ही बच्ची रो पड़ी। As soon as he came into the room the little girl burst into tears.

२ जब तक मुझे उधार का पैसा नहीं मिलेगा तब तक मुझे यहीं रहना पड़ेगा। Until I get the loan I'll have to stay right here.

३ जब आपको फ़ुरसत हो तो हमारे यहाँ खाना खाने आएँ। When you're free come and eat at our place.

४ ज्योंही मुझे महसूस हुआ कि उसे यह जगह अच्छी नहीं लगती त्योंही मैंने दूसरा घर ढूँढ़ लिया। As soon as I felt that he/she didn't like this place I [looked for and] found a different house.

५ जब तुम दिल्ली में रहने के लिए आओगे तब हम अवश्य मिलेंगे । When you come to live in Delhi we'll definitely meet.

६ जब तक तुम माफ़ी नहीं माँगोगी तब तक वह तुम्हें माफ़ नहीं करेगा । He won't forgive you until you apologise.

७ जब से मैंने उसे अपनी बहिन के बारे में बताया तब से मुझे उसकी एक भी चिट्ठी नहीं मिली । Since I told him/her about my sister I haven't had a single letter from him/her.

८ जब गाड़ी बिकेगी तभी हम तुम्हें तुम्हारा पैसा वापस देंगे । When the car gets sold, we'll return your money.

13b.1

१ जो दुकान मैंने आपको दिखाई थी उसमें विदेशी कपड़े मिलते हैं ।

२ जो किताबें आपको चाहिए, वे उस मेज़ पर मिलेंगी ।

३ जो पत्र मैंने आपको भेजा था, क्या वह मिल गया ?

४ जिन लोगों को मौक़ा मिले उन्हें अगले साल फिर मिलना चाहिए ।

५ जिन बच्चों को हमने कल देखा था वे मेरे दोस्त के बच्चे हैं ।

६ जो आदमी मेरे भाई जैसा लगता है वह असल में मेरा चाचा है ।

७ जा ताला हमने खाँ मार्केट में ख़रीदा, वह काफ़ी मज़बूत है ।

८ जो वाक्य तुमने कल लिखे, तुम्हें उनको सीखना चाहिए ।

९ जो लोग सिग्रेट पीते हैं उनको बाहर ही रहना चाहिए ।

13b.2

१ जब प्रताप की माँ ने उसे फ़ोन किया तभी उसने कहा कि उसे मेहनत करनी पड़ेगी ।

२ जब से प्रताप भारत आया है तब से वह हिन्दी सीख रहा है ।

३ जब प्रताप लन्दन जाएगा तो उसे हिन्दी-बोलनेवाले लोगों से मिलना चाहिए ।

४ उसको "जब"-वाले वाक्यों का अभ्यास करने का मौक़ा मिला ।

५ जो लड़का कोने में बैठा है, उसके बारे में खन्ना जी पूछ रहे हैं ।

६ जी नहीं, सुरेश संगीता का रिश्तेदार तो नहीं है, सिर्फ़ पड़ोसी है ।

७ जिस दिन डिनर हुआ, उस दिन अरुण को अपने प्रकाशक के यहाँ जाना था ।

८ कमला विषय को इसलिए बदलना चाहती है कि उसे डर है कि सुरेश की बातें खन्ना जी को बुरी लगें ।

13b.3 (sample answer)

१ जाने से पहले आपको "वीज़ा" का इंतज़ाम कर लेना चाहिए। जाने से पहले आप "वीज़ा" का इंतज़ाम कर लें।

२ अगर आपको ट्रेन से सफ़र करना हो तो आपको कई दिन पहले अपना टिकट ख़रीदना चाहिए। ... तो आप कई दिन पहले टिकट ख़रीदें।

३ आपको नल का पानी नहीं पीना चाहिए। आप नल का पानी न पिएँ।

४ आपको कोई हिन्दी फ़िल्म ज़रूर देखनी चाहिए।आप कोई हिन्दी फ़िल्म ज़रूर देखें।

५ भारत में आपको हिन्दी ही बोलनी चाहिए। भारत में आप हिन्दी ही बोलें।

६ अगर आपके पास काफ़ी पैसे हैं तो आपको कुछ बढ़िया कपड़े ख़रीदने चाहिए। ... तो आप कुछ बढ़िया कपड़े ख़रीदें।

14.a.1

१ तमिल तो दक्षिण भारत में बोली जाती है। Tamil is spoken in South India.

२ सारी तैयारियाँ ६ बजे तक की जाएँगी। All the arrangements will be made by 6 o'clock.

३ यह चिट्ठी हवाई डाक से भेजी जाएगी। This letter will be sent by airmail.

४ इस विश्वविद्यालय में संस्कृत भी पढ़ी जाती है। Sanskrit too is studied in this university.

५ मंदिर में फ़ोटो नहीं खींचा जाना चाहिए। Photographs ('a photograph') should not be taken in the temple.

६ ज़िन्दगी को थोड़ा और सरल बनाया जाना चाहिए। Life should be made a little simpler.

14.a.2

१ सबसे नए मकान पिछले साल ही बनाए गए थे।

२ सारी चिट्ठियों को एक बड़े लिफ़ाफ़े में रखा गया था।

३ अख़बार में कहा गया था कि चोरों को पकड़ा गया था।

४ भारतीय भाषाओं के बारे में कई अजीब किताबें लिखी गई हैं।

५ संगीता सोचने लगी कि रविवार कभी नहीं आएगा।

६ बारिश होने लगी, इसलिए कमला ने राज को बाहर जाने नहीं दिया।

७ जब बच्चों को भूख लगने लगी तो मैंने उन्हें खाना खाने दिया।

८ हमें बताया गया कि मेहमान आने लगे थे।

९ जब तक मैं तुम्हें न बताऊँ तब तक किसी को अन्दर आने न दो ।

१० भविष्य में जो लोग काम नहीं करते उन्हें पैसा नहीं दिया जाएगा ।

14.a.3 (sample answer)

जब सुरेश कमरे में आया तो उसने देखा कि संगीता ने कुछ नेपाली ज़ेवर पहने थे । जब उसने उनके बारे में पूछा, तो संगीता ने जवाब दिया कि इन्हें काठमांडु से लाया गया था । फिर सुरेश ने पूछा कि हरीश कल की दावत में क्यों नहीं आया; पर संगीता को मालूम नहीं था । संगीता ने कहा कि शायद हरीश के पिता ने उसे आने नहीं दिया था । सुरेश कहने लगा कि शायद खन्ना साहब चाहते थे... पर संगीता ने सुरेश को अपनी बात को ख़त्म करने नहीं दिया । विषय बदलने के लिए संगीता ने कहा कि दूरदर्शन को देखा जाए । पर उसकी गुस्ताख़ी सुरश को बहुत बुरी लगी थी इसलिए जब कमला कमरे में आई तो सुरेश ने उससे शिकायत की कि तुम्हारी बेटी ने मुझसे बुरी बातें कही हैं ।

14.b.1 (sample answer)

१ मेरे जितने दोस्त हैं, सभी छुट्टी पर गए हैं । All the friends I have, have gone on holiday.

२ तुम जितने ध्यान से पढ़ोगे, उतना सीखोगे । The harder you study the more you'll learn.

३ जितनी अच्छी यह नई किताब है, उतनी अच्छी तुम्हारी किताब नहीं हो सकती । Your book can't be as good as this new book.

४ जहाँ हम लोग रहते हैं, वहाँ कोई शराब की दुकान नहीं है । There's no liquor shop where we live.

५ छुट्टियों में हम वहाँ जाएँ जहाँ बहुत कम लोग जाते हों । On our holidays let's go to a place where very few people go.

६ जहाँ महँगी दुकानें और शानदार होटल हैं वहाँ अमीर लोगों की आबादी ज़रूर होगी । Where there are expensive shops and fancy hotels there are sure to be rich people living.

७ तुम्हारे पास जितने कपड़े हैं उतने ही हमारे पास भी हैं । We have just as many clothes as you do.

८ जितनी बड़ी दिल्ली है उतना बड़ा लखनऊ नहीं है । Lucknow is not as big as Delhi.

14b.2

Yesterday I was invited to Kamala and Prakash Kumar's dinner. It was a very fine dinner. I've never eaten as much as we were given to eat. When Kamala started giving me more for a third time I began saying 'Enough! Enough!' but she took no notice. Meat, vegetables, daal, roti, rice, chutney – so much food had been prepared that I just can't tell you! It wasn't the kind of Indian food you get in London; here everything was completely fresh, and it was as tasty as it was fresh! The sweet dish had been brought from some shop, but apart from the sweet everything had been made at home. Kamala ji is an expert at cooking.

But you must be wondering, who came to the dinner altogether? I'll tell you. I arrived late because of my studying. When I arrived I was sat in a corner of the room. Khanna ji had been sat in the middle, and next to him his wife, whom I thought very nice. Their son had been invited too, but for some reason he didn't come. Sangeeta had gone to see a film with her friend Pinkie (Khanna ji's younger sister); they got home when the film ended at about eleven and they ate whatever food was left. (The film was 'Hum Apke Hain Kaun', which was made several years ago; Sangeeta must have already seen it at least four or five times, and I don't understand why she wanted to see it again.) Suresh also came; Kamala ji sat him near her. Arun had gone to see some friend so he was '*anupasthit*' – absent. He's very fond of such words – he loads his speech with so many Sanskrit words that half of what he says goes right over my head.

Several interesting things about Hindi were said during the dinner. Suresh said that Delhi Hindi has become corrupted, because of Panjabi. (Sharma ji too was saying in class that Panjabis mostly say '*maine jānā hai*' [for 'I have to go'] which is a wrong usage – only '*mujhe jānā hai*' is correct. But when Suresh said this Prakash ji glared at him in such a way that Suresh fell silent, poor fellow. The thing is, you see, that Khanna is himself a Panjabi. And Prakash completely cowers in front of him – like a 'wet cat'! In the end Kamala changed the subject and made some joke about Rishi and Raj, and everyone started laughing. But afterwards Kamala ji must have given Suresh a good scolding!

Mrs Khanna is a very nice lady. She knows a lot about languages too. When I asked her why 'Rajasthan' has a '*th*' while Pakistan only has '*t*' she explained it to me by saying that '*sthān*' is a Sanskrit word while '*stān*' is Persian. Both words have the same meaning – 'place'. So even words have families! But not like the Kumar family. Not at all!

15a.1 (sample answers)

१ हम दिन भर काम करते रहेंगे । We'll go on working all day.

२ बेचारी छात्रा दस दिन तक पढ़ती रही । The poor student went on studying for ten days.

३ आप ध्यान से काम करते रहिए, तभी सफल होंगे । Keep working attentively, *then* you'll be successful.

४ सरकार की शक्ति बढ़ती गई, यहाँ तक कि हमें देश को छोड़ना पड़ा । The power of the government kept growing, to the point that we had to leave the country.

५ बादल और भी घने होते गए, फिर दस दिन तक बर्फ़ गिरती रही । The clouds went on thickening , then it kept snowing for ten days.

15a.2

१ पिताजी एक मशहूर सरकारी अख़बार चलाया करते थे । Father used to run a famous government newspaper.

२ वह बदमाश अपने बच्चों को मारा करता है । That scoundrel makes a habit of beating his children.

३ सच है कि किसी ज़माने में हमारे भी कई नौकर हुआ करते थे । It's true that at some time we too used to have several servants.

४ शाम को दादीजी हमेशा मंदिर जाया करती हैं । In the evening Grandmother always goes to the temple.

५ हमारे पड़ोसी हमें अक्सर धोखा दिया करते हैं । Our neighbours regularly trick us.

15a.3

१ जैसा आपने कहा था, वैसा ही हो गया । It happened just as you'd said.

२ जैसी फ़िल्में आजकल बन रही हैं, वैसी फ़िल्में मेरे बचपन में नहीं बनती थीं । The type of films that are being made today weren't made in my childhood.

३ जिस तरह की नौकरी मैं करती हूँ उस तरह की तुम क्यों नहीं करते ? Why don't you do a job like the one I do?

४ जिस तरह के मकान इस इलाक़े में बन रहे हैं उस तरह के मकान पुराने शहर में नहीं मिलते । The kind of houses that are being built in this area aren't to be found in the old city.

५ जैसा मौक़ा तुम्हें आज मिला है वैसा मौक़ा तुम्हें दुबारा नहीं मिलनेवाला है । You're not likely to get another chance like the one you got today.

15b.1

१ उस जैसे लोगों को नौकरी आसानी से नहीं मिलती ।
२ जैसे कि दर्ज़नों लोग मुझे बता चुके थे, वह आदमी पागल हो गया था ।
३ वह इस तरह सोया जैसे वह कई हफ़्तों से सोया न हो ।
४ हम लोग सन् १९४७ से इस देश में रह रहे हैं ।
५ जब से दुर्घटना हुई तबसे उसने गाड़ी नहीं चलाई है ।
६ अगर दवा से कुछ फ़ायदा न हो तो आपको डाक्टर से शिकायत करनी चाहिए ।
७ मैं मालिक से कुछ कहना चाहता था मगर डर के मारे मैं कुछ बोल नहीं पाया ।
८ आज आपको अख़बार ख़ुद लाने पड़ेंगे क्योंकि अख़बार-वाला बीमार है ।

15b.2 (includes sample answers)

१ प्रताप तीन साल से हिन्दी पढ़ रहा है । मैं तो एक साल से पढ़ रहा हूँ । मैंने पिछले साल ही हिन्दी सीखना शुरू किया ।
२ जो आदमी प्रताप को हिन्दी पढ़ाया करता था, वह उत्तर प्रदेश से था ।
३ जी हाँ, वह कभी कभी उच्चारण की गलतियाँ किया करता है; उदाहरण के लिए, जब उसे "मोड़" कहना था उसने "मोर" कहा ।
४ नहीं, उसके पास मोर क्यों होगा !
५ जी नहीं, दादी जी कहती हैं कि प्रताप को हिन्दी सीखनी रहनी चाहिए ।
६ क्योंकि उसको मालूम है कि खन्ना जी के पास ड्राइवर है ।
७ क्योंकि उसके पिताजी ने कहा था कि आज काम करनेवालों की छुट्टी है ।
८ ग़रीब लोगों की हालत ख़राब है; उनको छुट्टी नहीं मिलती, और बहुत मेहनत करने पर भी उन्हें पैसे की कमी रहती है ।
९ छोटू को खन्ना जी से बात करनी चाहिए ।
१० मेरे ख़याल से खन्ना जी छोटू के बारे में परवाह नहीं करते; लेकिन हरीश तो छोटू की मदद करना चाहता है ।

15b.3 (sample answer)

२१ जून १९९९। शनिवार है। आज कई काम करने थे; कालेज तो नहीं जाना था, लेकिन कालेज का काम बहुत था, और मैं जानता था कि आज नानी जी फ़ोन करेंगी, इसलिए मैंने सोचा कि मुझे बाहर नहीं जाना चाहिए, घर पर रुककर पढ़ाई का काम करूँगा। मगर ऐसा नहीं हुआ। क़रीब दस बजे रवि और रीता ने फ़ोन करके कहा कि हम लोग समुद्र के किनारे जा रहे हैं, तुम भी साथ चलो। मैंने जाने से इनकार तो नहीं किया, बस इतना कहा कि सुनो, एक छोटी-सी समस्या है – शनिवार को मेरी नानी जी अमरीका से फ़ोन किया करती हैं, इसलिए तुम्हारे साथ जाना मुश्किल होगा। फिर रवि गुस्सा होकर कहने लगा कि तुम्हारी नानी के सिवा तुम्हारा कोई नहीं है जिसके बारे में तुम परवाह करते हो! इसलिए मैंने कहा चलो ठीक है, चलता हूँ तुम्हारे साथ।

समुद्र के किनारे बहुत भीड़ थी। अच्छी-सी जगह थी लेकिन मेरे लिए तो रवि के गुस्से ने दिन को बरबाद कर दिया था। इतना डरपोक क्यों हूँ मैं? उसकी बातों पर ध्यान क्यों देता हूँ, जैसे कि वह मेरा बाप हो! मुझे उसे साफ़ कहना चाहिए था कि आज मुझे बाहर नहीं जाना है; मगर डर के मारे मैं कुछ बोल ही नहीं पाया; और दिन भर मैं नानी जी के फ़ोन के बारे में चिन्ता करता रहा।

मैं बड़ी देर से घर लौटा। जब मैं कमरे में आया तो फ़ोन पर नानी जी का मेसेज था – "बेटे, आज तुमसे बात नहीं कर पाऊँगी, कुछ दोस्तों के साथ समुद्र के किनारे जा रही हूँ। कल फ़ोन करूँगी। जीते रहो।"

16.a.1 (sample answers)

१ जी हाँ, मुझे साइकिल ठीक करना आता है; मगर साइकल चलाना तो नहीं आता।

२ आम तौर पर मैं काम साढ़े आठ बजे शुरू करता हूँ; पर जिस दिन मैं देर से उठता हूँ मैं साढ़े नौ से पहले नहीं शुरू करता।

३ मुझे तो पुरानी फ़िल्में ही पसंद हैं क्योंकि उनके गाने बहुत बढ़िया होते हैं।

४ जी हाँ, मैं लगभग हर काम के लिए कंप्यूटर का इस्तेमाल करता हूँ!

५ जी हाँ मैं अक्सर हिन्दी में ही ई-मेल भेजा करता हूँ, लेकिन ई-मेल में देवनागरी लिपि का इस्तेमाल करना थोड़ा मुश्किल है।

६ जी हाँ, मेरी शादी कई साल पहले हुई थी। हमारे तीन बच्चे भी हैं।

७ जी नहीं, आज तो मुझे किसी से नहीं मिलना है। मुझे अपनी साइकिल को ठीक करना है।

८ इस कमरे में कई चीज़ें दिखाई दे रही हैं – बहुत सारी किताबें, एक कंप्यूटर, कुछ पुराने अख़बार... और मेज़ पर कई चिट्ठियाँ पड़ी हैं जिनका मुझे जवाब देना चाहिए।

९ मैं उनको एक काग़ज़ पर लिख लेता हूँ और बार बार उनका सही उच्चारण करने की कोशिश करता हूँ ।

१० जी हाँ, एक साल पहले मैं उत्तर प्रदेश के एक छोटे-से गाँव में एक चाय की दुकान पर चाय पी रहा था ।

16a.2

१ हमें बताया गया है कि हमें दूसरे यात्रियों का इंतज़ार करना पड़ेगा ।

२ सामान तो ट्रेन पर लाद दिया गया है मगर हमारे खाने का इंतज़ाम किसी ने नहीं किया है ।

३ मालूम होता है कि किसी यात्री का देहान्त हो गया है ।

४ कृपया उन दूसरे यात्रियों का पीछा करें; आपके बच्चों की देखभाल हम लोग करेंगे ।

५ मैंने एक दोस्त को फ़ोन करने की कोशिश की लेकिन फ़ोन काम नहीं कर रहा था ।

६ आज वे कंप्यूटर का इस्तेमाल नहीं कर सकते क्योंकि बिजली नहीं है ।

७ जो लोग यहाँ नौकरी करते हैं, उनकी निंदा न करना, कसूर उनका तो नहीं है ।

८ जिस आदमी से मेरी मुलाक़ात स्टेशन पर हुई, उसी से मैंने शादी कर ली ।

16a.3 (sample answer)

हरीश ने छोटू को एक अच्छा-सा मज़ाक सुनाया, जिसे सुनकर छोटू हँसने लगा । छोटू को यह भी अच्छा लगा होगा कि उसके मालिक का बेटा उससे इस तरह से बात रहा है । हरीश छोटू से पूछने लगा कि खन्ना जी कहाँ हैं; और छोटू के जवाब से पता चला कि छोटू ख़ुश नहीं है; वह खन्ना जी से कुछ माँगना चाहता था मगर मारे डर के कुछ बोल न पाया था । हरीश ने कहा कि किसी से डरने की ज़रूरत नहीं, डरपोक मत बनना ।

बाद में जब खन्ना जी वापस आए तो छोटू ने फिर से उनसे बात करने की कोशिश की । शुरू में उसने हरीश की थोड़ी-सी तारीफ़ की, फिर यह पूछा कि हरीश की शादी कब हो जाएगी । लेकिन इन बातों का खन्ना जी पर कोई असर नहीं पड़ा, और जब छोटू ने खन्ना जी से अपनी हालत के बारे में कुछ कहना चाहा तो खन्ना जी ने उसकी बात काटकर कहा कि मैं बड़ी जल्दी में हूँ, मुझे एक मीटिंग का इंतज़ाम करना है । इसलिए फिर से निराशा हुई बेचारे छोटू को ।

16b.1

१ जहाँ मैं पैदा हुआ, वहाँ पुराने ज़माने में तरह तरह के जंगली जानवर घूमा करते थे ।
Where I was born, various kinds of wild animals used to roam in the olden days.

२ जहाँ जंगली जानवर रहते हैं वहाँ इमारतें नहीं बनाई जानी चाहिए थीं । Buildings should not have been put up where wild animals live.

३ जहाँ भी तुम बैठना चाहते हो, बैठ सकते हो । You can sit wherever you like.

४ जिस गाँव में नानी जी बचपन में रहती थीं मेरी शादी वहीं हुई थी । My wedding took place in the very village where my grandmother lived in her childhood.

५ गाँव के पुराने इलाक़े में जहाँ गाँधी जी रहा करते थे वहाँ बिजली का इस्तेमाल नहीं किया जाता है । In the old area of the village where Gandhi ji used to stay, electricity isn't used.

६ जब तक मेरे पड़ोसी घर पहुँचे तब तक उनके पिता का देहान्त हो चुका था । By the time my neighbours got home their father had already passed away.

16b.2

1 Which different places did you visit in India and what various things did you see?
2 In his childhood he must have had many kinds of experience.
3 All the people had become lost ('sunk') in their own thoughts.
4 After having piping hot tea we all went off to our own rooms.
5 Give the porters 20 rupees each.
6 Well Raju, are you in the pink? Like some tea or anything?
7 Why should I waste my time going to some useless meeting?

16b.3

१ हमें उनको दस दस रुपए देने चाहिए जिससे कि वे कुछ चाय-वाय लें ।

२ पाकिस्तान में तुम्हें कौन-कौन मिला ?

३ याद रखो कि ऐसी गंदी जगहों में तुम्हें खाना-वाना नहीं लेना चाहिए ।

४ रोज़ खाना खाने के बाद आप सबों को एक एक गोली खानी चाहिए ।

५ मेरे पास न पैसा है न वक़्त, इसलिए मेहमानों की देखभाल तुम्हें ख़ुद करनी होगी ।

17a.1

१ अगर आप हवाई जहाज़ से गए होते तो अब तक पहुँच जाते ।

२ हालाँकि मैंने उन्हें रोकने की कोशिश की, फिर भी उन्होंने मेरी सलाह पर ध्यान नहीं दिया ।

३ अगर दिल्ली यहाँ से इतनी दूर नहीं होती तो मैं तुरंत तुमसे मिलने आता ।

४ अगर मुझे मालूम होता कि उसकी हालत कितनी ख़राब थी तो मैं उसे सच नहीं बताता ।

५ अगर हीरो इतना लोकप्रिय नहीं होता तो ऐसी फ़िल्म देखने कोई भी नहीं आता ।

६ हालाँकि वह मेरे दादा जी को अच्छी तरह जानती थी फिर भी उसने सुझाव दिया कि हम उन्हें बुलाएँ ।

७ अगर तुमने मुझा बताया होता कि समस्या कितनी गंभीर थी तो मैं अपना समय नहीं गँवाता ।

८ हालाँकि मैंने कहा कि कसूर मेरा नहीं है, फिर भी उसने शिकायत की ।

17a.2

१ हालाँकि मैंने बहुत कोशिश की फिर भी मैं काम को पूरा नहीं कर पाया । Although I tried a lot, I couldn't complete the work.

२ हालाँकि मैं रात भर तलाश करती रही वह पुराना पत्र नहीं मिला । Although I went on searching all night I didn't find that old letter.

२ हालाँकि मैंने रस्सी को काटने की बहुत कोशिश की, फिर भी वह कटी नहीं । Although I tried hard to cut the string it wouldn't cut.

४ हालाँकि हमने शिकायत कर दी फिर भी कोई परवाह नहीं करता । Although we complained, nobody cares.

17a.3 (sample answer)

छोटू खन्ना जी, एक बात कहूँ ? अगर आपको फ़ुरसत हो तो...

खन्ना ज़रूर छोटू भैया, ज़रूर, क्या कहना चाहते हो ? तुम्हें किस चीज़ की चिन्ता है ? साफ़ साफ़ कहो !

छोटू सर, मैं अपना काम अच्छी तरह से करता हूँ न? इसलिए मुझे साल में पाँच हफ़्ते की छुट्टी मिलनी चाहिए । और... अगर ज़्यादा पैसा भी मिल जाता तो अच्छा होता ।

खन्ना अरे इतनी-सी बात ? इसका तो इंतज़ाम आज ही किया जाएगा । तुमने पहले क्यों नहीं कहा ?

छोटू सर, मैं आपको तकलीफ़ देना नहीं चाहता था । आप इतने व्यस्त रहते हैं कि...

खन्ना व्यस्त तो हूँ, फिर भी अगर मुझसे बात नहीं करोगे तो किससे करोगे छोटू? हम दोनों साथ साथ काम जो करते हैं, भाइयों के जैसे ।

छोटू खन्ना जी, किन शब्दों में आपसे धन्यवाद कहूँ ?

खन्ना अरे धन्यवाद-वन्यवाद को भूल जाओ । एक बात और – मैं तुमको अपना ड्राइवर बनाने की सोच रहा हूँ । मैं हर तरह से तुम्हारी देखभाल करूँगा, मेरे पुराने दोस्त !

17b.1

१ खन्ना जी को अपने बेटे हरीश की शादी के बारे में चिंता है ।

२ नहीं, उमा परेशान नहीं है । उसको उम्मीद है कि हरीश संगीता से ही शादी करेगा ।

३ खन्ना जी ऐसा सोचते हैं क्योंकि संगीता नौकरी नहीं करती है ।

४ मैं तो उमा से सहमत हूँ क्योंकि जिससे प्यार हो उसी से शादी करनी चाहिए ।

५ नहीं, बिलकुल नहीं । संगीता तो सुहास से ही प्यार करती है, हरीश से नहीं ।

६ क्योंकि शादी के मामले में संगीता अपने माता-पिता की बातें मानने को तैयार नहीं है ।

७ हाँ, प्रकाश अनीता से बात कर चुका है – पर रूबरू नहीं, फ़ोन पर ही ।

८ हाँ, मैं तो संगीता की गुस्ताख़ी को माफ़ कर देता, यह समझकर कि उसेकी अपनी ज़िन्दगी है ।

17b.2

१ एक साल के अन्दर मैंने पूरे सात लेख लिख डाले । Within a year I churned out a full seven articles.

२ उसने जो पैसे बड़ी मेहनत करके कमाये थे, सब को गँवा दिया है । He's squandered all the money he earned through hard work.

३ अरे, तुम किस तरह की पागल बातें बोल बैठे ? Oh, what kind of crazy things did you go and say?

४ मेरे बेटे ने गुस्से में अपने सबसे क़ीमती कपड़ों को फाड़ डाला । In anger my son ripped his most expensive clothes to shreds.

५ समाचार को सुनकर छोटू हँस उठा लेकिन दूसरे लोग रो पड़े । On hearing the news Chotu burst out laughing but the others started crying.

६ पुलिस ने कह रखा है कि बेचारा खिड़की से गिर पड़ा था । The police have maintained that the poor fellow had fallen from the window.

७ जैसे ही दूसरे लोग आ गए, हमने काम आरंभ कर दिया । As soon as the other people turned up we began work.

८ जिसने हमारे दोस्त को मार डाला, उससे हम रूबरू बात कर लें । Let's have a face-to-face talk with the person who killed our friend.

17b.3 (sample answers)

१ मेहरबानी करके आप हमारा खाना बनाने की भी तकलीफ़ करें – अगर वक़्त मिले तो ।

२ मुझे उम्मीद है कि इस साल के आख़िर तक यह किताब ख़त्म की जाएगी ।

३ अगर आपको फ़ुरसत हो तो अपने ख़ूबसूरत दोस्त को यह ख़त दे दें । शुक्रिया ।

४ शुरू में मुसाफ़िर को लगा कि सफ़र ज़्यादा मुश्किल होगा लेकिन इसका बहुत फ़ायदा होगा ।

५ सवाल – आम हिन्दी और आम उर्दू में कितना फ़र्क़ है ? जवाब – कौन कह सकता है कि दोनों ज़बानों में कोई ख़ास फ़र्क़ नहीं है ?

१ कृपा करके आप हमारा भोजन बनाने का भी कष्ट करें – यदि समय मिले तो ।
२ मुझे आशा है कि इस वर्ष के अन्त तक यह पुस्तक समाप्त की जाएगी ।
३ यदि आपको अवकाश हो तो अपने सुंदर मित्र को यह पत्र दे दें । धन्यवाद ।
४ आरंभ में यात्री को लगा कि यात्रा अधिक कठिन होगी किंतु इसका बहुत लाभ होगा ।
५ प्रश्न – "साधारण हिन्दी और साधारण उर्दू में कितना अंतर है ?" उत्तर – "कौन कह सकता है कि दोनों भाषाओं में कोई विशेष अंतर नहीं है ?"

18a.1 (sample answers)
१ इस शहर में रहते हुए मुझे कोई बीस साल हुए हैं ।
२ जिस कमरे में मैं बैठा हुआ हूँ, इसमें बहुत सारी किताबें हैं । फ़र्श पर भी किताबों के ढेर पड़े हुए हैं । मेज़ पर कुछ लकड़ी के बने हुए खिलौने हैं – एक छोटा-सा हाथी और तीन-चार चिड़ियाँ ।
३ आज मैं पुराने कपड़े पहने हुए हूँ क्योंकि मुझे बाहर नहीं जाना है, घर पर ही रहना है ।
४ हाँ, बिना भारत गए हिन्दी सीखी जा सकती है, लेकिन हिन्दी बोलने का पूरा आनंद तो भारत में ही आता है ।
५ जो लोग पैसे जोड़ते जोड़ते लाखों रुपए कमाते हैं उनको "लखपति" कहते हैं ।
६ मेरे लिए तो यह सवाल थोड़ा मुश्किल है क्योंकि अभी तक यह किताब छपी ही नहीं है !
७ जी हाँ, नहाते समय मैं अक्सर पुराने फ़िल्मी गाने गाता हूँ – जब घर में अकेला हूँ तो !
८ हाँ, जवाब लिखते लिखते थक तो गया हूँ, लेकिन मुझे मज़ा भी आ रहा है ।

18a.2
१ अपने दोस्तों का इंतज़ार करते करते हम ऊबने लगे । We began to get bored waiting for our friends.
२ फ़र्श पर पड़े हुए कपड़ों को उठाओ और उन्हें उस टूटी हुई कुरसी पर रख दो । Pick up the clothes lying on the floor and put them on that broken chair.
३ लखनऊ में रहते हुए मुझे सात महीने हुए हैं । I've been living in Lucknow for seven months.
४ वह गाती हुई लड़की कौन है ? उसे गाना सीखते कितने साल हुए हैं ? Who is that singing girl (that girl who is singing)? How many years has she been learning singing?

५ इस स्कूल में पढ़ते हुए बच्चे लोग काम करने का नाम नहीं लेते । The children studying in this school don't even think of working.
६ अंकल के पहुँचते ही सारे घरवाले चुप हो गए । As soon as Uncle arrived the whole family fell silent.

18b.1

१ अगर तुम्हें प्यास लगी तो चायवाले को बुलवाकर चाय बनवा लो ।
२ अगर आप कहानी को नहीं समझ पाते, तो किसी से उसका अँग्रेज़ी में अनुवाद करवा लीजिए ।
३ पंडित जी कहते हैं कि हमें बच्चों को संस्कृत के शब्द सिखवाने चाहिए, न कि उर्दू के ।
४ बिना कुछ कहे मैंने किताब को बंद करके अलमारी में रख दिया ।
५ पड़ोसियों से शिकायत करते समय मैं उनसे हिन्दी सीख रहा था ।
६ टी०वी० देखते देखते मैं समझने लगा कि बहुत-से लोग अपनी हिन्दी में बहुत-से अँग्रेज़ी के शब्द मिला लेते हैं ।
७ टूटे हुए खिलौने फ़र्श पर पड़े हुए थे ।
८ मेरी दोस्त के घर पहुँचते ही मैंने उसे बताया कि क्या हो गया था ।

18b.2

You perhaps might want to know what happened later in the Kumar family. It's a very long story; some day I'll write about it in detail. Meanwhile I'll just tell you that everybody lived very happily (except poor Suresh). No need to say that Sangeeta and Suhas got married, and in fine style; these days they're living in Delhi, and the Lucknow house has been let to some Hindi students who have come from London. If you ever find yourself in Delhi, go into some shop in Khan Market and you'll see Sangeeta and Suhas shopping – always together, always smiling, always happy. Sangeeta is about to have a baby too. One problem in the family has been that Dadi ji's health was poor for some time; for as long as two or three months there was much anxiety about her. But now she's recovered again.

You'll be pleased to know that Prakash is being promoted in the office, one result of which is that he is also able to help Chotu; at the moment Chotu is learning to drive – he'll become Prakash's driver. Arun and Prem's second book is selling like hot cakes; it seems that in the end they must have accepted Prakash's advice, because this second book of theirs is a love story – *A Tale of Two Hearts*, in which

Sangeeta's whole story has been told in detail. It's possible that a film will be made of it too, later on.

The enmity there used to be between Raj and Rishi is gradually coming to an end, and a kind of friendship is forming between them – although from time to time the old warfare breaks out again. What can be said about Suresh? For several reasons he has had to undergo much suffering, and, bored with life, he has started drinking rather heavily. Previously he was working in some hotel, but because of his excessive drinking his job too has come to an end. God knows what will become of him in the future. Khanna Sahib is about to go to London for some time, in connection with work, and Uma has got a good job in London too. Harish will go to do a BA at some American university – while Pinkie is about to marry an Englishman. And Pratap? His continuing story is very interesting (if Arun were here now he'd say it was *adbhut* – 'remarkable'!). You would be astonished to hear what happens in Pratap's life; but his story will be told in some other book!

18b.3

Friends, you are just finishing the 18th chapter of this book – you have worked very hard. The road was a little long; I very much enjoyed walking with you. I hope that your Hindi studies will continue in the future. This book is finishing, but there is no end to the road of studying. The question of how to study further may arise in your mind. My first suggestion is that you be sure to buy yourself one or two good dictionaries, so that reading books and newspapers will become a little easier. R.S. McGregor's *Hindi-English Dictionary*, which is published by the Oxford University Press, is very good indeed; this dictionary is printed from both Oxford and Delhi, and should be readily available. In addition, the several dictionaries by Hardev Bahri are also excellent. Keep these books with you. You shouldn't have too much difficulty reading simple stories.My second suggestion is that you make a habit of watching Hindi films, so that you get practice in hearing and understanding ordinary conversation. And if possible you should try to go to India – or to some other country where Hindi is spoken; then every Hindi-speaker will become your teacher, whether pandit, train passenger, or shopkeeper! Whatever happens, I am confident that you will very much enjoy learning and speaking Hindi. Goodbye.

HINDI–ENGLISH GLOSSARY

Key

inf = infinitive; ^{m} = masculine; ^{f} = feminine; ^{pl} = plural; $^{m\,f}$ (e.g. विद्यार्थी$^{m\,f}$) = used for both males and females; $^{m/f}$ (e.g. क़लम$^{m/f}$) = used in either gender; inv = invariable noun/adjective in *-ā*; ^{N} = always uses ने construction in perfective tenses; ^{n} = sometimes uses ने construction in perfective tenses; numbers (1 2 3 etc.) refer to the Unit in which a word first appears.

अ

अंकल^{m} *ankal* 5 uncle

अँग्रेज़^{m,f} *ãgrez* 1 English person

अंत^{m} *ant* 12 end

अंतर^{m} *ant ar* 17 difference

अंदर *andar* 8 inside, within

अँधेरा^{m} *ãdherā* 15 darkness

अकेला *akelā*; 4 **अकेले** (adv.) alone

अकेलापन^{m} *akelāpan* 6 loneliness

अक्सर *aksar* 6 often; usually

अख़बार^{m} *akhbār* 2 newspaper

अगर *agar* 9 if

अगला *aglā* 8 next

अगस्त^{m} *agast* 15 August

अचानक *acānak* 15 suddenly, unexpectedly

अच्छा *acchā* 1 good, nice; really? I see!; well, proficiently; **अच्छा-ख़ासा** really good

अजनबी^{m} *ajnabī* 17 stranger

अजीब *ajīb* 13 strange, odd

अठारह *aṭhārah* 8 eighteen

अद्भुत *adbhut* 12 remarkable

अधिक *adhik* 9 much, many, more; **अधिक से अधिक** at the most

अधेड़ *adheṛ* 18 middle-aged

अध्यापक^{m} *adhyāpak* 2 teacher

अनबन^{f} *anban* 13 discord

अनुपस्थित *anupasthit* 14 absent

अनुभव^{m} *anubhav* 16 experience

अनुवाद^{m} *anuvād* 18 translation

अनौपचारिक रूप से *anaupcārik rūp se* 15 informally

अपना *apnā* 6 (one's) own; **अपने आप** of one's own accord, oneself

अफ़सोस^{m} *afsos* 4 regret

अब *ab* 3 now; **अब की बार** this time

अभी *abhī* 2 at the moment, right now; still

अभ्यास^{m} *abhyās* 13 practice

अमरीकन *amrīkan* 1 American

अमरीका^{m} *amrīkā* 9 America

अमीर *amīr* 14 rich, wealthy
अरे *are* 4 oh! what! hey!
अर्ज़ी [f] *arzī* 18 application
अर्थ [m] *arth* 14 meaning
अलग *alag* 7 separate, different; separately
अलमारी [f] *almārī* 1 cupboard
अवकाश [m] *avkāś* leisure, free time
अवश्य *avaśy* 10 certainly
असंभव *asambhav* 10 impossible
असर [m] *asar* 17 effect, impact; असर पड़ना to have an effect
असल में *asal mẽ* 15 really, in fact
असली *aslī* 9 real
अस्पताल [m] *aspatāl* 8 hospital
अहम *aham* 16 important

आ

आँख [f] *ā̃kh* 8 eye; आँखें दिखाना [N] to look angrily
आकाश [m] *ākāś* 18 sky
आख़िर [m] *ākhir* 18 end; आख़िर (में) in the end, after all
आग [f] *āg* 13 fire
आगरा [m] *āgrā* 8 Agra
आगे *āge* 13 later, ahead; आगे चलकर in future, from now on
आज *āj* 2 today
आजकल *ājkal* 8 nowadays
आटो [m] *āṭo* 10 auto-rickshaw
आठ *āṭh* 7 eight; आठों पहर all day
आत्मीयता से *ātmīytā se* 18 cordially
आदमी [m] *ādmī* 1 man; person
आधा [m] *ādhā* 10 half
आधीरात [m] *ādhīrāt* 15 midnight
आनंद [m] *ānand* 11 joy, enjoyment; आनंद आना to feel enjoyment
आना *ānā* 5 to come
आप *āp* 1 you (formal)
आपका *āpkā* 3 your, yours
आपस में *āpas mẽ* 15 between/among themselves
आफ़ताब [m] *āftāb* 18 sun (poetic)
आबादी [f] *ābādī* 14 population, settlement
आम[1] [m] *ām* 12 mango
आम[2] *ām* 8 ordinary, general; आम तौर पर usually, normally
आरंभ [m] *ārambh* 17 beginning
आराम [m] *ārām* 3 rest, comfort; आराम करना [N] *to rest;* आराम से comfortably, easily
आर्थिक *ārthik* 14 financial
आलसी *ālsī* 16 lazy
आवश्यकता [f] *āvaśyaktā* 11 necessity
आवाज़ [f] *āvāz* 12 voice, sound
आशा [f] *āśā* 1 hope
आश्चर्य [m] *āścarya* 18 surprise; आश्चर्यजनक astonishing
आसान *āsān* 9 easy
आसानी से *āsānī se* 15 easily

इ

इंतज़ाम m *intazām* 9 arrangement(s), organisation; **का इंतज़ाम करना** N *to arrange*

इंतज़ार m *intazār* 16 wait, waiting; **का इंतज़ार करना** N to wait for

इकलौता *iklautā* 18 sole, only (child)

इक्कीस *ikkīs* 6 twenty-one

इतना *itnā* 10 so, so much

इतिहास m *itihās* 9 history

इधर *idhar* 5 here, over here; recently, latterly

इन *in* 3 oblique of **ये** *ye*

(से) इनकार करना N *(se) inkār karnā* 15 to refuse (to)

इनसान m *insān* 16 human being, person

इमारत f *imārat* 16 building

इरादा m *irādā* 9 intention

इलाक़ा m *ilāqā* 14 area

इलाज m *ilāj* 10 treatment, cure

इलाहाबाद m *ilāhābād* 13 Allahabad

इश्क़ m *iśq* 18 romantic love; **इश्क़ लड़ाना** N to have an affair

इस *is* 3 oblique of **यह**; **इस लिए** so; **इसी लिए** *that's* why

इस्तरी f *istrī* 18 clothes-iron; ironing

इस्तेमाल m *istemāl* 16 use; **का इस्तेमाल करना** N to use

ई

ईंट f *ī̃ṭ* brick

ई-पत्र m *ī-patr* 16 e-mail

ई-मेल f *ī-mel* 16 e-mail

ईव-टीज़िंग f *īv-ṭīzing* 9 'Eve-teasing' – sexual harassment of girls and women

उ

उँगली f *ũglī* 11 finger

उचित *ucit* 10 proper, appropriate

उच्चारण m *uccāraṇ* 6 pronunciation

उठना *uṭhnā* 6 to get up, rise

उठाना N *uṭhānā* 11 to pick up, lift; to take (**तकलीफ़** trouble etc.)

उड़ना *uṛnā* 15 to fly

उड़ाना N *uṛānā* 18 to make fly; to squander

उतरना *utarnā* 17 to get down, alight

उतारना N *utārnā* 10 to take down/off

उत्तर m *uttar* 17 reply

उदाहरण m *udāharaṇ* 16 example

उद्घाटन m *udghāṭan* 16 inauguration

उधर *udhar* 5 there, over there

उधार m *udhār* 11 loan; **उधार लेना** N to borrow

उन *un* 3 oblique of **वे** *ve*

उन्नीस *unnīs* 6 nineteen

उपन्यास m *upanyās* 15 novel

उपहार m *uphār* 11 present, gift

उबलना *ubalnā* 17 to boil; to rage

उम्मीद f *ummīd* 10 hope

उम्र f *umr, umar* 4 age

उर्दू f *urdū* 7 Urdu

उल्लू m *ullū* 16 'owl' – idiot

उषा f *uṣā* 9 dawn

उस *us* 3 oblique of वह *vah*

ऊ

ऊँचा *ū̃cā* 10 high

ऊपर *ūpar* 8 above; up; upstairs

ऊबना *ūbnā* 18 to be bored

ऊल-जलूल *ūl-jalūl* 14 silly, pointless

ऋ

ऋषि m *ṛṣi* 5 sage, seer

ए

एक *ek* 1 one; एक साथ together

एकदम *ekdam* 4 completely

एकाध *ekādh* 18 one or two, a couple (of)

ऐ

ऐनक f *ainak* 18 spectacles

ऐश m *aiś* 8 wanton luxury; ऐश करना N to live a life of pleasure

ऐसा *aisā* 6 such, thus, like this

ओ

ओ *o* 3 o!

ओहो *oho* 17 oho! oh no!

औ

औपचारिक रूप से *aupcārik rūp se* 15 formally

और *aur* 1 and; more, else, other; और कोई any other

औरत f *aurat* 7 woman

क, क़

कंजूस *kanjūs* 10 miserly, mean

कंपनी f *kampanī* 6 company, firm

कंप्यूटर m *kampyūṭar* 16 computer

कंबल m *kambal* 5 blanket

कई *kaī* 3 several

कटना *kaṭnā* 17 to be cut

कठिन *kaṭhin* 9 hard, difficult

कथक m *kathak* 18 kathak, a North Indian dance style

क़दम m *qadam* 18 step, pace

कपड़ा m *kapṛā* 3 cloth; garment

कब *kab* 11 when?; कब से since when?

कभी *kabhī* 6 sometime; कभी कभी sometimes; कभी नहीं never

कम *kam* 4 less; little; कम करना N *to reduce;* कम से कम at least

कमरा m *kamrā* 1 room

कमाना N *kamānā* 8 to earn

कमाल^m kamāl 18 miracle, wonder
कमी^f kamī 18 lack, want
करना^N karnā 5 to do
क़रीब qarīb 14 near; about, roughly
करोड़^m karoṛ 7 ten million
कल kal 4 yesterday; tomorrow
कलकत्ता^m kalkattā 8 Calcutta
क़लम^m/f qalam 3 pen
कवि^m kavi 17 poet
कविता^f kavitā 12 poem; poetry
कष्ट^m kaṣṭ 17 trouble, distress
क़सम^f qasam 18 oath
कसूर^m kasūr 16 fault, error
(से) कहना^N kahnā 5 to say (to); to call
कहलाना kahlānā 13 to be called, named
कहाँ kahā̃ 3 where?
कहानी^f kahānī 8 story
कहीं kahī̃ 16 somewhere; somehow; कहीं और somewhere else; कहीं का (in insult) complete, utter; कहीं ज़्यादा particularly; कहीं न कहीं somewhere or other; कहीं नहीं nowhere; कहीं भी anywhere at all
काँटा^m kā̃ṭā 10 fork; thorn
काँपना kā̃pnā 15 to shiver, tremble
का/की/के kā/kī/ke 5 (postposition indicating possession)
काग़ज़^m kāgaz 2 paper; a piece of paper
काटना^N kāṭnā 17 to cut
काठमांडु^m kāṭhmāṇḍu 8 Kathmandu
कान^m kān 18 ear
कानपुर^m Kānpur 7 Kanpur
काफ़ी^1 f kāfī 5 coffee
काफ़ी^2 kāfī 1 quite, very
काम^m kām 4 work
कामचोर kamcor 10 work shy, lazy
कामयाब kāmyāb 18 successful
कारण^m kāraṇ 14 reason, cause
कार्यक्रम^m kāryakram 16 programme
काल^m kāl 9 time, age, period
किंतु kintu 17 but
कि ki 4 (conjunction) that; or; when suddenly
कितना kitnā 2 how much/many
किताब^f kitāb 2 book
किधर kidhar 14 where? whither?
किन kin 3 oblique plural of कौन kaun and of क्या kyā
किनारा^m kinārā 15 edge, shore
किराया^m kirāyā 15 rent, fare
किस kis 3 oblique singular of कौन kaun and of क्या kyā
किसी kisī 7 oblique of कोई koī
क़िस्मत^f qismat 13 fate
की तरफ़ kī taraf 6 towards

की तरह *kī tarah* 6 like

की बग़ल में *kī bagal mẽ* 14 next to, close by

की वजह से *kī vajah se* 13 because of

क़ीमत f *qīmat* 11 price, value, cost; क़ीमती costly, valuable

कुछ *kuch* 7 some; somewhat; something; कुछ और something else, some more; कुछ न कुछ something or other; कुछ नहीं nothing

कुत्ता m *kuttā* 5 dog

कुरता m *kurtā* 5 kurta, Indian shirt

कुरसी f *kursī* 1 chair

कुली m *kulī* 16 porter

कृपया *kṛpayā* 2 please

कृपा f *kṛpā* 12 kindness, grace; कृपा करके kindly, please

के अंदर *ke andar* 6 inside

के आगे *ke āge* 6 in front of, ahead of

के आस-पास *ke ās-pās* 9 around, in vicinity of

के ऊपर *ke ūpar* 6 on top of

के कारण *ke kāraṇ* 14 because of

के द्वारा *(ke) dvārā* 14 by (means of)

के नज़दीक *ke nazdīk* 7 near

के नीचे *ke nīce* 6 beneath, below

के पहले *ke pahle* 6 before

के पास *ke pās* 6 near; in (one's) possession

के पीछे *ke pīche* 6 behind

के बजाय *ke bajāy* 15 instead of

के बाद *ke bād* 6 after

के बारे में *ke bare me* 6 about, concerning

के बाहर *ke bāhar* 6 outside

के बिना *ke binā* 15 without

के बीच *ke bīc* 14 between; के बीच में in the middle of

के मारे *ke māre* 15 on account of, through

के लिए *ke lie* 6 for

के यहाँ *ke yahā̃* 6 at the place of

के समान *ke samān* 7 like, equal to

के साथ *ke sāth* 6 with, in company of

के सामने *ke sāmne* 6 facing, opposite

के सिवा, सिवाय *ke sivā, sivāy* 15 apart from

कैमरा m *kaimrā* 11 camera

कैसा *kaisā* 2 of what kind, what like, how

को *ko* 3 to, on, at

कोई *koī* 7 anyone, someone; some, about; any; कोई और someone else; कोई न कोई some-one or other; कोई नहीं no-one

कोना m *konā* 13 corner

कोशिश f *kośiś* 16 attempt; की कोशिश करना N to try

कौन *kaun* 2 who?; कौन कौन which various people?

कौनसा/सी/से *kaunsā/sī/se* 5 which?

क्या *kyā* 1 what?; question-marker

क्यों *kyõ* 2 why

क्योंकि *kyõki* 2 because

क्लास m / f *klās* 4 class (in school etc.)

ख, ख़

खड़ा *khaṛā* 7 standing, waiting

ख़त m *khat* 5 letter

ख़त्म *khatm* 7 finished; ख़त्म करना N to finish

ख़बर f *khabar* 14 news, information

ख़याल m *khayāl* 5 opinion, thought; (का) ख़याल रखना N to take care of

ख़राब *kharāb* 2 bad

ख़रीदना N *kharīdnā* 9 to purchase

ख़रीदारी *kharīdārī* 10 buying, shopping

खाँ मार्केट m *khā̃ mārkeṭ* 5 Khan Market (in Delhi)

खाँसना *khā̃snā* 16 to cough

खाट f *khāṭ* 17 bedstead, 'cot'

खाना[1] m *khānā* 4 food

खाना[2] N *khānā* 5 to eat

ख़ाली *khālī* 1 empty, vacant, free; ख़ाली करना N *to vacate*

ख़ास *khās* 7 special, particular

खिड़की f *khiṛkī* 1 window

खिलाना N *khilānā* 5 to give to eat

खिलौना m *khilaunā* 5 toy

खींचना N *khī̃cnā* 10 *to draw; take (photograph)*

ख़ुद *khud* 10 oneself

ख़ुदा m *khudā* 18 God; ख़ुदा की क़सम by God; ख़ुदा जाने God knows

खुला *khulā* 18 open

ख़ुश *khuś* 2 happy

ख़ुशी f *khuśī* 4 happiness, pleasure

ख़ूब *khūb* 6 a lot (of); well

ख़ूबसूरत *khūbsūrat* 4 beautiful

खेद m *khed* 12 regret

खेलना n *khelnā* 6 to play (a game)

ख़ैर *khair* 3 well, anyway

खोना N *khonā* 12 to lose

खोलना N *kholnā* 11 to open

ग, ग़

गंगा f *gangā* 11 Ganges

गंदा *gandā* 2 dirty

गंभीर *gambhīr* 17 serious, profound

गँवाना N *gā̃vānā* 16 to waste, squander

गप f, गपशप f *gap, gapśap* 6 gossip

गरम *garam* 4 warm, hot

गरमी f *garmī* 7 heat; summer; गरमियाँ f.pl summer

ग़रीब *garīb* 15 poor

गर्व m *garv* 10 pride

ग़लत *galat* 8 wrong, incorrect

ग़लती f *galtī* 15 mistake

गला m *galā* 18 throat, neck; **गले लगाना** N to embrace
गली f *galī* 8 lane
गाँव m *gā̃v* 3 village
गाड़ी f *gāṛī* 1 car; train
गाना1 m *gānā* 9 song
गाना2 N *gānā* 9 to sing
गाय f *gāy* 10 cow
गाली f *gālī* 15 abuse, swearing; **गाली देना** N to abuse, swear at
गिरना *girna* 18 to fall
गिलास m *gilās* 11 tumbler (glass or metal)
गीत m *gīt* 11 song
गुंडा m *guṇḍā* 9 lout, hooligan
गुंडागर्दी f *guṇḍāgardī* 9 hooliganism
गुजराती *gujarātī* 1 Gujarati
गुज़ारना N *guzārnā* 11 to spend (time)
गुज़ारा m *guzārā* 16 livelihood, subsistence
गुरु m *guru* 13 teacher, guru
गुस्ताख़ी *gustākhī* 14 rudeness, impertinence
गुस्सा m, adj *gussā* 17 anger; angry
गुस्से *gusse* 10 angry
गृह मंत्री m, f *gṛh mantrī* 12 Home Minister
गोद f *god* 18 lap
गोरा adj /m *gorā* 15 fair; white person
गोली f *golī* 4 tablet, pill; bullet
गोश्त m *gośt* 6 meat
ग्यारह *gyārah* 9 eleven
ग्वालियर m *gvāliyar* 12 Gwalior

घ

घंटा m *ghaṇṭā* 8 hour
घंटी f *ghaṇṭī* 13 bell
घटिया *ghaṭiyā* 14 (inv.) inferior, low grade
घड़ी f *ghaṛī* 17 wristwatch
घना *ghanā* 15 dense, thick
घमंड m *ghamaṇḍ* 15 pride, arrogance
घर m *ghar* 3 house, home; **घर पर** at home
घाट m *ghāṭ* 11 (steps at) riverbank
घास f *ghās* 18 grass
घुमाना N *ghumānā* 18 to turn, make go round
घुसना *ghusnā* 17 to enter (forcibly, or uninvited)
घूमना *ghūmna* 11 to tour, roam, turn
घोड़ा m *ghoṛā* 5 horse

च

चटनी f *caṭnī* 14 chutney
चतुर्थ *caturth* 7 fourth, IVth
चपरासी m *caprāsī* 10 peon, orderly

चपाती f *capātī* 15 chapatti
चप्पल f *cappal* 2 sandal
चम्मच m *cammac* 10 spoon
चलना *calnā* 5 to move , walk; चल देना to set off; चला आना to come back, come away; चला जाना to go one's way
चलाना N *calānā* 8 to drive; to run, manage
चश्मा m *caśmā* 3 glasses, specs
चाँद m *cā̃d* 6 moon
चाँदी f *cā̃dī* 4 silver
चाचा m *cācā* 1 (inv.) paternal uncle, father's younger brother
चाबी f *cābī* 5 key
चाय f *cāy* 4 tea
चार *cār* 3 four
चावल m *cāval* 7 rice
चाहना N *cāhnā* 10 to want, wish; to be fond of
चाहिए *cāhie* 7 (is) needed; (with infinitive) should, ought to
चाहे... चाहे *cāhe ... cāhe* 16 whether... or
चिंता f *cintā* 16 anxiety, concern
चिट्ठी f *ciṭṭhī* 2 letter, note, chit
चिड़िया f *ciṛiyā* 1 bird
चिढ़ाना N *ciṛhānā* 12 to irritate, tease
चिल्लाना N *cillānā* 9 to shout
चीज़ f *cīz* 3 thing
चुकना *cuknā* 12 (after verb stem) to have already done
चुनना N *cunnā* 18 to choose
चुप *cup* 6 silent; चुप करना N to be quiet, shut up
चेहरा m *cehrā* 14 face, features
चोट f *coṭ* 13 hurt, injury; चोट लगना to get hurt
चोर m *cor* 11 thief
चोरी f *corī* 13 theft, robbery; चोरी करना N to steal
चौकीदार m *caukīdār* 15 watchman
चौथा *cauthā* 7 fourth
चौदह *caudah* 6 fourteen; चौदहवीं 14th of lunar month, full moon day

छ

छठा *chaṭhā* 7 sixth
छपना *chapnā* 9 to be printed
छह *chah* 3 six
छाता m *chātā* 13 umbrella
छात्र m *chātr* 2 student
छात्रवृत्ति f *chātravṛtti* 17 scholarship
छात्रा f *chātrā* 2 female student
छुटभैया m *chuṭbhaiyā* 18 a nobody, person of no importance
छुट्टी f *chuṭṭī* 7 holiday; free time
छुरी f *churī* 10 knife
छूटना *chūṭnā* 11 to depart; to be left, fall back

छूना N *chūnā* 5 to touch
छेड़ना N *cheṛnā* 18 to stir up, start up
छोकरी f *chokrī* 18 young girl, lass
छोटा *choṭā* 1 small, little
छोड़ना N *choṛnā* 6 to leave, abandon, give up
(को) छोड़कर *(ko) choṛkar* 12 apart from, except for

ज, ज़

जंगल m *jangal* 15 jungle, scrub
जंगली *janglī* 16 wild
जँभाई f *jabhāī* 15 yawn; जँभाई लेना N to yawn
जगह f *jagah* 13 place
जगाना N *jagānā* 5 to arouse
जनता f *jantā* 9 public, the people
जनवरी f *janvarī* 1 January
जनाब *janāb* 18 sir
जन्म m *janm, janam* 16 birth; का जन्म होना to be born
जन्मदिन m *janamdin* 8 birthday
जब 13 when; जब कि while; जब तक... तब तक for as long as... for that long; जब तक नहीं... तब तक until... until then; जब से.. .तब से since the time when... since then
ज़बान f *zabān* 14 language, tongue
ज़माना m *zamānā* 15 period, age, time
ज़मीन f *zamīn* 7 land
ज़रा *zarā* 5 just, a little
ज़रूर *zarūr* 1 of course
ज़रूरत f *zarūrat* 7 need
ज़रूरी *zarūrī* 7 necessary, urgent
जर्मन *jarman* 1 German
जलना *jalnā* 17 to burn
जल्दी *jaldī* 5 quickly; soon; early
जवान m *javān* 13 young, youthful, soldier
जवाब m *javāb* 2 reply, answer; जवाब देना N to reply
जहाँ... वहाँ *jahā̃... vahā̃* 14 where... there
जानना *jānnā* 6 to know; जान-बूझकर deliberately, knowingly; जाना-पहचाना recognised, well known
जाना *jānā* 5 to go
जानवर m *jānvar* animal
जापानी *jāpānī* 1 Japanese
जारी *jārī* 11 current, continuing; जारी रखना N to maintain
ज़ाहिर *zāhir* 18 clear, evident
ज़िंदगी f *zindagī* 16 life
जितना... उतना *jitnā... utnā* 14 as much as...
ज़िद f *zid* 18 obstinacy
ज़िद्दी *ziddī* 17 obstinate, stubborn
जिधर... उधर *jidhar... udhar* 14 whither...thither
ज़िम्मेदारी *zimmedārī* 10 responsibility
जियरा m *jiyrā* 18 soul, heart (poetic)

जी *jī* 1 (respect-marker); yes; **जी नहीं** no; **जी हाँ** yes

जी-हुज़ूरी f *jī-huzūrī* 12 sycophancy, flattery

जीना n *jīna* 15 to live, be alive; **के जीते जी** during the lifetime of; **जीते रहो** bless you ('stay living')

जीवन m *jīvan* 15 life

ज़ुकाम m *zukām* 4 a cold

जूता m *jūtā* 2 shoe; pair of shoes

जून m *jūn* 8 June

जेब f *jeb* 7 pocket

ज़ेवर m *zevar* 11 (item of) jewellery

जैसा *jaisā* 15 like, such as; **जैसा... वैसा** as... so...; **जैसे कि** as if, as though; **जैसे ही ...वैसे ही** as soon as

जो 13 (the one) who/ which; **जो कुछ** whatever; **जो कोई** whoever; **जो भी** whoever, whatever

जोड़ना N *joṛnā* 14 to add; to save

ज़ोर m *zor* 8 force, strength

ज़्यादा *zyādā* 4 much, many, more; **ज़्यादा से ज़्यादा** at the most

ज़्यादातर *zyādātar* 2 mostly, most

झ

झगड़ा m *jhagṛā* 5 quarrel, row

झट से *jhaṭ se* 18 suddenly, briskly

झाड़ना N *jhāṛnā* 18 to spout, pour

झूठ m *jhūṭh* 10 lie

झूमना *jhūmnā* 18 to sway

झेंपना *jhẽpnā* 15 to be embarrassed

ट

टकराना n *ṭakrānā* 18 to collide

टपकना *ṭapaknā* 18 to drop in, appear unexpectedly

टहलना *ṭahalnā* 18 to stroll

टिकट m / f *ṭikaṭ* 13 ticket; stamp

टुकड़ा m *ṭukṛā* 6 piece, bit

टूटना *ṭūṭnā* 18 to break, be broken

टेढ़ा *ṭeṛhā* 10 twisted, complex

टैक्सी f *ṭaiksī* 12 taxi

ट्रेकिंग f *ṭreking* 11 trekking

ट्रेन f *ṭren* 15 train

ठ

ठंड f *ṭhanḍ* 13 cold

ठंडा *ṭhanḍā* 4 cold

ठग m *ṭhag* 17 swindler, robber

ठहरना *ṭhaharnā* 5 to stop, wait, stay

ठीक *ṭhīk* 1 all right; exactly; **ठीक करना** N to put right, fix; **ठीक से** properly; exactly

ड

डर m *ḍar* 13 fear

(से) डरना *(se) ḍarnā* 6 to fear

डरपोक *ḍarpok* 15 timid

डाँटना N *ḍā̃ṭnā* 14 to scold

डाक f *ḍāk* 9 mail, post

डाकघर m *ḍākghar* 6 post office
डाकू m *ḍākū* 13 dacoit, bandit
डाक्टर m *ḍākṭar* 7 doctor
डॉयलॉग m *ḍāylāg* 18 dialogue
डाल f *ḍāl* 8 branch (of tree)
डालना N *ḍālnā* 13 to throw, cast, pour
डिगरी f *ḍigrī* 12 degree
डिनर m *ḍinar* 12 dinner
डिब्बा m *ḍibbā* 7 box; compartment
डूबना *ḍūbnā* 16 to sink, drown
डेढ़ *ḍeṛh* 10 one and a half
ड्राइवर m *ḍrāivar* 15 driver

ढ

ढंग m *ḍhang* 16 way, manner
ढाई *ḍhāī* 12 two and a half
ढूँढना N *ḍhū̃ṛnā* 5 to look for, find
ढेर m *ḍher* 17 pile, heap

त

तंग *tang* 8 narrow; तंग आना to get fed up; तंग करना N to harass
तक *tak* 3 up to, as far as; for (in time)
तकलीफ़ f *taklīf* 8 trouble, distress
तथापि *tathāpi* 17 nevertheless, even so
तबला m *tablā* 9 tabla (drum)
तबियत f *tabiyat* 3 health
तमाशा m *tamāśā* 11 spectacle, show
तमिल f *tamil* 14 Tamil
तरफ़ f *taraf* 7 side, direction
तरह f *tarah* 8 way, manner; तरह तरह का of various kinds
तलाक़ m *talāq* 13 divorce; तलाक़ होना a divorce to happen; तलाक़-शुदा divorced
तलाश f *talāś* 16 search; की तलाश करना N to search for
तलाशना N *talāśnā* 16 to search for
तस्वीर f *tasvīr* 3 picture
तहज़ीब f *tahzīb* 16 culture, refinement
ताज महल m *tāj mahal* 3 Taj Mahal
ताज़ा *tāzā* 14 fresh
तारीख़ f *tārīkh* 8 date
तारीफ़ f *tārīf* 16 praise; की तारीफ़ करना N to praise
ताला m *tālā* 13 lock
तालाब m *tālāb* 14 pond
ताली f *tālī* 8 clapping; तालियाँ बजाना N to clap
तिब्बती *tibbatī* 11 Tibetan
तीन *tīn* 1 three
तीसरा *tīsrā* 7 third; तीसरे पहर in the afternoon
तुझ *tujh* 3 oblique of तू *tū*
तुम *tum* 1 you (familiar)
तुम्हारा *tumhārā* 3 your, yours (from तुम)
तुरंत *turant* 10 immediately

तुराना N *turānā* 18 to have broken

तुलना *tulnā* 18 to be determined (to, पर)

तू *tū* 1 you (intimate); तू-तू मैं-मैं करना N to call names

तृतीय *tṛtīy* 7 third, IIId

तेज़ *tez* 18 quick, rapid, sharp, bright

तेरा *terā* 6 your, yours (from तू)

तैयार *taiyār* 5 ready; तैयार करना N to prepare

तैरना n *tairnā* 9 to swim

तो *to* 4 so, then; as for; तो सही for sure

तोड़ना N *toṛnā* 11 to break

तोहफ़ा m *tohfā* 11 a present

थ

थकना *thaknā* 15 to be tired

थकान f *thakān* 8 tiredness

था, थी, थे, थीं *thā, thī, the, thī̃* 4 was, were

थामना N *thāmnā* 18 to hold, support

थाली f *thālī* 8 platter

थैला m *thailā* 5 bag, cloth bag

थोड़ा *thoṛā* 6 a little, a few; थोड़ा-बहुत a certain amount; थोड़ा-सा a little; थोड़े (ही) by no means

द

दंगा m *dangā* 17 riot

दक्षिण m *dakṣiṇ* 14 south

दफ़ा f *dafā* 17 time, occasion

दफ़्तर m *daftar* 4 office

दबना *dabnā* 14 to yield, cower

दया f *dayā* 18 compassion

दरवाज़ा m *darvāzā* 3 door

दराज़ f *darāz* 3 drawer

दरी f *darī* 3 rug, mat

दर्जन f *darjan* 7 a dozen

दर्ज़ी m *darzī* 18 tailor

दर्शन m *darśan* 9 vision, audience or auspicious meeting

दल m *dal* 8 political party

दस *das* 3 ten

दवा f *davā* 11 medicine

दादा m *dādā* 11 (inv.) paternal grandfather

दादी f *dādī* 1 paternal grandmother

दाम *dām* 10 price

दाल f *dāl* 4 daal, lentils

दावत f *dāvat* 9 (invitation to) a dinner

दास्तान f *dāstān* 18 tale (poetic)

दाहिना *dāhinā* 8 right (opp. left)

दिखना *dikhnā* 8 to appear, seem

दिखाई देना/पड़ना *dikhāī dena/paṛnā* 15 to be visible, appear

दिन m *din* 6 day; दिन भर all day

दिल m *dil* 4 heart; दिल लगना to feel at home; to be in love

दिलचस्प *dilcasp* 14 interesting
दिलवाना N *dilvānā* 18 to cause to be given
दिली *dilī* 8 of the heart
दिल्ली f *dillī* 2 Delhi
दीखना *dīkhnā* 18 to appear, be visible, seem
दीवार f *dīvār* 3 wall
दुःख m *duḥkh* 18 grief, pain, suffering
दुकान f *dukān* 4 shop
दुकानदार m *dukāndār* 11 shopkeeper
दुनिया f *duniya* 16 world
दुबला *dublā* 2 thin; दुबला-पतला thin, slight of build
दुबारा *dubārā* 14 again, second time
दुर्घटना f *durghaṭnā* 11 accident
दूध m *dūdh* 5 milk
दूर *dur* 7 distant, far, remote
दूरदर्शन m *dūrdarśan* 14 television; Doordarshan (Indian TV network)
दूसरा *dūsrā* 1 other, second
देखना N *dekhnā* 5 to see, look
देखभाल f *dekhbhāl* 16 supervision, care; की देखभाल करना N to take care of
देन f *den* 13 contribution, gift
देना N *denā* 5 to give; (with oblique inf.) to allow to, let
देर f *der* 7 delay, a while; देर तक until late; देर से late
देवनागरी f *devanāgarī* 6 Devanagari script
देवर m *devar* 5 husband's younger brother
देश m *deś* 15 country
देहान्त m *dehānt* 16 death, demise; का देहान्त होना to die
दो *do* 1 two
दोनों *donõ* 1 both
दोपहर f *dopahar* 11 noon, afternoon; दोपहर का खाना m lunch
दोस्त m, f *dost* 4 friend
दौड़ना *dauṛnā* 12 to run
(के) द्वारा *(ke) dvārā* 14 by, by means of
द्वितीय *dvitīy* 7 second, IInd

ध

धंधा m *dhandhā* 18 work, occupation
धन्यवाद *dhanyavād* 2 thank you
धीमा *dhīmā* 12 low, faint
धुलना *dhulnā* 14 to be washed
धूमधाम m *dhūmdhām* 18 pomp, show
धोखा m *dhokhā* 15 trick, deceipt; धोखा देना N to trick, deceive
धोना N *dhonā* 5 to wash
धोबी m *dhobī* 5 dhobi, washerman

ध्यान ^{m} *dhyān* 5 attention; ध्यान देना ^{N} to pay attention; (का) ध्यान रखना ^{N} to take care of, mind; ध्यान से attentively

न

नंबर ^{m} *nambar* 8 number
न *na* 2 not; is it not so?; (with commands) don't; न कि and not; न... न neither... nor
नज़दीक *nazdīk* 8 near, nearby
नज़र ^{f} *nazar* 13 glance, look
नचवैया ^{m} *nacvaiyā* 18 dancer (derogatory)
नदी ^{f} *nadī* 14 river
नफ़रत ^{f} *nafrat* 6 hate, dislike
नमक ^{m} *namak* 9 salt
नमस्कार *namaskār* 2 hello; goodbye
नमस्ते *namaste* 1 hello; goodbye
नमूना ^{m} *namūnā* 15 example, sample, type, specimen
नया (नए, नई) *nayā (nae, naī)* 2 new
नरसों *narsõ* 18 three days ago/ahead
नर्तक ^{m} *nartak* 18 dancer
नल ^{m} *nal* 15 pipe, tap
नवाँ *navā̃* 7 ninth
नहाना *nahānā* 12 to bathe, wash
नहीं *nahī̃* 1 not; नहीं तो otherwise; not at all, of course not
नाक ^{f} *nāk* 11 nose
नाचना *nācnā* 17 to dance; नाच नचाना ^{N} to lead one a fine dance
नापसंद करना ^{N} *nāpasand karnā* 6 to dislike
नाम ^{m} *nām* 3 name; (का) नाम लेना ^{N} to mention; (का) नाम न लेना ^{N} to be far from doing something
नामुमकिन *nāmumkin* 17 impossible
नारा *nārā* 5 slogan
नाराज़ *nārāz* 2 angry, displeased
नाश्ता ^{m} *nāśtā* 12 breakfast
निंदा ^{f} *nindā* 16 blame, speaking ill; की निंदा करना ^{N} to blame
निकलना *nikalnā* 8 to come/go out, emerge; to turn out to be
निकालना ^{N} *nikālnā* 16 to extract, bring out, discover
निन्यानवे *ninyānve* 8 ninety-nine
निबंध ^{m} *nibandh* 16 essay
निराशा ^{f} *nirāśā* 14 disappointment, despair
निवेदन ^{m} *nivedan* 10 request
निहायत *nihāyat* 17 extremely
नींद ^{f} *nī̃d* 11 sleep; नींद आना to feel sleepy
नीचे *nīce* 8 below; down; downstairs
नुक़सान ^{m} *nuqsān* 9 harm
नृत्य ^{m} *nṛtya* 18 dance
नेक *nek* 18 good, virtuous, decent
नेता ^{m} *netā* 15 leader, politician

नेपाल m *nepāl* 8 Nepal
नेपाली *nepālī* 11 Nepali
नोट *noṭ* 10 note, banknote
नौ *nau* 2 nine
नौकर m *naukar* 5 servant; नौकर-चाकर m servants & domestics
नौकरी f *naukarī* 15 job, employment, service
नौजवान m *naujavān* 9 youth, young man

प

पंखा m *pankhā* 1 fan
पंचम *pancam* 7 fifth, Vth
पंजाबी *panjābī* 1 Panjabi
पंडित m *paṇḍit* 15 pandit
पकड़ना N *pakaṛnā* 10 to catch, grab, hold
पक्का *pakkā* 13 ripe
पच्चीस *paccīs* 11 twenty-five
पछताना N *pachtānā* 12 to regret
पड़ना *paṛnā* 10 to fall, befall
पड़ा *paṛā* 5 lying
पड़ोसी m *paṛosī* 4 neighbour
पढ़ना n *paṛhnā* 5 to read, study
पढ़ाई f *paṛhāī* 11 studies, studying
पढ़ाना N *paṛhānā* 7 to teach
पतंग f *patang* 18 kite (toy)
पतला *patlā* 2 thin
पता m *patā* 10 address; पता चलना to come to one's notice; पता नहीं don't know, no idea; पता होना to know, be aware
पति m *pati* 3 husband; पति-देव 'respected husband'
पत्थर m *patthar* 1 stone
पत्नी f *patnī* 3 wife
पत्र m *patr* 9 letter
परंतु *parantu* 9 but
पर[1] *par* 2 but
पर[2] *par* 3 on; at
परदा m *pardā* 3 curtain, veil, purdah
परवाह करना N *parvāh karnā* 15 to care
परसों *parsõ* 11 the day before yesterday; the day after tomorrow
परिवर्तन m *parivartan* 14 alteration
परिवार m *parivār* 3 family
परिस्थिति(याँ) f *paristhiti(yā̃)* 18 circumstance(s)
परीक्षा f *parīkṣā* 12 examination; परीक्षा देना N to sit an exam; (की) परीक्षा लेना N to examine (a student)
परेशान *pareśān* 2 troubled, upset
पल m *pal* 8 moment
पलंग m *palang* 1 bed
पवन m *pavan* 18 wind
पसंद *pasand* 4 'liked, pleasing': पसंद करना N to like, approve, choose; पसंद होना to appeal, be liked

पहचानना N *pahcānnā* 9 to recognise
पहनना N *pahannā* 11 to put on, wear
पहर m *pahar* 8 'watch', part of day
पहला *pahlā* 7 first
पहले *pahle* 4 previously; first
पहाड़ m *pahāṛ* 4 hill, mountain
पहिया m *pahiyā* 15 wheel
पहुँचना *pahũcnā* 9 to arrive, reach
पहुँचाना N *pahũcānā* 18 to convey, deliver
पाँच *pā̃c* 2 five
पाँचवाँ *pā̃cvā̃* 7 fifth
पाकिस्तान m *Pākistān* 14 Pakistan
पाकिस्तानी *pākistānī* 1 Pakistani
पागल *pāgal* 2 mad, crazy
पाठ m *pāṭh* 11 lesson, chapter
पान m *pān* 5 paan
पाना N *pānā* 11 to find, obtain; (after verb stem) to manage to
पानी m *pānī* 5 water; **पानी पड़ना** to rain
पापा m *pāpā* 5 (inv.) papa, father
पार करना N *pār karnā* 12 to cross
पारिवारिक *pārivārik* 18 familial
पास *pās* 18 nearby (adverb)
पास करना N *pās karnā* 12 to pass (exam etc.)
पिछला *pichlā* 8 last, previous
पिता m *pitā* 1 (inv.) father
पीछा m *pīchā* 16 rear; pursuit; **का पीछा करना** N to follow
पीछे *pīche* 11 behind
पीना N *pīnā* 5 to drink; to smoke
पुराना *purānā* 1 old (of things)
पुल m *pul* 14 bridge
पुलिस f *pulis* 10 *police*
पुस्तक f *pustak* 8 book
पूँछ f *pū̃ch* 15 tail
(से) पूछना N *pūchnā* 5 to ask (of)
पूरा *pūrā* 8 full, complete
पेंसिल f *pensil* 16 pencil
पे (= पर) *pe* 18 on, to
पेट m *peṭ* 11 stomach
पेड़ m *peṛ* 5 tree
पेशा m *peśā* 16 profession
पैदा होना *paidā honā* 18 to be born, produced
पैसा m *paisā* 5 money; paisa (hundredth of a rupee)
पौन, पौना *paun, paunā* 12 three-quarters
प्याज़ m *pyāz* 16 onion
प्यार m *pyār* 6 love, affection; **(को/से) प्यार करना** N to love
प्यारा *pyārā* 4 dear, lovely; beloved
प्याला m *pyālā* 11 cup
प्यास f *pyās* 13 thirst; **प्यास लगना** thirst to strike – to feel thirsty
प्रकाशक m *prakāśak* 12 publisher
प्रकाशित *prakāśit* 17 published
प्रति f *prati* 1 copy (of book etc.)

प्रतीत होना *pratīt honā* 18 to seem

प्रथम *pratham* 7 first, Ist

प्रदूषण m *pradūṣaṇ* 2 pollution

प्रदेश m *prades* 14 state, province

प्रधान मंत्री m, f *pradhān mantrī* 18 prime minister

प्रयोग m *prayog* 14 use, usage; **का प्रयोग करना** N to use

प्रश्न m *praśn, praśan* 17 question

प्राचीन *prācīn* 14 ancient

प्राध्यापक m *prādhyāpak* 9 lecturer

प्राप्त करना N *prāpt karnā* 14 to obtain, attain

प्रेम m *prem* 14 love

प्रसिद्ध *prasiddh* 11 famous

प्रिय *priy* 4 dear

प्रोग्राम m *progrām* 8 programme, plan, routine

फ, फ़

फँसना *phãsnā* 17 to be stuck, caught, snared

फ़रवरी f *farvarī* 8 February

फ़र्क m *fark* 7 difference, separation

फ़र्श m / f *farś* 3 floor

फल m *phal* 5 fruit

फाड़ना N *phāṛnā* 17 to tear

फ़ायदा m *fāydā* 9 profit, advantage

फ़ारसी f *fārsī* 14 Persian

फिर *phir* 6 then, so, again; **फिर भी** even so; **फिर से** again

फिरना *phirnā* 18 to turn, move

फ़िलहाल *filhāl* 18 in the meantime

फ़िल्म f *film* 11 film

फ़िल्मी *filmī* 11 of the films

फ़ुरसत f *fursat* 13 leisure, free time

फुसफुसाना *phusphusānā* 15 to whisper

फूल m *phūl* 14 flower

फ़ैक्स m *faiks* 11 fax

फ़ोटो m *foṭo* 11 photograph

फ़ोन करना N *fon karnā* 9 to phone

ब

बँगला f *bãglā* 13 Bengali (language)

बंद *band* 4 closed, shut; **बंद करना** N to close, shut

बंदर m *bandar* 15 monkey

बग़ीचा m *bagīcā* 1 garden

बचना *bacnā* 18 to escape, survive

बचपन m *bacpan* 6 childhood

बचा *bacā* 14 saved, left

बचाना N *bacānā* 18 to rescue, save

बच्चा m *baccā* 1 child

बजना *bajnā* 11 to resound, chime

बजाना N *bajānā* 9 to play (music)

बजे *baje* 6 o' clock

बड़ा *baṛā* 1 big

बढ़ना *baṛhnā* 15 to increase, grow, advance

बढ़िया *baṛhiyā* 14 (inv.) nice, of good quality

बताना N *batānā* 5 to tell
बत्ती f *battī* 13 light, lamp
बत्तीसी f *battīsī* 15 'set of 32' – full complement of teeth; बत्तीसी दिखाना N to grin broadly
बदमाश m *badmāś* 12 villain, rogue
बदलना n *badalnā* 12 to change
बदसूरत *badsūrat* 13 ugly
बधाई f *badhāī* 6 congratulation
बन m *ban* 18 forest, wood, jungle
बनना *bannā* 14 to be, become, be made, act
बनाना N *banānā* 8 to make
बनारस m *banāras* 9 Banaras, Varanasi
बरदाश्त करना N *bardāśt karnā* 17 to tolerate, endure
बरबाद करना N *barbād karnā* 13 to ruin
बर्फ़ f *barf* 15 snow, ice
बर्थ m / f *barth* 12 berth
बस[1] f *bas* 3 bus
बस[2] *bas* 14 enough! that's all!
बसना *basnā* 18 to settle, inhabit
बसाना N *basānā* 18 to settle, found
बस्ती f *bastī* 18 settlement, inhabited area; slum
बहिन f *bahin* 2 sister
बहुत *bahut* 1 very; बहुत-सारा lots of
बहू *bahu* 1 daughter-in-law
बाँटना N *bā̃ṭnā* 12 to divide
बाँसुरी f *bā̃surī* 17 bamboo flute
बाँह f *bā̃h* 11 (upper) arm
बाक़ी *bāqī* 17 remaining, left
बाज़ार m *bāzār* 4 market
बात f *bāt* 2 matter, thing; (से) बात करना N to talk, converse; बात काटना N to interrupt; बात बनना to go well, an aim to be achieved
बातचीत f *bātcīt* 17 conversation, negotiation
बाद (में) *bād (mẽ)* 8 later
बादल m *bādal* 15 cloud
बाप m *bāp* 6 father
बाबू m *babū* 7 clerk
बायाँ *bāyā̃* 8 left (opp. of right)
बार f *bār* 10 time, occasion; बार बार time and again
बारह *bārah* 6 twelve
बारिश f *bāriś* 13 rain; बारिश होना to rain
बारे में *bāre mẽ* 10 about, concerning
बाल-बच्चे mp *bāl-bacce* 4 children, family
बाहर *bāhar* 4 out; outside; away
बिकना *biknā* 9 to be sold
बिगड़ना *bigaṛnā* 17 to go wrong, get angry
बिजली f *bijlī* 7 electricity
बिठाना N *biṭhānā* 14 to make sit
बियर m/f *biyar* 13 beer

बिलकुल *bilkul* 2 completely; बिलकुल नहीं not at all
बिल्ली [f] *billī* 14 cat
बी० एच० यू० *bī.ec.yū.* 9 BHU (Banaras Hindu University)
बीतना *bītnā* 18 to pass (of time)
बीमार *bīmār* 2 ill
बीस *bīs* 11 twenty
बुख़ार [m] *bukhār* 4 fever
बुढ़िया [f] *buṛhiyā* 1 old woman
बुरा *burā* 2 bad
बुलाना [N] *bulānā* 5 to call, invite
बूढ़ा [adj/m] *būṛhā* 1 old (of people); old man
बेकार *bekār* 7 useless
बेचना [N] *becnā* 11 to sell
बेचारा [adj/m] *becārā* 13 poor, wretched, helpless; poor fellow
बेचैन *becain* 18 restless
बेटा [m] *beṭā* 2 son, child
बेटी [f] *beṭī* 2 daughter, child
बेवक़ूफ़ *bavaqūf* 16 stupid
बैठक [f] *baiṭhak* 18 sitting room
बैठना *baiṭhnā* 5 to sit
बैठा *baiṭhā* 7 seated, sitting
बोतल [f] *botal* 12 bottle
बोर करना [N] *bor karnā* 9 to bore
बोरियत [f] *boriyat* 10 boredom
बोलना [n] *bolnā* 5 to speak
बोली [f] *bolī* 14 speech, dialect
ब्राह्मण [m] *brāhmaṇ* 15 Brahmin

भ

भगवान [m] *bhagvān* 8 God
भतीजा [m] *bhatija* 9 nephew
भविष्य [m] *bhaviṣya* 9 future
भाई [m] *bhāī* 2 brother
भागना *bhāgnā* 17 to run away, flee
भाभी [f] *bhābhī* 12 elder brother's wife
भारत [m] *bhārat* 3 India
भारी *bhārī* 10 heavy
भाषा [f] *bhāṣā* 1 language
भिखारी [m] *bhikhārī* 15 beggar
भी *bhī* 2 also, too
भीगा *bhīgā* 14 wet; भीगी बिल्ली [f] 'drenched cat', timid person
भीड़ [f] *bhīṛ* 3 crowd; भीड़ लगना a crowd to gather
भूख [f] *bhūkh* 13 hunger; भूख लगना hunger to strike – to feel hungry
भूखा *bhūkhā* 13 hungry
भूत [m] *bhūt* 11 ghost
भूल *bhūl* 10 mistake; भूल करना [N] to make a mistake
भूलना *bhūlnā* 10 to forget, err; भूलकर भी even by mistake
भेंट [f] *bhẽṭ* 11 gift, presentation; meeting, encounter
भेजना [N] *bhejnā* 8 to send
भेद [m] *bhed* 17 difference
भैया [m] *bhaiyā* 5 (inv.) brother
भोजन [m] *bhojan* 12 food; भोजन करना [N] to dine, eat

भोला *bholā* 9 innocent, guileless
भौंकना *bhaũknā* 13 to bark
भ्रष्ट *bhraṣṭ* 14 corrupted; **भ्रष्ट करना** N to corrupt

म

मँगवाना N *mãgvānā* 9 to order, send for
मंदिर m *mandir* 10 temple
मकान m *makān* 1 house
मक्खन m *makkhan* 14 butter
मक्खी f *makkhī* 10 fly; **मक्खियाँ मारना** N to 'kill flies', laze about
मगर[1] m *magar* 12 crocodile
मगर[2] *magar* 10 but
मचना *macnā* 17 to break out, be caused
मचाना N *macānā* 9 to create (noise etc.)
मच्छर m *macchar* 14 mosquito
मज़दूर m *mazdūr* 17 labourer
मज़बूत *mazbūt* 4 strong
मजबूरी f *majbūrī* 11 compulsion
मज़ा m *mazā* 11 fun, pleasure, enjoyment; **मज़ा आना** to have fun
मज़ाक़ m *mazāq* 14 joke
मत *mat* 5 don't (in commands)
मतलब m *matlab* 4 meaning
मदद *madad* 10 help; **मदद देना** N *madad denā* to help; **की मदद करना** N to help
मन m *man* 6 mind; heart; **मन लगना** to feel at home
मना *manā* 9 forbidden, prohibited
मरना *marnā* 13 to die
मरम्मत f *marammat* 18 repair; **की मरम्मत करना** N to repair, set right
मर्द m *mard* 16 man, male
मशहूर *maśhūr* 15 famous
मसूरी f *masūrī* 9 Mussoorie
मस्त *mast* 18 joyous, delighted
महँगा *mahãgā* 2 expensive
महल m *mahal* 4 palace
महसूस करना N *mahsūs karnā* 6 to feel, experience; **महसूस होना** to be felt, experienced
महाभारत m *mahābhārat* 17 India's mythical epic war
महायुद्ध m *mahāyuddh* 7 great war
महाराजा m *mahārājā* 9 maharaja
महिला f *mahilā* 14 lady
महीन *mahīn* 14 fine, delicate
महीना m *mahīnā* 8 month
महोदय *mahoday* 14 gentleman; term of address
माँ f *mā̃* 4 ma, mother
माँस m *mā̃s* 17 meat
माता f *mātā* 1 mother
मानना N *mānnā* 11 to accept, believe
मानव m *mānav* 1 man
मापना *māpnā* 18 to measure, cover

माफ़ करना N *māf karnā* 11 to forgive, excuse

माफ़ी f *māfī* 11 forgiveness; **माफ़ी माँगना** N to apologise

मामला m *māmlā* 10 matter, affair

मारना N *mārnā* 5 to beat, hit, kill

मारुति f *māruti* 1 Maruti (car make)

मार्च m *mārc* 7 March

मालिक m *mālik* 6 boss

माला f *mālā* 16 garland

माली m *mālī* 11 gardener

मालूम *mālūm* 4 known; **मालूम नहीं** [I] don't know; **मालूम करना** N to ascertain

माहिर *māhir* 10 expert, skilled

मिठाई f *miṭhāī* 12 sweet, sweet dish

मित्र m, f *mitr* 4 friend

मिनट m *minaṭ* 12 minute

(से) मिलना *(se) milnā* 9 to meet; to be available; to resemble; **मिलना-जुलना** to resemble; **मिल-जुलकर** together, jointly

मिलाना N *milānā* 8 to dial, phone; to join (e.g. hands); to mix

मिस्तरी m *mistrī* 9 mechanic, artisan

मीटिंग f *mīṭing* 16 *meeting*

मीठा *mīṭhā* 11 sweet

मुँह m *mũh* 17 mouth, face

मुझ *mujh* 3 oblique of **मैं**

मुड़ना *muṛnā* 12 to turn

मुन्ना *munnā* 6 'Munna' – nickname for little boy

मुमकिन *mumkin* 11 possible

मुलाक़ात f *mulāqāt* 14 meeting, encounter

मुश्किल adj / f *muśkil* 6 difficult; difficulty

मुसलमान m, f *musalmān* 7 Muslim

मुसाफ़िर m *musāfir* 17 traveller

मुस्कराना *muskarānā* 18 to smile

मूर्ख m *mūrkh* 13 fool

मूर्ति f *murti* 1 statue, image

मूल m *mūl* 18 origin

में *mẽ* 3 in; **में से** from among, out of

मेज़ f *mez* 1 table

मेरा *merā* 3 my, mine; **मेरा सिर** 'my foot!'

मेहनत f *mehnat* 13 hard work

मेहनती *mehnatī* 4 hardworking

मेहमान m *mehmān* 6 guest

मेहरबानी f *meharbānī* 2 kindness; **मेहरबानी करके** 12 kindly, please

मैं *maĩ* 1 I

मैडम f *maiḍam* 2 madam

मोटा *moṭā* 2 fat, thick, coarse

मोड़ m *moṛ* 8 turn, bend

मोती m *motī* 7 pearl

मोर m *mor* 8 peacock

मौक़ा m *mauqā* 14 chance, opportunity

मौसम m *mausam* 2 weather

य

यक़ीन m *yaqīn* 10 confidence, faith
यदि *yadi* 10 if
यद्यपि *yadyapi* 17 although
यह *yah* 1 he, she, it, this
यहाँ *yahā̃* 1 here
यहीं *yahī̃* 9 right here, in this very place
या *yā* 2 or; **या तो... या** either... or
यात्रा f *yātrā* 17 journey, travel
यात्री m *yātrī* 15 traveller, passenger
याद f *yād* 16 memory; **याद आना** to be recalled, come to mind, be missed; **याद करना** N to remember, memorise; to think of, summon (e.g. an employee); **याद दिलाना** N to remind; **याद रखना** N to keep in mind, not to forget; **याद रहना** to be remembered; **याद होना** to be remembered
यानी *yānī* 18 that is to say
यार m, f *yār* 9 friend (esp. vocative)
यू० पी० m *yū. pī.* 15 UP, Uttar Pradesh
ये *ye* 1 these, they; he, she (formal)
योजना f *yojnā* 17 plan, scheme

र

रंग m *rang* colour
रखना N *rakhnā* 5 to put; to keep
रवानी f *ravānī* 9 fluency
रविवार m *ravivār* 1 Sunday
रसोईघर m *rasoīghar* 3 kitchen
रस्सी f *rassī* 17 string, cord
रहना *rahnā* 5 to stay, remain, live
राजधानी f *rājdhānī* 15 capital; name of some Delhi express trains
राजस्थान m *Rājasthān* 14 Rajasthan
राजा m *rājā* 1 king
राज़ी *rāzī* 17 agreeable, content
रात f *rāt* 3 night; **रात भर** all night
रामायण m *rāmāyaṇ* 2 Ramayan (epic poem)
राय f *rāy* 18 opinion
रिक्शा m *rikśā* 10 rickshaw
रिश्तेदार m, f *riśtedār* 4 relative
रुकना *ruknā* 9 to stop; to stay on
रुपया m *rupayā* 11 rupee; money
रूबरू *rūbarū* 17 face to face
रूसी *rūsī* 1 Russian
रे *re* 3 eh, oh, hey
रेडियो m *reḍiyo* 12 radio
रेलगाड़ी f *relgāṛī* 9 train
रेशम m *reśam* 18 silk
रोकना N *roknā* 17 to stop
रोज़ *roz* 13 every day, daily
रोटी f *roṭī* 7 bread; food
रोना n *rona* 11 to weep, cry
रोशनी f *rośnī* 9 light

ल

लंदन m *landan* 3 London

लंबा *lambā* 2 tall, high

लंबाई f *lambāī* 6 height, length

लकड़ी f *lakṛī* 17 wood; stick

लखनऊ m *lakhnaū* 6 Lucknow

लखपति m *lakhpati* 18 rich man, 'millionaire'

लगना *lagnā* 13 to strike; to appeal; to seem; to catch (of illness, fire); to be related, attached; to gather (of crowds); to be expended (of time); (with obl. inf.) to begin to

लगाना N *lagānā* 18 to apply, affix

लड़का m *laṛkā* 1 boy

लड़की f *laṛkī* 1 girl

(से) लड़ना n *(se) laṛnā* 13 to fight, quarrel

लदना *ladnā* 18 to be loaded

लहसुन m *lahsun* 16 garlic

लाख m *lākh* 7 hundred thousand

लाजवाब *lājavāb* 18 beyond compare

लाठी f *lāṭhī* 11 lathi, stick

लादना N *lādnā* 14 to load

लाना *lānā* 5 to bring

लाभ m *lābh* 17 profit, advantage

लायक़ *lāyaq* 9 worth (doing)

लाल *lāl* 1 red

लिखना N *likhnā* 5 to write

लिटाना N *liṭānā* 18 to make lie down

लिपि f *lipi* 6 script, alphabet

लिफ़ाफ़ा m *lifāfā* 13 envelope

लूटना N *lūṭnā* 17 to loot, steal

ले आना *le ānā* 12 to bring

ले जाना *le jānā* 12 to take away

लेकिन *lekin* 1 but

लेटना *leṭnā* 18 to lie, recline

लेख m *lekh* 14 article (written)

लेखक m *lekhak* 14 writer

लेना N *lenā* 5 to take, receive; लेना-देना m dealings, connection

लोकप्रिय *lokpriy* 17 popular

लोग m pl *log* 1 people

लोट-पोट *loṭ-poṭ* 18 rolling, helpless (with laughter)

लौटना *lauṭnā* 9 to return

व

वक़्त m *vaqt* 10 time

वग़ैरह *vagairah* 3 and so on, etc.

वजह f *vajah* 7 reason, cause

वर्णन m *varṇan* 18 description; (का) वर्णन करना N to describe

वर्ष m *varṣ* 17 year

वह *vah* 1 he, she, it, that

वहाँ *vahā̃* 3 there; वहीं right there, in that very place

वाक्य m *vāky* 13 sentence

वापस *vāpas* 10 'back': वापस आना to come back; वापस जाना to go back; वापस मिलना to be got back; वापस लेना N to take back

वाराणसी [f] *vārāṇasī* 4 Varanasi, Banaras
-वाला *-vālā* 10 suffix linking following word to preceding noun
वाह *vāh* 6 (expresses admiration or scorn) wonderful!
विचार [m] *vicār* 13 thought, idea, opinion
विदेश [m] *videś* 4 foreign country; abroad
विदेशी [m f] *videśī* 6 foreigner
विद्यार्थी [m, f] *vidyārthī* 2 student
विलंब [m] *vilamb* 8 delay
विवाह [m] *vivāh* 12 marriage, wedding
विषय [m] *viṣay* 13 subject
विशेष *viśeṣ* 12 particular
विश्वविद्यालय [m] *viśvavidyālay* 9 university
विश्वास [m] *viśvās* 10 belief, confidence
विस्तार से *vistār se* 18 at length, in detail
वे *ve* 1 those, they; he, she (formal)
वेतन [m] *vetan* 18 pay, salary
वैर [m] *vair* 12 hostility
वैसे *vaise* 6 actually, in fact
व्यंग्य [m] *vyangy* 6 sarcasm
व्यक्ति [m] *vyakti* 14 person, individual
व्यक्तिगत रूप से *vyaktigat rūp se* 15 personally
व्यवस्था [f] *vyavasthā* 9 arrangement

श

शंका [f] *śankā* 18 doubt, suspicion
शक्ति [f] *śakti* 15 power
शख़्स [m] *śa<u>kh</u>s* 18 individual, fellow
शनिवार [m] *śanivār* 7 Saturday
शब्द [m] *śabd* 11 word
शब्दकोश [m] *śabdkoś* 2 dictionary
शराब [f] *śarāb* 6 alcoholic drink
शराबी [m] *śarābī* 15 drunkard
शरारत [f] *śarārat* 6 mischief
शर्म [f] *śarm* 18 shame; **शर्म आना** to feel ashamed
शहर [m] *śahar* 3 town, city
शादी [f] *śādī* 13 marriage, wedding; **उमा की शादी राम से करना** [N] to marry Uma to Ram; **उमा की शादी राम से होना** Uma to marry Ram; **शादी-शुदा** (inv.) married
शानदार *śāndār* 14 magnificent
शाबाश *śābāś* well done! bravo!
शाम [f] *śām* 7 evening
शायद *śāyad* 3 perhaps
शिकायत [f] *śikāyat* 11 complaint; **शिकायत करना** [N] to complain; **उमा की शिकायत राम से करना** [N] to complain about Uma to Ram
शिष्य [m] *śiṣy* 13 disciple

शीघ्र *śīghr* 17 soon, quickly
शुक्रवार m *śukravār* 6 Friday
शुक्रिया *śukriyā* 1 thank you
शुद्ध *śuddh* 6 pure, unmixed
शुरू m *śurū* 15 beginning; **शुरू करना** N to begin (something); **शुरू होना** (something) to begin
शूटिंग f *śūṭing* 17 shooting, filming
शैतान m *śaitān* 5 devil
श्रावण m *śrāvaṇ* 18 Shravan, a monsoon month (July–August)
श्री *śrī* 2 Mr; Lord (with deity)
श्रीमती *śrīmatī* 2 Mrs

स

संतुष्ट *santuṣṭ* 17 satisfied
संतोष m *santoṣ* 17 satisfaction
संभव *sambhav* 10 possible
संस्कृत f *sanskṛt* 5 Sanskrit
सकना *saknā* 12 (after verb stem) to be able
सख़्त *sakht* 2 stern, strict, intense
सड़क f *saṛak* 3 street, road
सच *sac* 15 true
सचमुच *sacmuc* 5 really
सदस्य m *sadasy* 18 member
सदा *sadā* 16 always, ever
सन् m *san* 8 year (of calendar, era)
सपना m *sapnā* 7 dream; **सपना देखना** N to dream, have a dream
सप्ताह m *saptāh* 17 week
सफ़र m *safar* 17 journey, travel
सफल *saphal* 14 successful, fruitful
सफलता f *saphaltā* 14 success
सफ़ाई f *safāī* 10 cleaning
सफ़ेद *safed* 1 white
सब *sab* 2 everything, all; **सब कुछ** everything
सब्ज़ी f *sabzī* 8 vegetable(s)
समझ f *samajh* 9 understanding; **समझ में आना** to enter the understanding, be understood
समझना n *samajhnā* 6 to understand, consider, reckon
समझाना N *samjhānā* 18 to explain; to console
समय m *samay* 3 time
समस्या f *samasyā* 15 problem
समाचार m *samācār* 12 news; **समाचार-पत्र** m newspaper
समाप्त *samāpt* 17 finished, concluded
समुद्र m *samudr* 15 sea, ocean
समोसा m *samosā* 4 samosa
सर *sar* 2 sir
सरकार f *sarkār* 15 government
सरकारी *sarkārī* 15 governmental
सरल *saral* 5 simple
सलवार क़मीज़ f *salvār qamīz* 18 salwar qameez
सलाह f *salāh* 10 advice
सवा *savā* 12 one and a quarter

सवाल m *savāl* 2 question
सवेरा m *saverā* 8 early morning
सस्ता *sastā* 2 cheap
सहमत *sahmat* 17 in agreement
सही *sahī* 9 true, correct; **तो सही** for sure
सहेली f *sahelī* 6 girl's female friend
साँस f *sā̃s* 18 sigh; **ठंडी साँस भरना** N to heave a deep sigh
-सा *-sā* 15 -like, -ish
साइकिल f *sāikil* 1 bicycle
साड़ी f *sāṛī* 6 sari
साढ़े *sāṛhe* 12 plus a half
सात *sāt* 12 seven
साथ *sāth* 8 along, with, in company; **साथ साथ** together
साथी m, f *sāthī* 12 companion, friend
साधन m *sādhan* 16 means
साधारण *sādhāraṇ* 17 ordinary
साफ़ *sāf* 1 clean, clear; clearly; **साफ़ करना** N to clean
साबुन m *sābun* 12 soap
सामान m *sāmān* 3 furniture, things, luggage
सारा *sārā* 3 all, whole
साल m *sāl* 6 year
साला m, adj *sālā* 18 wife's brother; term of abuse
सावधानी f *sāvdhānī* 8 care
सावन m *sāvan* 18 = **श्रावण**
साहब m *sāhab* 2 Mr; sir
साहित्य m *sāhity* 14 literature
सिग्रेट f *sigreṭ* 5 cigarette
सितार m *sitār* 15 sitar
सितारा m *sitārā* 18 star
सिनेमा m *sinemā* 7 cinema
सिर m *sir* 8 head; **सिर खाना** N to plague, pester
सिर्फ़ *sirf* 1 only
सिलवाना N *silvānā* 18 to cause to be sewn
सिलसिला m *silsilā* 18 connection; **के सिलसिले में** in connection with
सीखना N *sīkhnā* 6 to learn
सीट f *sīṭ* 12 seat
सीढ़ी f *sīṛhī* 10 stair, step, staircase
सीधा *sīdhā* 8 straight, straightforward; **सीधे** straight; to the right
सुझाव m *sujhāv* 17 suggestion; **सुझाव देना** N to make a suggestion
सुधरना *sudharnā* 17 to improve, be put right
सुधारना N *sudhārnā* 15 to improve, put right
सुनना N *sunnā* 5 to listen, hear
सुनाई देना/पड़ना *sunāī dena/paṛnā* 16 to be heard, be audible
सुनाना N *sunānā* 11 to relate, tell, recite, sing
सुन्दर *sundar* 1 beautiful
सुबह f *subah* 3 morning

सुलाना^N *sulānā* 18 to make sleep
सूझना *sūjhnā* 18 to occur to the mind
सूरज^m *sūraj* 15 sun
से *se* 3 by, since, from, with
से पहले *se pahle* 6 before
सेब^m *seb* 12 apple
सैंतालीस *saintālis* 8 forty-seven
सैकड़ा^m *saikṛā* 7 a hundred
सैर^f *sair* 7 walk, trip; **सैर करना**^N to go for a walk, trip
सो *so* 13 he, she, it (archaic)
सोचना^N *socnā* 6 to think; **की [बात] सोचना**^N to think of doing
सोना^1 m *sonā* 4 gold
सोना^2 *sonā* 6 to sleep
सोमवार^m *somvār* 2 Monday
सोलह *solah* 2 sixteen
सौ *sau* 4 hundred
स्टेशन^m *sṭeśan* 6 station
स्थायी रूप से *sthāyī rūp se* 18 permanently
स्थिति^f *sthiti* 15 situation
स्नान *snān* 15 bath, ritual bathing
स्वभाव^m *svabhāv* 18 nature, disposition
स्वयं *svayam* 15 oneself
स्वर्ग^m *svarg* 7 heaven
स्वादिष्ट *svādiṣṭ* 14 tasty
स्वीकार करना^N *svīkār karnā* 18 to accept

ह

हँसना *hãsnā* 6 to laugh
हँसाना^N *hãsānā* 6 to make laugh
हँसी-मज़ाक^m *hãsī-mazāk* 18 laughter, fun, joking
हज़ार^m *hazār* 7 thousand
हड़ताल^f *haṛtal* 17 strike, lockout, **हड़ताल करना**^N to strike
हफ़्ता^m *haftā* 10 week
हम *ham* 1 we, us
हमारा *hamārā* 6 our, ours
हमेशा *hameśā* 6 always
हर, हरेक *har* 7 each, every; **हर कोई** *everyone*
हल^m *hal* 16 solution; **हल होना** to be solved
हलो, हेलो *halo, helo* 2 hello
हवा^f *havā* 2 air
हवाई जहाज़^m *havāī jahāz* 9 aeroplane
हवाई डाक^f *havāī ḍāk* 14 airmail
हवादार *havādār* 1 airy
हाँ *hā̃* yes
हाथ^m *hāth* 8 hand; **हाथ आना** to come to hand; **हाथ बँटाना**^N to lend a hand; **हाथ मिलाना** to join hands
हाल^m *hāl* 2 condition, state
हालत^f *hālat* 15 state, condition
हालाँकि *hālā̃ki* 17 although
हिन्दी^f *hindī* 2 Hindi
हिन्दुस्तानी *hindustānī* 1 Indian

हिन्दू *hindū* 1 Hindu

हिलना *hilnā* 9 to move, stir

ही *hī* 9 only; (emphatic)

हीरो [m] *hīro* 13 'hero', male film-star

हूँ *hū̃* 1 am

हे *he* 8 Oh!

है *hai* 1 is

हैं *haĩ* 1 are

होंठ [m] *hõṭh* lip

हो *ho* 1 are

होटल [m] *hoṭal* 7 hotel; cafe

होनहार *honhār* 6 promising

होना *honā* 5 to be, become, happen; (से) होकर via

होली [f] *holī* 12 Holi, springtime festival of colours

होल्ड करना [N] *hoḷḍ karnā* 12 to hold (phone line)

होशियार *hośiyār* 4 clever, intelligent

ह्विस्की [f] *hviskī* 18 whisky

ENGLISH–HINDI GLOSSARY

(For numbers, see Appendix 1)

Key

inf = infinitive; ^{m} = masculine; ^{f} = feminine; ^{pl} = plural; $^{m\,f}$ (e.g. **विद्यार्थी**$^{m\,f}$) = used for both males and females; $^{m/f}$ (e.g. **क़लम**$^{m/f}$) = used in either gender; inv = invariable noun/adjective in *-ā*; ^{N} = always uses ने construction in perfective tenses; ^{n} = sometimes uses ने construction in perfective tenses.

a **एक, कोई**
abandon, to **छोड़ना** ^{N}
able, to be **सकना** 12.3
about (approximately) **क़रीब, लगभग**; (with number) **कोई** 7.2; (concerning) **(के) बारे में**
above **(के) ऊपर**
abroad **विदेश**
absent **अनुपस्थित**
abuse, swearing **गाली** ^{f}; to abuse **गाली देना** ^{N}
accept, to **स्वीकार करना** ^{N}; **मानना** ^{N}
accident **दुर्घटना** ^{f}
actually **वैसे, असल में**
add, to **जोड़ना** ^{N}
address **पता** ^{m}
advice **सलाह** ^{f}
aeroplane **हवाई जहाज़** ^{m}
affection **प्यार** ^{m}
affix, to **लगाना** ^{N}
after **के बाद**
afraid (of), to be **(से) डरना** 15.3
afternoon **तीसरे पहर**
again **फिर, फिर से**
age (of person) **उम्र** ^{f}
Agra **आगरा** ^{m}
agreeable, content **राज़ी**
agreed, in agreement **सहमत**
ahead (of) **(के) आगे**
air **हवा** ^{f}
airmail **हवाई डाक** ^{f}
airy **हवादार**
alcoholic drink **शराब** ^{f}
alight, to **उतरना**
all **सब, सभी**; whole **सारा, तमाम**; all day **दिन भर**; all right **ठीक**
Allahabad **इलाहाबाद** ^{m}
allow, to: oblique inf. + **देना** ^{N} 14.4
alone **अकेला**; (adverb) **अकेले**
along with **साथ**

already अभी, अभी से (or use verb stem + चुकना 12.3)
also भी (*follows* word, 2.3)
alteration परिवर्तन m
although हालाँकि, यद्यपि 17.2
always हमेशा; as always, हमेशा की तरह
America अमरीका m; American अमरीकन
among के बीच; among themselves आपस में; from among में से
ancient प्राचीन
and और
angry गुस्से; displeased नाराज़; to become angry गुस्से होना, बिगड़ना
answer जवाब m; to answer जवाब देना N
anxiety परेशानी f; चिंता f
any कोई 7.2; (with uncountable, e.g. 'water') कुछ 7.2
anyone कोई 7.2; anyone at all कोई भी
anywhere (at all) कहीं (भी) 16.3
apart from के सिवा/ सिवाय; (को) छोड़कर
apologise (to), to (से) माफ़ी माँगना N 15.3
appear, to दिखना, दीखना, दिखाई देना/पड़ना 15b; to seem मालूम होना 6.1
apple सेब m
application अर्ज़ी f
appropriate उचित
area, district इलाक़ा m
arm, upper arm बाँह f
around, in vicinity of के आस-पास
arouse from sleep, to जगाना N
arrange, to का इंतज़ाम करना N 16.1
arrangement व्यवस्था f, इंतज़ाम m
arrive, to पहुँचना
arrogance घमंड m
article (written) लेख m
as if, as though जैसे, मानो (with subjunctive verb; 15.4)
as much as... जितना...उतना 14.5
as soon as जैसे ही 13.1
ask, to पूछना N 15.3
at को; at night रात को; (with place, e.g 'at home') पर; at least कम से कम
attempt कोशिश f; to attempt की कोशिश करना N 16.1
attention ध्यान m; to pay attention ध्यान देना N
attentively ध्यान से
August अगस्त m
auto-rickshaw आटो m
available, to be मिलना 13.5
back (in sense 'return') वापस
bad ख़राब, बुरा
bag, cloth bag थैला m
Banaras बनारस m, वाराणसी f

bandit डाकू ^{m}
bark, to भौंकना
bathe, to नहाना
bathroom बाथरूम ^{m}
be bored, to ऊबना
be cut, to कटना
be, to होना; बनना
beat, to मारना ^{N}
beautiful सुन्दर, ख़ूबसूरत
because क्योंकि
because of की वजह से, के कारण
become, to बनना
bedstead पलंग ^{m}, खाट ^{f}
beer बियर ^{m}
before (के/से) पहले
beggar भिखारी ^{m}
begin to, to oblique inf. + लगना;
direct inf. + शुरू करना ^{N}
beginning शुरू ^{m}, आरंभ ^{m}
behind (के) पीछे
belief विश्वास ^{m}
bell घंटी ^{f}
below (के) नीचे
beneath (के) नीचे
Bengali language बँगला ^{f}
berth बर्थ $^{m/f}$
between के बीच; between
themselves आपस में
bicycle साइकिल ^{f}
big बड़ा
bird चिड़िया ^{f}
birth जन्म ^{m}
birthday जन्मदिन ^{m}
black काला
blame, speaking ill निंदा ^{f};
to blame, censure दोष देना ^{N},
की निंदा करना ^{N} 16.1
blanket कंबल ^{m}
boil, to उबलना; उबालना ^{N}
book किताब ^{f}; पुस्तक ^{f}
bore, to बोर करना ^{N}, उबा देना ^{N}
boredom बोरियत ^{f}
born, to be पैदा होना; का जन्म होना
16.1
borrow, to उधार लेना ^{N}
boss मालिक ^{m}
both दोनों
bother, harass, to तंग करना ^{N}
bottle बोतल ^{f}
box डिब्बा ^{m}
boy लड़का ^{m}
Brahmin ब्राह्मण ^{m}
branch (of tree) डाल ^{f}
bravo वाह
bread रोटी ^{f}; (loaf) डबल रोटी ^{f}
break out (of noise, fight), to मचना
break, be broken, to टूटना
break, to तोड़ना ^{N}
breakfast नाश्ता ^{m}; to have
breakfast, नाश्ता करना ^{N}
brick ईंट ^{f}
bridge पुल ^{m}

bright (intelligent) होशियार, तेज़
bring, to लाना, ले आना
briskly झट से
broken टूटा
brother भाई m
brother-in-law (husband's younger brother) देवर m; (wife's brother) साला m
building इमारत f
bullet गोली f
burn, to जलना; जलाना N
bus बस f
but लेकिन, पर, मगर, किंतु, परंतु
butter मक्खन m
buy, to ख़रीदना N
buying, shopping ख़रीदारी
by से; by means of (के) द्वारा; (in time, e.g. 'by now') तक
cafe होटल m
Calcutta कलकत्ता m
call (invite), to बुलाना N; (give name, to) कहना 6.1; बुलाना N
called (named), to be कहलाना
camera कैमरा m
can: *see* 'able, to be'
capital city राजधानी f
car गाड़ी f, कार f
care सावधानी f; to take care of की देखभाल करना N 16.1
care , to परवाह करना N
cat बिल्ली f
catch, to पकड़ना N; (of fire, illness) लगना 13.6
cause कारण m
certain amount, a थोड़ा-बहुत
certainly ज़रूर, अवश्य
chair कुरसी f
chance, opportunity मौक़ा m
change, to बदलना N
chapatti चपाती f
cheap सस्ता
child बच्चा m
childhood बचपन m
choose, to चुनना N
chutney चटनी f
cigarette सिग्रेट f
cinema सिनेमा m
circumstance(s) परिस्थिति(याँ) f
city शहर m
clapping ताली f; to clap तालियाँ बजाना N
class (in school etc.) क्लास m/f
clean साफ़; to clean साफ़ करना N, की सफ़ाई करना N 16.1
cleaning सफ़ाई f
clear साफ़; evident ज़ाहिर, स्पष्ट
clearly साफ़
clerk बाबू m
clever (intelligent) होशियार; (cunning) चतुर
closed बंद; to close, बंद करना N
cloth कपड़ा m

clothing, item of कपड़ा m
cloud बादल m
coffee काफ़ी f
cold ठंड f; (adj.) ठंडा; (nose cold) जुकाम m 8.2
college कालेज m
collide, to टकराना n
colour रंग m
come, to आना
come out, emerge, to निकलना
comfort आराम m; comfortably आराम से
companion साथी m,f
company, firm कंपनी f
compartment (railway) डिब्बा m
compassion दया f
complain, to शिकायत करना N; to complain to Raj about Ram, राज से राम की शिकायत करना N 16.1
complaint शिकायत f
completely एकदम, पूरी तरह से, बिलकुल
compulsion मजबूरी f
computer कंप्यूटर m
concern चिंता f
condition, state हाल m, हालत f
confidence यक़ीन m; विश्वास m
congratulation बधाई f
connection सिलसिला m; in connection with के सिलसिले में
contribution देन f
conversation बातचीत f
copy (of book etc.) प्रति f
cordially आत्मीयता से
corner कोना m
correct सही
corrupt(ed) भ्रष्ट; to corrupt भ्रष्ट करना N
cough, to खाँसना
country देश m
couple (of), a एकाध (singular)
cow गाय f
crazy पागल
create (noise etc.), to मचाना N
crocodile मगर m
cross (road etc.), to पार करना N
crowd भीड़ f
culture, refinement तहज़ीब f
cup प्याला m
cupboard अलमारी f
cure इलाज m
current, ongoing जारी
curtain परदा m
cut, to काटना N
cycle, bike साइकिल f
daal, lentils दाल f
dacoit, bandit डाकू m
daily (adverb) रोज़
dance नृत्य m, नाच m; to dance नाचना
dancer नर्तक m
dark; darkness अँधेरा; अँधेरा m

date तारीख़ ^{f} 8.4
daughter बेटी ^{f}
daughter-in-law बहू ^{f}
dawn उषा ^{f}
day दिन ^{m}; all day दिन भर, round the clock आठों पहर
day before yesterday/ after tomorrow परसों
dear प्रिय; (beloved) प्यारा
death देहान्त ^{m}, मौत ^{f}, मृत्यु ^{f} 16.1
degree (academic) डिगरी ^{f}
delay देर ^{f}, विलंब ^{m}
Delhi दिल्ली ^{f}, देहली ^{f}
deliberately जान-बूझकर
dense घना
depart, to छूटना, चला जाना
description वर्णन ^{m}; to describe का वर्णन करना ^{N} 16.1
despair निराशा ^{f}
detail, in विस्तार से
Devanagari script देवनागरी ^{f}
devil शैतान ^{m}
dhobi, washerman धोबी ^{m}
dial (phone), to नंबर मिलाना ^{N}
dialect बोली ^{f}
dialogue डॉयलॉग ^{m}
dictionary शब्दकोश ^{m}
die, to मरना; का देहान्त होना, की मौत/मृत्यु होना 16.1
difference फ़र्क ^{m}, भेद ^{m}
different भिन्न; (separate) अलग
difficult मुश्किल, कठिन
difficulty मुश्किल ^{f}, कठिनाई ^{f}
dinner डिनर ^{m}
direction तरफ़ ^{f}, ओर ^{f}
dirty गंदा, मैला
disappointment निराशा ^{f}; disappointed निराश
disciple शिष्य ^{m}
discord अनबन ^{f}
dislike, to नापसंद करना ^{N}
distant दूर
distribute, to बाँटना ^{N}
divide, to बाँटना ^{N}
divorce तलाक़ ^{m}; to become divorced का तलाक़ होना; divorced तलाक़-शुदा
do, to करना ^{N}; do not (with command) न, मत
doctor डाक्टर ^{m}
dog कुत्ता ^{m}
don't (with commands) न, मत 5.2
door दरवाज़ा ^{m}
doubt शंका ^{f}
down, downstairs नीचे
dozen दर्ज़न ^{f}
draw, to खींचना ^{N}
drawer दराज़ ^{f}
dream सपना ^{m}; to dream (of) (का) सपना देखना ^{N} 16.1
drink, to पीना ^{N}
drive, to चलाना ^{N}

driver ड्राइवर ^{m}
drop in, to टपकना
drown, to डूबना
drunkard शराबी ^{m}
each हर, हरेक
ear कान ^{m}
early जल्दी; (in morning) सवेरे-सवेरे
earn, to कमाना ^{N}
easily आसानी से, आराम से
easy आसान; simple सरल
eat, to खाना ^{N}
edge, shore किनारा ^{m}
effect असर ^{m}; to have an effect असर पड़ना
either... or या तो... या 16.6
electricity बिजली ^{f}
e-mail ई-पत्र ^{m}; ई-मेल ^{f}
embarrassed, to be झेंपना
embrace, to गले लगाना ^{N}
emerge, to निकलना
employment नौकरी ^{f}
end अंत ^{m}; in the end, after all आख़िर (में)
English person अँग्रेज़ $^{m, f}$
enjoy, feel enjoyment आनंद आना
enough! that's all! बस
enter, to घुसना
envelope लिफ़ाफ़ा ^{m}
escape, to बचना
essay निबंध ^{m}
etc. वग़ैरह, इत्यादि
even भी (*follows* word, 2.3)
evening शाम ^{f}; this evening आज शाम (को)
every हर; every day रोज़, हर रोज़
everything सब, सब कुछ
exactly, precisely ठीक
examination परीक्षा ^{f}; to take (sit) an exam; परीक्षा देना ^{N}; to examine की परीक्षा लेना ^{N}
example उदाहरण ^{m}, नमूना ^{m}
except for (को) छोड़कर, के सिवाय
excuse, to माफ़ करना ^{N} 5.2
expensive महँगा
experience अनुभव ^{m}; to experience अनुभव/ महसूस करना ^{N}
expert, skilled माहिर
explain, to समझाना ^{N}
extract, to निकालना ^{N}
extremely बहुत ही, निहायत
face मुँह ^{m}; चेहरा ^{m}; face to face रूबरू
facing, opposite के सामने
fall, to गिरना
family परिवार ^{m}
famous मशहूर, प्रसिद्ध
fan पंखा ^{m}
far away दूर
fare (taxi etc.) किराया ^{m}
fat मोटा
fate क़िस्मत ^{f}
father पिता ^{m}(inv.), बाप ^{m}, पापा ^{m} (inv.)

fault, guilt कसूर m, दोष m
fax फ़ैक्स m
fear डर m; to fear (से) डरना
fed up (with), to become (से) तंग आना
feel, to महसूस करना N; to be felt, महसूस होना; to feel at home दिल/मन लगना; I feel hungry / thirsty मुझको भूख/प्यास लगी है 13.6
fetch, to लाना, ले आना
fever बुख़ार m
fight, to (से) लड़ना n
film फ़िल्म f; film-shooting शूटिंग f
film-star (male) हीरो m
financial आर्थिक
find out, ascertain, to मालूम करना N
find, to पाना N; मिलना (with 'thing found' as subject) 13.5
fine, delicate महीन
finger उँगली f
finish, to ख़त्म करना N, समाप्त करना N; to complete पूरा करना N
finished ख़त्म, समाप्त
fire आग f
first पहला; (adverb) पहले
fix, put right, to ठीक करना N
flee, to भागना
floor फ़र्श m/f
flower फूल m
fluency रवानी f
flute बाँसुरी f
fly (insect) मक्खी f
fly, to उड़ना
follow, to का पीछा करना N
food खाना m, भोजन m
fool मूर्ख m, उल्लू (lit. 'owl')
for के लिए
forbidden मना (inv.)
force, strength ज़ोर m
foreign विदेशी; foreign country विदेश m; foreigner विदेशी m
forest बन m
forget, to भूलना, भूल जाना
forgive, to माफ़ करना N
forgiveness माफ़ी f
fork (utensil) काँटा m
formally औपचारिक रूप से
free (vacant) ख़ाली; (gratis) मुफ़्त
free time फ़ुरसत f, अवकाश m
fresh ताज़ा
friend दोस्त m, f, मित्र m, f; girl's girlfriend सहेली f
from से
fruit फल m
full (complete) पूरा; (filled) भरा
fun मज़ा m
furniture सामान m
future भविष्य m
Ganges गंगा f
garden बग़ीचा m
gardener माली m
garland माला f

garlic लहसुन ^{m}
German जर्मन
get, to मिलना 13.5
get up, to उठना
ghost भूत ^{m}
gift भेंट ^{f}, तोहफ़ा ^{m}
girl लड़की ^{f}
give, to देना ^{N}; to give up छोड़ना ^{N}; to give back वापस देना ^{N}
glance, look नज़र ^{f}
glare, glower, to आँखें दिखाना ^{N}
glass (tumbler) गिलास ^{m}
glasses, spectacles चश्मा ^{m}; ऐनक ^{f}
go, to जाना
go out, emerge, to निकलना
God भगवान ^{m}; ख़ुदा ^{m}, God knows भगवान/ख़ुदा जाने
gold सोना ^{m}
good अच्छा; decent नेक
goodbye नमस्ते, नमस्कार; (Muslim) ख़ुदा हाफ़िज़
good-quality बढ़िया (inv.)
gossip गप ^{f}, गपशप ^{f}
government सरकार ^{f}; governmental सरकारी
grandfather (paternal) दादा ^{m} (inv.); (maternal) नाना ^{m} (inv.)
grandmother (paternal) दादी ^{f}; (maternal) नानी ^{m}
grass घास ^{f}
grief दुःख ^{m}
grin broadly, to बत्तीसी दिखाना ^{N}
guest मेहमान ^{m}
Gujarati गुजराती
guru गुरु ^{m}
Gwalior ग्वालियर ^{m}
half आधा ^{m}; half past साढ़े 12.2
hand हाथ ^{m}; to come to hand हाथ आना; to lend a hand हाथ बँटाना ^{N}; to join hands हाथ मिलाना ^{N}
handsome ख़ूबसूरत, सुंदर
happen, to होना, हो जाना
happiness ख़ुशी ^{f}
happy ख़ुश
hard, difficult मुश्किल, कठिन
hardworking मेहनती
harm नुक़सान ^{m}
harass, hassle, to तंग करना ^{N}
hate नफ़रत ^{f}; to hate (से) नफ़रत करना ^{N} 15.3
have (possess), to के पास होना 8.2; (be obliged), to: inf.+ पड़ना 13.3
he वह, वे
head सिर ^{m}
health तबियत ^{f}
heap ढेर ^{m}
hear, to सुनना ^{N}
heard, to be सुनाई देना/पड़ना 15b
heart दिल ^{m}
heat गरमी ^{f}
heaven स्वर्ग ^{m}
heavy भारी

height लंबाई f
hello नमस्ते, नमस्कार
help मदद f; to help मदद देना N, की मदद करना N 16.1
here यहाँ, इधर
hero हीरो m
high ऊँचा
hill पहाड़ m
Hindi हिन्दी f
Hindu हिन्दू
history इतिहास m
hit, to मारना N
hold, to पकड़ना N; (phone line) होल्ड करना N
Holi होली f
holiday छुट्टी f
home घर m; at home घर पर
Home Minister गृह मंत्री m, f
hooligan गुंडा m; hooliganism गुंडागर्दी f
hope आशा f, उम्मीद f; I hope मुझे उम्मीद/आशा है
horse घोड़ा m
hospital अस्पताल m
hostility वैर m
hot गरम
hotel होटल m
hour घंटा m
house मकान m, घर m
how (what like?) कैसा; (in what way?) कैसे
how much/many कितना
human being मानव m, इनसान m
hunger भूख f
hungry भूखा; I feel hungry, मुझको भूख लगी
hurt चोट f; to get hurt, चोट लगना 13.6
husband पति m
I मैं
ice बर्फ़ f
idea विचार m, ख़याल m
if अगर, यदि 10.4, 17.1
ill बीमार
immediately तुरंत
important ज़रूरी, अहम
impossible असंभव, नामुमकिन
improve, to सुधरना; सुधारना N
in में
in front (of) (के) आगे
inauguration उद्घाटन m
incomparable लाजवाब
increase, to बढ़ना
India हिन्दुस्तान m, भारत m
Indian हिन्दुस्तानी, भारतीय
individual, person व्यक्ति m
inferior (in quality) घटिया (inv.)
informally अनौपचारिक रूप से
injury चोट f; I got injured, मुझको चोट लगी
innocent, guileless भोला
inside (के) अंदर

instead of के बजाय
intelligent होशियार, तेज़
intention इरादा ^{m}
interesting दिलचस्प
interrupt (की) बात काटना ^{N}
invite, to बुलाना ^{N}
iron, ironing इस्तरी ^{f}
irritate, to चिढ़ाना ^{N}, तंग करना ^{N}
-ish -सा (redish लाल-सा)
it वह
Japanese जापानी
jewellery (item of) ज़ेवर ^{m}
job, employment नौकरी ^{f}
joke मज़ाक़ ^{m}; joking हँसी-मज़ाक ^{m}
journey यात्रा ^{f}, सफ़र ^{m}
joy, enjoyment आनंद ^{m}
jungle जंगल ^{m}
just, a little ज़रा
Kanpur कानपुर ^{m}
kathak कथक ^{m}
Kathmandu काठमांडु ^{m}
keep, to रखना ^{N}
key चाबी ^{f}
Khan Market खाँ मार्केट ^{m}
kill, to मारना ^{N}, मार डालना ^{N}
kind, type तरह ^{f}, प्रकार ^{m}; of various kinds तरह तरह का
kindly, please मेहरबानी करके
kindness मेहरबानी ^{f}, कृपा ^{f}
king राजा ^{m} (inv.)
kitchen रसोईघर ^{m}
kite (toy) पतंग ^{f}
knife छुरी ^{f}
know, to जानना ^{N}; मालूम होना 4.4
kurta कुरता ^{m}
lack, want कमी ^{f}
lady महिला ^{f}
lamp; electric light बत्ती ^{f}
land ज़मीन ^{f}
lane गली ^{f}
language भाषा ^{f}, ज़बान ^{f}
lap गोद ^{f}
lass छोकरी ^{f}
last (previous) पिछला; (final) आख़िरी
late, delayed देर से
later बाद (में), आगे चलकर
lathi, stick लाठी ^{f}
laugh, to हँसना ^{n}; to make laugh हँसाना ^{N}
laughter, joking हँसी-मज़ाक ^{m}
laze about, to मक्खियाँ मारना ^{N}
lazy आलसी, कामचोर
leader, politician नेता ^{m}
learn, to सीखना ^{N}; to study पढ़ना
leave, to छोड़ना ^{N}
lecturer प्राध्यापक ^{m}
left (opp. of right) बायाँ; to the left (hand) बायें/ उलटे (हाथ)
left (remaining) बाक़ी
leisure, free time फ़ुरसत ^{f}, अवकाश ^{m}
lend, to उधार देना ^{N}

length लंबाई ^{f}
lentil(s) दाल ^{f}
less कम
lesson, chapter पाठ ^{m}
letter ख़त ^{m}, पत्र ^{m}, चिट्ठी ^{f}
let, to: *see* 'allow, to'
lie झूठ ^{m}; to lie झूठ बोलना ^{n}
lie, recline, to लेटना
life ज़िंदगी ^{f}, जीवन ^{m}
lift, to उठाना ^{N}
light (brightness) रोशनी ^{f}; (lamp, electric light) बत्ती ^{f}
light (in weight) हल्का
like (in manner of) की तरह; (equal to) (के) समान; (such as, similar to) जैसा 15.4
like, to पसंद करना ^{N}/होना 4.4
lip होंठ ^{m}
listen, to सुनना ^{N}
literature साहित्य ^{m}
little छोटा; a little थोड़ा-सा 15.5
live, to (reside) रहना; (be alive, live life) जीना ^{N}
livelihood गुज़ारा ^{m}
load, to लादना ^{N}
loaded, to be लदना
loan उधार ^{m}
lock ताला ^{m}
London लंदन ^{m}
loneliness अकेलापन ^{m}
look, glance नज़र ^{f}
look, to देखना ^{N}; to look after की देखभाल करना ^{N} 16.1; to look for ढूँढ़ना ^{N}; to look like जैसा लगना 13.6
lose, to खोना ^{N}
lots of बहुत-से 15.5, बहुत-सारा
lout, hooligan गुंडा ^{m}
love प्रेम ^{m}, प्यार ^{m}; to love Raj, राज से प्रेम/प्यार करना ^{N} 15.3
lovely प्यारा; सुन्दर
low (of sound, voice) धीमा
Lucknow लखनऊ ^{m}
luggage सामान ^{m}
lunch दोपहर/दिन का खाना ^{m}
luxury ऐश ^{m}
lying (e.g. मेज़ पर) पड़ा, पड़ा हुआ 18.1
Ma माँ ^{f}
mad पागल
madam मैडम ^{f}
magnificent शानदार
Mahabharata महाभारत ^{m}
maharaja महाराज(ा) ^{m} (inv.)
mail, post डाक ^{f}
maintain, keep current, to जारी रखना ^{N}
make, to बनाना ^{N}
male, man मर्द ^{m}
manage (succeed), to: verb stem + पाना 12.3
man, person आदमी ^{m}
mango आम ^{m}
many बहुत, बहुत-से 15.5, कई

manner, way ढंग m; तरह f
market बाज़ार m
marriage शादी f, विवाह m
married शादी-शुदा (inv.)
marry, to शादी करना N; to marry Ram, राम से शादी करना N; to marry Ram to Sita, राम की शादी सीता से करना N 16.1
Maruti मारुति f
matter, affair मामला m, बात f
me मैं, मुझ
mean, miserly कंजूस
meaning मतलब m, अर्थ m
means साधन m
meantime, in the फ़िलहाल
meat गोश्त m, माँस m
mechanic मिस्तरी m
medicine दवा f
meet (with), to (से) मिलना 15.3
meeting मुलाक़ात f, भेंट f; (formal) मीटिंग f
member सदस्य m
memory याद f 16.2
middle of, in the के बीच में
middle aged अधेड़ (उमर का)
midnight आधीरात f
milk दूध m
mind मन m
mine मेरा
minute मिनट m
miracle कमाल m
mischief शरारत f
mistake ग़लती f, भूल f; to make a mistake, गलती/भूल करना N
mix, to मिलाना N
moment पल m, क्षण m; at the moment अभी
Monday सोमवार m
money पैसा m
monkey बंदर m
month महीना m
moon चाँद m
more और, ज़्यादा, अधिक
morning सुबह f; in the early morning सवेरे; this morning आज सुबह
mosquito मच्छर m
most ज़्यादा, अधिक; at the most अधिक से अधिक, ज़्यादा से ज़्यादा; most people ज़्यादातर लोग
mostly ज़्यादातर
mother माता f, माँ f
mountain पहाड़ m
mouth मुँह m
move , to चलना; हिलना; to move house शिफ़्ट करना N, घर बदलना N
Mr श्री, मिस्टर
Mrs श्रीमती, मिसेज़
much ज़्यादा, अधिक
Muslim मुसलमान m,f
Mussoorie मसूरी f
my मेरा
name नाम m

narrow तंग
nature, disposition स्वभाव ^{m}
near (के) नज़दीक, (के) पास
nearby (adv.) पास; (adj.) पास-वाला
necessary ज़रूरी, आवश्यक
necessity आवश्यकता ^{f}
neck गरदन ^{f}
need ज़रूरत ^{f} 7.4
need, to: *see* 7.4 and 13.2-3
needed चाहिए 7.4
neighbour पड़ोसी ^{m}
neither... nor न... न 16.6
Nepal नेपाल ^{m}
Nepali नेपाली
nephew भतीजा ^{m}
never कभी नहीं
new नया (नये/नए, नयी/नई)
news ख़बर ^{f}, समाचार ^{m}
newspaper अख़बार ^{m}, समाचार-पत्र ^{m}
next अगला
next to, close by की बग़ल में
night रात ^{f}; all night रात भर
no नहीं, जी नहीं
nobody कोई नहीं
noise, tumult शोर ^{m}
noon, afternoon दोपहर ^{f}
no one कोई नहीं 7.2
nose नाक ^{f}
not नहीं, न
note (written) नोट ^{m}, चिट्ठी ^{f}; (banknote) नोट ^{m}
nothing कुछ नहीं 7.2
novel (book) उपन्यास ^{m}
now अब
nowadays आजकल
nowhere कहीं नहीं
number नंबर ^{m}; (figure) संख्या ^{f}
obstinacy ज़िद ^{f}
obstinate, stubborn ज़िद्दी
obtain, to प्राप्त करना ^{N}, पाना ^{N}; (मिलना 'to be obtained' 13.5)
occur to the mind, to सूझना
ocean समुद्र ^{m}
o'clock बजे (e.g. तीन बजे)
of का; half of this इसका आधा; of course ज़रूर, अवश्य
office दफ़्तर ^{m}
often अक्सर
OK ठीक
old (elderly, of people) बूढ़ा; old man बूढ़ा ^{m}; old woman बुढ़िया ^{f}; (of things) पुराना
on पर; on account of के मारे; on top (of) के ऊपर
one एक; one and a half डेढ़; one and a quarter सवा; one or two, a couple (of) एकाध $^{(sg)}$
oneself ख़ुद, स्वयं 15.7; of one's own accord अपने आप 15.7
onion प्याज़ ^{m}
only सिर्फ़, केवल; ही 9.4
open खुला; to open खुलना; खोलना ^{N}

opinion राय ^{f}, ख़याल ^{m}; in my opinion मेरे ख़याल में/से
opposite (के) सामने
opportunity मौक़ा ^{m}
or या 16.6
order (send for), to मँगवाना ^{N}
ordinary आम, साधारण
origin मूल ^{m}
other, second दूसरा
otherwise नहीं तो
our, ours हमारा
out बाहर; out of, from among में से
outside (के) बाहर
own, one's own अपना 6.3
paan पान ^{m}
pain दर्द ^{m}, दु:ख ^{m}
paisa पैसा ^{m}
Pakistan पाकिस्तान ^{m}
Pakistani पाकिस्तानी
palace महल ^{m}
pale (complexioned) गोरा
pandit पंडित ^{m}
Panjabi पंजाबी
papa पापा ^{m} (inv.)
paper; piece of paper काग़ज़; newspaper अख़बार ^{m}
particular ख़ास, विशेष
party (political) दल ^{m}, पार्टी ^{f}
pass (exam etc.), to पास करना ^{N}; (of time), to बीतना; बिताना ^{N}; to pass away: *see* 'die'
passenger यात्री ^{m}, मुसाफ़िर ^{m}, सवारी ^{f}
pay, salary वेतन ^{m}
pay attention (to), to (पर) ध्यान देना ^{N}
peacock मोर ^{m}
pearl मोती ^{m}
pen क़लम $^{m/f}$
pencil पेंसिल ^{f}
peon, orderly चपरासी ^{m}
people लोग $^{m\ pl}$; the public जनता $^{f\ sg}$
perhaps शायद
period, age ज़माना ^{m}, युग ^{m}
permanently स्थायी रूप से
Persian language फ़ारसी ^{f}
person, individual व्यक्ति ^{m}
personally व्यक्तिगत रूप से
phone फ़ोन ^{m}
phone, to फ़ोन करना ^{N}
photograph फ़ोटो ^{m}; to take photo फोटो खींचना ^{N}
pick up, to उठाना ^{N}
picture तस्वीर ^{f}, चित्र ^{m}
piece, bit टुकड़ा ^{m}
pile ढेर ^{m}
pill गोली ^{f}
place जगह ^{f}
place of, at the के यहाँ 6.4
plan योजना ^{f}, प्रोग्राम ^{m}
plane, aeroplane हवाई जहाज़ ^{m}
play (a game), to खेलना ^{n}
play (music etc.), to बजाना ^{N}

please कृपया, मेहरबानी करके
pleased ख़ुश
pleasure ख़ुशी f, मज़ा m, आनंद m
pocket जेब f
poem; poetry कविता f
poet कवि m
point, advantage फ़ायदा m
police पुलिस f. sg
politician नेता m
pollution प्रदूषण m
pomp धूमधाम m
pond तालाब m
poor ग़रीब
popular लोकप्रिय
population आबादी f
porter कुली m
possible मुमकिन, संभव
post, mail डाक f
post-office डाकघर m
pour, to डालना N
power शक्ति f
practice अभ्यास m
praise तारीफ़ f; to praise की तारीफ़ करना N 16.1
prepare, to तैयार करना N
present, gift तोहफ़ा m, उपहार m, भेंट f
previous पिछला; previously पहले
price दाम m, क़ीमत f
pride गर्व m; (arrogance) घमंड m
prime minister प्रधान मंत्री m
printed, to be छपना
problem समस्या f
profession पेशा m
profit फ़ायदा m, लाभ m
programme प्रोग्राम m, कार्यक्रम m
prohibited मना (inv.)
promising, up-and-coming होनहार
pronunciation उच्चारण m
proper, appropriate उचित
properly ठीक से
public, the people जनता f sg
published प्रकाशित
publisher प्रकाशक m
pure, unmixed शुद्ध
put, to रखना N
put on (wear), to पहनना N
quarrel झगड़ा m
quarter to the hour पौने (e.g. पौने तीन) 12.2
question सवाल m, प्रश्न m
quick तेज़; quickly जल्दी
quite (fairly, very) काफ़ी; (completely) बिलकुल
radio रेडियो m
rain बारिश f; to rain बारिश होना/आना, पानी पड़ना
Rajasthan राजस्थान m
Ramayan रामायण m
rather (very) बहुत; (a little) कुछ, थोड़ा; (with adj.) -सा 15.5
reach, to पहुँचना
read, to पढ़ना N

ready तैयार
real असली
realise, to समझ जाना
really (genuinely) सचमुच; (in reality) असल में
reason कारण^{m}, वजह^{f}
recently इधर, हाल में, अभी
recite, to सुनाना^{N}
recognise, to पहचानना^{N}
red लाल
reduce, to कम करना^{N}
refuse (to), to (से) इनकार करना^{N}
regret अफ़सोस^{m}, खेद^{m}
regret, to पछताना^{N}
relative रिश्तेदार^{m,f}
remain, to रहना
remaining बाक़ी
remarkable अद्भुत
remember, to याद रखना^{N}/ करना^{N}/होना 16.1
remind, to याद दिलाना^{N}
rent किराया^{m}; to rent किराये पर लेना^{N}/ देना^{N}
repair मरम्मत^{f}; to repair की मरम्मत करना^{N} 16.1
reply उत्तर^{m}, जवाब^{m}; to reply जवाब देना^{N}
request निवेदन^{m}
rescue, to बचाना^{N}
resemble, to (से) मिलना, मिलना-जुलना 13.5
resound, to बजना
responsibility ज़िम्मेदारी^{f}
rest, ease आराम^{m}; to rest आराम करना^{N}
restless बेचैन
return, to लौटना, वापस आना/जाना
rice चावल^{m}
rich, wealthy अमीर; rich man, 'millionaire' लखपति^{m}
rickshaw रिक्शा^{m}
right (opp. of left) दाहिना; to the right (hand) दाहिने/ सीधे (हाथ)
right here, in this very place यहीं 9.4
right now अभी 9.4
riot दंगा^{m}
ripe पक्का
river नदी^{f}
riverbank, steps घाट^{m}
robbery चोरी^{f}
room कमरा^{m}
rudeness, impertinence गुस्ताख़ी^{f}
rug दरी^{f}
ruin, to बरबाद करना^{N}
run (manage), to चलाना^{N}
run, to दौड़ना; run away भागना
rupee रुपया^{m}
Russian रूसी
sage, seer ऋषि^{m}
salary वेतन^{m}
salt नमक^{m}
salwar qameez सलवार क़मीज़^{f}

same, the same one वही 9.4
samosa समोसा ^{m}
sandal चप्पल ^{f}
Sanskrit संस्कृत ^{f}
sarcasm व्यंग्य ^{m}
sari साड़ी ^{f}
satisfaction संतोष ^{m}; satisfied संतुष्ट
Saturday शनिवार ^{m}
save, to बचाना ^{N}
saved, left over बचा, बाक़ी
say(to), to (से) कहना ^{N}
scholarship छात्रवृत्ति ^{f}
scold, to डाँटना ^{N}
script (alphabet) लिपि ^{f}
sea समुद्र ^{m}
search तलाश ^{f}; to search for की तलाश करना ^{N} 16.1
seat सीट ^{f}
seated, sitting बैठा
see, to देखना ^{N}; (to visit) मिलना 15.3
seem, to लगना 13.6; मालूम होना 6.1
sell, to बेचना ^{N}
send, to भेजना ^{N}
sentence वाक्य ^{m}
separate, separately अलग
serious गंभीर
servant नौकर ^{m}
serve (food), to खिलाना ^{N}
several कई
shame शर्म ^{f}; to feel ashamed शर्म आना
she वह, वे
shiver, to काँपना
shoe; pair of shoes जूता ^{m}
shop दुकान ^{f}; shopkeeper दुकानदार ^{m}; shopping दुकानदारी ^{f}
should: infinitive + चाहिए 13.2
shout, to चिल्लाना ^{N}
show, spectacle तमाशा ^{m}
show, to दिखाना ^{N}
shut बंद; to shut, बंद करना ^{N}
sick, ill बीमार
side, direction तरफ़ ^{f}, ओर ^{f}
sigh साँस ^{f}; to heave a (deep) sigh (ठंडी) साँस भरना ^{n}
silent चुप, ख़ामोश
silk रेशम ^{m}
silly, pointless ऊल-जलूल, बेकार
silver चाँदी ^{f}
simple, easy सरल
since से; since Monday सोमवार से; since the time when... since then जब से... तब से 13.1
sing, to गाना ^{N}
sir साहब, सर, जनाब
sister बहिन ^{f}
sister-in-law (elder brother's wife) भाभी ^{f}
sit, to बैठना; sitting बैठा, बैठा हुआ; sitting room बैठक ^{f}
sitar सितार ^{m}
situation स्थिति ^{f}

sky आकाश ^{m}, आसमान ^{m}
sleep नींद ^{f}
sleep, to सोना
slogan नारा ^{m}
slum बस्ती ^{f}
small छोटा
smile, to मुस्कराना ^{n}
smoke, to (सिग्रेट) पीना ^{N}
snow बर्फ़ ^{f}
so (then) तो, सो, इसलिए; so (+ adj.) इतना (e.g. इतना पुराना); so that ताकि + subjunctive
soap साबुन ^{m}
sold, to be बिकना
soldier जवान ^{m}
sole, only (child) इकलौता
solution (to problem) हल ^{m}
solve, to हल करना ^{N}; to be solved हल होना
some (with countable noun) कोई; (with uncountable noun) कुछ; something कुछ; something else कुछ और, और कुछ; something or other कुछ न कुछ 7.2
somehow कहीं
someone कोई; someone else और कोई, कोई और; someone or other कोई न कोई 7.2
sometime कभी; sometimes कभी कभी
somewhere कहीं; somewhere else कहीं और; somewhere or other कहीं न कहीं
son बेटा ^{m}
song गाना ^{m}, गीत ^{m}
soon जल्दी; as soon as जैसे ही 13.1
sorry (regret) अफ़सोस ^{m}; I apologise, forgive me माफ़ कीजिए
sound आवाज़ ^{f}
south दक्षिण ^{m}
speak, to बोलना ^{n}
special ख़ास
spend (time), to गुज़ारना ^{N}
spoon चम्मच ^{m}
squander, to उड़ाना ^{N}
stair, staircase सीढ़ी ^{f}
stamp टिकट $^{m/f}$
standing खड़ा
star सितारा ^{m}
start, to: *see* 'begin, to'
state (condition) हालत ^{f}
state (province) प्रदेश ^{m}
station स्टेशन ^{m}
statue, image मूर्ति ^{f}
stay, to रहना; (e.g. in hotel) ठहरना
steal, to चोरी करना ^{N}
step, pace क़दम ^{m}
stern सख़्त
stick लकड़ी ^{f}; (truncheon) लाठी ^{f}
still (even now, up to now) अभी (अभी तक, अभी भी)
stir up, start up, to छेड़ना ^{N}

stomach पेट m

stone पत्थर m

stop, to रुकना; रोकना N

story कहानी f

straight सीधा; (adv.) सीधे; straight away तुरंत, अभी; straightforward सीधा

strange अजीब

stranger अजनबी m

street सड़क f

strict सख़्त

strike, lockout हड़ताल f

string रस्सी f

stroll, to टहलना

strong मज़बूत, तेज़

stubborn ज़िद्दी

stuck, to be फँसना

student विद्यार्थी m f, छात्र m, छात्रा f

studies, studying पढ़ाई f

study, to पढ़ना

stupid बेवक़ूफ़; stupid person उल्लू (lit. 'owl')

subject, topic विषय m

success सफलता f; successful सफल, कामयाब

such (of such a kind) ऐसा; (so much) इतना

suddenly, unexpectedly अचानक

suggestion सुझाव m; to suggest सुझाव देना N

summer गरमियाँ f pl

sun सूरज m; sunlight, sunshine धूप f

Sunday रविवार m

surprise आश्चर्य m; I'm surprised मुझको आश्चर्य है; surprising आश्चर्यजनक

sway, to झूमना

swear, to (curse, swear at) गाली देना N; (make oath) क़सम खाना N

sweet मीठा; sweet dish मिठाई f

swim, to तैरना n

swindler ठग m

sycophancy जी-हुज़ूरी f

tabla तबला m

table मेज़ f

tablet, pill गोली f

tail पूँछ f

tailor दर्ज़ी m

Taj Mahal ताज महल m

take, to (receive) लेना N; (transport, deliver, take away) ले जाना; take care of का ख़याल/ध्यान रखना N 16.1; take down उतारना N; take off (clothes) उतारना N

talk, converse, to (से) बात/बातें करना N

tall लंबा; (of buildings etc.) ऊँचा

Tamil तमिल f

tap नल m; tapwater नल का पानी m

tasty स्वादिष्ट

taxi टैक्सी f

tea चाय f; teaboy चाय-वाला m

teach, to पढ़ाना N, सिखाना N

teacher अध्यापक ^{m}
tear, to फ़ाड़ना ^{N}
tease, to चिढ़ाना ^{N}
television दूरदर्शन ^{m}, टी० वी० ^{m}
tell, to बताना ^{N}
temple मंदिर ^{m}
thank you शुक्रिया, धन्यवाद
that (pronoun) वह; (conjunction) कि; (relative, 'which') जो 13.4; that is to say यानी
theft चोरी ^{f}
them वे, उन
then फिर, तब
there वहाँ; right there वहीं; over there उधर; there is/are है/ हैं
these ये
they ये, वे
thick (coarse) मोटा; (dense) घना
thief चोर ^{m}
thin पतला; (lean) दुबला-पतला
thing चीज़ ^{f}
think, to सोचना ^{N}
thirst प्यास ^{f}; I'm thirsty मुझको प्यास लगी है 13.6
this यह
thorn काँटा ^{m}
those वे
thought विचार ^{m}, ख़याल ^{m}
three days ago/ahead नरसों
three-quarters पौन, पौना
throat गला ^{m}
throw, to डालना ^{N}, फेंकना ^{N}
Tibetan तिब्बती
ticket टिकट $^{m/f}$
time समय ^{m}, वक़्त ^{m}; age, season काल ^{m}; occasion बार ^{f}, दफ़ा ^{f}; what's the time? कितने बजे हैं ?; 12.2; at the time of leaving चलते समय 18.1
timid डरपोक
tired, to be थकना
tiredness थकान ^{f}
to को
today आज
together (in company with) एक साथ, के साथ; (jointly) मिल-जुलकर
tolerate, to बरदाश्त करना ^{N}
tomorrow कल
too (also) भी (*follows* word, 2.3); (excessive) बहुत ज़्यादा
tonight आज रात (को)
top of, on के ऊपर
touch, to छूना ^{N}, हाथ लगाना ^{N}
tour, to घूमना
towards की तरफ़/ ओर
town शहर ^{m}
toy खिलौना ^{m}
train ट्रेन ^{f}, गाड़ी ^{f}, रेलगाड़ी ^{f}
translation अनुवाद ^{m}; to translate (का) अनुवाद करना ^{N}
travel यात्रा ^{f}, सफ़र ^{m}
traveller यात्री ^{m}, मुसाफ़िर ^{m}

treatment (medical) इलाज m
tree पेड़ m
trekking ट्रेकिंग f
tremble, to काँपना
trick, deceipt धोखा m; to trick धोखा देना N
trouble तकलीफ़ f, कष्ट m
troubled, upset परेशान
true सच
trust भरोसा m, विश्वास m
truth, the सच m
try, to की कोशिश करना N
tumbler गिलास m
turn, bend मोड़ m
turn, to मुड़ना, मोड़ना N
twisted टेढ़ा
two and a half ढाई
UP (Uttar Pradesh) उत्तर प्रदेश m; उ० प्र०; यू० पी०
ugly बदसूरत
umbrella छाता m
uncle अंकल m
uncle (father's younger brother) चाचा m (inv.)
understand, to समझना n
understanding समझ f
university विश्वविद्यालय m
until तक; जब तक न... 13.1
up to तक
up, upstairs ऊपर
upset परेशान
Urdu उर्दू f
urgent ज़रूरी
us हम
use, usage प्रयोग m; to use का इस्तेमाल/ प्रयोग करना N 16.1
'used to': see 7.1
useless बेकार
usually आम तौर पर, अक्सर
vacant ख़ाली
vacate, to ख़ाली करना N
valuable क़ीमती
Varanasi वाराणसी f
vegetable(s) सब्ज़ी f
very बहुत
via से होकर 12.1
village गाँव m
villain बदमाश m
visible, to be दिखाई देना
voice आवाज़ f
wait, waiting इंतज़ार m; to wait (for) (का) इंतज़ार करना N
walk, to पैदल चलना/जाना
wall दीवार f
want, to चाहना 10.2 (in past , use imperfective: मैं चाहता था)
warm गरम
wash, to धोना N; (bathe) नहाना
washed, to be धुलना
washerman धोबी m
waste, to गँवाना N; (squander) उड़ाना N

watch, wristwatch घड़ी ^{f}
watch, to देखना ^{N}
watchman चौकीदार ^{m}
water पानी ^{m}
way, manner ढंग ^{m}, तरह ^{f}, प्रकार ^{m}
we हम
weak कमज़ोर
wear, to पहनना ^{N}
weather मौसम ^{m}
wedding शादी ^{f}
week हफ़्ता ^{m}, सप्ताह ^{m}
weep, to रोना ^{n}
well, abundantly ख़ूब
well (anyway) ख़ैर; (in a good way) अच्छा, अच्छी तरह (से)
wet (soaked) भीगा; (damp) गीला
what? क्या; what like? what kind of? कैसा
wheel पहिया ^{m}
when... then जब... तब 13.1; when? कब
where... there जहाँ... वहाँ 14.7; where? कहाँ, किधर
whether ... or चाहे ...चाहे
which (relative pronoun) जो; which/what ever जो भी; which? कौनसा
while (on the other hand) जब कि; while doing करते समय, करते करते
whisky व्हिस्की ^{f}
whisper, to फुसफुसाना
white सफ़ेद; white person गोरा ^{m}
who (relative pronoun) जो; whoever जो भी 13.4
who? कौन; whom? किस, किन; whose? किसका, किनका
why क्यों
wife पत्नी ^{f}
wild, untamed जंगली
wind हवा ^{f}
window खिड़की ^{f}
with से; (in company of) के साथ
without के बिना; without doing बिना किए
woman औरत ^{f}
wood लकड़ी ^{f}
word शब्द ^{m}
work काम ^{m}; (occupation) धंधा ^{m}; (employment) नौकरी ^{f}
work, to काम करना ^{N}; to function (of machine) काम करना ^{N}; to have an effect (का) असर पड़ना
worker, labourer मज़दूर ^{m}
world दुनिया ^{f}
worth, worthy लायक़; worth doing करने लायक़
wretch, poor fellow बेचारा ^{m}
write, to लिखना ^{N}
writer लेखक ^{m}
wrong, incorrect ग़लत

yawn जँभाई ^{f}; to yawn जंभाई लेना ^{N}

year साल ^{m}, वर्ष ^{m}; (of calendar or era) सन् ^{m}

yes हाँ, जी हाँ

yesterday कल

you (intimate) तुम; (familar) तुम; (formal) आप 1.1

young छोटा, जवान

your, yours (intimate) तेरा; (familiar) तुम्हारा; (formal) आपका; yourself ख़ुद

youth, young man नौजवान ^{m}

INDEX

Other related titles

TEACH YOURSELF

URDU

David Matthews and Mohamed Kasim Dalvi

This is a complete course in spoken and written Urdu. If you have never learnt Urdu before, or if your Urdu needs brushing up, *Teach Yourself Urdu* is for you.

The authors have created a practical course that is both fun and easy to work through. They explain everything along the way and give you plenty of opportunities to practise what you have learnt. The course structure means that you can work at your own pace, arranging your learning to suit your needs.

The course contains:

- a range of graded units of dialogues, culture notes, grammar and exercises
- a step-by-step guide to pronunciation
- an Urdu–English vocabulary.

By the end of the course you'll be able to cope with a whole range of situations and participate fully and confidently in all aspects of Urdu life in India, Pakistan and the United Kingdom.